Ama Dablam, Khumbu Himal, Nepal

MOUNTAINEERING AND ITS LITERATURE

A descriptive bibliography of selected works published in the English language, 1744–1976.

W. R. NEATE

THE MOUNTAINEERS
Seattle

The Mountaineers: Organized 1906 ". . . to explore, study, preserve and enjoy the natural beauty of the Northwest."

Published by
The Mountaineers
719 Pike Street, Seattle, Washington 98101

Published simultaneously in Canada by
Douglas & McIntyre Ltd.
1615 Venables St.
Vancouver, B.C. V5L 2H1

Published in Great Britain by Cicerone Press, Harmony
Hall, Milnthorpe, Cumbria, England

Manufactured in the United States of America

Cover photo by Walt Unsworth: Head of the Khumbu
Valley. Khumbutse, Lingtrense and Pumoro sweep from
front cover to back.

Library of Congress Cataloging in Publication Data

Neate, W R
    Mountaineering and its literature.

    1. Mountaineering—Bibliography.   I. Title.
Z6016.M7N4   1980   [GV200]   016.795'22   80-7785
ISBN 0-89886-004-0

ACKNOWLEDGEMENTS

I wish to thank:

Alpine Club Library; American Alpine Club Library;
University of Cape Town Library; Mr. Warren Elsby,
Librarian, Keswick Public Library; Mrs. Muriel Files, Hon.
Librarian, Fell & Rock Climbing Club; Mrs. Audrey
Salkeld for the use of her library and records.

CONTENTS

ILLUSTRATIONS

Photographs by W. Unsworth

PUBLISHER'S NOTE

This American edition has been produced from the same plates used to produce the British edition. The author has subsequently obtained some missing dates and has identified some errors; those which are significant are noted below. Any minor and obvious typographical misfortunes will be corrected in the next edition.

The author is currently collecting and organizing information for a thoroughly updated and enlarged edition. Readers having any such information are encouraged to send it to the author, in care of the publisher:

> The Mountaineers
> 719-B Pike Street
> Seattle, Washington 98101

ADDITIONS AND CORRECTIONS:

Page

19. Bolivia paragraph (line 13). Delete 'and 1900'

24. Canada (first para, lines 13-14). Amend to read 'others, including Americans'.

29. Fiction (line 4). Delete 'novels'.

73. Korjenevskoi - delete existing line and insert:
    Korjenevskoi 23,310 1953 A. Ugarov & party
    -Lower summit 22,671 1937 Guschtschin, Golofist, Korsun, Prokudajew

91. ANDERSON (Line 1) Delete 'soldier' & substitute 'solicitor'

105. No. 216 Pagination details omitted; should read:
     London: Allen & Unwin, 1954. } 256 p, 25 plates (1 col);
     New York: Harper, [1954]. } ill, maps; 22 cm

121. No. 444 Delete '?:?,1832' & sub 'London: Seeley & Burnside, 1832. iv, 349 p; map; 23 cm'

128. No. 539. Pagination statement omitted. Should read:
     London: Eyre & Spottiswoode, 1968. } 288 p, 25 plates
     New York: Dodd Meade, 1968. } (incl. ports); 23 cm

128. Muir (biog. detail) Line 12 should run on 'Biographies: The Life and letters (etc.)'

128. No. 545. Pagination statement. Should read:
     New York: The Century Co., 1894 } xvi [xii], 381 p; ill,
     London: Fisher Unwin, 1894 } 2 maps; 20 cm

139. No. 707. Pagination should read 'xiv, 212 p, 41 plates (etc)'

140. SMITH Delete 'English' & sub. 'Scottish' in line 1.

143. No. 792. (Line 9) After 'follows:' delete '1953,'

145. TILMAN Line 3 - delete 'has' at end of line

150. No. 896. (Lines 6-8) Delete 'Also published . . . & 1874' & sub. 'Further editions in 1870, 1871 & 1874.'

157. Appendix II. Amend 'Ascent' entry by deleting '?' & sub. '1967-in progress'

157. Appendix II. Add
     Mazama
     Portland: The Mazamas, 1896-in progress

157. Appendix II. Add after 'Scottish Mountaineering Club Journal' a new item, viz:
     Sierra (Club Bulletin)
     San Francisco: Sierra Club, 1893-in progress

158. Appendix III. Column 2, line 3. After 'snakes and ladders' add new sentence 'Illustrated in [417].'

The Brenta Dolomites, Italy

INTRODUCTION

INTRODUCTION

Explanatory notes

The Subject Index provides access to the literature of mountaineering, and the Author Index, by means of a series of articles, e.g. Alps, Anthologies, Autobiographies. The object of each article is to identify the salient points, interpolating references to books in the Author Index wherever suitable. These references appear in [ ] within the main text and/or as lists. The overall result is a very condensed history of mountaineering and an appraisal of its literature. Fortunately much of this is available in English, the worst gaps being German mountaineering in the Andes, and Japanese mountaineering. Where no English references to important ascents and developments are available, foreign language titles have been interpolated.

The Mountain Index is intended for use as a supplement to, and not as a substitute for, the Subject Index. Most of such detailed information is traceable in guidebooks (see Appendix VI).

The works listed in the Author Index are restricted to printed books and pamphlets (being more than a few pages), which are principally concerned with some aspect of mountaineering, or which contain important references. The work must have been published in English, either originally or in translation.

Subject to a few historical and authoritative items, the following are excluded from the Author Index:

  (i)   leaflets and ephemera
  (ii) magazine articles (unless collected into book form)
 (iii) club journals
 (iv) books having only isolated chapters on mountaineering
  (v) books on rambling, hiking, and mountain countryside
 (vi) camping, caving, ski-ing and polar travel
 (vii) manuscripts
(viii) geology, and mountain flora and fauna
 (ix) foreign language works not available in English
  (x) bibliographies and library catalogues (see Appendix I)
 (xi) guidebooks (see Appendix V & VI).

The Anglo-American Cataloguing Rules (British text) published by The Library Association have been used as a model for cataloguing the principal entries. The majority of mountaineering books being post-eighteenth century, problems of precise collation and identification of first editions/issues are the exception rather than the rule. First editions, and first English editions, have been catalogued in full wherever possible. Subsequent editions have been noted in such detail as is thought necessary to identify them and indicate their individual points.

Where a popular book runs through many editions and printings entries may be condensed. Book club editions have been ignored throughout. Contrary to strict bibliographical practice, foreign language editions of English works have been omitted.

Suggested reading is indicated by * against the book title, while † indicates that the book contains a specialist reading list.

References and sources consulted

Apart from the books themselves, the following references and sources have been consulted:

Alpine Journal
American Alpine Club, **Library working list**
American Alpine Journal
Bridge, G. **Rock climbing in the British Isles 1894–1970: a bibliography of guidebooks**
British National Bibliography
Booksellers' catalogues
Campbell, J. I. **Bibliography of mountains and mountaineering in Africa**
Dictionary of National Biography
Encyclopaedia Britannica
Fell & Rock Climbing Club, **Library catalogue**
International Who's Who
Krawczyk, C., **Mountaineering: a bibliography of books in English to 1974**
Library Association, **Readers' guide to books on mountaineering**
Meckly, E. P., **Bibliography of privately printed mountaineering books**
Montagnier, H. F., **Bibliography of the ascents of Mont Blanc from 1786–1853** (and supplement)
Mumm, A. L., **Alpine Club Register**
National Library of Scotland, **Shelf catalogue of the Lloyd Collection of Alpine Books**
Read, B. J. **Mountaineering, the literature in English: a classified bibliography, and an introductory survey**
Who's Who
Who was Who
Yakushi, Y., **Catalogue of Himalayan literature**

Paperback series (Publishers)

Ace Books (New English Library)
Aldine (Dent)
Anchor Books (W. H. Allen)
Arrow Books (Hutchinson)
Bantam Books (Transworld Publishers)
Batsford Paperbacks (Batsford)
Bestseller Library (Elek)
Calderbooks (John Calder)
Cambridge Paperbacks (C.U.P.)
Cherry Tree Books
Consul Books (World Distributors)
Corgi Books (Transworld Publishers)
Coronet (Hodder)
Digit Books (Brown, Watson)
Dolphin Books (Mayflower: W. H. Allen)
Dover Books (Constable)
Evergreen Books (John Calder)
Everyman Paperbacks (Dent)
Faber Paperbacks (Faber)
Fontana Books (Collins)
Four Square Books (New English Library)
Galaxy Books (O.U.P.)
Grey Arrow (Hutchinson)
Guild Books (C.U.P.)
Mentor Books (New English Library)
Mercury Books (Heinemann)
Murray Paperbacks (Murray)
Muses Library Paperbacks (Routledge)

Oxford Paperbacks (O.U.P.)
Pan Books
Panther Books (Hamilton)
Papermacs (Macmillan)
Pelican; Penguin; Peregrine; Puffin (Penguin Books)
St. Martins Library (Macmillan)
Torchbooks (Hamilton)
University Paperbacks (Methuen)
Unwin Books (Allen & Unwin)
Wyvern Books (Epworth Press)

List of abbreviations

A.C. – Alpine Club
A.A.C. – American Alpine Club
A.A.J. – American Alpine Journal
A.B.M.S.A.C. – Association of British Members of Swiss
    Alpine Club
A.J. – Alpine Journal
A.S.C.C. – (See M.C. of S.)
B.M.C. – British Mountaineering Council
C.C. – Climbers' Club
C.C.P.R. – Central Council of Physical Recreation
C.U.P. – Cambridge University Press
D.Ö.A.V. – Deutscher Österreichischer Alpen Verein
F. & R.C.C. – Fell & Rock Climbing Club (of the English
    Lake District)
G.H.M. – Groupe de Haute Montagne
L.A.C. – Ladies Alpine Club
M.C. of S. – Mountaineering Council of Scotland (form-
    erly Association of Scottish Climbing Clubs)
O.U.P. – Oxford University Press
S.A.C. – Swiss Alpine Club
S.F.A.R. – Swiss Federation for Alpine Research
S.M.C. – Scottish Mountaineering Club

The Mischabel peaks above Saas Fee

SUBJECT INDEX

SUBJECT HEADINGS

Accidents and rescue
Africa
— Ahaggar (Hoggar) Mountains
— Atlas Mountains
— Ethiopia
— Mount Kenya
— Kilimanjaro
— Virunga Mountains
— Ruwenzori
— South Africa
Alaska
Alpine Club (publications and library)
Alps (See also: 'Golden Age', Mont Blanc, Pre-'Golden Age', 'Silver Age')
Andes
Antarctica (See: Polar regions)
Anthologies
Arctic (See: Polar regions)
Artificial (aid) climbing (See: Technique)
Artists (See: Illustrators)
Asia (excluding Himalaya, Hindu Kush & Karakoram)
— Turkey and Iran
— Ta Hsueh Shan
— Kun Lun
— Pamirs
— Tien Shan
— Altai
— Siberia
— Japan
Australasia (excluding New Zealand)
— Australia
— New Guinea
Autobiographies
Biographies
British Isles
Canada
— Rocky Mountains
— Interior Ranges
— Coast Mountains of British Columbia
Caucasus (See: Europe)
Caving (Spelaeology)
Central America (See: Latin America)
Children's books
Climbing memoirs
Corsica (See: Europe)
Dictionaries and encyclopaedias
Dolomites (See: Alps)
Eiger (North Wall) (See: Alps (Bernese))
Eight-thousand metre peaks (See also: Everest)
Equipment (and clothing) (See: Technique)
Essays
Europe (excluding the Alps & British Isles)
— Caucasus
— Pyrenees
— Norway
— Polish Tatras
— Other European mountains
Everest
Fiction (novels and short stories)
Fifty books in mountaineering
Flora and fauna
General reference books
Geology and glaciation
'Golden Age' of mountaineering (1854–65)
Guidebooks
Guides
Himalaya (See also: Eight-thousand metre peaks; Everest)
Hindu Kush

ACCIDENTS AND RESCUE

The first British mountain rescue manual was Lionel West's little book [883], published in 1907, in which he described and illustrated methods of crag rescue and first aid. It pre-dates by some twenty-five years the start of the mountain rescue movement in Britain, which only came to maturity with the post-1945 surge in outdoor pursuits. Hamish MacInnes, who has written an account of the work of one of the Scottish rescue teams [482], also founded the search dog organization in Britain [227]. The work of the Royal Air Force mountain rescue teams is described in [528].

There are several authoritative manuals on mountain rescue equipment and techniques, including books by L. D. Bridge [108], Wastl Mariner [498], and Hamish MacInnes [481]. See also [495], which describes self-help for rock-climbers. Emil Zsigmondy's classic, **Die Gefahren der Alpen,** originally published in 1885, is at last available in English in its newest form [606].

Charles Gos has written the stories of over twenty well-known Alpine accidents from the past [318]. One of the most publicized rescues of recent times was the drama of Corti and Longhi on the Eigerwand in 1957 [587]; see also [709].

Further references to Author Index

81. Bernhard, O. – First aid to the injured
281. Fraser, C. – The avalanche enigma
326. [Royal Air Force] – Mountain rescue handbook
412. Jones, A. S. G. – Some thoughts on the organisation of mountain search and rescue operations
437. LaChapelle, E. R. – ABC of avalanche safety
505. May, W. G. – Mountain search and rescue techniques
544. Mountain Rescue Committee – Mountain rescue and cave rescue
591. Orlob, H. – Mountain rescues
823. Townsend, J. H. – The two climbers: a cry from the Alps
884. Westmorland, H. – Adventures in climbing

Note also:

Mitchell, R. – Mountaineering first aid: a guide to accident response and first aid care

AFRICA

Mountaineering in Africa is reasonably well covered by English-language books, with the exception of the Atlas and Ahaggar ranges, which have been more the province of French climbers.

Ahaggar (Hoggar) Mountains

A remote desert range in southern Algeria, about 1,000 miles inland. It was not really penetrated until this century, since when French climbers have shown great interest in the mountaineering possibilities. The Ahaggar is a region of bare, eroded rock, rising to nearly 10,000' at its highest point. Bernard Pierre climbed a number of virgin peaks here in 1951 [**Escalades au Hogger** (Paris: Arthaud, 1952)].

Atlas Mountains

An irregular mountain mass, comprising several chains, e.g. Middle Atlas, Anti-Atlas, Rif Atlas. The principal range is the High (or Great) Atlas. Exploration began in the second half of the nineteenth century. In 1871 a scientific expedition led by Sir Joseph Hooker, with John Ball, explored the central part of the High Atlas [381]. Other Victorian explorers of this area included W. B. Harris [350] and Joseph Thomson [806].

The mountaineering pioneers of the High Atlas included many well-known members of the G. H. M. such as Jacques and Tom De Lépiney, L. Neltner and A. Stofer, but particularly Marquis de Segonzac and Louis Gentil. Bentley Beetham and A. de Pollitzer-Pollenghi, from England, were also active in the area. References will be found in the A. J.

Ethiopia

There is a complex of mountain groups over most of the country and parts of the Ethiopian mountains remain unexplored. The highest peak is Ras Dashan (which has nine tower-like tops) in the Semien (Simen) Mountains, located in the north of the country. They were not explored or surveyed until the Italian occupation of Ethiopia in the 1930s. The mountaineering interest in Ethiopia is limited according to Sir Douglas Busk [139].

Mount Kenya

The main interest in Kenyan mountaineering is Mount Kenya itself, one of the most difficult and impressive mountains in Africa. The principal summits are Batian, the highest, and Nelion. Batian was climbed in 1899 but Nelion remained unclimbed until 1929 when it was conquered by Eric Shipton [698] & [814]. The principal reference is a beautiful book by E. A. T. Dutton [233]. During the last war three Italian prisoners of war broke camp to climb Mount Kenya. With only makeshift equipment and hoarded rations they found it too difficult to reach either of the highest peaks and finally set up their home-made Italian flag on Point Lenana [79]. See also [825].

Kilimanjaro

Kilimanjaro is the highest mountain in Africa, being over 2,000' higher than Mount Kenya, although the main peak Kibo is an easy, albeit laborious climb. It was attempted in 1884 by Sir Harry Hamilton Johnston (1858–1927), a British colonial administrator who also explored the Ruwenzori. Hans Meyer made the first ascent in 1889 after a dispute over his attempt in 1887 [517]. Mawenzi, which is the second peak of Kilimanjaro, is much lower and its ascent involves rock-climbing; it was first climbed in 1912.

Virunga Mountains

A group of eight volcanoes, all more or less inaccessible. The hardest, or most dangerous, climbing is encountered on Mikeno. The first of the Virungas to be sighted was Muhavura, seen by J. H. Speke in 1861, and by H. M. Stanley in 1876. The region was thoroughly explored in 1912. Although the Virungas are remote people have climbed there – notably King Albert of the Belgians – and there are some references [80] & [209]. The Virungas are the home of the mountain gorilla.

Ruwenzori

(Ptolemy's 'Mountains of the Moon')
A range of mountains some sixty-five miles long near the equator, first sighted by H. M. Stanley in 1888. He was followed by over twenty expeditions before the Duke of Abruzzi's expedition arrived in 1906. Two of the earlier expeditions are described in books by J. E. S. Moore and A. F. R. Wollaston. Grauer Rock, on Mount Baker, was the first Ruwenzori summit to be climbed.

It was the aim of the Duke of the Abruzzi to climb every peak and to map every mountain, valley and glacier accurately, and in all this the expedition was entirely successful. Filippo de Filippi's account [265] is one of the most important books in mountaineering literature. All the highest peaks have been climbed, although very infrequently, despite the numerous visits to the area. Some accounts will be found in [80], [139] & [794].

South Africa

South Africa has a strong history of mountaineering, an account of which was published in 1966 [136]. The principal reference source, however, is the 'Annual' of the Mountain Club of South Africa, the authoritative mountaineering body. Table Mountain [464] in Cape Province and the Drakensberg in Natal are probably the best climbing areas. Interest in the Drakensberg [457] & [609] centres on the fifty mile section from Cathkin Peak to Mont-aux-Sources. See also [753–4] and **Appendix VI.**

Further references to Author Index

27. Amery, L. – Days of fresh air
28. Amery, L. – In the rain and the sun
502. Mason, G. – Minus three [Kilimanjaro]
586. Oliver, W. D. – Crags and craters: rambles in the island of Réunion
698. Shipton, E. E. – Upon that mountain
794. Synge, P. M. – Mountains of the Moon
814. Tilman, H. W. – Snow on the equator
825. Truffaut, R. – From Kenya to Kilimanjaro

Note also:

Johnston, H. H. – The Kilima-Njaro expedition (Kegan Paul, 1886)

Kingsley, Mary – Travels in West Africa (1897) [Ascent of Mt. Cameroon in 1895 by a new route.]

Maydon, H. C. – Simien, its heights and abysses: a record of travel and sport in Abyssinia (1925)

Moore, J. E. S. – To the Mountains of the Moon (Hurst & Blackett, 1901)

New, C. – Life, wanderings and labours in Eastern Africa: with an account of the first successful ascent [sic] of the equatorial snow mountain, Kilima Njaro (Hodder, 1873)

Scott, H. – Journey to the Gughé Highlands (1952) [Ethiopia]

Stuart-Watt, E. – Africa's dome of mystery: comprising . . . a girl's pioneer climb to the crater of Kilimanjaro (Marshall, 1930)

Wells, C. – In coldest Africa (New York, 1931)

Wollaston, A. F. R. – From Ruwenzori to the Congo (Murray, 1908)

ALASKA

Alaska is deemed to have been discovered in 1741 by the Russian Vitus Bering, and during the late eighteenth century the region was explored by Cook, Vancouver and Mackenzie. In 1867 Alaska was formally purchased by the United States from Russia. By the onset of the first world war most of the mountain ranges had been explored and some of the principal peaks climbed, including McKinley and St. Elias. The major difficulties of Alaskan travel have now been largely diminished, firstly by the road system built during the last war and secondly by the use of aeroplanes. In 1934 the A. A. C. published a bibliography on the mountains of Alaska [**Appendix I**].

Mount McKinley

Much of the literature concerns the various attempts to make the first ascent of Mount McKinley, which is the highest mountain in North America, rising 17,000' from base to summit, a greater rise than any other mountain in the world. Wickersham made the first attempt in 1903, reaching 10,000'.

In 1903 also Dr. Frederick Cook led his first expedition to attempt McKinley [184]. See also [229]. Cook returned in 1906 with a larger party, which included Belmore Brown and Herschel C. Parker. After further unsuccessful attempts they returned to base. Shortly afterwards Cook disappeared into the wilds again, returning to claim the first ascent. Browne and others were extremely suspicious and several years later were able to prove that Cook's claim was fraudulent.

In 1910 the lower North Peak was climbed by four sourdough prospectors, who had no mountaineering experience or equipment. Instinctively they picked the northerly and most feasible approach via the Muldrow Glacier. In a 4,000' summit bid they set up their flagpole on the North Peak, which is separated from the highest point by several miles and a considerable descent.

At this time another attempt was being made from the south by Browne and Parker. Although they failed in 1910, they made a virtually complete ascent in 1912, being beaten back by a blizzard only a few hundred yards from the gently sloping summit [121]. The following year Hudson Stuck and his party made the first complete and undisputed ascent of the South Peak [768]. In another book [45] E. S. Balch tried to resolve the conflicting claims but his conclusions are void because he used Dr. Cook's false evidence. The first winter ascent of McKinley is described in [202]. The pioneer climbs are summarized in [536].

Mount St. Elias

Another famous mountain in Alaskan mountaineering history is Mount St. Elias, probably the most difficult peak over 16,000' in North America. In 1886 Schwatka and Seton Karr [416] were in the area and in 1888 Topham and Williams reached 12,000' [112]. On the second of two attempts (1890–1) Russell reached 14,500'. Bryant made a less successful attempt in 1897, to be followed the same year by the very large expedition organized by the Duke of Abruzzi [264]. This expedition, which made the first ascent, was one of three outstanding expeditions led by the Duke, all mountaineering land-marks. Mount St. Elias was not climbed again until 1946.

As part of Canada's Centennial Celebrations in 1967, more than 250 climbers converged on the St. Elias Mountains in Yukon Territory. The record of this enterprising and successful expedition [271] includes **A short history of mountaineering in the St. Elias Mountains** by Walter A. Wood covering the period 1886-1966.

Further references to Author Index

26. Brooks, A. H. – Mountain exploration in Alaska [Alpina Americana 3]
413. Jones, C. – Climbing in North America
518. Mills, E. J. E. – Airborne to the mountains
547. Muir, J. – Travels in Alaska
655. Roberts, D. S. – The mountain of my fear [Mt. Huntingdon]
656. Roberts, D. S. – Deborah

876.   Washburn, H. B. – Bradford on Mount Fairweather
944.   Young, S. H. – Alaska days with John Muir

Note also:

Beach, W. N. – In the shadow of Mt. McKinley (New York: Derrydale Press, 1931)
Brower, K. – Earth and the great weather [Brooks Range]
Sheldon, C. – The wilderness of Denali [McKinley]
Whymper, F. – Travel and adventure in the territory of Alaska (Murray, 1868)

ALPINE CLUB

(Publications and Library)

The Alpine Club was formed at an inaugural meeting held on 22 December, 1857, E. S. Kennedy presiding. It was conceived as a dining club for the pooling of information on Alpine matters. The formal life of the Club began early in 1858, with the election of John Ball as the first President.

Ball was free to devote his leisure and talents to the development of mountaineering generally and of the Alpine Club in particular. Although he was an indefatigable pioneer in all aspects of mountain exploration, his distinction lies not in his record as a conqueror of peaks but in his creation of a readily available body of knowledge of mountaineering and the establishment of the Alpine Club as an authority on such matters.

Late in 1858 Ball and William Longman, the publisher, agreed that there was a market for an annual volume of contributions by Alpine travellers. This resulted in the publication in 1859 of **Peaks, passes and glaciers** [18]. In his editorial introduction Ball explained that the success or otherwise of the venture was to determine the prospect of further series. The book ran through four printings and was followed in 1862 by a two volume sequel [20].

By 1863 the Club, recognizing the continuing demand, had decided to branch out by producing the first volume of the **Alpine Journal.** This was, and still is, sub-titled 'a record of mountain adventure and scientific observation'. The stated policy was to report club proceedings, new mountain expeditions worldwide, new scientific and geographical knowledge, details of new books, and in fact everything useful to mountaineers. 'The prospect of starvation for want of material', said the introduction, 'may be deferred beyond the scope of our calculations'.

Ball was yet to make his greatest contribution – his **Alpine Guide** [46]. This had an even greater influence on the development of mountaineering than the other Alpine Club publications. He had pointed out as early as 1861 that there was no book dealing with the whole Alpine chain. When commissioned to prepare one, he commandeered members' services, sifting and editing their contributions with his own considerable knowledge of the various areas. The results appeared in three volumes through the years 1863–8 [47–51]. The guide went through several printings and remained unaltered until the turn of the century. Although it was still regularly consulted, it was seriously out of date by 1890. About this time Martin Conway proposed a series of guidebooks to be called 'The Alpine Club guide to the high Alps'. The Alpine Club however preferred to undertake a revision of Ball's guide, which was started but not finished by W. A. B. Coolidge.

There are two other major Alpine Club publications. The first, in 1932, was a further series of **Peaks, passes and glaciers** made up of articles from the first five volumes of

the **Alpine Journal** and not previously published in book form. The other venture was the adaptation of the issues of the **Alpine Journal** for 1949 and 1950; this was called the **Alpine Annual** [118–9]. Neither can be counted a success. As reprints from the **Alpine Journal** they should command respect but in fact, in a collection of mountaineering books, they stick out like sore thumbs.

The Library

Over the years the Alpine Club has amassed one of the most important Alpine and mountaineering libraries in the world. The Club soon began collecting books, the first librarian being appointed in 1861. The first library catalogue containing 600 entries was published in 1880. Today the library comprises some 16,000 volumes. Latterly conditions have been such that the Club has not been able to keep up the collection to the desired standard. To enable the library to draw on wider financial resources and to extend its traditional services to non-members, it has now been made over to a charitable trust, with a full-time professional librarian. Once the necessary remedial work has been accomplished it is intended that the library shall be maintained to a high standard.

ALPS

(See also: 'Golden Age', Mont Blanc, Pre-'Golden Age', 'Silver Age')

Alpine exploration covers several centuries. The exploits of early Alpine travellers and of the originators of mountaineering are covered in a number of scholarly books by writers such as T. G. Brown [120]; Gavin De Beer [204–6]; W. A. B. Coolidge [185] & [187]; and Francis Gribble [333]. As a reference source Coolidge is unequalled for meticulous attention to detail and accuracy.

With the 'Golden Age' well under way, members of the Alpine Club were expected to write up their mountaineering expeditions for the benefit of fellow members [18] & [20]. This period of mountaineering attracted many gifted men – Wills, Hudson, Whymper, Tyndall, Ball, Moore, Stephen – and their talents are reflected in the high order of their writing, which surpasses the literature of other sports. The **Cambridge History of English Literature** notes particularly Forbes, Stephen and Tyndall. The great Alpine explorers include Forbes [274] & [276], Ball, F. F. Tuckett [830], and Coolidge [157].

The story of the early Alpine guides is covered in [149] and [197], the latter illustrated by Abney with superb photographic portraits. W. M. Conway produced two memorable books on the Alps; one recording his climbing tour across the Alps in 1894 [176], the other a general description [181]. Other general surveys include [159] and [401]. A useful one-volume history of Alpine mountaineering is [246]. The most comprehensive source for details of the activities and writings (books and articles) of early Alpine Club members is [554]. Appreciations of Alpine literature will be found in [246] and [470].

Western Alps

Nowadays the Alps are generally referred to as the Western Alps and the Eastern Alps, the dividing point being, roughly speaking, the Swiss frontier with Austria. Alpine historians and guidebook writers used to subdivide the Western Alps into western and central blocks. The most important groups in the Western Alps are: (i) the Dauphiné and the chain of Mont Blanc, where the emphasis is on rock-climbs: (ii) the Bernese Oberland and the Pennine Alps, where snow and ice peaks predominate.

Maritime Alps An almost sub-alpine group, the highest peak being Punta dell'Argentera, first climbed by Coolidge. See [188] & [293].

Cottian Alps A wild, craggy mountain system, occasionally rising above 11,000'. Hannibal's crossing of the Cottian Alps is examined by several authors, notably De Beer [**Alps and elephants** (Bles, 1955)] and Freshfield [291]. James Forbes circumambulated the region in 1839, the year that his career as a mountain explorer may be said to begin. See [188] & [830].

Dauphiné Alps The last main Alpine massif to be surveyed, explored and climbed. The pioneers were hampered by the primitive conditions which prevailed and the region had a reputation for inaccessibility until the 1860s. The principal peaks include Les Ecrins, Pelvoux and the Meije, the last great Alpine peak to be climbed. The first mountaineer to visit the district was Forbes [276]. Other explorers of note were Tuckett, who made three attempts on Les Ecrins [830]; T. G. Bonney [97]; Whymper and Moore, conquerors of Les Ecrins [897] & [535]; and Coolidge, who systematically climbed most of the remaining virgin peaks during the 1870s. See also [87] and [539].

Graian Alps A region with many peaks rising to 13,000', the highest and most famous being Gran Paradiso. English climbers were active in making first ascents in this area, including searching for the legendary Mont Iseran – eventually traced to a cartographic confusion. The principal reference is [936]. See also [513].

Chain of Mont Blanc See separate section of bibliography: MONT BLANC.

Pennine Alps (Central) This group includes some of the famous giants – Dent Blanche; Weisshorn (Tyndall's great first ascent [839]); and of course the Matterhorn, the first ascent of which remains the greatest of all mountaineering stories. Whymper's own account is the standard and definitive one [897]. Tyndall also had several goes at the mountain [839]. For a modern consideration of the Matterhorn disaster see [158]. The first 100 years' climbing is summarized in [476]. See also Guido Rey's important monograph [647] and Mummery's book [555]. One of the greatest achievements on the Matterhorn was a new route put up by Walter Bonatti, solo and in winter – the North Face Direct [89].

Pennine Alps (Eastern) Dominated by Monte Rosa, a massif having ten different summits. Local climbers made first ascents of the lower points during the first quarter of the nineteenth century. The highest point was climbed by Hudson in 1855 [388]. Tyndall made a solo ascent [836]. One of the delightful Victorian travel books is Mrs Cole's account of her tour round Monte Rosa [167]. See also [568], [622], [839], & [942].

Bernese Alps This range divides naturally into three sections, the central Bernese Oberland being the most important. This major Alpine group rises to 14,000' and is historically most important. The Meyers' ascents of the Finsteraarhorn and Jungfrau laid the foundations of Swiss mountaineering (but see [256]). Thirty years later in 1841 Forbes made the first British ascent of the Jungfrau, while visiting the scientists studying the glaciers. In 1854 Alfred Wills made his historic ascent of the Wetterhorn, which ushered in the 'Golden Age'. The Bernese Alps are almost equal to the Pennine Alps in the quality of their attractions for the mountaineer.

During the first British ascent of the Finsteraarhorn in 1857 the idea of an alpine club was first mooted. Other notable events are F. F. Roget's ski-traverse [664] and the first complete ascent of the north-east wall by Miriam Underhill [850]. Although the Jungfrau was climbed relatively early, the more difficult ascent from the Wengern Alp was not made until 1865 [305]. Another famous Oberland peak is the Schreckhorn, which inspired Leslie Stephen's most famous Alpine observation [766]. However, the most notorious peak is the Eiger, more specifically its north wall, the 'Eigerwand'. The definitive history is [347]. The first British ascent was in 1962 [90]. Other specific references include the first winter ascent [368]; the direct route in winter [314] & [849]; and the rescue of Corti [587] & [709]. See [355] for the most recent climbs.

Lepontine Alps A large group suited to mountain walking. The highest peaks, headed by Monte Leone, are all in the eastern part, sometimes referred to as the Adula Alps. See [284].

Glarus Alps (Tödi) and Alps of N.E. Switzerland The great pioneer was Father Placidus a Spescha, who made the first ascents of many secondary, but none the less difficult, peaks in this region. His climbs include Piz Urlaun and the Stockgron. [**Placidus à Spescha, Sein Leben und Seine Schriften.**Edited by F. Pretti & K. Hager (Berne, 1913)]. See also [333]. D. W. Freshfield was one of the later visitors to the Range of the Tödi.

Eastern Alps

The Eastern Alps are concentrated in the western tongue of Austria, which is bounded on the north, west and south respectively by Germany, Switzerland and Italy. The mountains may be divided into two catergories – the northern limestone ranges providing most severe rock-climbing and the southern groups, which provide fairly modest Alpine climbing suitable for novices. Two important groups lie outside this rough framework; they are the Bernina Alps of south-east Switzerland and the Italian (formerly Austrian) Dolomites.

The story of nineteenth century climbing in the Eastern Alps belongs principally to German and Austrian climbers. Outstanding among the early pioneers and guideless climbers were Paul Grohmann [**Wanderungen in den Dolomiten** (Vienna, 1877)]; Ludwig Purtscheller [**Der Hochtourist der Ostalpen** (1894)]; Otto and Emil Zsigmondy [**Im Hochgebirge** (Leipzig, 1889)]; and Hermann von Barth [**Aus der nördlichen Kalkalpen** (Gera, 1874)]. English mountaineers who visited the Eastern Alps were Freshfield, Ball, and Stephen, but especially Tuckett [830]. Since 1900 Italian climbers have gradually challenged the supremacy of the Germans and Austrians, most particularly in the Dolomites in the 1930s. The best summary of big wall climbing in the Eastern Alps is [692].

Bernina Alps An important group, with a number of high peaks rising to 13,300' in Piz Bernina, and giving climbs of all grades and types. Christian Klucker was the outstanding guide from this region [425], making some of his climbs with Norman-Neruda [572]. The north-east face of Piz Badile is a famous climb [88], [131] & [639].

Albula Group Also referred to as the Rhaetian Alps: a minor range, providing fine viewpoints for the Bernina.

Silvretta-Rhatikon Alps A group on the Austro-Italian border, with good opportunities for high mountain walking and rock-climbing rather than serious Alpine mountaineering. See [176] & [732].

Bavarian, Vorarlberg and Salzburg Alps   Sub-alpine ranges, containing several well-known mountains such as Dachstein, Watzmann, and Zugspitze. Better known as the Wetterstein, Karwendel, and Kaisergebirge (Wilder Kaiser). Hermann Buhl made many sensational climbs in these ranges [131]. The east face of the Watzmann was the scene of a dramatic rescue in 1937 [508].

Ortler, Ötztal and Stubai Alps   Three groups with a number of relatively easy snow peaks, although some harder climbs exist. They provide a useful introduction to Alpine climbing. Originally part of Austria, the Ortler Alps now lie inside Italy. See [176] & [732].

Lombard Alps   A pleasant but minor area, which includes the Adamello-Presanella groups, the Brenta Dolomites, and Bergamasque Alps. See [286].

Tauern (Venediger-Glockner groups) & Zillertal Alps   Two areas also used by beginners and including Austria's highest peak, the Gross Glockner. The first ascent of this peak in 1800 was a significant milestone in the history of climbing in the Eastern Alps. Other well-known peaks are Gross Venediger and Hochpfeiler. See [176] & [732].

Dolomites   A region of extremely severe limestone rock peaks, exhibiting a variety of spectacular shapes and colours. Originally in Austria, but part of Italy since 1918, there is now a confusing duality of nomenclature in Alpine literature. Early English travellers included Gilbert and Churchill, whose classic book [309] convinced English mountaineers of the climbing attractions of the Dolomites. See also [236]. Among the first climbers were Stephen, Freshfield, Tuckett and John Ball, who made the very first Dolomite ascent in 1857. However, the greatest pioneer was Austrian climber Paul Grohmann. Prominent towards the end of the first phase of Dolomite climbing (i.e. 1914) were Norman-Neruda [572], Guido Rey [648], and Leone Sinigaglia [708]. Giusto Gervasutti [307] was one of the leaders in the 1930s heyday of Italian Dolomite climbing. The best all-round book on the area is [523].

Julian, Carnic and Karawanken Alps   The eastern outposts of the Alps, the most impressive mountain being Triglav (Terglou) in the Julian Alps. The great authority on this area was Julius Kugy [434].

Further references to Author Index

Note also:

ANDES

The Andes stretch over 4,000 miles from Cape Horn to Venezuela. Basically the chain is Y-shaped, splitting halfway and continuing northwards as the West and East Cordilleras. In the far north the branches of the Y become more diffuse, breaking into smaller ranges and isolated masses. The general height of the chain is about 20,000', the highest peak being Aconcagua. The character of the mountaineering is somewhere between Alpine and Himalayan; it approaches its most Himalayan in the Peruvian cordilleras. Since 1945 the Andes have attracted climbers in considerable numbers but large areas are still imperfectly known. A good many expeditions and ascents have been made by German climbers and the Santiago-based German community has always had a strong presence. Hardly any of their records are available in English.

Venezuela

Interest centres on a small range, the Sierra Nevada de Merida, explored in 1885 by W. Sievers, who attempted La Columna [**Die Cordillere von Mérida** (Vienna: Holzel, 1888)]. It is a range of alpine rock and ice peaks and Merida has become an important mountaineering centre, very accessible from the United States. The main peaks were first climbed around 1940.

Colombia

The highest coastal mountains in the world, only thirty miles from the sea, are the Sierra Nevada de Santa Marta, an isolated mountain mass little visited or known. Sievers reached the snowline during his travels [**Reise in der Sierra Nevada de Santa Marta** (Leipzig, 1887)]. The mountains were investigated by De Brettcs in 1898 and by A. F. R. Wollaston in 1923. In 1939 Walter A. Wood penetrated the area and climbed several peaks including Pico Christobal Colon.

Another range is the small but beautiful Sierra Nevada de Cocuy, stretching only fifteen miles north-south. The highest peak was climbed in 1942, since when many climbing parties have visited the area, including a Cambridge University group in 1957, who made three first ascents.

Ecuador

The most impressive collection of volcanoes in the world, about thirty in all, make up the Ecuadorian portions of the West and East Cordilleras: the main railway line from the coast to Quito runs between them for about 200 miles. The earliest scientific exploration took place during the years 1736–44, led by the Frenchmen Pierre Bouguer and Charles de La Condamine, who climbed Corazon. The next important traveller to visit the region was Alexander von Humboldt, who climbed Pichincha and attempted Antisana, Cotopaxi and Chimborazo in 1802. Various further attempts were made to climb Cotopaxi until Wilhelm Reiss succeeded in 1872. He was followed by A. Stubel, who made first ascents of several other volcanoes [**Die Vulkanberge von Ecuador** (1897)]. Whymper systematically completed the climbing exploration of the region in 1880, climbing a number of peaks. His book [899] is the great classic of Andean mountaineering. Another expedition was made in 1903 by Hans Meyer [**In den Hochanden von Ecuador** (Berlin, 1907)]. Cotopaxi, Altar and Illiniza are the most interesting from a mountaineering point of view.

Peru

When considering mountaineering in Peru the emphasis switches very definitely to contemporary climbing and Himalaya-style expedition books, with a growing literature in English, either as written or in translation.

Cordillera Blanca These are the greatest tropical mountains in the world, making up the most spectacular range in the Andean chain, with about forty peaks approaching 20,000'. This is a mountaineer's paradise, which since 1945 has offered great climbing rewards for relatively low cost, coupled with ease of access.

Early climbing interest concentrated on Huascaran, the north peak of which was climbed in 1908 by Miss Annie Peck [610], while Sievers explored the valleys in 1909 [**Reise in Peru und Ecuador** (Leipzig, 1914)]. The range was very comprehensively tackled by three D.Ö.A.V. expeditions in the 1930s, led by Phillip Borchers [**Cordillera Blanca** (Munich, 1933)] and [**Die Weisse Kordillere** (Berlin: Scherl, 1935)]. Never has a major range been conquered so quickly; for instance, in 1932 the party made five major first ascents and fourteen others of mountains over 16,000'.

In 1952 two Dutchmen with Lionel Terray climbed Nevados Huantsan and Pongos [239] & [802]. In 1956 a French expedition climbed Taulliraju and Chacraraju

[802], the latter having repulsed several previous parties. A Franco-Belgian party was successful in 1951 on Alpamayo and Quitaraju [430]. Günther Hauser and his companions made several first ascents in the range in 1957 [356].

Cordillera Huayhuash The area was explored by Sievers in 1909 but not visited by climbers until the 1930s. The principal peak is Yerupaja, for many years the highest unclimbed mountain in South America. It was attempted by the Germans in 1936 and climbed by American students,in 1950 [678]. Rondoy has been climbed also [866].

Cordillera de Vilcabamba This range is headed by Salcantay, climbed in 1952 by Bernard Pierre and party [**La conquête du Salcantay** (Paris: Dumont, 1953)]. Veronica and Soray (Humantay) were climbed in 1956. Pumasillo was for a long time something of a mystery mountain, its true position being discovered only in 1956. It was climbed the next year by a Cambridge University party [161].

Cordillera Veronica de Urubamba Malcolm Slesser's party made eight first ascents in this range in 1964 [711].

Cordillera Vilcanota Günther Hauser's party made several first ascents in this range in 1957 [356].

Cordillera Occidental Peru's volcanoes include Charchani and El Misti [610], both climbed by the Incas, perhaps in the fifteenth century. Coropuna was climbed in 1911 by American historian Hiram Bingham.

Bolivia

Like most, Bolivia has its share of volcanoes, in the West Cordillera, topped by Sajama. The snow line is very high and they do not provide very interesting climbing. The main mountaineering interest concentrates on the Cordillera Real, a range some seventy-five miles long, extending from the Sorata massif near Lake Titicaca, on the Peru-Bolivia frontier, south-east to Illimani. The range lies very near to La Paz, the capital of Bolivia. It is the most alpine of Bolivia's ranges, with many glaciers, and is dominated by four huge massifs – Sorata (Anchohuma-Illampu); the Chachacomani-Chearoco complex; Huayna Potosi; and Illimani. Illimani was attempted by Wiener in 1877 but it was Conway's expeditions of 1898 and 1900 that marked the birth of Bolivian mountaineering [179]. Conway achieved a fair measure of success on Anchohuma, Illampu and Illimani. Twenty years later the Germans, Schulze and Dienst, had reached the highest points, also the top of Huayna Potosi [R. Dienst, **Im Dunkelsten Bolivia** (Stuttgart, 1926)]. Most of the other peaks fell to light expeditions, notably a D.O.A.V. party in 1928 and two English parties in 1964 and 1968. See also [335].

On the other side of the deeply-cut La Paz River there is another range of beautiful ice-peaks, the Cordillera Quimsacruz. They are generally lower, although the highest point exceeds 19,000'. Professor Herzog made several ascents here in 1911 [**Bergfahrten in Sudamerika** (Stuttgart, 1925)].

Puna de Atacama (Northern Chile)

An arid, high-level plateau, averaging 12,000', extending 400 miles and bordered by numerous peaks rising to over 20,000'. They carry little permanent snow and are technically easy. The main climbing obstacles are inaccessibility, altitude, cold and wind. Archaeological remains have been found on a number of peaks over

18,000', dating back 500 years or more. [See: Walter Penck, **Puna de Atacama** (Stuttgart, 1933)].

Argentina/Chile

The main Andean cordillera forms the boundary between the two countries and for the first 750 miles southwards (as far as Santiago) it maintains a height of about 20,000', rising to 22,835' in Aconcagua, the highest mountain in the western hemisphere. All the high peaks are of volcanic formation. Thereafter the height of the mountains decreases substantially, while still offering good mountaineering opportunities in places.

Aconcagua Region (Mercedario to Maipu) South of a relatively uninteresting stretch, Mercedario rises up suddenly into a broad massif, ice-capped and glaciated: it was first attempted in 1933 by A. Maass. From here southwards to Aconcagua and Tupungato the mountains are precipitous and craggy: further south the high Andes culminate in Maipu. The first exhaustive exploration of the area, and of Aconcagua, was carried out by Dr. Paul Güssfeldt in 1883 [**Reisen in den Andes** (Berlin, 1888)]. He made the first attempt on Aconcagua, which has now been climbed many times since the first ascent in 1897. It is one of the best documented mountains in the Andes and the subject of important books by Conway [180] and Fitzgerald [273]. See also [948]. In 1954 a French team climbed the very severe south face [262]. The most accessible area for most Chilean mountaineers is the Santiago hinterland, an area which had been thoroughly explored by the late 1930s by resident German climbers. The most frequently climbed peaks include Marmolejo, San Jose and Cerro Plomo.

Lakes District Known as the 'Chilean Switzerland', this area is chiefly in Chile and includes well-known peaks such as Lanin, Osorno, the difficult Tronador, and Puntiagudo, the Chilean 'Matterhorn'.

Patagonia One expert on Patagonia was Eric Shipton, who crossed the ice-cap during his expeditions from 1958 to 1962 [703].

Patagonia is also famous for its stupendous rock-spires such as Fitzroy and the Towers of Paine. Fitzroy was climbed in 1952 by the French [39]. Italians climbed the North Tower of Paine in 1958, while an English party climbed the higher Central Tower in 1963.

Tierra del Fuego Conway was one of the first explorers and attempted Sarmiento [180]. Shipton's party climbed Darwin in 1962, and he also explored Mount Burney, a hitherto unknown mountain [705].

Further reference to Author Index
192. Coverley-Price, V. – An artist among mountains

Note also:
Bingham, H. – Inca Land (Boston, 1922) [Coropuna]
Humboldt, A. von – Personal narrative of travels to the equinoctial regions of America during the years 1799–1804 by... and Aimé Bonpland (Bohn, 1870–1) [Pichincha & others]
Larden, W. – Argentine plains and Andine glaciers (Fisher Unwin, 1911)
Radau, H. – Illampu: adventure in the Andes (Abelard Schumann, 1961)
Tilman, H. W. – 'Mischief' in Patagonia (C.U.P. 1957)
Tschudi, J. J. von – Travels in Peru during the years 1838–42, on the coast, in the Sierra, across the Cordilleras and the Andes, into the primaeval forests (London, 1847)

ANTHOLOGIES

The anthologies included in this bibliography can be grouped into three categories:

(i) on specific subjects, e.g. Mont Blanc
(ii) consisting principally of passages selected from mountaineering books (and journals)
(iii) mixed prose and verse anthologies drawn from all literature (either Alpine only or universal)

Principal references to Author Index
41. Baker, E. A. – The voice of the mountains
245. Engel, C. E. – Mont Blanc
400. Irving, R. L. G. – The mountain way
469. Lunn, A. H. M. – The Englishman in the Alps
583. Noyce, C. W. F. – The climber's fireside book
630. Pyatt, E. C. – British crags and climbers
759. Spender, H. – In praise of Switzerland
771. Styles, F. S. – The mountaineer's weekend book
795. Talbot, D. – Treasury of mountaineering stories
871. Ward, M. P. – The mountaineer's companion

Further references to Author Index
104. Bozman, E. F. – Mountain essays by famous climbers
114. Broughton, G. – Climbing Everest
191. Corbett, E. V. – Great true mountain stories
404. Irwin, W. R. – Challenge
452. Lee, F. H. – The lure of the hills
488. Maeder, H. – The lure of the mountains
514. Merrick, H. – The perpetual hills
722. Smith, G. A. – The armchair mountaineer
743. Smythe, F. S. – The mountain top
785. Styles, F. S. – Men and mountaineering
842. Ullman, J. R. – Kingdom of adventure Everest
941. Young, G. W. – In praise of mountains

Note also:
Lunn, A. H. M. – Switzerland in English prose and poetry (Eyre & Spottiswoode, 1947)

ASIA
(Excluding the Himalaya, Hindu Kush and Karakoram)

Turkey and Iran

The best known mountain in Turkey is Ararat, first climbed in 1829 by Dr. Parrot [599]. Viscount Bryce made the third ascent in 1876 [128]. See also [285]. Ararat is the traditional resting place of Noah's Ark, which people think they have glimpsed [564].

The most alpine ranges are situated in eastern Turkey, little visited by mountaineers until recently. The Rize Mountains, though small in area, are among the finest with many rock, snow and ice routes to be made from the north. The Munzur Mountains are the least known of all the major ranges. They were visited in 1964 by an Austrian party, who claimed the ascent of sixteen virgin peaks ranging from 9,850'–11,150'. Lastly there are the Cilo-Sat Mountains, which have some high peaks with formidable walls. The Cilo-Sat were first explored in 1937 by a German geological and cartographical expedition led by Dr. H. Bobek: several high peaks were climbed. The region remained practically closed until 1965, since when British climbers have been active there. Monica Jackson and a friend made the first all-women ascent of Gelyasin

[408]. In a book by Gwyn Williams [**Eastern Turkey: a guide and history** (Faber, 1972)] there is an appendix on eastern Turkey for the alpinist traveller (written by S. E. P. Nowill), which provides a useful introduction to the eastern ranges and also includes a bibliography of the Cilo-Sat.

The mountaineering possibilities in Iran are chiefly found in the central portion of the Elburz Mountains, south of the Caspian Sea, where the average height of the range is about 13,000'. The principal peak is Demavend, a volcano revered by Iranians. The most alpine part of the range is the Takht-e Soleyman group, which includes Alam Kuh. This mountain boasts a 2,000' rock-wall with considerable scope for rock-climbing. See [138]; also [116].

Central Asia

Not a great deal is known about the vast mountain ranges of central Asia. Certainly there are no peaks which rival the Himalaya for size, the highest being only around 25,000'. The outstanding western explorers of this region were Sven Hedin and Sir Aurel Stein, who between them made many expeditions during 1890–1910. Hedin's **Transhimalaya** is a fascinating record of travel and includes an historical survey of Himalayan exploration. See also [945].

Ta Hsueh Shan The most easterly mountains approaching Himalayan proportions, the best known being Minya Konka. It was climbed in 1932 by members of an American light-weight expedition [134]. See also [612].

Kun Lun The longest mountain system in Asia, rising to over 25,000'. No peaks are known to have been climbed by westerners, W. H. Johnson being mistaken in his claim to have climbed E.61 (Ulugh Muztagh) in 1805. The main Kun Lun range, which separates Tibet from China, has two parallel crests. The northern Altyn Tagh (rising to 17,000') was discovered in 1876 and is vividly described by Hedin. The southern crest, the Arka Tagh, is still largely unknown and to the east breaks up into other ranges such Amne Machin: see [612].

Pamirs The Pamirs lie partly in U.S.S.R. (the Trans-Alai Range) and partly in Chinese Sinkiang. The Trans-Alai was first explored in 1928 by a Russo-German expedition led by W. Rickmer Rickmers [**Alai: Alai** (Leipzig, 1930)]. Members of the party climbed Pik Lenin. There was a great deal of Russian activity in the area in the 1930s, the highest peak being climbed in 1933 [665]. In 1962 a British-Soviet party visited the region: while climbing Wilfrid Noyce was killed [710]. See also [116]. The greatest Pamir peaks are in Sinkiang and include Muztagh Ata [935]. Hedin made four attempts on this peak in 1894. Shipton and Tilman got to within a few feet of the top in 1947 [699] & [819].

Tien Shan A range as long as the Himalaya, otherwise known as the Celestial Mountains. It was explored in 1903 by an expedition led by Professor Merzbacher [515]. A lot of exploration has been carried out in recent years in the north-west (U.S.S.R.) sector. Very little is known of the rest. There is some confusion over the heights and ascents. For many years Khan Tengri was considered to be the highest peak but in 1943 the Russians claimed to have discovered another nearby, which they named Pik Pobeda (Victory Peak). A Russian climbing party visited the area in the 1950s [706]. At the eastern extremity of the Tien Shan is the Bogdo Ola massif, visited by Shipton and Tilman in 1948 [699] & [819]. See also [685].

Altai Another major mountain system but considerably lower. It was explored in the early nineteenth century by Karl von Ledebour and 100 years later by Hedin and Sir Aurel Stein. The U.S.S.R. sector, know as the Great Altai, includes the Katun Range, a truly Alpine area, headed by Gora Beluhka, which Samuel Turner attempted in 1903 [831–2]. The Mongolian Altai is extremely barren and not fully explored.

Siberia The Sayan Mountains form part of the boundary between Siberia and Mongolia. The highest point is 11,453'. Other Siberian ranges of very moderate height include the Chersky Mountains and the Stanovoi Range.

Japan

Mountains cover three-quarters of the total area of Japan but the principal peaks are concentrated in a small section of the main island Honshu. They are known as the North and South Alps, and are separated by a belt of volcanoes, including Fujiyama. The Northern Alps are Japan's most impressive mountains and are more alpine than might be expected from their height and location. Mountaineering as a recreation began in Japan in the 1890s. It was pioneered by Walter Weston, who wrote two classic books on the 'playground of the Far East' [885–6]. Another classic is [869]. The Japanese have since become the world's most enthusiastic mountaineers, both at home and abroad. It is estimated that there are five million climbers and ramblers in the country.

Further references to Author Index

32. Ashenden – The mountains of my life [Includes Turkish climbs]
242. Elwood, H. – Queen's University expedition to the Taurus, 1969
374. Hills, D. C. – My travels in Turkey
422. Kingdon-Ward, F. – Burma's icy mountains

Note also;

Enriquez, C. M. – Kinabalu, the haunted mountain of Borneo (1927)
Gregory, J. W. – To the alps of Chinese Tibet (Seeley Service, 1923)
Hedin, S. – Through Asia (1898) [Muztagh Ata]
Hedin, S. – Transhimalaya (Macmillan, 1909–12) [Includes his discovery of the Altyn Tagh]
Shaw, R. B. – Visits to High Tartary (Murray, 1871)
Stark, F. – The Valleys of the Assassins (1934) [Iran]
Whitehead, J. – Exploration of Mount Kina Balu (Gurney & Jackson, 1893)

AUSTRALASIA
(Excluding New Zealand)

Australia

Australia offers less mountaineering opportunity than any other major world land mass. The highest point is Mount Kosciusko in the Snowy Mountains, which provide fine high mountain skiing [526]. One of the first European mountaineers to visit Australia was R. von Lendenfeld, who went on to do pioneer work in the New Zealand Alps [**Australische Reise** (Innsbruck: Wagner, 1892)]. A great deal of rock-climbing is done nowadays in Australia but the best climbing is on the island of Tasmania, where the colder climate makes the mountains more alpine.

New Guinea

This second largest island in the world is divided territorially between West Irian (formerly Dutch New Guinea) and Australia. The most important peaks lie in former Dutch territory, which constitutes the western third of the island. The (apparently) highest point is Carstensz Pyramid. The original exploration was carried out by A. F. R. Wollaston in 1911 and 1913 but he was only able to reach the foot of the mountains. Using an aeroplane to overcome the jungle approach, a Dutch party managed to climb Ngapalu in 1936 [A. H. Colijn, **Naar de eeuwige Sneeuw van tropisch Nederland** (Amsterdam: Scheltens & Giltay, 1937)]. This party and a New Zealand expedition in 1961 [**799**] both failed to climb the highest peak but Heinrich Harrer was more successful the following year, climbing all thirty-one tops of the Carstenz complex [**348**]. In 1959 a Dutch scientific expedition climbed Juliana in the Antares Mountains further east [**113**]. There is considerable confusion over heights and nomenclature in the Carstenz group.

Note also:

Barrett, C. – Isle of Mountains (Cassell, 1944) [Tasmania]

Groom, A. – One mountain after another (Angus & Robertson, 1949) [MacPherson Range, eastern Australia]

Wollaston, A. F. R. – Pygmies and Papuans: the Stone age today in Dutch New Guinea (1912)

AUTOBIOGRAPHIES

Principal references to Author Index

17. Alack, F. – Guide aspiring [New Zealand]
90. Bonington, C. – I chose to climb
94. Bonington, C. – The next horizon
102. Bowie, M. – The Hermitage years [New Zealand guide]
116. Brown, J. – The hard years: an autobiography
165. Clyde, N. – Norman Clyde of the Sierra Nevada
214. Diemberger, K. – Summits and secrets
322. Graham, P. – Peter Graham: mountain guide
373. Hillary, E. P. – Nothing venture, nothing win
415. Kain, C. – Where the clouds can go [Austrian guide in Canada]
425. Klucker, C. – Adventures of an Alpine guide
527. Moffat, G. – Space below my feet
529. Moffat, G. – On my home ground
530. Moffat, G. – Survival count
574. Noyce, C. W. F. – Mountains and men
704. Shipton, E. E. – That untravelled world
948. Zurbriggen, M. – From the Alps to the Andes

Further references to Author Index

27. Amery, L. C. M. S. – Days of fresh air
28. Amery, L. C. M. S. – In the rain and the sun
304. Geiger, H. – Alpine pilot

Note also:

Bonney, T. G. – Memories of a long life (Cambridge, privately, 1921)

Browning, O. – Memories of sixty years at Eton, Cambridge and elsewhere (Lane, 1910)

Bryce, J. – Memories of travel (Macmillan, 1923)

Clark, J. I. – Pictures and memories (Moray Press, 1938)

Conway, W. M. – Episodes in a varied life (Country Life, 1932)

Harper, A. P. – Memories of mountains and men (Christchurch: Simpson & Williams, 1946)

Le Blond, Mrs. – Day in, day out (Lane Bodley Head, 1928)

Lunn, A. H. M. – Unkilled for so long (Allen & Unwin, 1968)

Mannering, C. E. – Eighty years in New Zealand (1943)

BIOGRAPHIES

Principal references to Author Index

25. Ament, P. – Master of rock [John Gill]
148. Clark, R. W. – The splendid hills: the life and photographs of Vittorio Sella 1859–1943
157. Clark, R. W. – An eccentric in the Alps: the story of the Rev. W. A. B. Coolidge
238. [Edwards, J. M.] – Samson: the life and writings of Menlove Edwards
292. Freshfield, D. W. – The life of Horace-Bénédict de Saussure
343. Hankinson, A. – Camera on the crags: a portfolio of early rock climbing photographs by the Abraham Brothers
597. Palmer, H. – Edward W. D. Holway: a pioneer of the Canadian Alps
602. Pascoe, J. D. – Mr. Explorer Douglas [New Zealand]
615. Petzoldt, P. – On top of the world [Grand Teton guide]
636. Pye, D. R. – George Leigh Mallory
658. Robertson, D. – George Mallory
736. Smythe, F. S. – Edward Whymper
808. Thorington, J. M. – Mont Blanc sideshow: the life and times of Albert Smith
845. Ullman, J. R. – Man of Everest [Tenzing Norgay]
849. Ullman, J. R. – Straight up: the life and death of John Harlin
923. Wolfe, L. M. – John of the mountains: unpublished journals of John Muir

Further references to Author Index

426. Knoop, F. Y. – A world explorer: Sir Edmund Hillary
435. Kugy, J. – Son of the mountains [Anton Oitzinger]
490. Malartic, Y. – Tenzing of Everest
534. Moon, K. – Man of Everest: the story of Sir Edmund Hillary
673. Russell, J. – Climb if you will [Geoff Hayes]
784. Styles, S. – Mallory of Everest
853. Unsworth, W. – Matterhorn man: being the life and adventures of Edward Whymper
854. Unsworth, W. – Tiger in the snow: the life and adventures of A. F. Mummery

Note also:

Annan, N. G. – Leslie Stephen: his thought and character in relation to his time (1951)

Badé, W. F. – Life and Letters of John Muir (Boston: Houghton Mifflin, 1903)

Barker, R. – One man's jungle: a biography of F. Spencer Chapman (Chatto, 1975)

Douglas, W. O. – Muir of the mountains (1961)

Eve, A. S. – Life and work of John Tyndall. By ... and C. H. Creasey (Macmillan, 1945)

Fitzsimons, R. – The Baron of Piccadilly (Bles, 1967) [Albert Smith]

Maitland, F. W. – Life and letters of Leslie Stephen (Duckworth, 1906)

Shairp, J. C. – Life and letters of James David Forbes. By . . . , P. G. Tait and A. H. W. Adams-Reilly (Macmillan, 1873)

Wilkins, T. – Clarence King (New York: Macmillan, 1958)

Wolfe, L. M. – Son of the wilderness: the life of John Muir (New York: Knopf, 1945)

[Wollaston, A. F. R.] – Life and letters of A. F. R. Wollaston (C.U.P. 1933)

Biographical sketches

The following references are to **The climber's bedside book** by Showell Styles [786] and **Because it is there: famous mountaineers, 1840–1940** by Walter Unsworth [855].

Subject	[786]	[855]
Duke of Abruzzi	*	
John Ball	*	
Meta Brevoort	*	
Lily Bristow		*
C. G. Bruce	*	*
H. Buhl	*	
J. N. Collie	*	*
W. M. Conway	*	*
W. A. B. Coolidge	*	
C. T. Dent	*	
H. B. de Saussure	*	
O. Eckenstein		*
J. M. Edwards		*
J. D. Forbes	*	
D. W. Freshfield	*	
H. B. George	*	
W. S. Green	*	
D. Hadow	*	
S. W. Herford		*
Hopkinson Brothers		*
C. Hudson	*	
A. C. Irvine	*	
O. G. Jones	*	*
E. S. Kennedy	*	
C. F. Kirkus		*
Mrs. Le Blond	*	
T. G. Longstaff	*	
G. L. Mallory	*	*
C. E. Mathews	*	
W. Mathews	*	
A. W. Moore	*	
A. F. Mummery	*	*
C. W. F. Noyce	*	
Michel Paccard	*	
Pilkington Brothers		*
G. Rey		*
W. C. Slingsby	*	*
Albert Smith		*
F. S. Smythe	*	*
L. Stephen	*	
Miss Straton	*	
Eustace Thomas	*	
'Tschingel'	*	
C. C. Tucker	*	
F. F. Tuckett	*	
J. Tyndall	*	
Walker Family	*	*
E. Whymper	*	*
A. Wills	*	
Mr. & Mrs. Workman	*	
Winthrop Young		*
F. E. Younghusband	*	

BRITISH ISLES

Although British hills are pygmies in the mountain scale they have played a considerable part in the achievements of British climbers. Originally they were used by the Victorian alpinists to practise their snow and ice climbing during the winter but they quickly came to be recognized as mountain playgrounds in their own right. British rock-climbing is dated from W. P. Haskett Smith's solo ascent of Napes Needle in 1886: he subsequently produced the first British guidebook [725]. The British hills are still excellent training grounds for the most severe modern mountaineering exploits. The principal mountain areas are Snowdonia in North Wales; the English Lake District; and Scotland. There are also numerous lesser climbing grounds, the most famous being the Peak District.

Climbing in Britain has seen three great advances. The turn of the century was the era of O. G. Jones and the Abraham brothers, whose three books on rock-climbing [1], [2] & [414] are an important and highly prized trilogy. Other important figures include Collie [170] and Oppenheimer [590]. See also [4] & [40]. The period between the wars also saw considerable progress in rock-climbing but particularly in Scottish climbing. One of the great Scottish all-round climbers of this period is W. H. Murray [558–9]. One of his contemporaries, J. H. B. Bell, emphasizes the value of Scottish winter climbing as preparation for the Alps [75]. See also [238] & [879]. The greatest advance in rock-climbing came after 1945, led by Joe Brown and Don Whillans [116] & [893]. Eric Byne [140] attributed the success of the Joe Brown school to their training on Derbyshire gritstone. Two fine records of modern Welsh rock-climbing are [745] & [752]. See also [921].

Several histories have been published covering the following: mountaineering in Britain [155]; Lake District rock-climbing [342]; Snowdonia [142] & [943]; Skye [392]; Peak District [140]. An interesting anthology by Pyatt and Noyce [630] demonstrates the progress of British rock-climbing.

Other books on various aspects of the British climbing scene include: fiction [193]; mountain rescue [482] & [528]; outcrops [852] and sea cliffs [162]; photo-albums [626]; professional guiding [527] & [931]; Scottish islands [767].

Further references to Author Index

5. Abraham, G. D. – Mountain adventures at home and abroad
7. Abraham, G. D. – On Alpine heights and British crags
15. Airey, A. F. – Irish hill days
42. Baker, E. A. – The Highlands with rope and rucksack
43. Baker, E. A. – The British highlands with rope and rucksack
60. Barrow, J. – Mountain ascents in Westmoreland and Cumberland
74. Bell, J. H. B. – British hills and mountains
76. Benson, C. E. – Crag and hound in Lakeland
84. Bicknell, P. – British hills and mountains
100. Borthwick, A. – Always a little further
218. Docharty, W. M. – Selection of 900 British and Irish tops
222. Doughty, J. H. – Hill-writings of J. H. Doughty
283. Frere, R. B. – Thoughts of a mountaineer [Scotland]

339.   Hall, R. W. – The art of mountain tramping
391.   Humble, B. H. – On Scottish hills
419.   Kilgour, W. T. – Twenty years' on Ben Nevis [Observatory service]
533.   Monkhouse, F. – Climber and fellwalker in Lakeland 541.
541.   Mould, D. D. C. P. – Mountains of Ireland
604.   Paterson, M. – Mountaineering below the snowline
614.   Perry, A. W. – Welsh mountaineering
631.   Pyatt, E. C. – Where to climb in the British Isles
633.   Pyatt, E. C. – Mountains of Britain
634.   Pyatt, E. C. – Climber in the West Country
635.   Pyatt, E. C. – Climbing and walking in south-east England
680.   Salt, H. S. – On Cambrian and Cumbrian hills
681.   Sandeman, R. R. – A mountaineer's journal [Scotland]
770.   Styles, S. – A climber in Wales
788.   Styles, S. – Mountains of North Wales
862.   Walker, J. H. – Mountain days in the Highlands and Alps
863.   Walker, J. H. – On hills of the North
865.   Wall, C. W. – Mountaineering in Ireland
933.   Wright, J. E. B. – Rock-climbing in Britain

CANADA

(See Alaska for the Canadian portion of the St. Elias Mountains).

The principal mountain chain in Canada is the Rocky Mountains, with 675 named peaks over 10,000'. They are limestone mountains, which accounts for their distinctive appearance. Despite their relatively modest height they are mountains of truly Alpine character, many of them demanding considerable mountaineering skill. There are forty-seven peaks over 11,000' and four over 12,000'. The highest is Mount Robson. This vast area of western Canada was almost unknown when W. S. Green explored the Selkirks in 1888. Today the mountain names testify to the subsequent presence and activity of British climbers. In the period 1897–1902 Professor Collie and various friends made four expeditions, and there were others. Additionally, Americans Howard Palmer and J. Monroe Thorington have carried out much exploratory work and produced authoritative books on the region.

Rocky Mountains

The main range stretches approximately 450 miles north from the United States border. The principal groups were discovered and mapped by Dr. Hector during the Palliser Expedition (1857–60). Among the early travellers were fur traders, then railway engineers. One notable journey was that of Viscount Milton and Dr. Cheadle, who crossed the mountains in 1863 from the headwaters of the Athabasca to those of the Fraser River, over the Yellowhead Pass. The climbers arrived in the 1890s. Collie was chiefly responsible for exploring and mapping the very mountainous area between Fortress Lake and Lake Louise, all subsequent maps being based on his. During his climbs he discovered the Columbia ice-field, the largest permanent body of ice outside the polar regions [769]. Others who were climbing in the area at this time included Sir James Outram [592] and W. D. Wilcox [905]. One of the most interesting of all the accounts of Canadian mountain exploration and climbing is a book [168] by Arthur Coleman.

The standard climber's guide to the Rockies [596] sub-divides the main range into twenty-nine sections. The most important of these are:

(i) south of Kicking Horse Pass – Assiniboine (Grp 6) and the Lake Louise area (Grp 10)
(ii) Kicking Horse Pass to Yellowhead Pass – Freshfield-Forbes (Grps 16–17) and Columbia group (Grp 19)
(iii) north of Yellowhead Pass – Mount Robson (Grp 26).

Mount Robson is a most impressive mountain, rising 10,000' above the valley in its southern aspect, and presenting Himalaya-style problems in its north-west ridge. Five attempts were made in 1908–9, It was climbed in 1913, the party being led by the Austrian guide Conrad Kain [415]. This was his greatest climb, up the very difficult east face and down the south glacier and SSW ridge.

Edward Whymper was another visitor to the Rockies in the period 1901–5. He was chiefly engaged on the preparation of publicity material for the Canadian Pacific Railway [141] and did no serious climbing, much to the disgust of his guides, including Christian Klucker [425]. One of the most knowledgeable men on the subject of Canadian mountaineering is J. Monroe Thorington, who recorded his own explorations and ascents (1914–24) [807] and who has been closely involved with the principal Canadian guidebooks.

About 400 miles north of Mount Robson lies the Lloyd George Range, explored by Frank Smythe in 1947 [744]. He also climbed on the main range.

Interior Ranges

The first mountaineering visitor was W. S. Green, who explored the Selkirk Range in 1888 and climbed Mt. Bonney [328]. The period 1890–1910 saw most of the Selkirk peaks climbed, many of the first ascents being made by E. W. D. Holway [597] and Howard Palmer, who produced the principal book on the range [595]. Arthur Wheeler was another authority on the area [887–8]

There are three other interior ranges – Purcells [810], Cariboo and Monashee (Gold Range). The Cariboo to the north is still partly unsurveyed: the first climbers to visit the range were Holway and Gilmour in 1916. The dense undergrowth makes the approaches to the peaks very difficult. A similar situation obtains in the Monashee Mountains to the west of the Selkirks, first visited by Milton and Cheadle in 1863.

Coast Mountains of British Columbia

It was not until the 1920s that it gradually became obvious that there was at least one peak in these ranges that equalled or over-topped Mt. Robson in height. The climber who did most to unravel the uncertainties surrounding 'Mystery Mountain' (Mt. Waddington) was Don Munday [556]. Another party explored the area and made the first ski crossing of the Coast Mountains [877].

Further references to Author Index

26.   Fay, C. E. – The Canadian Rocky Mountains [Alpina Americana 2]
27.   Amery, L. C. M. S. – Days of fresh air
28.   Amery, L. C. M. S. – In the rain and the sun
44.   Baker, G. P. – Mountaineering memories of the past
137.   Burpee, L. J. – Among the Canadian Alps
170.   Collie, J. N. – Climbing on the Himalaya and other mountain ranges

208. Delville, E. – Description of & guide to Jasper Park
282. Freeman, L. R. – On the roof of the Rockies: the great Columbia icefield of the Canadian Rockies
411. Jeffers, L. – The call of the mountains: rambles among the mountains and canyons of the United States and Canada
413. Jones, C. – Climbing in North America
460. Longstaff, T. G. – This my voyage
695. Sherman, P. – Cloud walkers: six climbs on major Canadian peaks
912. Williams, M. B. – Jasper National Park

Note also:
Milton/Cheadle – The North-west passage by land (Cassell, 1865)
Phillips, W. J. – Colour in the Canadian Rockies (Nelson Canada, 1937)
Williams, M. B. – Through the heart of the Rockies and Selkirks (1921)

CAVING (Spelaeology)
Caving books are excluded from this bibliography. However, there are a few books which include this subject.

References to Author Index
40. Baker, E. A. – Moors, crags and caves of the High Peak
598. Palmer, W. T. – The complete hillwalker, rock climber and cave explorer
649. Richard, C. – Climbing blind

CHILDREN'S BOOKS
This is a large, indefinite category as it is not always easy to draw a line between adult and juvenile reading. In the past many famous mountaineers have grown up on a reading diet consisting largely of the Alpine classics and the **Alpine Journal.** Most mountaineering books, if they are at all readable, may be enjoyed by old and young alike; a very good example of this is a book [804] by Lowell Thomas. Some books clearly declare their intended audience. The following lists are by no means exhaustive.

Principal references to Author Index
151. Clark, R. W. – Come climbing with me
153. Clark, R. W. – Great moments in mountaineering
154. Clark, R. W. – Six great mountaineers
156. Clark, R. W. – The true book about mountaineering
248. Evans, R. C. – Eye on Everest [Sketchbook]
453. Lefebure, M. – Scratch & Co. [Fiction]
632. Pyatt, E. C. – Boy's book of mountains and mountaineering
775. Styles, S. – Getting to know mountains
776. Styles, S. – How mountains are climbed
777. Styles, S. – Look at mountains
804. Thomas, L. – Lowell Thomas' book of the high mountains
851. Unsworth, W. – The young mountaineer
853. Unsworth, W. – Matterhorn man [Whymper]
854. Unsworth, W. – Tiger in the snow [Mummery]
855. Unsworth, W. – Because it is there: famous mountaineers, 1840–1940
856. Unsworth, W. – The book of rock-climbing
874. Washburn, H. B. – Among the Alps with Bradford
875. Washburn, H. B. – Bradford on Mount Washington
876. Washburn, H. B. – Bradford on Mount Fairweather
895. White, A. T. – All about mountains and mountaineering

Further references to Author Index
14. Ahluwalia, H. P. S. – Climbing Everest
56. Banks, M. E. B. – Snow commando
109. Briggs, R. – First up Everest
220. Dodderidge, M. – Man on the Matterhorn
306. George, M. M. – A little journey to Switzerland: for home and school
378. Hoare, R. J. – The high peaks
389. Huf, H. – English mountaineers
418. Kennett, J. – The story of Annapurna
485. McMorris, W. B. – The real book of mountaineering
534. Moon, K. – Man of Everest: the story of Sir Edmund Hillary
577. Noyce, C. W. F. – Everest is climbed
623. Platt, W. – The joy of mountains
701. Shipton, E. E. – The true book about Everest
746. Snaith, S. – At grips with Everest
747. Snaith, S. – Alpine adventure
762. Stead, R. – Daring deeds of great mountaineers
873. Warwick, A. R. – With Whymper in the Alps

CLIMBING MEMOIRS
This is a diffuse category, which is liable to include too many books to be useful. Of those listed below, some are almost autobiographies, while others are only fragments of a varied (or not so varied) climbing career.

Principal references to Author Index
88. Bonatti, W. – On the heights
89. Bonatti, W. – The great days
105. Braham, T. – Himalayan odyssey
122. Bruce, C. G. – Twenty years in the Himalaya
123. Bruce, C. G. – Kulu and Lahoul
125. Bruce, C. G. – Himalayan wanderer
131. Buhl, H. – Nanga Parbat pilgrimage
170. Collie, J. N. – Climbing on the Himalaya and other mountain ranges
267. Finch, G. I. – The making of a mountaineer
307. Gervasutti, G. – Gervasutti's climbs
313. Gill, M. – Mountain midsummer: climbing in four continents
325. Gray, D. D. – Rope boy
354. Haston, D. – In high places
360. Heckmair, A. – My life as a mountaineer
406. Jackson, J. A. – More than mountains
434. Kugy, J. – Alpine pilgrimage
442. Larden, W. – Recollections of an old mountaineer
460. Longstaff, T. G. – This my voyage
507. Mazeaud, P. – Naked before the mountain
516. Messner, R. – The seventh grade: most extreme climbing
539. Morin, N. – A woman's reach: mountaineering memoirs
555. Mummery, A. F. – My climbs in the Alps and Caucasus
600. Pascoe, J. D. – Unclimbed New Zealand: alpine travel in the Canterbury and Westland Ranges, Southern Alps
601. Pascoe, J. D. – Land uplifted high
605. Patey, T. W. – One man's mountains: essays and verses
621. Pilley, D. – Climbing days
662. Roch, A. – Climbs of my youth

674. Russell, R. S. – Mountain prospect
688. Schuster, C. – Peaks and pleasant pastures
689. Schuster, C. – Men, women and mountains: days in the Alps and Pyrenees
690. Schuster, C. – Postscript to adventure
737. Smythe, F. S. – The adventures of a mountaineer
802. Terray, L. – Conquistadors of the useless: from the Alps to Annapurna
832. Turner, S. – My climbing adventures in four continents
872. Ward, M. P. – In this short span
893. Whillans, D. D. – Don Whillans: portrait of a mountaineer
939. Young, G. W. – On high hills: memories of the Alps
942. Young, G. W. – Mountains with a difference

Further references to Author Index

5. Abraham, G. D. – Mountain adventures at home and abroad
7. Abraham, G. D. – On Alpine heights and British crags
13. Ahluwalia, H. P. S. – Higher than Everest: memoirs of a mountaineer
32. Ashenden – The mountains of my life: journeys in Turkey and the Alps
42. Baker, E. A. – The Highlands with rope and rucksack
44. Baker, G. P. – Mountaineering memories of the past
54. Banks, M. E. B. – Commando climber
138. Busk, D. L. – The delectable mountains
146. Chapman, F. S. – Helvellyn to Himalaya: including an account of the first ascent of Chomolhari
192. Coverley-Price, V. – An artist among mountains
196. Croucher, N. – High hopes
232. Durham, W. E. – Summer holidays in the Alps 1898–1914
277. Fox, J. H. – Holiday memories
283. Frere, R. B. – Thoughts of a mountaineer
341. Hamilton, H. – Mountain madness
410. Javelle, E. – Alpine memories
411. Jeffers, L. – The call of the mountains: rambles among the mountains and canyons of the Unites States and Canada.
456. Lewin, W. H. – Climbs
462. Lowe, W. G. – Because it is there
471. Lunn, A. H. M. – The mountains of youth
473. Lunn, A. H. M. – Mountains of memory
502. Mason, G. – Minus three
622. Pius XI – Climbs on Alpine peaks
649. Richard, C. – Climbing blind
713. Smeeton, M. – A taste of the hills
723. Smith, J. A. – Mountain holidays
779. Styles, S. – Blue remembered hills
805. Thompson, D. – Climbing with Joseph Georges
862. Walker, J. H. – Mountain days in the Highlands and Alps
884. Westmorland, H. – Adventures in climbing

DICTIONARIES AND ENCYCLOPAEDIAS

129. Bueler, W. M. – Mountains of the world: a handbook for climbers and hikers
172. Collomb, R. G. – A dictionary of mountaineering
195. Crew, P. – Encyclopaedic dictionary of mountaineering

397. Huxley, A. J. – Standard encyclopaedia of the world's mountains
458. Livani, M. – Encyclopaedia of the world's mountains
584. McMorrin, I. – World atlas of mountaineering
858. Unsworth, W. – Encyclopaedia of mountaineering

EIGHT-THOUSAND METRE PEAKS

The ascent of Annapurna in 1950 was mountaineering's equivalent of the four-minute mile and ushered in the 'Golden Age' of Himalayan ascents. The history of the 8,000-metre peaks to end-1954 is summarized in [234]. See also [337] & [503].

Annapurna

The first big post-war expedition and the first success. Climbed by the French in 1950 [366]. The South Face was climbed by a British party in 1970 [91].

Broad Peak

First attempted in 1954 by Karl Herligkoffer [Deutsche am Broad Peak, 8047m (Munich: Lehmanns, 1955)] and climbed in 1957 by an Austrian expedition, which included Buhl and Diemberger [M. Schmuck, Broad Peak, 8047 (Stuttgart: Berglandbuch, 1958)]. See also [214].

Cho Oyu

Reconnoitred by Hillary in 1952 [362]. It was climbed by three Austrians in 1954 under the noses of a French expedition, which included Claude Kogan [438] Later she was killed on the mountain with an all-women expedition [346].

Dhaulagiri

Reconnoitred by French and Swiss expeditions in 1950 and 1953 [M. Eichelberg, Dza, dza-dem Himalaya zu (Zurich: Arche, 1953)]. Attempted by Argentine climbers in 1954. Many others followed and failed. Finally climbed by the Swiss in 1960 [241]. See also [214] & [353].

Everest

The Everest literature is so extensive that a separate section has been devoted to it: see EVEREST.

Gasherbrum II

Reconnoitred by Dyrenfurth's international expedition in 1934 and climbed by an Austrian party in 1956.

Gosainthan (Shisha Pangma)

The main summit is in Tibet and therefore inaccessible. Tilman brought back a little information [820], also an Austrian party [H. Kruparz, Shisha Pangma (Vienna: Kremayr & Sherian, 1954)]. The Chinese claim the first ascent in 1964 [612].

Hidden Peak (Gasherbrum I)

Attempted by a French expedition in 1936 [247] and climbed by an American party in 1958.

K2

The second highest mountain in the world. Attempted by a powerful expedition under Eckenstein and Crowley in 1902, followed by the Duke of Abruzzi in 1909 [266]. The next major attempt was by Americans in 1938 [65] & [615]. This was followed in 1939 by a disastrous expedition [223] & [840]. They returned to the attack in 1953 when the whole party were nearly swept away

[385]. The Italians were successful in 1954 [212].

Kanchenjunga

Freshfield did important exploratory work in 1899 [289] and was followed by others in 1905, 1920 and 1925. In 1929 the first serious attempt was made by the Germans under Bauer [66]. They were followed in 1930 by an international group [728]. The Germans returned in 1931 [66]. A reconnaissance in 1954 [826] paved the way for British success the following year [249]. See also [116].

Lhotse

A satellite of Everest, it has virtually no literature of its own. First climbed by the Swiss in 1956 [240].

Makalu

The French succeeded in 1956 after failure the previous year [279] & [802]. Hillary's 1961 expedition came to grief [371] & [550]. See also [313] & [872].

Manaslu

Formerly known as Kutang I. The great Japanese Himalayan ascent. Reconnoitred by them in 1952, followed by an attempt in 1953. They finally got there in 1956.

Nanga Parbat

Plucky but ill-fated attempt by Mummery and his friends in 1895 [170]. Thereafter it became a German preserve. There were repeated attacks – in 1932 [429]; in 1934, which ended in disaster [71]; 1937, another disaster [67]; 1938 and 1939. In 1950 three Englishmen made a winter attempt; two died. The Germans and Austrians returned in 1953 and managed to settle the score [364]. Success came with Hermann Buhl's solo dash for the summit, an achievement which will always rank high among the great feats of mountaineering and human endurance [131]. See also [69].

Further references to Author Index

68. Bauer, P. – Kanchenjunga challenge
418. Kennett, J. – The story of Annapurna

ESSAYS

References to Author Index

64. Basterfield, G. – Mountain lure [Essays and verses]
222. Doughty, J. H. – Hill-writings of J. H. Doughty
402. Irving, R. L. G. – Ten great mountains
468. Lunn, A. H. M. – Oxford mountaineering essays
532. Molony, E. – Portraits of mountains
576. Noyce, C. W. F. – Scholar mountaineers
605. Patey, T. W. – One man's mountains: essays and verses
690. Schuster, C. – Postscript to adventure
859. Van Dyke, J. C. – The mountain: renewed studies in impressions and appearances

Note also:
Chorley, K. – Hills and highways (Dent, 1928)

EUROPE

(Excluding the Alps and British Isles)

Caucasus

The Caucasus is a range lying between the Black Sea and the Caspian Sea. It runs in the direction NW–SE for 600 miles and has only one main crest. Conditions are very similar to the Alps and the principal peaks are situated in the 120-mile central portion from Elbruz, in the west, to Kazbek in the east.

The first climbing expedition was made in 1868 by Freshfield. This marked the start of modern mountaineering beyond the Alps. Freshfield's party made the first undisputed ascent of the lower summit of Elbruz, and also the first ascent of Kazbek [285]. In 1874 A. W. Moore and his companions climbed the higher peak of Elbruz and made a further journey of exploration through the range [336]. The period 1886–96 was one of intensive English attack and most of the main peaks were climbed. Mummery made the first ascent of Dykh-tau in 1888 [555]. Freshfield produced a magnificent two-volume history of the exploration of the Caucasus [288].

The higher peak of Ushba was finally climbed in 1903 after a great struggle [402]. There were many visits by continental climbers between the wars, particularly Germans and Austrians. Russian climbers have progressively tackled the hardest peaks, while thousands make easy expeditions annually. In 1957 Joyce Dunsheath climbed with a Russian party [231] and the following year saw a full-scale Anglo-Russian expedition in the area [396]. This book includes a useful summary of the mountaineering history of the Caucasus. See also [359].

It should be borne in mind, when reading the early books, that in the nineteenth century some of the peaks were known by different or erroneous names, viz:

Modern name	Old references
Koshtan-tau	Dykh-tau
Shkhara	Koshtan-tau
Dykh-tau	Guluku: or, Koshtan-tau
Katuin-tau	Saddle Peak: or, Adish-tau
Gestola	Tetnuld
Tetnuld	Totonal

Pyrenees

Straddling the Franco-Spanish frontier the Pyrenees average about 10,000', rising to 11,168' in the Maladetta. A good deal has been written about the area but very little in English which can be classed as mountaineering literature. Hilaire Belloc's **The Pyrenees** (1900) is one of the best introductions to the range.

The pioneer of Pyrenean mountaineering was Baron Ramond de Carbonnières, who explored the range and eventually made the first ascent of Mont Perdu [638]. See also [333]. However it was Charles Packe who was chiefly responsible for opening up the Pyrenees as a mountaineering district in the 1860s. His guidebook [594], which is in the style of Ball's **Alpine Guide,** remained the standard work until the turn of the century, although it was long out of print. Another pioneer was Packe's friend, the eccentric Count Henri Russell-Killough, whose principal interest in life was 'le Pyrénéisme' and who devoted his later years to building grottoes on the Vignemale. The principal record of holiday exploration and climbing is Harold Spender's book [758] published in 1898. It includes an extensive bibliography. See also [258] & [689].

Norway

James Forbes visited Norway in 1851 to study the glaciers [276] but Norwegian mountaineering did not really commence until 1872 when W. C. Slingsby paid the first of sixteen visits spanning the next thirty years. His favourite climb was his first ascent of Skagastolstind, still considered a difficult route. His book on Norway [712] is one of the best-loved mountaineering classics. Around the turn of the century Mrs. Le Blond climbed on the Lyngen Peninsula [450] and E. C. Oppenheim recorded details of new climbs in the Sondmore district [588]. More recently Showell Styles and Tom Weir have written about their climbs on the Lyngen Peninsula [772] and Lofoten Isles [881].

All the important climbing areas of Norway are described in detail in [629]. See also [263] & [379].

Polish Tatras

A small region of rocky peaks and serrated ridges, rising to nearly 9,000'. Mountaineering did not commence in earnest until the 1880s when Dr. Chalubinski reached most of the easier virgin summits. Two important ascents preceded his activities; that of Lomnica in 1793 by Robert Townson and the ascent of Ladovy in 1843 by John Ball. Leslie Stephen and James Bryce visited the Tatra in 1878 and made a few minor ascents. What little has been written in English about this important range will be found mostly in the A.J. See [269].

Other European mountains

Other mountain regions of Europe offer possibilities for climbing. Corsica is one of the most mountainous islands in the world, with fine rock peaks, and snow in winter. References include [267], [293], [621], & [727]. Useful notes on the principal peaks and areas of the rest of Europe will be found in Bueler's excellent hand-book [129]. See also [190].

Note also:

Bryce, J. – Memories of travel (Macmillan, 1923) [Tatras]

Townson, R. – Travels in Hungary (1797) [Tatras]

EVEREST

Everest climbing and literature is so extensive that it must be analysed in detail but basically there have been three phases, viz:

(i) exclusively British attempts via Tibet and the North Col (1921-38)

(ii) reconnaissance, Swiss failure and British success via Nepal and the South Col (1950-3)

(iii) attempts and ascents by various nationalities and by various routes (1956 onwards).

Summary of expeditions		Principal References	
		Chief Accounts	Other Accounts
1913	Noel's exploration of Tibetan approaches	570	
1921	Major reconnaissance	387	
1922	Climbing expedition	124	570, 751
1924	Mallory and Irving disappear near the summit	573	570, 751
1933	Further attempt	675	733
1933	First flight over summit	260	166
1934	Solo attempt by Maurice Wilson	657	
1935	Reconnaissance		698
1936	Major attempt	677	
1938	Light climbing expedition	817	
1947	Earl Denman's solo attempt	209	
1950	First approached from the south by Tilman and Houston		820
1951	Shipton's party reconnoitre Western Cwm	700	369, 872
1951	Solo attempt by R. B. Larsen		
1952	Swiss almost succeed via South Col	216	663, 793
1953	British success via South Col	393	248, 332, 369, 540, 576
1956	Swiss ascent. Ascent of Lhotse	240	
1960	Chinese claim ascent via North Col	612	
1960	First Indian attempt	707	
1962	Unauthorized American climbing party	683	
1962	Second Indian attempt	213	
1963	American expedition. Three parties reached the summit, including West Ridge route and traverse	848	383, 478
1965	Indian expedition which put four parties on summit	432	
1966	Chinese attempt from north		
1968	Chinese attempt		
1969	Japanese reconnoitre SW face		
1970	Japanese ascents via South Col		
1971	International expedition		764
1971	Argentine expedition		

1972	International expedition		
1972	Major British attempt on SW Face	92	
1973	Italian ascents		
1973	Japanese expedition to SW Face		
1975	British success on SW Face	96	

Mention should also be made of two summaries. The first is Younghusband's account of the 1921–24 expeditions [946], which in some ways were the most exciting of all, and the other is W. H. Murray's summary up to 1953 and the first ascent [561].

Further references to Author Index

109. Briggs, R. – First up Everest
114. Broughton, G. – Climbing Everest [Anthology]
127. Bryant, L. V. – New Zealanders and Everest
221. Dolbier, M. – Nowhere near Everest
267. Finch, G. I. – The making of a mountaineer
268. Finch, G. I. – Climbing Mount Everest
321. Goswami, S. M. – Everest, is it conquered?
354. Haston, D. – In high places
395. Hunt, J. – Our Everest adventure: the pictorial history from Kathmandu to the summit
405. Izzard, R. W. B. – The innocent on Everest
484. MacIntyre, N. – Attack on Everest
499. Marshall, H. – Men against Everest
507. Mazeaud, P. – Naked before the mountain
538. Morin, M. – Everest – from the first attempt to the final victory
577. Noyce, C. W. F. – Everest is climbed
694. Serraillier, I. – Everest climbed [Poem]
701. Shipton, E. E. – The true book about Everest
746. Snaith, S. – At grips with Everest
842. Ullman, J. R. – Kingdom of adventure Everest: a chronicle of Man's assault on the Earth's highest mountain
872. Ward, M. P. – In this short span
903. Wibberley, L. – The epics of Everest
947. Younghusband, F. – Everest the challenge

FICTION

Mountaineering novels and stories probably appeal more to the non-technical reader, who does not mind the distortions and exaggerations which seem to be an almost inevitable feature. A few novels avoid these pitfalls. Two items stand out particularly. These are Elizabeth Coxhead's **One green bottle** [193], a superb story of love and rock-climbing in North Wales, and C. E. Montague's short story **In Hanging Garden Gully** [400]. Among the rest of the better known titles are novels by W. E. Bowman [103]; Roger Frison-Roche [296]; A. E. W. Mason [501]; C. W. F. Noyce [578]; Frank Smythe [741]; and James Ramsay Ullman [841] & [846]. Mention should also be made of an anthology of short stories [795], and some detective stories by Glyn Carr [Appendix IV]. See Appendix IV for more titles not otherwise included in this bibliography.

Further references to Author Index

199. Daudet, A. – Tartarin on the Alps
453. Lefebure, M. – Scratch & Co.: the great cat expedition [Scafell]
749. Sneyd-Kynnersley, E. A. – A snail's wooing: the story of an Alpine courtship [Zermatt]

FIFTY BOOKS IN MOUNTAINEERING

Many of the books listed in the Author Index are author-itative and readable, and over 400 have been marked (*) as suggested reading. Even this culling leaves an unwieldy collection from which to assimilate the real substance of mountaineering and its literature. In choosing the following fifty books, regard has been had to:

    (i) coverage of the whole field
    (ii) historical importance
    (iii) literary quality
    (iv) material quality
    (v) exceptional achievements.

The titles are arranged in alphabetical order.

1. Abraham, A. P. – Rock-climbing in Skye
2. Abraham, G. D. – Rock-climbing in North Wales
18/20. Alpine Club – Peaks, passes and glaciers [Series I & II]
58. Barker, R. – The last blue mountain
79. Benuzzi, F. – No picnic on Mount Kenya
88. Bonatti, W. – On the heights
116. Brown, J. – The hard years: an autobiography
117. Brown, T. G. – Brenva
131. Buhl, H. – Nanga Parbat pilgrimage
148. Clark, R. W. – The splendid hills: the life and photographs of Vittorio Sella 1859-1943
168. Coleman, A. P. – The Canadian Rockies: new and old trails
170. Collie, J. N. – Climbing on the Himalaya and other mountain ranges
176. Conway, W. M. – The Alps from end to end
193. Coxhead, E. – One green bottle [Fiction]
202. Davidson, A. – The coldest climb: the winter ascent of Mt. McKinley
262. Ferlet, R. – Aconcagua: South Face
265. Filippi, F. de – Ruwenzori: an account of the expedition of H.R.H. Prince Luigi Amadeo of Savoy, Duke of the Abruzzi
272. Fitzgerald, E. A. – Climbs in the New Zealand Alps: being an account of travel and discovery
274. Forbes, J. D. – Travels through the Alps of Savoy and other parts of the Pennine chain with observations on the phenomena of glaciers
288. Freshfield, D. W. – The exploration of the Caucasus
333. Gribble, F. – The early mountaineers
347. Harrer, H. – The White Spider
366. Herzog, M. – Annapurna: conquest of the first 8000-metre peak (26,493 feet)
383. Hornbein, T. F. – Everest: the west ridge
400. Irving, R. L. G. – The mountain way: an anthology in prose and verse
413. Jones, C. – Climbing in North America
414. Jones, O. G. – Rock-climbing in the English Lake District
420. King, C. – Mountaineering in the Sierra Nevada
425. Klucker, C. – Adventures of an Alpine guide
434. Kugy, J. – Alpine pilgrimage
460. Longstaff, T. G. – This my voyage
474. Lunn, A. H. M. – A century of mountaineering 1857-1957
494. Maraini, F. – Where four worlds meet: Hindu Kush 1959

503. Mason, K. – Abode of snow
535. Moore, A. W. – The Alps in 1864: a private journal
546. Muir, J. – My first summer in the Sierra
555. Mummery, A. F. – My climbs in the Alps and Caucasus
558. Murray, W. H. – Mountaineering in Scotland.
576. Noyce, C. W. F. – South Col: one man's adventure on the ascent of Everest, 1953
621. Pilley, D. – Climbing days
692. Scott, D. K. – Big wall climbing
696. Shipton, E. E. – Nanda Devi
712. Slingsby, W. C. – Norway: the northern playground. Sketches of climbing and mountain exploration in Norway between 1872 and 1903
731. Smythe, F. S. – The spirit of the hills
766. Stephen, L. – The playground of Europe
807. Thorington, J. M. – The glittering mountains of Canada: a record of exploration and pioneer ascents in the Canadian Rockies 1914-1924
897. Whymper, E. – Scrambles amongst the Alps in the years 1860-69
899. Whymper, E. – Travels amongst the great Andes of the equator
938. Young, G. W. – Mountain craft
940. Young, G. W. – Collected poems

FLORA AND FAUNA

Botanists and hunters were among the first to scramble around mountain crags and to explore the higher reaches. The east terrace of Clogwyn du'r Arddu is thought to have been first climbed by botanists in the eighteenth century, while in the Alps many of the chamois hunters became mountain guides following the first ascent of Mont Blanc. Many of the late nineteenth century expeditions to remote mountain regions included valuable details of plantlife and wildlife among the scientific data and specimens which they collected. One famous naturalist-mountaineer was A. F. R. Wollaston, who explored the Ruwenzori, Dutch New Guinea (Carstenz) and the Colombian Andes. In the United States John Muir (1838-1914), an ardent lover of nature and open-air life, exercised great influence over American concepts of mountains [545-9]. One of the greatest twentieth century planthunters was F. Kingdon-Ward, whose pre-war expeditions to the high mountains of Burma are described in [422].

Chapters on Alpine flora and fauna will be found in [98], [187], and [757]; and on those of Snowdonia in [142]. The most famous botanical story in mountaineering literature is C. E. Montague's **A Botanist in Hanging Garden Gully** [400].

One of the most controversial topics in recent years is the nature of the yeti, or 'Abominable Snowman', which apparently exists in the Himalaya. The quest was sparked off by tracks seen in 1951 by Eric Shipton [704]. In 1960 Sir Edmund Hillary mounted an expedition to discover a yeti [371] and was subjected to an elaborate hoax. Don Whillans made one of the most recent sightings in 1970.

Further references to Author Index

80. Bere, R. M. – The way to the Mountains of the Moon
113. Brongersma, L. D. – To the mountains of the stars [New Guinea]
734. Smythe, F. S. – The valley of flowers [Garhwal]
868. Walton, E. – Flowers from the upper Alps

Note also:

Izzard, R. W. B. – The Abominable Snowman adventure (Hodder, 1955)
Kingdon-Ward, F. – Land of the blue poppy
Kingdon-Ward, F. – Riddle of the Tsangpo gorges (1926)
Kingdon-Ward, F. – Assam adventure (Cape, 1941)
Long, A. – Mountain animals (Macdonald, 1971)
Wollaston, A. F. R. – From Ruwenzori to the Congo (Murray, 1908)

GENERAL REFERENCE BOOKS
References to Author Index

163. Cleare, J. S. – Mountains
171. Collins, F. A. – Mountain climbing
376. Hindley, G. – The roof of the world
382. Shipton, E. E. – Mountain conquest
397. Huxley, A. J. – Standard encyclopaedia of the world's mountains
439. Lane, F. C. – The story of mountains
519. Milne, L. J. – The mountains
520. Milne, M. – The book of modern mountaineering
721. Smith, G. A. – Introduction to mountaineering
755. Spectorsky, A. C. – The book of the mountains
804. Thomas, L. – Lowell Thomas' book of the high mountains
895. White, A. T. – All about mountains and mountaineering

GEOLOGY AND GLACIATION

One of the aspects of mountains which fascinated eighteenth and nineteenth century scientists was glaciation. At least two of them became enthusiastic and well-known mountaineers – James Forbes and John Tyndall. Their experiments, observations and travels are recorded in [274], [276], and [836]. T. G. Bonney wrote one of the best books on the geology of the Alps [99].

Further references to Author Index

101. Bourrit, M. T. – Relation of a journey to the glaciers in the Dutchy of Savoy
646. Rendu, L. – Theory of the glaciers of Savoy
834. Tutton, A. E. H. – The natural history of ice and snow: illustrated from the Alps

Note also:

Bakewell, R. – Travels . . . in the Tarentaise and various parts of the . . . Pennine Alps (Longman, 1823)
Collet, L. – The structure of the Alps (Arnold, 1927)
Ramsay, A. C. – Old glaciers of Switzerland and North Wales (Longmans, 1860)

'GOLDEN AGE' (1854-1865)

The Golden Age of mountaineering was ushered in by Alfred Wills' ascent of the Hasle Jungfrau peak of the Wetterhorn from Grindelwald. This climb is generally accepted as marking the start of mountaineering as a popular outdoor pursuit. The Golden Age ended with the first ascent of the Matterhorn. During this period English climbers dominated the scene in as much as they made thirty-one first ascents of major peaks against only eight ascents by other climbers. However it is wrong to assume that the early English climbers made more first ascents in the Alps than the Continental climbers: prior to 1854 their contribution was minimal.

The three most important records of their achievements during the Golden Age are Whymper's 'Scrambles' [897] and the books by Leslie Stephen [766] and A. W. Moore [535]. The first two are world famous and have gone through many editions and translations: Moore's journal has had a very limited publication. The other major literary events of the Golden Age emanated from the Alpine Club, formed in 1857. Two series of accounts of members' climbs appeared under the title **Peaks, passes and glaciers** [18] & [20]. In 1863 the A.C. began publication of the **Alpine Journal**, one of the most authoritative mountain journals. The other venture was the decision to commission John Ball to prepare a mountaineer's guide to the Alps. The first two volumes of his **Alpine guide** [46] appeared in 1863-4.

Other famous books relating to this period include [305], [309], [375], [388], [830], [836], [837], [839], [913] and [915].

Principal British first ascents during the Golden Age, with references to Author Index

1854
Monte Rosa (Ostspitze)
Strahlhorn
Cima di Jazzi

1855
Mont Blanc du Tacul 388
Monte Rosa (Dufourspitze) 388

1856
Allalinhorn 18
Laquinhorn

1857
Grand Combin (Graffeneire) 18
Trugberg (Lowest point)
Pelmo

1858
Dome de Miage (169)
Dom 18
Eiger

1859
Grivola 20
Rimpfischhorn
Aletschhorn 535 830 839
Bietschhorn 469

1860
Gran Paradiso 20
Grande Casse
Alphubel
Blümlisalphorn

1861
Monte Viso 20
Weisshorn 837
Monte Rosa (Nordend) 20
Castor
Lyskamm 20
Gross Schreckhorn 766

1862
Dent Blanche 22 897
Täschhorn
Gross Fiescherhorn 22
Monte Della Disgrazia 22

1863
Dent d'Herens 22
Monte Rosa (Parrotspitze)
Balfrin
Piz Roseg (Lower point)

1864
Les Ecrins 535 897
Grivola (Punta Rossa)
Dent Parrachée
Grande Motte
Aiguille d'Argentière 897
Aiguille de la Trélatête 897
Aiguille du Tour
Mont Dolent 897
Zinal Rothorn 766
Balmhorn
Piz Kesch (Higher point)
Königspitze
Presanella 286

1865
Aiguille Verte 897
Grandes Jorasses (Lower point) 535 897
Aiguille du Chardonnet
Matterhorn 897
Ober Gabelhorn
Grand Cornier 535 897
Wellenkuppe
Trifthorn
Pigne d'Arolla
Ruinette 897
Lauterbrunnen Breithorn [5 minutes behind first party]
Gross Nesthorn 305
Piz Roseg (Higher point) 22
Punta San Matteo 830
Piz Tresero 830
Care Alto
Mösele 830

Further references to Author Index

97. Bonney, T. G. – Outline sketches in the high Alps of Dauphiné
167. Cole, Mrs. – A lady's tour round Monte Rosa
284. Freshfield, D. W. – Across country from Thonon to Trent
294. Freshfield, Mrs. – Alpine byways: or, Light leaves gathered in 1859 and 1860
295. Freshfield, Mrs. – A summer tour in the Grisons and Italian valleys of the Bernina
421. King, S. W. – The Italian valleys of the Pennine Alps
669. Roth, A. – The Doldenhorn and Weisse Frau
827. Tuckett, E. F. – How we spent the summer: or, A 'Voyage en Zigzag' in Switzerland and Tyrol, with some members of the Alpine Club

GUIDEBOOKS

In 1881 W. M. Conway published his **Zermatt pocket book** [174], thus creating the format which, by and large, has been adopted for all mountaineering guidebooks ever since. More directly, his guidebook led to the creation of the series known as 'Conway and Coolidge's Climbers' Guides' [189].

Conway was constantly seeking new routes and had to rely for his basic information on Ball's **Alpine Guide** [46-52], which had remained unaltered since the 1860s. To determine whether a proposed route had been climbed necessitated a great deal of laborious research through the journals of the various alpine clubs and was not conclusive, as Conway found to his chagrin on Monte Rosa. His dismay at finding that his cherished route had already been accomplished resolved him to collect every scrap of information together to save himself, and others, from similar errors in the future. He sought advice on the need for such a publication, its format and possible market from W A. B. Coolidge, who responded enthusiastically. This was the start of the remarkable partnership between Conway, the explorer, and Coolidge, who provided the fund of historical information and records of ascents for **Zermatt pocket book** and its successors. The 500 copies printed took several years to sell (@ 2/6d each) but their value soon rose so dramatically that Conway felt justified in charging £1 each for the new volumes which followed.

When the revision of **Zermatt pocket book** was at an advanced state Conway proposed that it should form the start of a series to be called the 'Alpine Club guide to the High Alps'. The Alpine Club, however, with their eyes on the revision of Ball's **Alpine Guide** declined and it was left to Conway to persuade T. Fisher Unwin to undertake publication of the new series, which appeared in fifteen volumes through the years 1890-1910. Fisher Unwin was clearly apprehensive about Coolidge's verbosity and irascibility, and without Conway's skilful and at times devious mediation it is doubtful whether the series would have been completed. Unlike Ball's guide, it did not cover the Eastern Alps.

Ball's **Alpine Guide** is discussed in the section on Alpine Club publications. Another guidebook produced about the same time is that by Charles Packe [594], who was chiefy responsible for opening up the Pyrenees as a mountaineering district. His guide to the Pyrenees remained the standard work until the turn of the century.

The first guide to British rock-climbing was prepared by W. P. Haskett Smith, who found himself in much the same situation as Conway, that is to say information about climbs was passed by word of mouth, or recorded in hotel books, or occasionally published as magazine articles. The first part of his guide came out in 1894 [725] and the second part the following year. The projected third volume covering Scotland was abandoned when it was found that the Scots were preparing one of their own. His guide is an informative and academic survey of the sport, full of topographical, technical, historical and etymological detail, but there is little attempt to describe routes in detail and no attempt at all at classification. Three years later O. G. Jones included such matters in his book [414], laying down the basis of the modern adjectival grading system.

In the forty or so years it was in print Haskett Smith's guide-book sold about 3,000 copies of each volume Presumably many have perished over the years as copies are more scarce than those of some books theoretically more difficult to find. The trilogy [1], [2], [414] produced by O. G. Jones and the Abraham brothers, which are not guidebooks in the accepted sense, are the direct descendants of Haskett Smith's first steps in the popularization of British climbing, but the real bridge between Haskett Smith and the modern guidebook is George Abraham's **British mountain climbs** [4]. Of course there have been changes down the years. Narrative has given way very largely to tabulations of pitch by pitch detail. Background information is relegated to introductions and appendices and the traditional humour hardly survives.

See also Appendix V and Appendix VI.

GUIDES

The story of guiding goes back to the first ascent of Mont Blanc. Originally the guides had no more experience of the mountains than their employers, except that they lived amongst them and probably were chamois hunters. Their skill grew with the sport. The lives of the best of the early guides are recorded in a handsome volume by Cunningham and Abney [197]. More recent is [149], which contains a table of the principal ascents made by the early guides. The table below gives individual references from these two books. See also [786].

Name	References to Author Index		
	[149]	[197]	Other books
Christian Almer	*	*	
Ulrich Almer		*	
Jakob Anderegg	*	*	
Melchior Anderegg	*	*	With Leslie Stephen [766]
Franz Andermatten	*	*	With Dent [210]
Auguste Balmat	*	*	With Forbes [274] and Wills [913], [915]
Jacques Balmat			See [120], [333] & [504]
Johann Baumann		*	
Peter Baumann		*	
Johann Joseph Bennen	*	*	With Tyndall [839]
Johann von Bergen	*	*	
Peter Bohren	*	*	
Alexander Burgener	*	*	With Mummery [555]
Jean-Antoine Carrel	*	*	See [647]
Francois Couttet	*	*	
Michel Croz	*	*	With Whymper [897]
Edouard Cupelin	*	*	With Mrs. Le Blond [445-6]
François Devouassoud	*	*	
Johann Fischer		*	
Josef Imboden	*	*	

Name			Notes
Ferdinand Imseng	*	*	
Johann Jaun		*	
Ulrich Kaufman	*	*	
Peter Knubel	*	*	
Laurent Lanier		*	
Christian Lauener	*	*	With Tuckett [830]
Ulrich Lauener	*	*	With Wills [913]
Jean Joseph Macquignaz	*	*	
Andreas Maurer		*	
Christian Michel		*	
Alphonse Payot	*	*	
Michel Payot	*	*	
Aloys Pollinger		*	
Emile Rey	*	*	
Peter Rubi		*	
Auguste Simond	*	*	
Mathias Zurbriggen	*		With Conway [175] and Fitzgerald [272-3]

Further references to Author Index

HIMALAYA

(See also: Eight-thousand metre peaks; Everest)

The Himalaya include most of the world's highest mountains (the only comparable range is the much less extensive Karakoram) and their mountaineering history may be deemed to date from 1883. In this year W. W. Graham visited Garhwal and Sikkim solely to climb, taking with him an Alpine guide. The first attempt on a 8000-metre peak, Nanga Parbat, was made in 1895 and in 1907 the first ascent was made of a 7000-metre peak, Trisul. Everest dominated British mountaineering ambition from 1921 onwards, while the 1930s saw strong German attacks on Nanga Parbat and Kanchenjunga. The post-war explosion in Himalayan mountaineering, resulting from access to Nepal, was triggered off by the French ascent of Annapurna in 1950. Since then the Himalaya have become an international playground, with the Japanese playing an increasingly important role. The absence of books in English relating to their climbs constitutes a serious gap in Himalayan literature.

Himalayan mountaineering has developed in two streams – (i) the major climbing expedition, with many climbers, hundreds of porters and tons of stores; and (ii) the light-weight expedition consisting of two or three climbers and a few porters, largely living off the land. Both streams have produced a body of Himalayan literature. As a class the books produced by the major expeditions are rather repetitive, with their details of the approach march, build-up, success (or failure), and finally retreat. They have been satirized by W. E. Bowman in his book **The ascent of Rum Doodle** [103]. In contrast the books written by members of small expeditions are, generally speaking, eminently readable and include some classics of mountain exploration, such as Freshfield's **Round Kanchenjunga** [289] and Shipton's **Nanda Devi** [696]. One pioneer of the light expedition, and a great mountain traveller, was T. G. Longstaff [460]; another was C. G. Bruce [122-5]. Probably the greatest of all mountaineer-explorers was Eric Shipton, who travelled extensively through the Asian ranges as well as other parts of the world. Another very experienced Himalayan mountaineer is Trevor Braham, also editor of the **Himalayan Journal** [105].

The intense activity in Himalayan mountaineering during the past quarter-century has left the history books far behind. Kenneth Mason's book [503] is an authoritative reference source for the historical and geographical background to the entire Himalayan range and contains a concise and comprehensive history of Himalayan exploration up to 1955. Also published in 1955, Dyrenfurth's **To the third pole** [234] summarizes the attempts on the 8000-metre peaks, most of which have been climbed since the book was written. Another book deals with mountaineering in Nepal during the period 1950-1960 [337].

Kashmir

Nanga Parbat, described by Kenneth Mason as 'the cruellest and most vengeful of mountains', dominates this section of the Himalaya. After Mummery's fateful attempt in 1895 [170] the mountain became a German preserve. Many lives were lost and the ascent became something of a crusade, culminating in Hermann Buhl's outstanding solo climb to the summit. For details see 'Eight-thousand metre peaks' section of this bibliography.

The only other mountains over 7000 metres in the 400 miles between Nanga Parbat and Garhwal are the twin peaks Nun and Kun. This area was explored in 1906 by Dr. and Mrs. Workman [928]. The easier Kun was climbed in 1913 but Nun resisted British attempts in 1934 and 1946, being climbed by a French party in 1953 [617]. The other mountains in Kashmir are on a more modest scale. A lot of wartime climbing was done in the Sonamarg district after the establishment of the Aircrew Mountain Centre [406] & [574]. See also [433].

Kulu, Spiti and Lahul

This small area, approximately sixty miles square, contains a number of peaks about 21,000' in height, mostly bordering the central Bara Shigri glacier. It has attracted numerous small expeditions, including all-women parties [230] & [684]. See also [380] & [433].

Garhwal-Kumaon

In the old days of British India, and with Nepal closed to foreigners, this region attracted considerable mountaineering attention as, apart from Sikkim, it contained the highest peaks then readily accessible (more than 100 over 20,000'). The three most famous peaks are Nanda Devi, Kamet and Trisul. The first climber to reconnoitre them was W. W. Graham [323].

Nanda Devi is an isolated peak guarded by a ring of 20,000' mountains and consequently exceedingly difficult to approach. Many climbers, including Longstaff, Bruce and A. L. Mumm [553], failed in their efforts until finally, after thirty years, Shipton and Tilman penetrated the Rishi Ganga gorge in 1934, entering the Inner Sanctuary and reconnoitring the peak. This was one of the finest pieces of mountain exploration ever carried out [696]. Nanda Devi was climbed two years later [815]. See also [441].

The slightly lower Kamet, which was the first peak over 25,000' to be climbed, also resisted many attempts, the first of which was made by Adolf and Robert Schlagintweit in 1855, during their work on the Magnetic Survey of India. Among those who tried were Longstaff, Bruce and Mumm [553] and C. F. Meade [508]. Kamet was climbed by F. S. Smythe in 1931 [729]. He subsequently made more ascents in the area and explored the Bhyundar Valley [734]. Trisul, second only to Nanda Devi in beauty, was climbed by Longstaff in 1907 [460]. A small Scottish expedition, including W. H. Murray and Tom Weir, visited the area in 1950 [560] & [880]. See also [406] & [433]. In 1974 Bonington and his companions climbed the difficult Changabang [95].

The year 1936 saw the first Swiss expedition to the Himalaya, their route taking them through north-east Kumaon and over the frontier into Tibet (Kailas). The story of this expedition, the purpose of which was mainly geological, is told in the superbly illustrated **Throne of the gods** [362].

Nepal

The Nepalese section of the Himalaya contains seven of the fourteen 8000-metre peaks – Annapurna, Cho Oyu, Dhaulagiri, Everest. Lhotse, Makalu and Manaslu. They were climbed in the decade 1950–60 [337]. Details are given in the 'Eight-thousand metre peaks' and 'Everest' sections of this bibliography. Cho Oyu is probably the only mountain of this magnitude to have been climbed by a light-weight expedition. It is also closely associated with Claude Kogan, a leading French woman mountaineer, who was eventually killed on the mountain [346].

The Dhaulagiri massif and the Annapurna Himal, which are separated by the deep gorge cut by the Kali Gandaki, form a major section of the Nepalese Himalaya. In 1950 Tilman explored the area north of the main peaks [820]. The first ascents of Annapurna II and III are reported in [324] & [431]. Wilfrid Noyce led an expedition to Machapuchare in 1957 [579]. See also [773]. Eastwards is another important peak, Gaurisanker. A French team, including Claude Kogan, attempted it in 1954 [438] and the Japanese tried in 1959.

Further east is the large and important Everest group, which includes Lhotse, Makalu and Cho Oyu (qv). Sir Edmund Hillary has been very active in this region. Apart from his 'school-house' and scientific projects his parties climbed Ama Dablam, Taweche and Kantega [371] & [372]. See also accounts by other members of the expeditions .[313] & [872]. An earlier attempt on Ama Dablam is described in [539]. Hillary also led a New Zealand party to the Barun Valley, east of Everest [370]. See also [882].

All-women expeditions have climbed a number of peaks in the Jagdula and Jugal Himal [407] & [684].

Sikkim

A semi-autonomous state now administered by India. The country came increasingly under British control from 1817 onwards, one of the earliest well-known travellers being the naturalist Sir Joseph Hooker. The first pleasure mountaineering was done by W. W. Graham in 1883 [323]. His claim to have climbed Kabru has always been disputed but never disproved. Freshfield and Longstaff (as late as 1950) both recorded their acceptance of his claim: Conway rejected it. Three principal records of travel in Sikkim are those by L. A. Waddell, J. C. White and D. W. Freshfield [289]. Freshfield's dangerous and exhausting circuit of Kanchenjunga was a classic model for mountain exploration. The most active climber in the pre-1914 period was A. M. Kellas, who climbed a number of peaks well over 20,000'. Mountaineering in the 1930s was mainly concerned with Kanchenjunga. In 1936 a German party made the first ascent of the very beautiful Siniolchu [67]. Another fine peak is Jannu, on the Nepal side of the Kanchenjunga massif. The French ascent of Jannu in 1962 was the most difficult Himalayan climb accomplished at that time [280]. For a New Zealand attempt on the North Face see [214b].

Bhutan

An independent kingdom under Indian protection, which has never been freely accessible to foreigners. It is a mountainous country, still largely unmapped. There are several peaks approaching 25,000'; the best known is Chomolhari, climbed by F. Spencer Chapman in 1937 [146]. The country was explored by J. C. White and F. M. Bailey, among others, around the turn of the century. Most of the peaks are still unclimbed. Two mountaineers, who have been to Bhutan in recent years as medical advisors, are Peter Steele [763] and Michael Ward [872], whose book includes a short reading list of books about Bhutan.

Assam Himalaya

The least known part of the Himalayan chain, extending 450 miles from north of Bhutan through Assam to Namche Barwa, the highest peak, in Tibet. A route, known as the Mönyul Corridor, leading from India to Tibet was gradually opened up and has been used by travellers who included F. M. Bailey in 1913 and F. Kingdon-Ward in 1935 and 1938. Just to the east of this route lies a group of some dozen peaks over 20,000', explored by H. W. Tilman in 1939 [816].

Tibet

The Tibetan peaks of the Himalaya have been visited by only a handful of western mountaineers, disregarding the Tibetan side of Everest. The highest is Gosainthan (Shisha Pangma), an 8000-metre peak (see separate section). Tilman surveyed the area north of the Langtang Himal in 1949 in an effort to fix the exact position of Gosainthan, which is now reckoned to lie on the true boundary between Nepal and Tibet, not north of it [820].

Additionally there are several 7000-metre peaks inside Tibet, including Namche Barwa. Lying at the eastern extremity of the Himalaya this peak is separated from another 7000-metre peak, Gyali Peri, by the Tsangpo gorge. Very little is known about it and apparently no mountaineer has set foot on it, although Bailey and Morshead explored the area in 1912-3. Another peak near the Kumaon-Nepal border is Gurla Mandhata, attempted by Longstaff and Sherring during their 1905 journey through Tibet. Not far away is Kailas, an unclimbed holy mountain: Col. R. C. Wilson reached a height of over 20,000' in 1926. The Swiss expedition circumambulated the mountain in 1936 [362].

Further references to Author Index

170. Collie, J. N. – Climbing on the Himalaya and other mountain ranges
225. Douglas, W. O. – Exploring the Himalaya
436. Kumar, N. – Nikalantha: story of the Indian expedition of 1961 [Garhwal]
479. McCormick, A. D. – An artist in the Himalayas
537. Mordecai, D. – The Himalaya: an illustrated summary of the world's highest mountain ranges
566. Neve, A. – Thirty years in Kashmir
797. Taylor, P. – Coopers Creek to Langtang II
813. Tichy, H. – Himalaya
947. Younghusband, F. E. – Everest the challenge

Note also:

Bailey, F. M. – No passport to Tibet (Hart-Davis, 1957)
Hooker, J. – Himalayan journals (Murray, 1855. Revised ed.)
Kingdon-Ward, F. – Riddle of the Tsangpo gorges (1926)
Kingdon-Ward, F. – Assam adventure (Cape, 1941)
[Mazuchelli, E. S.] – The Indian Alps and how we crossed them (Longmans, 1876)
Moorcroft, W. – Travels in the Himalayan Provinces . . . from 1819 to 1825. Edited by H. H. Wilson (1841)
Sherring, C. A. – Western Tibet and the British borderland (Arnold, 1906)
Sleen, W. G. N. van der – Four months camping in the Himalaya (Philip Allan, 1929) [Kailas]
Waddell, L. A. – Among the Himalayas (Constable, 1899)
White, J. C. – Sikkim and Bhutan: experiences of twenty years on the north-east frontier of India (Arnold, 1909)
Wilson, A. – Abode of snow: observations on a journey from Chinese Tibet to the Indian Caucasus through the upper valleys of the Himalaya (Blackwood, 1875)

HINDU KUSH

The Hindu Kush is a range of mountains lying to the west of the Karakoram, containing the most westerly of the mountains of truly Himalayan stature. The highest peaks (c.25,000') lie across the Afghanistan-Pakistan frontier and are usually approached through Pakistan. The remaining two-thirds of this 800-mile chain lie wholly within north-east Afghanistan, comprising the Central Mountains of Nuristan (c. 20,000') and the less important Koh-i-Baba Range (highest point 16,874'), which is the most westerly extension of the Hindu Kush. A few people including Alexander the Great and Marco Polo journeyed through the area; otherwise it appears to have been unvisited until the first half of the nineteenth century. At that time the British were engaged in surveying the range but this work was cut short by the Afghan wars, which closed the frontier with India. It is certain that the first major peak to be climbed was the highest, Tirich Mir. As late as 1965 very little was known about the mountains of Nuristan. Although most of the principal peaks have been climbed since then there are scarcely half a dozen books on the range. A good many references will be found in the **Alpine Journal** etc.

It is the eastern Hindu Kush, with its Himalaya-style peaks, which has attracted most attention. Ignoring a few isolated visits before 1939, Hindu Kush mountaineering dates from 1950 when a Norwegian expedition climbed Tirich Mir [563]. In 1959 an Italian party climbed another fine peak, Saraghrar, further east. Fosco Maraini's book [494] recording this expedition is of a very high standard. In 1960 the most important feature of Hindu Kush climbing began to flourish, i.e. the small group of friends spending a month's holiday in true expedition style. These parties were from many countries, including for example Poles, Czechs, Austrians and Japanese. Kurt Diemberger made the first ascent of Tirich Mir (West IV) [214].

The first climbing sortie into the mountains of Nuristan was made by Eric Newby and a companion. They were not expert mountaineers but they attempted 19,880' Mir Samir [567]. In 1965 a four-man Scottish expedition climbed and surveyed in the hitherto unexplored country at the head of the Bashgal Valley [824].

Further references to Author Index

687. Schomberg, R. C. F. – Kafirs and glaciers: travels in Chitral
691. Scott, D. K. – The Midlands Hindu Kush expedition, 1967
699. Shipton, E. E. – Mountains of Tartary
819. Tilman, H. W. – China to Chitral

Note also:

Dunsheath, J. – Afghan quest (Harrap, 1961)
Schomberg, R. C. F. – Between the Oxus and the Indus (Hopkinson, 1935)

HISTORIES

The post-1945 explosion in mountaineering has far outpaced the history books, many of which were written twenty years ago. There are signs however that today's climbers are turning their attention to this side of mountaineering literature, after a spate of expedition books and climbing memoirs. Some areas are still without any proper summary, particularly the Andes where there is no collected record at all, a situation exacerbated by the fact that much of the source material is written in German or Spanish. Of the rest, the Himalaya is the section most seriously out of date.

Principal references to Author Index
General

149. Clark, R. W. – The early Alpine guides
150. Clark, R. W. – The Victorian mountaineers
403. Irving, R. L. G. – A history of British mountaineering
474. Lunn, A. H. M. – A century of mountaineering 1857-1957
554. Mumm, A. L. – The Alpine Club Register
692. Scott, D. K. – Big wall climbing
801. Temple, R. P. – The world at their feet: the story of New Zealand mountaineers in the great ranges of the world
908. Williams, C. – Women on the rope: the feminine share in mountain adventure

Alpine

120. Brown, T. G. – The first ascent of Mont Blanc
187. Coolidge, W. A. B. – The Alps in nature and history
246. Engel, C. E. – Mountaineering in the Alps: an historical survey
333. Gribble, F. – The early mountaineers [Includes Pyrenees]
347. Harrer, H. – The White Spider: the history of the Eiger's North Face
476. Lunn, A. H. M. – Matterhorn centenary
524. Milner, C. D. – Mont Blanc and the Aiguilles
647. Rey, G. – The Matterhorn
809. Thorington, J. M. – A survey of early American ascents in the Alps in the nineteenth century

British Isles

140. Byne, E. – High Peak: the story of walking and climbing in the Peak District
142. Carr, H. R. C. – The mountains of Snowdonia: in history, the sciences, literature and sport
155. Clark, R. W. – Mountaineering in Britain: a history from the earliest times to the present day
342. Hankinson, A. – The first tigers: the early history of rock-climbing in the Lake District
392. Humble, B. H. – The Cuillin of Skye
752. Soper, J. N. – The Black Cliff: the history of rock-climbing on Clogwyn du'r Arddu
943. Young, G. W. – Snowdon biography

Caucasus

288. Freshfield, D. W. – The exploration of the Caucasus

Himalaya

234. Dyrenfurth, G. O. – To the third pole: the history of the high Himalaya
337. Gurung, H. B. – Annapurna to Dhaulagiri: a decade of mountaineering in Nepal
503. Mason, K. – Abode of snow: a history of Himalayan exploration and mountaineering
860. Verghese, B. G. – Himalayan endeavour [Summary of Indian mountaineering]

New Zealand

603. Pascoe, J. D. – Great days in New Zealand mountaineering
920. Wilson, J. G. – Aorangi: the story of Mount Cook

North America

130. Bueler, W. M. – Roof of the Rockies: a history of mountaineering in Colorado
413. Jones, C. – Climbing in North America
536. Moore, T. – Mount McKinley: the pioneer climbs

South Africa

136. Burman, J. – A peak to climb: the story of South African mountaineering

Further references to Author Index

127. Bryant, L. V. – New Zealanders and Everest
152. Clark, R. W. – A picture history of mountaineering
185. Coolidge, W. A. B. – Swiss travel and Swiss guide-books
204. De Beer, G. R. – Early travellers in the Alps
205. De Beer, G. R. – Alps and men: pages from forgotten diaries of travellers and tourists in Switzerland
206. De Beer, G. R. – Travellers in Switzerland
244. Engel, C. E. – They came to the hills
334. Gribble, F. – The story of Alpine climbing

399. Irving, R. L. G. – The romance of mountaineering
417. Keenlyside, F. – Peaks and pioneers: the story of mountaineering
470. Lunn, A. H. M. – The Alps
740. Smythe, F. S. – British mountaineers
783. Styles, S. – On top of the world: an illustrated history of mountaineering
787. Styles, S. – First on the summits
843. Ullman, J. R. – The age of mountaineering
857. Unsworth, W. – North Face: the second conquest of the Alps

HUMOUR

Mountaineering literature is short on humour, although rock-climbing guidebooks have some tradition of scholarly punning and dry humour in the naming and description of climbs. One humorous book is the Badminton Library volume edited by Clinton Dent [211], which is full of delightful sketches by H. G. Willink. Other memorable items are C. E. Montague's story In Hanging Garden Gully [400] and W. E. Bowman's satire about expedition books [103]. One of the best is Tom Patey's book of essays and verses [605].

Further references to Author Index

199. Daudet, A. – Tartarin on the Alps
344. Harding, W. – Downward bound: a mad guide to rock climbing
937. Young, G. W. – Wall and roof climbing

ILLUSTRATORS (Artists and Photographers)

Most mountaineering books have some illustrations; many are profusely and superbly illustrated. Most forms of book illustration may be found – steel engravings, wood engravings, chromolithographs, reproductions of water-colours and oils, photogravures and full-colour photographs. The method of illustration is not the only thing that has changed: artists' representations of the mountains have altered radically over the years.

It was not until the nineteenth century that artists began to achieve a more natural representation of mountains. One of the earliest collections of mountain pictures is Brockedon's Illustrations of the passes of the Alps, published in 1828-9 [110]. A few years later John Ruskin began to publish Modern Painters (Part V – 'Of mountain beauty'), which was written primarily to exalt the art of J. M. W. Turner as the greatest English painter for sincerity and fidelity to nature.

The latter part of the nineteenth century produced several mountain artists, the best known being Edward Whymper. Many Victorian books contain some of his illustrations (sketched and/or engraved by him). He had been trained originally as a wood engraver and his Alpine career was sparked off when he was commissioned by William Longman to prepare sketches for the second series of Peaks, passes and glaciers [20]. There are also the delightful sketchbooks produced by Elizabeth Tuckett, recording family holidays with her mountaineer brother Francis Fox Tuckett [827-9]. Another artist, who delighted in mountain scenery and atmospheric effects, was Elijah Walton: T. G. Bonney supplied the text accompanying his folios [868]. One other name crops up frequently at the turn of the century, before photographs became the standard form of book illustration, and that is A. D. McCormick. He illustrated three of Conway's books [175-6] & [181], and also wrote an account of his own work in the Himalaya [479].

One of the earliest mountaineering books to contain photographs is H. B. George's **Oberland and its glaciers** [305], published in 1866 and containing twenty-eight high level plates taken by Ernest Edwards. Each plate is an individually mounted print. Another prized volume contains Abney's superb photographic portraits of the early Alpine guides [197]. Photographic illustration of mountaineering books began to flourish in the early 1900s with the appearance of Vittorio Sella, possibly the greatest mountain photographer, and the Abraham brothers of Keswick. Vittorio Sella was expedition photographer to the Duke of the Abruzzi [264-6] and a short biography and selection of his pictures is given in [148]. See also [16]. One of the famous mountain pictures is his photograph of K2. In the British Isles the Abraham brothers with their friend O. G. Jones were busy recording their rock-climbs [1], [2] & [414]. See also [343].

Coming more up to date, Everest has been the subject of several finely illustrated books including Gregory's **Picture of Everest** [332], Hornbein's **West Ridge** [383] and Charles Evans' sketchbook [248]. One of the leading mountain photographers today is John Cleare, who has developed techniques for filming climbers on the most extreme rockfaces [162-3] & [745]. Two other photographers who have produced approximately thirty quarto volumes of mountain pictures between them are W. A. Poucher [626] and F. S. Smythe [739]. Poucher's books concentrate on the British hills, whereas Smythe's are mostly Alpine or further afield.

There are also books on the techniques of mountain photography by Arthur Gardner [302] and C. D. Milner [521], who has also published a picture book of rock-climbing [522] and an attractive book on the Dolomites [523].

Further references to Author Index

KARAKORAM

The Karakoram is a range of mountains approximately 200 miles long, lying to the north of the western end of the Himalayan chain. It is the most heavily glaciated region in the world excepting the polar areas. South of the main crest lies a secondary line of peaks, which includes Rakaposhi, Haramosh, Masherbrum and Saltoro Kangri. Sir Francis Younghusband travelled through the region in the 1880s and the first mountaineering expedition arrived in 1892, led by W. M. Conway. They surveyed the Hispar and Baltoro glaciers and climbed 23,000' Pioneer Peak, achieving a height record. Conway was knighted for his efforts. His account of the expedition is [175]. Other members of the party recorded their experiences in [125], [479] & [948].

Two Americans, Fanny Bullock Workman and her husband Dr. William Hunter Workman led many expeditions to the area, including six during the period 1898-1908. They explored, surveyed and climbed, Mrs. Workman achieving a height record for women. They produced several handsome books recounting their travels [926-7], [929-30].

Just as Mummery's ambition had led him to Nanga Parbat in 1895, so thoughts began to turn to the Karakoram giants. In 1902 a powerful expedition (led by the notorious Aleister Crowley and the eccentric Oscar Eckenstein) made an attempt on K2. Although the time was premature for tackling such an undertaking they made a poor showing on the mountain compared with the Duke of the Abruzzi's 1909 expedition. The Duke's party also managed to get near the summit of Bride Peak (Chogolisa), the peak on which Hermann Buhl was to fall to his death nearly fifty years later. Filippo de Filippi records the expedition in [266]. The next major attempt on K2 was made by an American party in 1938 [65] & [615], followed by another attempt in 1939. They returned to the attack in 1953, when the whole party were very nearly swept away [385]. The Italians were successful in 1954. [212].

The Karakoram boasts three other 8000-metre peaks. Gasherbrum I (Hidden Peak) was attempted by a French expedition in 1936 [247] but it was eventually climbed by Americans in 1958. Gasherbrum II was reconnoitred by G. O. Dyrenfurth's international expedition in 1934 and climbed by Austrians in 1956. The last, Broad Peak, was attempted in 1954 by Karl Herligkoffer [**Deutsche am Broad Peak, 8047m** (Munich:Lehmanns, 1955)] and was climbed by an Austrian team [M. Schmuck, **Broad Peak, 8047** (Stuttgart:Berglandbuch, 1958)], which included Hermann Buhl and Kurt Diemberger [214].

Other peaks about which there are accounts include: Rakaposhi [53] & [55]: Trivor [581]; Haramosh [58]; Masherbrum and Saltoro Kangri [867]; and Gasherbrum IV [493]. This last is a particularly fine book. For travel, exploration and surveying in the region to the north of the main Karakoram crest see books by Schomberg [686] and Shipton [697].

Further references to Author Index

LATIN AMERICA

(Excluding the Andes)

This section comprises the mountains of Mexico, Guatemala and the rest of Central America, the Guiana Highlands and Brazil. Many of these mountains are volcanic. The principal reference to this diffuse group is Bueler's handbook [129], pp. 83-93.

One of the most spectacular climbs recently was the ascent of the Great Prow of Roraima, in the Guiana Highlands, recorded by Hamish MacInnes [483] and also filmed and shown on television. Roraima was the model for Conan Doyle's lost world of prehistoric monsters.

Note also:

Burton, R. – The Highlands of Brazil (1869)

Clementi, Mrs. C. – Through British Guiana to the summit of Roraima (Fisher Unwin, 1920)

MISCELLANEOUS

References to Author Index

MONT BLANC (and the Aiguilles)

The chain of Mont Blanc is the most important section of the Alps in mountaineering terms: every climber with Alpine ambitions finds his way to Chamonix sooner or later. For the first 100 years, from Windham to Wills, Mont Blanc dominated the climbing scene; during this period sixty-one complete ascents were made. Subsequently, the conquests of the Aiguilles and the Brenva Face have provided some of the finest mountaineering stories. As a starting point Douglas Milner's book, **Mont Blanc and the Aiguilles,** provides a useful summary of the climbing history and opportunities of the Mont Blanc range [524].

First ascent of Mont Blanc

Prior to William Windham's excursion in 1741 Chamonix was quite 'off the map', the reputation of Savoy being generally unfavourable. Conveniently the continuous story of Alpine climbing may be said to commence with Windham's visit to the Montenvers and Mer de Glace, as his is the earliest mountaineering record in English. It was published in 1744 [922]. A facsimile appears in [504] and the text is reproduced in [333].

As a result of Windham's publicity Chamonix found itself to be a place of interest to scientists and fashionable travellers. One of the scientists who visited the village in 1760 was Horace Bénédict de Saussure. He immediately offered a reward to the man who could find a route to the summit of Mont Blanc. He had to wait until Jacques Balmat and Dr. Paccard achieved this in 1786. A great deal of unpleasantness arose out of claims to the honours for this ascent and the affair is examined very thoroughly in a scholarly book by Brown and De Beer [120]. De Saussure made his own ascent in 1787 [500]. Many interesting and useful references to early attempts and ascents of Mont Blanc, updated through the editions, will be found in William Coxe's **Travels in Switzerland.** The fourth edition, which appeared in 1801, was considered by W. A. B. Coolidge to be the best.

Mont Blanc in the nineteenth century

In the early days the ascent of Mont Blanc was not only most fashionable but also a much more considerable feat than it would be for a tourist today. Understandably most of those who accomplished the ascent wrote some account of their experiences. Out of the numerous records the following may be noted: the Hamel accident [31]; Auldjo's lavish quarto volume [38]; first route variation [261] & [357]; first American ascent [386]; other early ascents [36], [61], [164] & [302]; Albert Smith's ascent [616] & [714]. For full details of the very extensive and complicated bibliography of this period see [120] and [Appendix I (Montagnier)].

The story of Albert Smith's involvement with Mont Blanc has been written many times. From childhood he was fascinated almost to the point of obsession with the mountain and the idea of climbing it. Although he visited Chamonix many times it was not until 1851, when he was thirty-five, that he could afford to finance his own ascent. His critics considered his ascent a stunt, made with the object of creating a popular attraction out of it, despite his genuine emotional involvement. His illustrated lecture opened on March 15, 1852 at the Egyptian Hall, Piccadilly and ran for six years. All sorts of sidelines appeared [Appendix III] until London was fairly buzzing: had the expression been possible at that time he must inevitably have been referred to as 'The Abominable Showman'. As it was, for a large section of the public he became in effect 'Mr. Mont Blanc', and it was this publicity which helped to usher in the Golden Age of mountaineering. His book appeared in a bewildering variety of guises and editions [714-9]. For a biography see [808].

With the advent of the Golden Age of mountaineering the ascent of Mont Blanc by the traditional route lost much of its lustre, as the climbers became more adventurous. One example of this was Hudson and Kennedy's ascent in 1855 guideless and by a new route [388], while the end of the Golden Age witnessed the first ascent of the Brenva face, by the Brenva ice-ridge [535], a route immortalized by A. E. W. Mason in his novel **Running water** [501]. The Mont Blanc story down to the end of the nineteenth century is covered in Charles Mathews' fine monograph [504].

The conquest of the Aiguilles

The first ascents of the Aiguilles were accomplished almost exclusively by English climbers, mostly during the Silver Age of mountaineering. Accounts of most of these climbs will be found in the **Alpine Journal**: in book form there are – Whymper (Grandes Jorasses and other climbs) [897]; Clinton Dent's battle for the Grand Dru [210]; and Mummery's classic climbs on the Charmoz, Grépon and others [555]. Mummery's climbs were typical of the development of rock-climbing towards the end of the nineteenth century. See also [445] & [939].

Twentieth century

This period is characterized by the development of mixed rock and ice routes of exceptional severity on the Aiguilles and on the Brenva face of Mont Blanc. Between the wars many fine routes were put up by Continental climbers such as the De Lépiney brothers [207]; Gervasutti [307]; and Roch [662]; while T. G. Brown pioneered three major routes on the Brenva face [117]. Since 1945 the Continental supremacy, typified by climbers like Magnone [489] and Rébuffat [639], but particularly Bonatti [88–9], has been challenged by, among others, the leading British climbers, for example Bonington [90], Brown [116] and Whillans [893].

Further references to Author Index

593. Oxley, T. L. – Jacques Balmat: or, The first ascent of Mont Blanc
645. Rébuffat, G. – The Mont Blanc massif: the 100 finest routes
900. Whymper, E. – Chamonix and the range of Mont Blanc
914. Wills, A. – The ascent of Mont Blanc, together with some remarks on glaciers

Note also:

Browne, J. D. H. – Ten scenes in the last ascent of Mont Blanc including five views from the summit (McLean, 1853)
Cheever, G. – Wanderings of a pilgrim in the shadow of Mont Blanc (Wiley & Putnam, 1846)
Coxe, H. – The travellers' guide in Switzerland, . . . and Mont Blanc (Sherwood, 1816)
Coxe, William – Travels in Switzerland and in the country of the Grisons (Cadell, 1789)
Trench, F. C. – A walk round Mont Blanc (Bentley, 1847)
White, W. – To Mont Blanc and back again (Routledge, 1854)

MYSTICISM AND SPIRITUAL INFLUENCE

Although many mountain lovers and mountaineers have felt the power of the mountains, only one book [509] by Charles Meade specifically investigates the subject of mountains and mysticism. In his book Meade quotes passages from various mountaineering books and books on mysticism. Among the mountain authors often quoted is Geoffrey Winthrop Young [939]; others mentioned include Irving [399] and Kugy [434], and Meade's own book **Approach to the hills** [508].

Note also:

Arundale, G. S. – Mount Everest: its spiritual attainment (Wheaton, Ill: Theosophical Press, 1933)
Irving, R. L. G. – The mountains shall bring peace (Blackwell, 1947)
Seaver, G. – Francis Younghusband: explorer and mystic (Murray, 1952)
Younghusband, F. E. – Wonders of the Himalaya (Murray, 1924)

NATIONALITIES

Mountaineering as an outdoor pursuit developed in the Alps. The nationalities specifically associated with Alpine mountaineering are the British, French, Italians, Swiss, and the Germans and Austrians, whose climbing history is interwoven. Although there are now many nations who climb, both at home and oversea, only the British (and to a lesser extent the Germans) have climbed extensively for 100 years all over the world.

References to Author Index

24. Ament, P –Swaremandal [American rock-climbers]
127. Bryant, L. V. – New Zealanders and Everest
136. Burman, J. – Peak to climb: the story of South African mountaineering
149. Clark, R. W. – The early Alpine guides
403. Irving, R. L. G. – A history of British mountaineering
413. Jones, C. – Climbing in North America
475. Lunn, A. H. M. – The Swiss and their mountains: a study of the influences of mountains on man
603. Pascoe, J. D. – Great days in New Zealand mountaineering
612. Mountaineering in China
692. Scott, D. K. – Big wall climbing

740. Smythe, F. S. – British mountaineers
801. Temple, R. P. – The world at their feet: the story of New Zealand mountaineers in the great ranges of the world
809. Thorington, J. M. – A survey of early American ascents in the Alps in the nineteenth century
860. Verghese, B. G. – Himalayan endeavour [Indian mountaineering]

NEW ZEALAND

The mountaineering interest is almost entirely confined to South Island, the principal area being the Southern Alps containing Mount Cook and numerous other high peaks. Another important area further south is the Darran Mountains, first explored by Samuel Turner [833]. See also [313]. In North Island there is some interest in climbing on volcanoes such as Ruapehu, Ngauruhoe and Tongariro [73].

The history of New Zealand climbing starts with W. S. Green's visit and almost successful ascent of Mount Cook in 1882 [327]. This was a remarkable effort for, while Mount Cook was climbed in 1894, Green's route was not completed for nearly thirty years. The continuous story of mountaineering in the Southern Alps really dates from the first complete ascent of Mount Cook at Christmas, 1894. Learning that E. A. Fitzgerald was coming out from England for the express purpose of climbing Mt. Cook, three New Zealanders took their chance to snatch the prize from under his nose. Fitzgerald had to make do with four other first ascents, including that of Tasman [272]. During 1906-7 Teichelmann and Newton carried off six more first ascents. The Australian woman, Miss Freda Du Faur, who was the first woman to accomplish much serious climbing in New Zealand, also has a first ascent to her credit apart from her famous traverse of Mount Cook [228]. See [920] for a history of climbing on Mount Cook.

The 'father' of New Zealand mountaineering is A. P. Harper. He founded the New Zealand Alpine Club and together with C. E. Mannering did much exploratory and survey work in the 1890s [345] & [492]. Another pioneer and founder member of the New Zealand Alpine Club was Malcolm Ross [667]. Foremost amongst the early guides were Peter and Alex Graham [322]. The most famous New Zealand mountaineer is Sir Edmund Hillary [373]. See also [214a] [313] & [600-1].

Further references to Author Index

17. Alack, F. – Guide aspiring
70. Baughan, B. E. – Mt. Egmont
102. Bowie, M. – The Hermitage years
108. Bridge, L. D. – Mountain search and rescue in New Zealand
310. Gilkinson, W. S. – Peaks, packs and mountain tracks
311. Gilkinson, W. S. – Aspiring, New Zealand: the romantic story of the 'Matterhorn' of the Southern Alps
312. Gilkinson, W. S. – Earnslaw, monarch of Wakatipu
349. Harris, G. – The Mount Cook alpine region
367. Hewitt, L. R. – The mountains of New Zealand
602. Pascoe, J. D. – Mr. Explorer Douglas
603. Pascoe, J. D. – Great days in New Zealand mountaineering
627. Powell, P. – Men aspiring
628. Powell, P. – Just where do you think you've been?

Note also:
Pascoe, J. D. – Exploration New Zealand (Reed, 1972)

OUTCROP CLIMBING
(Outcrops, quarries, sea-cliffs and stacks)
Outcrops are a significant feature of British rock-climbing, as there are over 400 such locations in England alone, providing the only home climbing ground for many enthusiasts. The most famous are the gritstone edges of Derbyshire. The principal references are books by E. C. Pyatt [631], [634] & [635] and Walt Unsworth [852].

Sea-cliff climbing has also been popular for many years although it has only achieved prominence in recent years through the development of big cliffs such as Craig Gogarth on Anglesey, North Wales. The principal references are books by John Cleare [162] and E. C. Pyatt [634].

For greater detail reference should be made to George Bridge's bibliography of guidebooks [Appendix I].

Further references to Author Index
140. Byne, E. – High Peak: the story of walking and climbing in the Peak District
539. Morin, N. – A woman's reach: mountaineering memoirs [S.E. England: Harrison's Rocks]
605. Patey, T. – One man's mountains: essays and verses

POETRY
It is a chastening thought that probably the best mountain poems have been written by non-mountaineers such as Shelley and Byron. In one of his books [470] Arnold Lunn observes that whereas in prose there are half a dozen Alpine books that would satisfy a severe critic, in poetry only one mountaineer, namely Geoffrey Winthrop Young, has achieved outstanding success. Young's poems were published in several volumes and in collected form [940].

D. W. Freshfield belonged to the generation before Young and although he was a mountaineer and writer of the same high quality, he is scarcely remembered as a poet. His volume of poems [290] was published in 1914, but they date from 1870 and are essentially Victorian in character. Several of his poems survive in anthologies, the best known being his epitaph to his friend W. F. Donkin, lost in the Caucasus.

Moving right into the twentieth century Wilfrid Noyce's poems [580] deserve mention, the best being those written during the successful 1953 attack on Everest. His poetry may be contrasted with that of his contemporary Menlove Edwards [238].

Further references to Author Index
64. Basterfield, G. – Mountain lure [Includes verses]
86. Blakeney, E. H. – Alpine poems
287. Freshfield, D. W. – A tramp's wallet of Alpine and roadside rhymes
568. Nichols, S. H. – Monte Rosa: the epic of an alp
589. Oppenheim, E. C. – The reverberate hills
619. Pilkington, L. – An Alpine valley and other poems
620. Pilkington, L. – The hills of peace and other poems
694. Serraillier, I. – Everest climbed

Note also:
McSpadden, J. W. – The Alps as seen by the poets (1912)

POLAR REGIONS
Arctic and northern waters
Arctic mountaineering dates from 1870 with the ascent of Payer Peak in East Greenland by three members of the German Arctic expedition. Conway made two very important expeditions to Spitsbergen in 1896-7, climbing and establishing the basic pattern for Arctic exploration [177-8]. Since 1918 there have been numerous expeditions to Greenland and Spitsbergen, in which climbing has figured prominently. See also [460] & [757].

Greenland Cambrige University parties were in Greenland in 1926 and 1929. Spencer Chapman took part in the Watkins Arctic Air Route expedition in 1931 [147]. N. E. Odell made some new climbs in East Greenland in 1933. Expeditions to the mountains of Greenland have become popular again in recent years. See [792] for an account of mountaineering in Greenland 1870-1966; this includes bibliographical references (chiefly articles).

Spitsbergen Conway's expeditions were not repeated for over twenty years until Oxford University parties went out in 1921, 1923 and 1933. In this year they climbed in the Stubendorff Mountains. In 1962 a Swiss expedition made several ascents in the north-west sector [585].

Iceland The mountains of Iceland are volcanoes, some still active, covered with ice-caps, Vatnajökull being the largest. The highest point is Hvannadalshnuker, on the rim of the crater of Oraefajökull. The crater rim (c. 6,000') was reached by the Icelandic naturalist Sveinn Palsson in 1794.

Antarctica and southern waters
The two great Antarctic volcanoes, Erebus and Terror, were first sighted in 1841 by the expedition under Sir James Ross. Amundsen discovered the Queen Maud Range in 1911 and an attempt was made on the highest peak, Mt. Fridtjof Nansen, during the American expedition of 1928-30 led by Admiral Byrd. The highest mountains of all are in the Sentinel Range of the Ellsworth Mountains, discovered in 1957. A number of peaks were climbed during December 1966-January 1967 by an A.A.C. party. It is now certain that there are no undiscovered mountains of greater height in Antarctica. See [792] for an article on Antarctica during the International Geophysical Year (1957), with a supplement on mountains and the first mountaineers. Since 1957 there have been many scientific and survey parties in Antarctica, who have climbed numerous peaks: see [801].

Most of the islands in Antarctic waters are mountainous, many of them consisting of little more than ice-covered volcano. One of the better known is Big Ben on Heard Island in the southern Indian Ocean. This peak defied several attempts to climb it [800]. Mount Ross in the Kerguelen Islands may be still unclimbed. Atrocious weather conditions are the climber's worst problem in these latitudes.

Further references to Author Index
340. Hallworth, R. – The last flowers on Earth [Schweizerland, Greenland]
462. Lowe, G. – Because it is there [Chiefly Antarctica]
692. Scott, D. K. – Big wall climbing [Baffin Island]
790. Sutton, G. – Glacier Island: the official account of the British South Georgia Expedition 1954-55

Note also:
Ahlmann, H. W. – Land of ice and fire (Kegan Paul,

1938) [Iceland]

Banks, M. E. B. – High Arctic (Dent, 1957)

Banks, M. E. B. – Greenland (1974)

Beckett, J. A. – Iceland adventure: the double traverse of Vatnajökull by the Cambridge expedition (Witherby, 1934)

Clinch, N. B. – 'First conquest of Antarctica's highest peaks', *National Geographic Magazine* Vol. 131 No. 6 June, 1967

Conway, W. M. – No man's land: a history of Spitsbergen from its discovery in 1596 to the beginning of the scientific exploration of the country

Glen, A. R. – Young men in the Arctic: Oxford University Arctic expedition to Spitsbergen, 1933 (Faber, 1935)

Hillary, E. P. – No latitude for error (Hodder, 1961) [Antarctica]

Irish M.C. – Irish Greenland expedition 1968

Lindsay, M. – Sledge: the British Trans-Greenland expedition, 1934 (Cassell, 1935) [Discovered new mountains]

Tilman, H. W. – 'Mischief' among the penguins (Hart-Davis, 1961) [Voyage to the Crozet and Kerguelen Islands]

PRE-'GOLDEN AGE' MOUNTAINEERING

(Up to 1854)

(See also: Mont Blanc)

Men have climbed mountains all over the world for hundreds of years for religious and military purposes, but mountaineering as a leisure activity developed out of Alpine travel and scientific enquiry. It becomes discernible as a continuous thread from the middle of the eighteenth century and gathers momentum rapidly after 1800. Even before the start of the 'Golden Age' over 100 principal Alpine peaks had been climbed, including Mont Blanc, Monte Rosa (but not the highest point), the Finsteraarhorn and the Jungfrau. British names are conspicuously absent from this role of honour, only accounting for five relatively insignificant peaks.

The highlights of this long period, in approximate chronological order, are:

(i) the activities of the sixteenth century Swiss scholars Conrad Gesner [308] and Josias Simler, [W. A. B. Coolidge, **Josias Simler et les origines de l'alpinisme jusqu'en 1600** (Grenoble, 1904)], and later Johann Jacob Scheuchzer [**Itinera per Helvetiae Alpinas Regiones facta annis 1702-1711.** Collected edition. 4 vols. (Leyden, 1723)]

(ii) the 'discovery' of Chamonix by Windham and Martel [922] and the fight for Mont Blanc

(iii) the climbs of H. B. de Saussure [292] and Placidus à Spescha [**Pater Placidus à Spescha, Sein Leben und Seine Schriften.** Edited by F. Pretti & K. Hager (Berne: Benteli, 1913)], the leading mountaineers of the late eighteenth century (and their contemporary Ramond de Carbonnières [638], the pioneer of the Pyrenees

(iv) the pioneers of the Bernese Oberland, the Meyer brothers [**Reise auf den Jungfrau-Gletscher und Ersteigung seines Gipfels** (Aarau, 1811)]; and the pioneers of Monte Rosa

(v) the work of the scientists, particularly Forbes [274] & [276] and Agassiz, alongside the climbs of men such as Coaz, Desor, Ulrich and Studer [**Berg-und Gletscher-Fahrten.** By . . ., Ulrich & Weilenmann (Zurich, 1859)].

Among the Alpine historians are Francis Gribble, W. A. B. Coolidge and Gottlieb Studer [**Uber Eis und Schnee.** Edited by A. Wäber & H. Dübi (Berne, 1896)]. Gribble's **Early mountaineers** [333] covers the subject up to about 1820 and is standard reading. Coolidge's works, although unsurpassed in accuracy and wealth of details, are by and large unreadable. The best is **Alps in nature and history** [187] which gives a good account of the progress of mountaineering from 1800 to 1850. Several books by G. R. De Beer provide useful and interesting background [204-6].

One of the most important figures of this period was James Forbes, a professor at Edinburgh University, whose principal study was of glaciers. Forbes began exploring the Alps in 1832, visiting as many glaciers as possible. He also pursued his researches in Norway and the Dauphiné Alps. In 1841 he made the fourth (first British) ascent of the Jungfrau, and the following year the first British ascent of a virgin peak, the Stockhorn. He published his accounts of his travels and scientific observations in 1843 and 1853 [274] & [276]. These two books are the first accounts (in English) of systematic Alpine exploration and description. The 1900 edition of **Travels through the Alps** contains all Forbes' Alpine writings, revised and annotated by W. A. B. Coolidge.

Further references to Author Index

101. Bourrit, M. – Relation of a journey to the glaciers in the Dutchy of Savoy
111. Brockedon, W. – Journals of excursions in the Alps
185. Coolidge, W. A. B. – Swiss travel and Swiss guide-books
291. Freshfield, D. W. – Hannibal once more
443. Latrobe, C. J. – The alpenstock: or, Sketches of Swiss scenery and manners
444. Latrobe, C. J. – The pedestrian: a summer's ramble in the Tyrol and some of the adjoining provinces
470. Lunn, A. H. M. – The Alps
575. Noyce, C. W. F. – Scholar mountaineers

Note also:

Bakewell, R. – Travels . . . in the Tarentaise and various parts of the . . . Pennine Alps (Longmans, 1823)

PRIVATELY PUBLISHED BOOKS

The starting point for any study of this interesting field, which contains much of the esoteric in mountaineering literature, is a bibliography [**Appendix I**] compiled by an American, Eugene P. Meckly. Meckly's forenote to his bibliography states that it has been compiled from the **Alpine Journal, Appalachia,** the catalogues of the libraries of the Alpine Club and the Swiss Alpine Club, and various booksellers' catalogues. It includes privately printed books that relate to mountains, mountaineering exploits, and the men who took part in these exploits. It includes certain foreign language books. The **Alpine Journal** editor comments: 'This list . . . is not of course exhaustive, and, for instance, it omits some privately reprinted accounts of the early ascents of Mont Blanc, which had been published in magazines and were reproduced with new title pages; but it is a valuable beginning in an interesting field.' The most recently published book listed in Meckly's bibliography is dated 1948.

PUBLISHERS

William Longman, one of the principals of the publishing house of Longman, Green and later to become President of the Alpine Club (1872-4), made his first Alpine tour in 1856 at the age of forty-three. Keen though he was, circumstances prevented him from devoting himself seriously to mountaineering. Stimulated perhaps by the chance that brought Longman, Green and Charles Hudson together [388], Longman was quick to sense the increasing public interest in mountaineering and gladly published T. W. Hinchliff's book [375] in 1857. During the next forty or so years Longman's firm went on to publish many of the leading mountaineering books of the period, including all those produced under the aegis of the Alpine Club. Longman was one of the first to envisage the Alpine Club as a really important society, rather than the dining club it was created and, with John Ball, was one of the moving spirits in the publication of **Peaks, passes and glaciers** [18]. In 1860 Longman asked the young Edward Whymper to prepare a series of sketches for the second series of **Peaks, passes and glaciers** [20], thus diverting to the Alps all Whymper's energy and cherished ambition for Arctic travel. Years later Longman wrote a short history of the Alpine Club, but he died before he could complete his history of mountaineering.

William Longman's successor in the publishing world, as the 'patron' of mountaineering books was undoubtedly T. Fisher Unwin, who was responsible for publishing many of the leading works during the period 1890-1920. Unwin's association with climbing literature began when he was wheedled into publishing the Conway-Coolidge guidebooks. Conway acted as mediator between publisher and editor, namely W. A. B. Coolidge. Unwin is said to have remarked that because he loved the mountains he was very interested in the guidebooks, though he doubted they would ever repay him.

More recently the mountaineer-writer-publishers have included E. F. Bozman, who was largely responsible for Dent's publication of T. G. Brown's **Brenva** [117] and W. H. Murray's books [558-61], and Robin Collomb who specializes in guidebooks.

RÉSUMÉS
References to Author Index

10. Adams, W. H. D. – Alpine adventure: or, Narratives of travel and research in the Alps
11. Adams, W. H. D. – Alpine climbing: narratives of recent ascents of Mont Blanc, the Matterhorn, the Jungfrau and other lofty summits of the Alps
12. Adams, W. H. D. – Mountains and mountain climbing: records of adventure and enterprise among the famous mountains of the world
78. Benson, C. E. – Mountaineering ventures
153. Clark, R. W. – Great moments in mountaineering
194. Crabb, E. W. – The challenge of the summit: stories of mountains and men
200. Daunt, A. – Crag, glacier and avalanche: narratives of daring and disaster
298. Frith, H. – Ascents and adventures: a record of hardy mountaineering in every quarter of the globe
428. Knowles, A. C. – Adventures in the Alps
448. Le Blond, Mrs. – True tales of mountain adventure for non-climbers young and old
449. Le Blond, Mrs. – Adventures on the roof of the world
467. Lukan, K. – Mountain adventures
552. Muller, E. – They climbed the Alps
557. Mundell, F. – Stories of alpine adventure

651. Robbins, L. H. – Mountains and men
720. Smith, B. W. – Pioneers of mountaineering
747. Snaith, S. – Alpine adventure
748. Snaith, S. – The mountain challenge
762. Stead, R. – Daring deeds of great mountaineers
919. Wilson, H. S. – Alpine ascents and adventures: or, Rock and snow sketches
949. Zurcher, F. – Mountain adventures in the various countries of the world: selected from the narratives of celebrated travellers

SERIES AND EDITIONS
Many mountaineering books have been published as part of a series – educational, sporting, children's books. A few examples are:

Badminton Library [211]; 'Britain in pictures' [84] & [740]; Everyman's Library [21], [836]; Nelson Shilling Library [176] [555] [897] & [899].

However, several series have been created more or less specifically for mountaineering:

Blackwell's Mountaineering Library Quite attractive reprints of several mountaineering classics, e.g. [535], [555], [712], & [913], substituting photographs for the original illustrations.

Eyre & Spottiswoode: New Alpine Library A post-war venture urged on the publisher by Arnold Lunn, with one or two good titles [690] & [942]. Generally an undistinguished series, the production of which suffered no doubt from post-war economies, particularly the covers which fade badly.

Hodder & Stoughton: Black Jacket edition An unattractive pocket edition, reprinting a number of mountaineering and exploration books, e.g. [696], [733] & [751]. **Uniform edition** Very adequate reprints of some of Frank Smythe's books.

Sierra Club Exhibit-Format Series Lavishly produced monographs on aspects of mountaineering and the mountain world, chiefly North America. See [383]. Real collectors' items.

'SILVER AGE' OF MOUNTAINEERING
The Silver Age started when the Golden Age ended, namely with the ascent of the Matterhorn in 1865. When it ended is arguable but for the purpose of these notes Arnold Lunn's definition has been adopted, i.e. that the end was marked by W. W. Graham's ascent of the higher summit of the Dent du Géant in 1882. The basis of his assertion is that the Dent du Géant was the last great virgin peak in the Alps (i.e. a 4000-metre peak, not being a satellite of a greater mountain). One of his books [474] includes a useful chapter on the principal events and personalities characterizing the Silver Age.

Briefly the Silver Age was chiefly characterized by the following developments and events (references are to Author Index):

(1) the conquest of the Dauphiné Alps, principally by W. A. B. Coolidge [157]

(ii) the conquest of the Chamonix peaks [22] & [555]; and the Dolomites and Eastern Alps [692]

(iii) new routes, such as Mummery's ascent of the Zmutt Ridge on the Matterhorn [555]

(iv) exploration and climbing in new areas, e.g. Freshfield [285] & Grove [336] in the Caucasus, Slingsby in Norway [712], W. S. Green's visit to New Zealand

[327] and Whymper in the Andes [899]

(v) development of guideless climbing [316] & [474]

(vi) surveys of the American Rockies and Sierra Nevada, when the numerous peaks were climbed and identified [107] [420] & [896].

SIMULATION

The great demand in outdoor pursuits after 1945 led to the development of artificial climbing walls, or 'climbing simulators'. The first purpose-built wall is thought to be Schurmann Rock in William G. Long Camp, Seattle; this was erected in 1941. The first in Britain was constructed with concrete flanges and ledges; the best example of this type is at Liverpool University. Climbing walls are either exterior, e.g. incorporated into some architectural feature, or interior, e.g. on a gymnasium wall. The subject is covered in [511]. Other simulators which have been devised in the field of mountaineering include holding a falling leader and ice-axe braking. Climbers, including Whymper and Mummery, have been known to simulate snow climbing on the chalk cliffs of Beachy Head, Eastbourne.

Another form of simulation is the sport of wall and roof climbing ('Stegophily'), which has been described as a 'tradition peculiar to Cambridge, its history filled with mystery, absurdity, interest and anonymity'. The sport appears to have passed through three periods of intense activity, although Geoffrey Winthrop Young in his humorous history [937], remarks that 'it is of enormous antiquity, possessing extensive history and a literature which includes the greatest verse and prose writers of all ages.' Young was a leading nightclimber in the 1890s and published a guide to Trinity. In the 1930s (the great heyday) the classic routes were accomplished and recorded [894]. In the 1960s modern rock-climbing techniques were brought into service to achieve even harder climbs, culminating in 1965 with the raising of a 'Peace in Vietnam' banner between the pinnacles of Kings College Chapel [361]. See also [Appendix I (Bridge)].

SKI-MOUNTAINEERING

Briefly, ski-mountaineering means the use of skis as an aid to mountaineering (equivalent to the use of ice-axe and crampons) coupled with the sport of ski-running. It has been described as a marriage between two great sports — skiing and mountaineering, but in fact it has a technique all its own, bringing in different problems of route-finding etc. A modern manual of ski-mountaineering is [798]. See also Gerald Seligman's classic work Snow structures and ski fields [693].

The first great ski-mountaineering expeditions were traverses in the Bernese Oberland, made during the period 1897-1903. Monte Rosa was almost climbed on ski in 1898. The first ski ascent of Mont Blanc was in 1904. One of the outstanding pioneers of this new sport was F. F. Roget, whose book is the classic (in English) on the subject [664]. The most famous ski-mountaineering route in the Alps is the High-Level Route from Chamonix to Zermatt [257].

Ski-mountaineering (and trekking) is popular in other parts of the mountain world. Norway has a long tradition of ski-touring and skis have been used in the Himalaya. Some of the easier Alaskan giants are largely climbed on skis; Mount Waddington in British Columbia was the scene of a famous ski expedition in the 1930s [877]. See also [526] for high mountain skiing in Australia.

Further references to Author Index

35. A.B.M.S.A.C. – Mountaineering handbook
115. Brower, D. R. – Manual of ski mountaineering
267. Finch, G. I. – The making of a mountaineer
472. Lunn, A. H. M. – A history of skiing
474. Lunn, A. H. M. – A century of mountaineering 1857-1957
727. Smythe, F. S. – Climbs and ski-runs: mountaineering and skiing in the Alps, Great Britain and Corsica
757. Spencer, S. – Mountaineering
934. Wyatt, C. – The call of the mountains
938. Young, G. W. – Mountain craft

Note also:

Rickmers, W. R. – Ski-ing for beginners and mountaineers (Fisher Unwin, 1910)

SONGBOOKS
References to Author Index

62. Basterfield, G. – Songs of a cragman [2 versions]
226. Downer, A. C. – Mountaineering ballads
377. Hirst, J. – Songs of the mountaineers
390. Humble, B. H. – Songs for climbers
605. Patey, T. – One man's mountains: essays and verses [Includes two famous items, 'Ballad of Joe Brown' and 'The Manchester Delinquent']

Note also:

Meany, E. S. – Mountain camp fires (Seattle: Lowman & Hanford, 1911)

STAGE-PLAYS

W. H. Auden and Christopher Isherwood collaborated in writing three plays in which the influence of the German expressionist theatre is strong. These are Brechtian, topical plays, with songs and choruses; satirical verse dramas embodying political protest. The ascent of F6 [37] is one of these plays. In the 'Expressionist Theatre' the action on the stage represented psychological conflicts, the torment in man's soul. Every character was heavily symbolic and humour, when it appeared at all, was usually harsh and scarifying. The despair, disillusionment and hysteria of post-World War I Europe flooded onto the stage. The plot of The ascent of F6 involves a race for the first ascent between climbers from Britain and a rival power, the prize being domination over the local territory and peoples. It does not rate as a play of any particular importance and would appear to have been but rarely performed.

Further reference to Author Index

506. Mayhew, H. & A. – Mont Blanc: a comedy in three acts

SURVIVAL AND MOUNTAIN MEDICINE
(See also: Accidents and Rescue)

References to Author Index

83. Bhattacharja, B. – Mountain sickness
459. Longstaff, T. G. – Mountain sickness and its probable cause
543. Mountaineers – Medicine for mountaineering
582. Noyce, C. W. F. – They survived: a study of the will to live
756. Speer, S. T. – On the physiological phenomena of the mountain sickness, as experienced in the

ascent of the higher Alps
764. Steele, P. R. C. – Doctor on Everest
765. Steele, P. R. C. – – Medical care for mountain climbers

Note also:

Darvill, F. T. – Mountaineering medicine (1965)
Edholm, O. G. – Exploration medicine: a practical guide for those going on expeditions (Bristol: John Wright, 1965)
Greenbank, A. – A book of survival (Wolfe, 1967)
Merrill, B. – The survival handbook (Prior, 1972)
Roget, F. F. – Altitude and health (Constable, 1919)
Troebst, C. C. – Art of survival (W. H. Allen, 1965)
Ward, M. P. – Man at high altitude (1974)
Ward, M. P. – Mountain sickness: a clinical study of cold and high altitude (Crosby Lockwood Staples, 1975)

TECHNIQUE

(Equipment, clothing, methods, instruction)

The many books dealing with mountaineering technique started in the 1890s and are of several types. There are omnibus books dealing with all aspects of mountaineering (technique, climbing areas, photography etc.); books which are solely technique, some profusely illustrated; and some which combine instruction with personal reminiscence.

Principal references to Author Index

3. Abraham, G. D. – The complete mountaineer [Omnibus]
57. Barford, J. E. Q. – Climbing in Britain
75. Bell, J. H. B. – Progress in mountaineering [Includes reminiscences]
77. Benson, C. E. – British mountaineering
85. Blackshaw, A. – Mountaineering from hill walking to Alpine climbing [Handbook currently approved by B.M.C./M.C. of S.]
211. Dent, C. T. – Mountaineering [Omnibus]
251. Evans, C. – On climbing [Includes reminiscences]
363. Henderson, K. A. – The handbook of American mountaineering
424. Kirkus, C. F. – 'Let's go climbing'
440. Langmuir, E. – Mountain leadership: the official handbook of the Mountain Leadership Training Boards of Great Britain
455. Leonard, R. M. – Belaying the leader
496. March, W. – Modern snow and ice techniques
497. March, W. – Modern rope techniques in mountaineering
542. Mountaineers – Mountaineering: the freedom of the hills
637. Raeburn, H. – Mountaineering art
641. Rébuffat, G. – On snow and rock [Superbly illustrated]
652. Robbins, R. – Basic rockcraft
653. Robbins, R. – Advanced rockcraft
666. Roscoe, D. T. – Mountaineering: a manual for teachers & instructors
692. Scott, D. K. – Big wall climbing [Artificial climbing]
757. Spencer, S. – Mountaineering [Omnibus]
890. Wheelock, W. – Ropes, knots and slings for climbers
916. Wilson, C. – Mountaineering
938. Young, G. W. – Mountain craft [Omnibus]

Further references to Author Index

8. Abraham, G. D. – First steps to climbing

9. Abraham, G. D. – Modern mountaineering
34. A.B.M.S.A.C. – The technique of Alpine mountaineering
35. A.B.M.S.A.C. – Mountaineering handbook
82. Bernstein, J. – Ascent: of the invention of mountain climbing and its practice
126. Brunning, K. – Rock-climbing and mountaineering
133. Bunting, J. – Climbing
135. Burlingham, F. – How to become an alpinist
143. Casewit, C. W. – The mountaineering handbook, an invitation to climbing
144. C.C.P.R. – Safety on mountains
151. Clark, R. W. – Come climbing with me
215. Disley, J. – Tackle climbing this way
217. Dixon, C. M. – Rock-climbing
259. F.M.C.N.Z. – Safety in the mountains
278. Francis, G. – Mountain climbing
329. Greenbank, A. – Instructions in rock-climbing
330. Greenbank, A. – Instructions in mountaineering
339. Hall, R. W. – The art of mountain tramping
362a. Heine, A. J. – Mountaincraft manual [New Zealand]
398. Ingram, J. A. – Fellcraft: some advice for fell-walkers
409. James, R. – Rock face: techniques of rock climbing
461. Lovelock, J. – Climbing
477. Lyman, T. – The field book of mountaineering and rock climbing
480. MacInnes, H. – Climbing
491. Mandolf, H. I. – Basic mountaineering
512. Mendenhall, R. – Introduction to rock and mountain climbing
562. Murray, W. H. – The craft of climbing
569. Nock, P. – Rock-climbing
598. Palmer, W. T. – The complete hillwalker, rock climber and cave explorer
608. Peacocke, T. A. H. – Mountaineering
625. Porter, E. C. – Mountaineering: essays on safety and technique
721. Smith, G. A. – Introduction to mountaineering
724. Smith, P. D. – Knots for mountaineering
774. Styles, S. – Introduction to mountaineering
775. Styles, S. – Getting to know mountains
776. Styles, S. – How mountains are climbed
778. Styles, S. – Modern mountaineering
780. Styles, S. – The foundations of climbing
782. Styles, S. – Rock and rope
789. Sutton, G. – Artificial aids in mountaineering
796. Tarbuck, K. – Nylon rope and climbing safety
851. Unsworth, W. – The young mountaineer
856. Unsworth, W. – The book of rock-climbing
878. Wedderburn, E. – Alpine climbing on foot and with ski
932. Wright, J. E. B. – The technique of mountaineering
933. Wright, J. E. B. – Rock-climbing in Britain

UNITED STATES OF AMERICA

(Excluding Alaska)

(In the following notes references to the United States (U.S.A.) are to be taken as excluding Alaska).

In height the principal mountains of the U.S.A. are not unlike the Alps, there being hundreds of peaks ranging from 10,000'-14,000'. There is however relatively little snow and ice and many of the highest peaks are what American climbers term 'walk-ups'. There are many lesser peaks and spires which present far greater problems. The principal reference is a recently published history, **Climbing in North America** [413]. For a useful introduction on a state by state basis see [129]. See also [254].

Rocky Mountains

This interlocking chain runs for over 1,000 miles from the Canadian border to New Mexico. There are more than 100 defined and named groups, mainly within the states of Montana, Wyoming and Colorado. They form a series of mountains interspersed with extensive tablelands but only in Colorado do they constitute a real barrier between east and west.

In places the mountains are known to have been penetrated first by the Spanish and by Indian tribes, who undoubtedly climbed a number of peaks. American exploration commences at the beginning of the nineteenth century with such discoveries as Pikes Peak (1806), Grand Teton (1807) and Longs Peak (1820). Still it was not until the latter part of the century that these areas began to be colonized. Most of the early systematic exploration of the mountains was done by government survey teams, who alone had the necessary time and money. Much of the work was carried out under the leadership of Dr. F. V. Hayden, who was for twelve years (1867-79) U.S. geologist-in-charge of the western territories. Members of his survey teams made quite a number of first (recorded) ascents. By the end of 1916 there were no virgin summits over 14,000' in the Rockies and few peaks of major importance remained unclimbed for much longer after that date.

Montana Glacier National Park is an area of steep, serrated rock peaks, most of which are moderately easy. The main crest is the Lewis Range, and there are numerous small glaciers. To the south lies the Absaroka Range, with some peaks which are among the most rugged in the U.S.A., although the highest, Francs Peak, is easy. The Beartooth Range forms the north-east spur of the Absarokas but although it is one of the major alpine regions of the U.S.A. it is one of the least visited. See [850].

The ranges along the Montana-Idaho boundary – chiefly the Bitterroot and Salmon River mountains – are strictly not part of the Rockies, being linked to the Purcell and Selkirk ranges in British Columbia. There are mountains here to rival any range in the U.S.A. and much of the region remains impenetrable to vehicles. The first Americans to traverse Montana into Idaho and back again were Lewis and Clark in 1805-6, who crossed the Bitterroot Mountains [811].

Wyoming The first American travellers into this region were John Colter, who crossed Yellowstone in 1807, and the Hunt expedition in 1811. The principal ranges – the Tetons and Wind River Mountains – are claimed by some as the best climbing areas in the American West.

The Tetons are a compact group with a few small glaciers, offering high-quality rock-climbing. They are dominated by Grand Teton which rises a dramatic 7,000' from the valley floor. It was attempted as early as 1843, and many times by Indians, but was not climbed until 1898 (subject to a possible ascent by the Hayden Survey). Mt. Moran was climbed in 1919 [411] and the most difficult peak, Mt. Owen, in 1930. New routes in this period were pioneered by climbers such as Henderson, Underhill and Fryxell [299]. See also [615].

The Wind River Range carries the most extensive glaciers in the American Rockies and also offers rock-climbing comparable to the Tetons, all in one of the vastest tracts of roadless wilderness in the U.S.A. Fremont Peak (more probably Mt. Woodrow Wilson) was climbed in 1842 by a government expedition. In 1878 an Englishman, James Eccles, made ascents of Fremont Peak and Wind River Mountain while accompanying the Hayden Survey. Apparently there was no further climbing in the district until Gannett Peak was climbed in 1922.

Colorado This is the highest state in the U.S.A., with an average elevation of nearly 7,000'. Fifty-two of the sixty-seven mountains over 14,000' in the U.S.A. are in Colorado (most of the others in the Sierra Nevada) and also three-quarters of all the peaks over 10,000'. Nevertheless there are scarcely any snow and ice climbs: the attractions are all for rock-climbers and walkers. Well over half of Colorado's highest peaks can be climbed by walking routes.

The Front Range provides some good climbing, particularly in the Rocky Mountain National Park [23], [145] & [821], including Longs Peak [565]. The Sawatch Range contains the highest peak in the Rockies, Mt. Elbert, which was a Hayden survey point in the 1870s. This range also contains Pikes Peak, America's most famous mountain. Other ranges with more challenging peaks are the beautiful Sangre de Christo; the San Juan and the mountains to the south-west; and the Elk Mountains (west of the Sawatch) [338]. For history of Colorado rock-climbing see [130]. See also [352].

Sierra Nevada

A great mountain range in eastern California, some 400 miles long. Interest concentrates on the southern half known as the High Sierra. Roughly speaking, the most important climbing areas lie within three National Parks – Sequoia, Kings Canyon and Yosemite. The highest peak is Mt. Whitney, named after Professor Whitney, who was California State geologist in the 1860s. Another well-known pioneer was Clarence King, also a geologist and member of Whitney's team. One of the most famous names is that of John Muir. This Scottish-born naturalist and explorer was very active in the mountains of California and became founder and President of the Sierra Club. He was largely responsible for the establishment of Yosemite and other areas as national parks [545-6]. Between the wars the leading climber was Norman Clyde [165].

Sequoia Park This area contains several of the highest peaks, including Mt. Whitney [889]. The headwaters of the Kings and Kern rivers run up to the Kings-Kern Divide, the principal obstacle in Clarence King's epic ascent of Mt. Tyndall [420]. King's book is the great mountain classic of American mountaineering literature: it has a most complicated publishing history.

Kings Canyon Park The Palisade group is the most alpine section of the High Sierra, North Palisade and Thunderbolt Peak being two of the most difficult mountains in the U.S.A.

Yosemite This is a region of canyons, peaks, cliffs and waterfalls. Yosemite Valley is flanked by remarkable rock walls such as El Capitan and Half Dome, providing thousands of feet of excessively severe rock-climbing [670]. See also [549], [896] & [911].

Cascades

Known as the 'American Alps', the Cascades run from Lassen Peak (California) north to the Canadian border, linking the Sierra Nevada with the Coast Mountains of British Columbia. They have an average elevation of 8,000', punctuated by a number of high volcanoes. Of these, Shasta and Hood [910] are easy climbs; Jefferson is the most difficult. The highest is Rainier, which has the largest glacial system of any mountain in the U.S.A. Rainier is a great favourite and is well documented [510] & [531], including a beautiful little book by J. H. Williams [909]. The North Cascades is a superb region of jagged peaks and glaciers, the most alpine of all the ranges in the U.S.A. Fred Beckey, one of America's leading climbers, has written a book on this area [72].

Olympic Mountains

In the extreme north-west is a small range averaging 7,000'-8,000'. On the western slopes the rare climatic conditions (temperate rain forest) produce prodigious forest growth and vast snow and ice fields (as much as 250' of snow each year). The Olympic Mountains were first explored in 1889-90 [924-5].

Further references to Author Index

24. Ament, P. – Swaremandal
25. Ament, P. – Master of rock
30. Anderson, J. – The book of the White Mountains [Eastern U.S.A.]
106. Brewer, W. H. – Up and down California in 1860-1864
107. Brewer, W. H. – Rocky Mountain letters, 1869
224. Douglas, W. O. – Of men and mountains [Cascades]
252. Farquhar, F. P. – Exploration of the Sierra Nevada
253. Farquhar, F. P. – Place names of the High Sierra
255. Farquhar, F. P. – History of the Sierra Nevada
300. Fryxell, F. N. – The Tetons: interpretations of a mountain landscape
358. Hazard, J. F. – Snow sentinels of the Pacific North-west
411. Jeffers, L. – The call of the mountains: rambles among the mountains and canyons of the United States and Canada
451. Le Conte, J. N. – Journal of ramblings through the High Sierra of California by the University Excursion Party
486. McNeil, F. H. – Wy' East 'The Mountain' [Mount Hood]
548. Muir, J. – Steep trails
668. Rossit, E. A. – Northwest mountaineering
672. Rusk, C. E. – Tales of a western mountaineer: a record of mountain experiences
760. Spring, B. – High adventure
761. Spring, B. – High worlds of the mountain climber
822. Toll, R. W. – The mountain peaks of Colorado
875. Washburn, H. B. – Bradford on Mount Washington

Note also:

Atwood, W. W., – The Rocky Mountains
Baggs, M. L. – Colorado, Queen Jewel of the Rockies
Barnes, A. H. – Our greatest mountain (1911)
Carson, A. C. – Colorado, the top of the world
Cumming, C. F. G. – Granite crags (Blackwood, 1884)
Fremont, J. C. – Narrative of the exploring expedition to the Rocky Mountains (Washington: Gales & Seaton, 1845)
Hayden, F. V. – Geological Survey of the Territories,
U.S. Geological Survey, 1875-1878. 13 vols. (Washington)
Lewis, M. – Travels to the source of the Missouri River and across the American continent to the Pacific Ocean (1814)
Morris, M. O. – Rambles in the Rocky Mountains (London, 1864)
Peattie, R. – Sierra Nevada: range of light (New York: Vanguard Press, 1947)
Peattie, R. – Friendly mountains (New York: Vanguard Press, 1943)
Sabin, E. L. – The peaks of the Rockies (Denver Railroad, 1916)
Schmoe, F. W. – Our greatest mountain (1925) [Rainier]
Steel, W. G. – The mountains of Oregon
Ward, J. H. – The White Mountains
Wickham, R. S. – Friendly Adirondack peaks (Adirondack M.C., 1924)

VOLCANOES

Volcanoes generally do not provide very interesting or difficult climbing. There are about 430 volcanoes with recorded eruptions, the majority being in the northern hemisphere. Volcanic activity is chiefly confined to three regions:

(i) a horseshoe-shaped chain extending round the Pacific Ocean from New Zealand through Indonesia, Japan, Alaska, Central America and on into the Andes

(ii) a belt stretching from the Canary Islands eastwards to the Pacific, through Italy, Iran and the Caucasus; and south to Kilimanjaro and the Virunga Mountains of the Congo

(iii) isolated submarine areas in the Pacific, Atlantic and Indian oceans.

Most activity occurs in the Pacific area (2,000 out of 2,500 recorded eruptions). From a mountaineering point of view the most famous volcanoes are probably the giants of Ecuador, explored and climbed by Edward Whymper in 1880 [899], while the most obscure are the Virunga Mountains [209]. The most severe climb is the South Face of Aconcagua [262].

WINTER MOUNTAINEERING

Winter climbing in the Alps has been in vogue since Victorian times. Horace Walker, one of the pioneers of the Golden Age, was an early advocate. When Mrs. Le Blond went to the Alps to recuperate, she took up winter climbing [445]. Since the first war it has become commonplace for the leading climbers of the day to pit themselves against the hardest summer routes under winter conditions. Much of this climbing takes place in the Alps but two climbers who were quick to see the possibilities of Scottish winter climbing were J. H. B. Bell [75] and W. H. Murray [558-9]. Specific references are: the winter ascent of Mt. McKinley [202]; winter ascents of the Eigerwand [314], [355] & [368]; and the first winter traverse of the Southern Alps of New Zealand [214a].

WOMEN MOUNTAINEERS

A useful summary of women's climbing has been written by Cecily Williams [908]. Further references to the nineteenth century pioneers, and to later climbers, will be found in [135], [150], [333], [786] & [855]. A good deal of information about Meta Brevoort is available in R. W. Clark's biography of her nephew, W. A. B. Coolidge

[157], with whom she shared many climbs. The best ladies' accounts of mid-Victorian Alpine travel were written by Mrs. Cole [167] and Mrs. Freshfield [294-5].

Linking the Victorian era to the modern is Mrs. Le Blond (1861-1934), first President of the Ladies Alpine Club. She climbed extensively in the Alps in the 1880s [445-6] and later in Norway [450]. At the beginning of the twentieth century three other women were making history in remote mountain areas. Annie Peck, an American, climbed Huascaran in Peru in 1908 [610] and Miss Freda Du Faur accomplished many fine routes in New Zealand [228], while Fanny Bullock Workman, another American, carried out no less than seven important Himalayan expeditions [926-30].

The next and possibly most important development occurred in the 1930s – manless climbing. Two leaders in this drive were Nea Morin [539] and Miriam Underhill [850], one of the few leading American climbers of that period to climb in the Alps. Nea Morin's book contains a useful check-list of feminine first ascents. One of the finest climbing records of this period is Dorothy Pilley's **Climbing days** [621]. The post-1945 period has witnessed the development of women's high altitude climbing, with a number of all-women expeditions to the Himalaya. Outstanding among these was Claude Kogan [346] & [438]. Other expeditions are recorded in [230], [407] & [684]. The first woman professional guide in Britain is Gwen Moffat [527, 529-30].

Further references to Author Index

236.　　Edwards, A. – Untrodden peaks and unfrequented valleys: a mid-summer ramble in the Dolomites
341.　　Hamilton, H. – Mountain madness
384.　　Hornby, E. – Mountaineering records
430.　　[Leininger, N.] – The ascent of Alpamayo
618.　　Pigeon, A. – Peaks and passes
624.　　Plunket, F. – Here and there among the Alps
649.　　Richard, C. – Climbing blind
723.　　Smith, J. A. – Mountain holidays
805.　　Thompson, D. – Climbing with Joseph Georges
861.　　Visser-Hooft, J. – Among the Kara-korum glaciers in 1925

Note also:

Clark, J. I. – Pictures and memories (Moray Press, 1938)
Clementi, Mrs. – Through British Guiana to the summit of Roraima (Fisher Unwin, 1920)
Deacock, A. – No purdah in Padam (Harrap, 1960)
Le Blond, Mrs. – Day in, day out (Lane, Bodley Head, 1928)
[Mazuchelli, E. S.] – The Indian Alps and how we crossed them (Longmans, 1876)

Pumori, Khumbu Himal, Nepal

MOUNTAIN INDEX

SECTION HEADINGS

Notes:
(i) The names of guides, sherpas and other employees are shown in italic type.
(ii) Principal book references are shown in bold type.

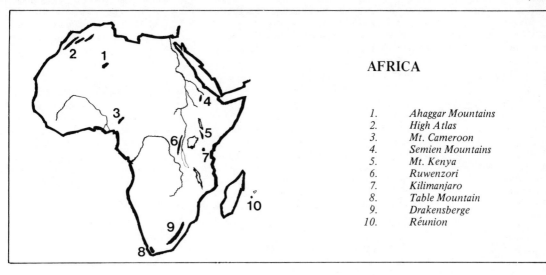

AFRICA

1.	*Ahaggar Mountains*
2.	*High Atlas*
3.	*Mt. Cameroon*
4.	*Semien Mountains*
5.	*Mt. Kenya*
6.	*Ruwenzori*
7.	*Kilimanjaro*
8.	*Table Mountain*
9.	*Drakensberge*
10.	*Réunion*

AFRICA

Name of Peak	Height (Feet)	Date	Details of first recorded ascent Names of Party, etc.	References to Books
Ahaggar Mtns				
Tahat	9,574	1912		
Ilamane	9,050			
Iharen		1935		
Garet el Djenoun	7,667			
High Atlas				
Jebel Toubkal	13,665	1923	Berger, Dolbeau, Segonzac	
Ouanoukrim Sud	13,416			
Mgoun	13,356			
Afella	13,265			
Likimt	13,150	1888	J. Thomson	806
Iferouane	13,127			
Tazarharht	13,058			
Biiguinnoussene	13,006			
Aksoual	12,828			
Anrhemer	12,773			
Jebel Ayachi	12,303			
Jebel Tezah	11,972	1871	J. Hooker, J. Ball, G. Maw	381
Angour	11,745			
Mt. Cameroon				
Fako Peak	13,350	1861	R. Burton	
Ethiopia				
Semien Mtns				
Ras Dashan	15,159	1841	Ferret, Galinier	
Bwahit	14,793			
Kollo	14,107			139
Guna	13,881			
Uara Sahia	13,000			
Mt. Kenya				
—Batian	17,058	1899	H. Mackinder, *C. Ollier, J. Brocherel*	233, 698, 814, 825
—Nelion	17,022	1929	E. E. Shipton, P. W. Harris	233, 698, 814
—Point Lenana	16,355			79, 233
Ruwenzori				
Stanley				
—Margherita	16,763	1906	Abruzzi party	265, 814
—Alexandra	16,703	1906	Abruzzi party	265, 814

Africa

—Albert	16,690	1932	X. de Grunne & party	
—Savoia	16,330	1906	Abruzzi party	265
—Elena	16,300	1906	Abruzzi party	265
—Elizabeth	16,170	1953	D. L. Busk, A. Firmin	139
—Philip	16,140	1954	H. Osmaston, A. Stuart	139
—Moebius	16,134	1906	Abruzzi party	265

Speke

—Vittorio Emanuele	16,042	1906	Abruzzi party	265
—Ensonga	15,961	1926	G. N. Humphreys	
—Johnston	15,860	1926	G. N. Humphreys	
—Trident	15,000			

Baker

—Edward	15,889	1906	Abruzzi party	265, 814
—Semper	15,730	1906	Abruzzi party	265, 814
—Wollaston	15,286	1906	A. F. R. Wollaston, R. E. Woosman, R. E. Dent.	265
—Moore	15,170	1906	V. Sella, E. Botta, *J. Brocherel*	
—Cagni	14,720	1906	U. Cagni, *J. Petigax, J. Brocherel*	
—Grauer Rock	14,710	1906	R. Grauer, H. W. Tegart, H. E. Maddox.	
—Kinyangoma	14,536	1947	A. J. Haddow, E. J. Holmes	

Emin

—Umberto	15,740	1906	Abruzzi party	265
—Kraepelin	15,720	1932	X. de Grunne & party	

Gessi

—Iolande	15,470	1906	Abruzzi party	265
—Bottego	15,418	1906	Abruzzi party	265

Luigi di Savoia

—Sella	15,178	1906	Abruzzi party	265
—Weismann	15,157	1932	G. N. Humphreys	794
—Stairs	14,910	1906	Abruzzi party	265

Virunga Mtns

Karisimbi	14,782			
Mikeno	14,557	1927	Pere Van Hoef, M. & Mme Leonard	
Muhavura	13,532			
Vishoke	12,175			80, 209
Sabinyo	11,922			
Mgahinga	11,397			
Nyiragongo	11,381			
Nyamuragira	10,056			

Kilimanjaro

—Kibo	19,340	1889	H. Meyer, L. Purtscheller	502, 517, 825
—Mawenzi	16,890	1912	F. Klute, E. Ohler	814

South Africa
Table mountain

Table mountain	3,567	1503	Antonio de Saldanha	464

Drakensberge

Thabantshonyana	11,425			
Champagne Castle	11,079	1888	A. H. Stocker, F. R. Stocker	
Giants Castle	10,878	1864	R. Spiers, A. Bovill, H., E. & F. Bucknall	
Mont-aux-Sources	10,768	1836	T. Arbousset, F. Daumas	457, 609
—Sentinel	10,740	1910	Wybergh, McLeod	
Cathkin Peak	10,330	1912	G. T. Amphlett, W. C. West, A. D. Kelly, T. Casement	
Cathedral Peak	9,856	1917	D. W. Bassett-Smith, R. G. Kingdon	

Réunion

Piton des Neiges	10,069			586

General References
[129], [136], [139], [Appendix VI]

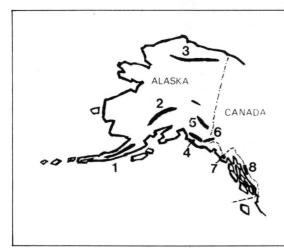

ALASKA

1. *Aleutian Range*
2. *Alaska Range*
3. *Brooks Range*
4. *Chugach Mtns.*
5. *Wrangell Mtns.*
6. *St. Elias Mtns.*
7. *Fairweather Range*
8. *Coast Mtns.*

ALASKA

Name of Peak	Height (Feet)	Date	Details of first recorded ascent — Names of Party, etc.	References to Books
Aleutian Range				
Torbert	11,413			
Spurr	11,190			
Redoubt	10,197			
Iliamna	10,016			
Shishaldin	9,387			
Katmai	6,715			
Alaska Range				
McKinley	20,320	1913	H. Stuck, H. C. Karstens, W. Harper, R. Tatum	45, **121, 184,**
—North Peak		1910	Andersen, Taylor	**202,** 229, 502,
				536,750,**768**
Foraker	17,400	1934	C. S. Houston, T. G. Brown, C. Waterston	
Hunter	14,570	1954	F. Beckey, H. Harrer, H. Meybohm	
Hayes	13,832			
Cathedral Peak	12,540			
Deborah	12,339	1954	F. Beckey, H. Harrer, H. Meybohm	**656**
Huntington	12,240	1964	[French party]	**655**
Russell	11,500			
Kimball	10,350			
Mooses Tooth	10,335	1964	[German party]	
Revelation Mtns	9,828			
Allen	9,500			
Dall	9,000			
Kichatna Spire	8,985			
Brooks Range				
Isto	9,060			
Arrigetch Peaks				
Chugach Mtns				
Marcus Baker	13,176	1938	H. B. Washburn	
St. Agnes		1938	H. B. Washburn, N. Dyrenfurth, N. Bright, P. Gabriel.	
Gilbert	10,194			
Wrangell Mtns				
Blackburn	16,390	1958		
—SE Summit	16,286	1912	Miss D. Keen, G. W. Handy	
Sanford	16,237	1938	H. B. Washburn, T. Moore	
Wrangell	14,163	1908	R. Dunn, W. Soule	
Jarvis	12,230			

St. Elias Mtns

Logan	19,850	1925	A. H. MacCarthy, H. F. Lambart	402
St. Elias	18,008	1897	Abruzzi party	112, 264, 416
Lucania	17,147	1937	H. B. Washburn, R. Bates	
King	17,130			
Steele	16,440	1935	W. A. Wood & party	
Bona	16,420	1930	A. Carpe, T. Moore, A. M. Taylor	
Wood	15,855			
Vancouver	15,825	1949	N. E. Odell, W. Hainsworth, R. McCarter, Bruce-Robertson	
Cook	15,760			
Churchill	15,638			
Slaggard	15,575			
McCauley	15,475			
Hubbard	15,015	1951	W. A. Wood	
Bear	14,831			
Walsh	14,780			
Alverstone	14,516	1951	W. A. Wood	
McArthur	14,500			
University Peak	14,470			
Augusta	14,070			
Natazhat	13,480	1913	H. F. Lambart & party	
Craig	13,250			

Fairweather Range

Fairweather	15,318	1931	A. Carpe, T. Moore	695, 876
Quincy Adams	13,560			
Root	12,860			
Crillon	12,725	1934	H. B. Washburn & party	
Watson	12,495			
Lituya	11,750			
La Perouse	10,750			
Lodge	10,530			
Bertha	10,182	1940	H. B. Washburn & party	

Coast Mtns

Kates Needle	10,002	1946	F. Beckey, R. Craig, C. Schmidtke	
Devil's Thumb	9,077	1946	F. Beckey, R. Craig, C. Schmidtke	413
Devil's Paw		1949	W. Putnam & 2 others	

General References:
[129], [271 (Appendix on St. Elias Mtns history)], [757], **Appendix VI.**
[See also many articles in A.A.J.]

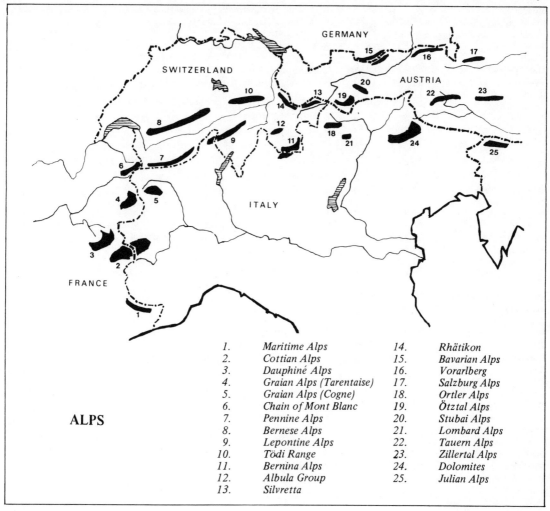

ALPS

1.	Maritime Alps	14.	Rhätikon
2.	Cottian Alps	15.	Bavarian Alps
3.	Dauphiné Alps	16.	Vorarlberg
4.	Graian Alps (Tarentaise)	17.	Salzburg Alps
5.	Graian Alps (Cogne)	18.	Ortler Alps
6.	Chain of Mont Blanc	19.	Ötztal Alps
7.	Pennine Alps	20.	Stubai Alps
8.	Bernese Alps	21.	Lombard Alps
9.	Lepontine Alps	22.	Tauern Alps
10.	Tödi Range	23.	Zillertal Alps
11.	Bernina Alps	24.	Dolomites
12.	Albula Group	25.	Julian Alps
13.	Silvretta		

ALPS

Name of Peak	Height (Feet)	Details of first recorded ascent Date	Name of Party, etc.	References to books
Maritime Alps				
P.dell'Argentera	10,794	1879	W. A. B. Coolidge, *C. & C. Almer*	
Monte Stella	10,699	1871	C. Isaia	
Cima dei Gelas	10,286	1864	P.de St. Robert	188, 293
Cima di Nasta	10,197	1878	D. W. Freshfield	
Monte Matto	10,128	1879	W. A. B. Coolidge, *C. & C. Almer*	
Cottian Alps				
Monte Viso	12,609	1861	W. Mathews, F. W. Jacomb, *M. & J. B. Croz*	
Aig.de Scolette	11,500	1875	M. Baretti	
A.de Chambeyron	11,155	1879	W. A. B. Coolidge, *C. & C. Almer*	
B.de Chambeyron	11,116	1878	P. Agnel, J. Risoul	188, 830
Rognosa d'Etche	11,106	1875	F. Montaldo	
Dents d'Ambin	11,096	1875	M. Baretti	
Roches d'Ambin	11,080	1822	[Piedmontese & Austrian surveyors]	
Dauphiné Alps				
Pointe des Ecrins	13,462	1864	A. W. Moore, H. Walker, E. Whymper, *M. Croz, C. Almer*	535, 897

Meije	13,081	1877	E. Boileau de Castelnau, *P. & P. Gaspard*	**188, 244,** 318
–Central Peak	13,025	1870	W. A. B. Coolidge, M. Brevoort, *C. Gertsch*	
			C. & U. Almer	
–East Peak	12,832	1878	H. Duhamel, *Giraud-Lezin, F. Gonet*	
Ailefroide	12,989	1870	W. A. B. Coolidge, *C. & U. Almer, Gertsch*	307
Mont Pelvoux	12,973	1848	V. Puiseaux	897
–Pyramide	12,921	1830	A. A. Durand, *J. E. Matheoud, A. Liotard*	
Pic Sans Nom	12,845	1877	J. B. Colgrove, R. Pendlebury,	
			G. & J. Spechtenhauser	
Pic Gaspard	12,730	1878	H. Duhamel, *P. & P. Gaspard, C. Roderon*	
Le Pavé	12,570	1879	W. A. B. Coolidge, *C. & C. Almer*	
Grande Sagne	12,399	1877	W. A. B. Coolidge, *C. & C. Almer*	
Pic Coolidge	12,323	1877	W. A. B. Coolidge, *C. & C. Almer*	
Râteau	12,317	1873	W. A. B. Coolidge, M. Brevoort, *C. Almer,*	
			P. Michel, P. Bleuer, C. Roth	
Grande Ruine	12,317	1873	W. A. B. Coolidge, M. Brevoort, *C. Almer,*	
			P. Michel, P. Bleuer, C. Roth	
Roche Faurio	12,192	1873	F. Gardiner, R. & W. M. Pendlebury, C. Taylor,	
			T. Cox, H. & P. Baumann	
Pic Bourcet	12,130	1887	F. E. L. Swan, *P. Gaspard Sr, J. B. Rodier, C. Clot*	
Le Fifre	12,074	1881	W. A. B. Coolidge, *C. & C. Almer*	
Pic de la Grave	12,051	1874	W. A. B. Coolidge, *C. Almer, R. Kaufmann*	
Mont Aiguille	6,880	1492	A. de Ville	333

Graian Alps
(Tarentaise)

Grande Casse	12,668		W. Mathews, *M. Croz*	
Mont Pourri	12,428		*M. Croz* [directed by W. Mathews]	
Dent Parrachée	12,179	1864	R. M. Cuthbert, T. Blanford	
Grande Motte	12,018	1864	E. P. Rowsell, R. M. Cuthbert, T. Blanford	

(Mountains of Cogne)

Grand Paradiso	13,324	1860	J. J. Cowell, W. Dundas, *M. Payot, Tairraz*	
Grivola	13,022	1859	J. Ormsby, R. Bruce, *Z. Cachat, Tairraz*	
–Punta Nera	12,113	1888	W. A. B. Coolidge	
Petit Paradis	12,920	1869		
Cresta Gastaldi	12,671	1888	W. A. B. Coolidge	936
B. di Montandeyné	12,632	1875		
Mont Herbetet	12,396	1873	S. Barale	
Punta Budden	12,153	1885		

Chain of Mont Blanc

Mont Blanc	15,782	1786	M. Paccard, J. Balmat	See SUBJECT
Mont Blanc de	15,595	1877	J. Eccles	INDEX
Courmayeur				
Mont Maudit	14,669	1878	H. S. Hoare, W. E. Davidson	
Dôme du Goûter	14,118	1784	F. Cuidet, J. M. Couttet	
Mont Blanc du Tacul	13,941	1855	C. Hudson	388
Grandes Jorasses	13,797	1868	H. Walker	88, **388, 445**
–Lower Peak		1865	E. Whymper, *C. Almer, F. Biener*	535, **639, 897, 939**
Aig. Verte	13,541	1865	E. Whymper, *C. Almer, F. Biener*	207, **535,** 897
Aig. Blanche de Peuterey	13,482	1885	H. S. King, *C. Klucker*	**425**
A. de Bionnassay	13,341	1865	F. C. Grove, E. N. Buxton, R. J. S. Macdonald	**22**
Aig. du Géant	13,170	1882	W. W. Graham	318, **446**
Dome de Rochefort	13,163	1881	J. Eccles	
Aig. de Rochefort	13,134	1873	J. Eccles	
Mont Mallet	13,085	1871	L. Stephen, F. A. Wallroth, Loppé, *Cachat,*	
			M. Anderegg, Tournier	
Aig. de Trélatête	12,832	1864	E. Whymper, A. Adams-Reilly	22, **897**
Aig. d'Argentière	12,819	1864	E. Whymper, A. Adams-Reilly	22, **897**
Aig. de Triolet	12,717	1874	J. A. G. Marshall	**662**
Les Courtes	12,648	1876	T. Middlemore, J. O. Maund, H. Cordier	
Aig. du Midi	12,609	1856	F. de Bouille	22, **445, 939**
–North Peak		1818	Count Malczewski	
Tour Noir	12,586	1876	E. Javelle	**410**
Mont Dolent	12,543	1864	E. Whymper, A. Adams-Reilly	22, **897**
A. du Chardonnet	12,540	1865	R. Fowler	**539**
Tour Ronde	12,441	1867	D. W. Freshfield	

Aig. Noire de Peuterey	12,402	1877	Lord Wentworth	
Grand Dru	12,320	1878	C. T. Dent, J. W. Hartley, *A. Burgener, K. Maurer*	**210**
Aig. de Talèfre	12,268	1879	F. F. Cullinan, G. Fitzgerald, *J. Baumann*	
Petit Dru	12,245	1879	J. Charlet-Straton, *P. Payot*	88, 489, 639
Dome de Miage	12,100	1858	E. T. Coleman	
Aig. du Plan	12,061	1871	J. Eccles, *M. & A. Payot*	535, 662, 939
Aig. du Tour	11,615	1864	R. B. Heathcote	
A. de Blaitière	11,549	1874	E. R. Whitwell, *C. & J. Lauener*	207, 539
Aig. de Grépon	11,447	1881	A. F. Mummery, *A. Burgener, B. Venetz*	539, 555, 662, 939
Grands Charmoz	11,293	1880	A. F. Mummery, *A. Burgener, B. Venetz*	555
Dent du Requin	11,218	1893	A. F. Mummery, J. N. Collie, G. Hastings, W. C. Slingsby	539, 535, 662
Aig. du Moine	11,198	1871	I. Straton, E. Lewis-Lloyd	

Pennine Alps (Central)

Weisshorn	14,804	1861	J. Tyndall, *J. J. Bennen, Wenger*	837
Matterhorn	14,782	1865	E. Whymper, C. Hudson, D. Hadow, Lord Francis Douglas, *M. Croz, Taugwalders*	89, 158, 476 555, 639, 647 839, 897
Dent Blanche	14,318	1862	T. S. Kennedy, W. Wigram	318, 850, 897
Grand Combin	14,164	1860	M. Delville	
Zinal Rothorn	13,856	1864	L. Stephen, F. C. Grove, *J. Anderegg*	766
Dent d'Hérens	13,715	1863	W. E. Hall, F. C. Grove, R. S. Macdonald, M. Woodmass, *M. Anderegg, Perrn, Cachat*	410
Bieshorn	13,652	1884	Mrs. Le Blond	**446**
Ober Gabelhorn	13,364	1865	A. W. Moore, H. Walker, *J. Anderegg*	
Grand Cornier	13,022	1865	E. Whymper	535, 897
Ruinette	12,727	1865	E. Whymper	897
Pigne d'Arolla	12,471	1865	A. W. Moore, H. Walker, *J. Anderegg*	
Mont Vélan	12,353	1779	L. J. Murith	

Pennine Alps (Eastern)

Monte Rosa				
—Dufourspitze	15,217	1855	C. Hudson, E. J. Stevenson, C. & G. Smyth, J. Birbeck, *U. Lauener*	338, 836
—Ostspitze		1854	J. G. Smyth, C. Smyth, E. Smyth	
—Grenzgipfel	15,194	1848	J. Madutz. M. zum Taugwalder	
—Nordend	15,132	1861	T. F. Buxton, E. N. Buxton, J. J. Cowell, *M. Payot*	
—Zumsteinspitze	15,004	1820	J. Zumstein, A. & J. N. Vincent, Molinatti	
—Signalkuppe	14,965	1842	G. Gnifetti	
—Parrotspitze	14,643	1863	R. J. S. Macdonald, F. C. Grove, M. Woodmass, *M. Anderegg, Perrn*	
—Ludwigshöhe	14,259	1822	Baron von Welden	
—Schwarzhorn	13,882	1873	Baron von Rothschild, Marchese Maglioni	
—Vincent Pyramide	13,829	1819	J. N. Vincent	
Dom (Mischabel)	14,942	1858	J. L. Davies	18
Lyskamm	14,889	1861	J. F. Hardy, A. C. Ramsay, F. Gibson, T. Rennison, J. A. Hudson, W. E. Hall, C. H. Pilkington, R. M. Stephenson	318
Täschhorn	14,758	1862	J. L. Davies, J. W. Hayward	555
Nadelhorn	14,220	1858	J. Zimmermann, A. Supersaxo, B. Epiney, *F. Andermatten*	
Lenzspitze	14,108	1870	C. T. Dent, *A. & F. Burgener*	210
Hohberghorn	13,865	1869	R. B. Heathcote	
Castor	13,879	1861	W. Mathews	
Alphubel	13,803	1860	L. Stephen, T. W. Hinchliff	
Rimpfischhorn	13,790	1859	L. Stephen, R. Liveing, *M. Anderegg*	535
Strahlhorn	13,751	1854	E., J. G. & C. Smyth, *F. Andermatten*	
Zermatt Breithorn	13,685	1813	H. Maynard	
Pollux	13,433	1864	J. Jacot	
Allalinhorn	13,236	1856	E. L. Ames	
Weissmies	13,226	1855	Häusser	
Laquinhorn	13,140	1856	E. L. Ames, *F. Andermatten, P. Imseng*	
Klein Matterhorn	12,750	1792	H. B. de Saussure	

Bernese Alps

Finsteraarhorn	14,026	1812	A. Volker, J. Bortis, A. Abbuhl	836, 850
Aletschhorn	13,721	1859	F. F. Tuckett, *J. J. Bennen, Tairraz, Bohren*	535, 830, 839

Alps

Jungfrau	13,669	1811	J. R. & H. Meyer	**256**, 305, 839
Mönch	13,468	1857	S. Porges, *C. Almer, U. & C. Kaufmann*	
Schreckhorn	13,386	1861	L. Stephen	318, **766**
Fiescherhorn	13,285	1862	A. W. Moore, H. B. George, *C. Almer, U. Kaufmann*	
Lauteraarhorn	13,265	1842	E. Desor	
Eiger	13,042	1858	C. Barrington, *C. Almer, P. Bohren*	88, 90, **314**, 347, 355, **368**, 587, 709
Ebnefluh	13,006	1868	T. L. M. Browne	
Agassizhorn	12,980	1872	W. A. B. Coolidge	
Bietschhorn	12,970	1859	L. Stephen	469
Dreieckhorn	12,540	1868	T.L.M. Browne	
Gross Nesthorn	12,533	1865	H. B. George	
Geisshorn	12,291	1880	W. A. B. Coolidge	
Balmhorn	12,176	1864	F., H. & Lucy Walker, *J. & M. Anderegg*	
Wetterhorn	12,166	1845	S. T. Speer	
Blümlisalphorn	12,044	1860	L. Stephen, R, Liveing	

Lepontine Alps

Monte Leone	11,684	1859		⎫
Rheinwaldhorn	11,149	1789	Placidus à Spescha	⎬ 284
Güferhorn	11,132	1806	Placidus à Spescha	
Blindenhorn	11,103	1866		⎭

Tödi Range

Tödi (Piz Rusein)	11,887	1824	P. Curschellas, A. Bisquolm
—Glarner	11,815	1853	M. Ulrich, G. Studer
Bifertenstock	11,241	1863	A. Roth, G. Sand, Raillard, Stähelin
Stockgron	11,214	1788	Placidus à Spescha, C. M. Huonder
Piz Urlaun	11,060	1793	Placidus à Spescha

Bernina Alps

Piz Bernina	13,304	1850	J. Coaz	
Piz Zupo	13,151	1863	L. Enderlin, Serardi	
Monte di Scersen	13,016	1877	P. Güssfeldt	
Piz Roseg	12,934	1865	A. W. Moore, H. Walker, *J. Anderegg*	
Piz Palü	12,835	1886	K. Digby, *J. Anderegg*	
Crast' Agüzza	12,704	1865	J. J. Weilenmann, J. A. Specht	
Piz Morteratsch	12,317	1858	G. Brügger, P. Gensler	839
Disgrazia	12,067	1862	L. Stephen, E. S. Kennedy, *T. Cox, M. Anderegg*	286
Bellavista	11,884	1868	E. Burckhardt	
Piz Tschierva	11,693	1850	J. Coaz	
Pizzo di Verona	11,358	1865	F. F. Tuckett, D. W. Freshfield, H. E. Buxton, *F. Devouassoud, P. Michel, J. B. Walther*	
Piz Corvatsch	11,339	1850	J. Coaz	
Piz Tremoggia	11,326	1859	J. J. Weilenmann	
Cima di Castello	11,155	1866	D. W. Freshfield, C. C. Tucker, *F. Devouassoud, A. Fluri*	
Il Chapütschin	11,126	1850	J. Coaz	
Piz Cengalo	11,070	1866	D. W. Freshfield, C.C. Tucker, *F. Devouassoud*	88
Piz Badile	10,863	1867	W. A. B. Coolidge, *F. & H. Devouassoud*	88, 131, 639

Albula Group

Piz Kesch	11,228	1864
Piz Vadret		
Alplihorn		
Piz Ela		
Tinzenhorn		

Silvretta/Rhätikon

Piz Linard	11,201	1835	O. Heer	⎫
Fluchthorn	11,165	1861		⎪
Piz Buin	10,880	1865		⎬ 176, 732
Muttler	10,821	1858		⎪
Silvrettahorn	10,657	1865		⎭

Bavaria, Vorarlberg & Salzburg

Dachstein	9,830	1832

Zugspitze	9,738	1820		
Watzmann	8,901	1801	V. Stanig, Beck, Von Buch	131, 508

Ortler Alps

Ortler	12,802	1804	J. Pichler, J. Leitner, J. Klausner	
Königspitze	12,655	1864		
Monte Cevedale	12,382	1865		
Monte Zebru	12,254	1866	J. Payer	176, 732, 830
P. San Matteo	12,113	1865	J. H. Backhouse, D. W. Freshfield, F. F. Tuckett	
Punta Taviela	11,880	1866	F. A. Y. Browne	
Pizzo Tresero	11,818	1865	J. H. Backhouse, D. W. Freshfield, F. F. Tuckett	
Trafoier Eiswand	11,657	1872	M. de Déchy	

Ötztal Alps

Wildspitze	12,382	1861		
Weisskugel	12,291	1846	[2 local men]	
Similaun	11,821	1834		176, 732
Hochvernagtspitze	11,585	1865		
Finailspitze	11,259	1865		

Stubai Alps

Zuckerhütl	11,520	1863		
Schrankkogel	11,483	1840		
Ruderhofspitze	11,392	1865		176, 732
Wilder Pfaff	11,388	1870		
Wilder Freiger	11,241	1865		

Lombard Alps

Presanella	11,694	1864	D. W. Freshfield	**286**
Adamello	11,661	1864		**286**

Tauern Alps

Gross Glockner	12,461	1800	Bishop of Gurk & party	
Gross Venediger	12,008	1841		176, 732
Rainerhorn	11,684	1859		

Zillertal Alps

Hochfeiler	11,559	1865	Grohmann	
Mösele	11,438	1865	J. H. Backhouse, D. W. Freshfield, F. F. Tuckett	830
Olperer	11,418	1867		
Thurnerkamp	11,228	1872		
Schrammacher	11,208	1847	P. C. Thurwieser	

Dolomites

Marmolata	11,024	1864	P. Grohmann	
Antelao	10,706	1863	P. Grohmann	
Tofana	10,633	1863	P. Grohmann	
Sorapiss	10,594	1864	P. Grohmann	
Monte Civetta	10,564	1867	F. F. Tuckett, Blackstone, Howard, Hare	
Vernel	10,519	1879	W. Merzbacher	
Monte Cristallo	10,496	1865	P. Grohmann	
Langkofel	10,427	1869	P. Grohmann	
Cima di Vezzana	10,470	1872	C. C. Tucker, D. W. Freshfield	
C. della Pala	10,453	1870	E. R. Whitwell	307, 523, 692
Pelmo	10,397	1857	J. Ball	708
Dreischusterspitze	10,375	1869	P. Grohmann	
Zwölferkofel	10,142	1874	M. Innerkofler	
Grosse Zinne	9,853	1869	P. Grohmann	
Vajolet Towers	9,256	1881	W. Merzbacher	
—Stabelerthurm		1892	H. Stabeler	
—Winklerthurm		1887	G. Winkler	
—Delagothurm		1895	H. Delago	

Julian Alps   **434**

General references:
[88–9], [131], [157], [189], [307], [333]

Venezuela
1. *Sierra Nevada de Merida*

Colombia
2. *Sierra Nevada de Santa Marta*
3. *Sierra Nevada de Cocuy*
4. *Cordillera Central*

Ecuador
5. *Cord. Occidental*
6. *Cord. Oriental*

Peru
7. *Cord. Occidental*
8. *Cord. Blanca*
9. *Cord. Huayhuash*
10. *Cord. Vilcabamba*
11. *Cord. Veronica de Urubamba*
12. *Cord. Vilcanota*
13. *Nudo de Apolobamba*

Bolivia
14. *Cord. Quimsacruz/ Cochabamba*
15. *Cord. Occidental*
16. *Cord. Real*
17. *Puna de Atacama*

Argentina-Chile
18. *Aconcagua Region*
19. *Lakes District*
20. *Patagonia*
21. *Tierra del Fuego*

ANDES

ANDES

Name of Peak	Height (Feet)	Details of first recorded ascent Date	Names of Party, etc.	References to books
Venezuela				
Sierra Nevada de Merida				
Pico Bolivar	16,411	1936	F. Weiss [disputed ascent 1934]	
Pico Humboldt	16,214	1911	A. Jahn, L. Hedderich	
La Concha	16,148	1939	F. Weiss, A. E. Gunther, D. Pena, La Garza	
La Columna	16,076	1940	A. E. Gunther	
Pico Bonpland	16,027	1940	A. E. Gunther	
El Toro	15,611	1910	A. Jahn	
El Leon	15,571	1946	H. Mathews, B. Trujillo	
Colombia				
Sierra Nevada de Santa Marta				
P. Simon Bolivar	18,947	1939	G. Pichler, E. Kraus, E. Praolini	
Christobal Colon	18,947	1939	W. A. Wood, A. Bakewell, A. Praolini	
Pico Simmons	18,570	1943	D. & F. Marmillod	
Pico Santander	18,175	1943	A. Gansser	
La Reina	18,158	1941	E. Cowles, M. Eberli, P. Petzoldt, E. Knowlton	
Pico Ojeda	18,012	1941	E. Cowles, M. Eberli, P. Petzoldt, E. Knowlton	
El Guardian	17,338	1941	E. Cowles, M. Eberti, P. Petzoldt, E. Knowlton [Possibly J. de Brettes in 1898]	
Sierra Nevada de Cocuy				
Alto Ritacuba	17,926	1942	G. Cuenet, A. Gansser, E. Dress, E. Kraus, H. Hüblitz	
Ritacuba Negro	17,680	1942	G. Cuenet, A. Gansser, E. Dress, E. Kraus, H. Hüblitz	
Ritacuba Norte	17,247	1942	G. Cuenet, A. Gansser, E. Dress, E. Kraus, H. Hüblitz	
Concavo	17,342	1939	A. Gansser	
Pichacho	17,133	1959	J. Rucklidge, C. Smythe	
Cord. Central/Occidental				
Huila	17,844	1944	H. Hüblitz, E. Kraus	

Pico Daniel	17,388	1939	A. Gansser	
Ruiz	17,181	1936	M. Rapp	
Quindiu	16,900			
Santa Isabel	16,732	1943	H. Hüblitz, E. Kraus	
Tolima	16,732	1926	H. Huber, Klein, Schimmer, Baptiste, Riveros, Vergara	
Tairona	16,404	1939	E. Kraus, E. Praolini	
Cumbal	15,630	1848	J. D. Boussingault	
Chiles	15,574	1869	W. Reiss	

Ecuador
Cord. Occidental

Chimborazo	20,551	1880	E. Whymper	899
Illiniza	17,277	1880	E. Whymper	899
Carihuarirazo	16,496	1951	A. Eichler, H. Lopez	899
Cotacachi	16,204	1880	E. Whymper	899
Pichincha	15,718	1802	A. von Humboldt [Spanish ascent 1582]	
Corazon	15,718	1738	P. Bouguer, C. M. de La Condamine	
Sincholagua	13,126	1880	E. Whymper	899

Cord. Oriental

Cotopaxi	19,347	1872	W. Reiss, A. M. Escobar	899
Cayambe	18,993	1880	E. Whymper	899
Antisana	18,717	1880	E. Whymper	899
Sangay	17,464	1966	J. Larrea, S. Snow, C. Bonington	94
Cerro Altar	17,447	1963	F. Gaspard, M. Trementi, C. Zardini	
Tunguragua	16,420	1873	A. Stübel, W. Reiss, Farrand	
Quilindaña	16,069	1953	A. Eichler, H. Lopez, G. Vergani, A. Vinci	
Saraurcu	15,341	1880	E. Whymper	899

Peru
Cord. Occidental

Coropuna	21,706	1911	H. Bingham, Tucker, Prof. Coello, Corporal Camarra	
Ampato	20.702	1972	[German party]	
Solimana	20,341	1938	A. Bolinder	
Charchani	19,970	1889	A. Hettner	
El Misti	19,098	1878	R. Falb	610

Cord. Blanca

Huascaran (South)	22,205	1932	P. Borchers, E. Schneider, H. Hoerlin, E. Hein, H. Bernhard		
Huascaran (North)	21,834	1908	Miss A. S. Peck, *G. zum Taugwald, R. Taugwalder*	610	
Chopicalqui	20,998	1932	P. Borchers & party		
Huandoy	20,981	1932	E. Schneider, E. Hein		
Nev. Santa Cruz	20,537	1948	F. Marmillod		
Pamparaju	20,351	1932	P. Borchers & party		
Chacraraju	20,056	1956	L. Terray, M. Davaille, C. Gaudin, R. Jenny, M. Martin, R. Sennelier, P. Souriac	802	
–East Peak		1963	L. Terray, G. Magnone, L. Dubost, P. Gendre J. Soubis	802	
Quitaraju	19,850	1936	E. Schneider	430	
Yanaraju	19,803	1939	W. Brecht, H. Schweitzer, S. Rohner		
Artesonraju	19,766	1932	E. Schneider, E. Hein		
Hualcan	19,575	1932	P. Borchers & party		
Alpamayo	19,455	1951	R. Leininger, C. & G. Kogan	356	430
Aguja Nevada	19,311	1965	G. Frigieri		
Piramide de Garcilaso	19,306	1957	G. Hauser, B. Huhn, F. Kraus, H. Wiedmann	356	
Ocshapalca	19,292	1965	[Japanese party]		
Taulliraju	19,128	1956	L. Terray	802	
Nevado Cayesh	18,770	1960	L. R. Stewart, D. Ryan, L. S. Crawford	870	
Nevado Pongos	18,737	1952	C. G. Egeler, T. de Booy, *L. Terray*	239	802
Caullaraju	18,654	1952	A. Vinci		
Yahuarraju	18,620	1965	H. A. Carter & party		
Nev. de Parron	18,537	1957	G. Hauser, B. Huhn, F. Knaus, H. Wiedmann	356	
Loyacjirca	18,373	1957	G. Hauser, B. Huhn, F. Knaus, H. Wiedmann	356	

Cord. Huayhuash

Yerupaja (Carincero)	21,758	1950	D. Harrah, J. C. Maxwell	678

Nevada Suila	20.841	1936	E. Schneider, A. Awerzger	
Jirishanca	20,099	1957	T. Egger, S. Jungmaier	
Rassac	19,816	1936	E. Schneider	
Rondoy Sur	19,301	1963	V. Walsh, P. Farrell, P. Bebbington, C. Powell	
			D. Condict, G. Sadler	866
Rondoy Nord	19,100	1961	W. Bonatti, A. Oggioni	88

Cord. de Vilcabamba

Salcantay	19,951	1952	B. Pierre, Mme C. Kogan, G. I. Bell, F. D. Ayres	
			D. Michael, W. V. G. Matthews	
Pumasillo	19,916	1957	H. Carslake, J. H. Longland	161
Sacsarayoc	19,800	1963	P. Farrell	
Soray	18,964	1956	C. G. Egeler, T. de Booy, *L. Terray*	802

Cord. Veronica de Urubamba

Nevado Veronica	18,865	1956	C. G. Egeler, T. de Booy, *L. Terray*	802
Chainapuerto				
Cancan	c. 18,000	1964	M. Slesser & party	711
Sirijuani				
Yucay				

Cord. Vilcanota

Ausangate	20,946	1953	H. Harrer, H. Steinmetz J. Wellenkamp	
Jatunhuma	20,151	1957	G. Hauser, B. Huhn, T. Achilles	356
Yayamari	19,709	1957	G. Hauser, B. Huhn, T. Achilles	356
Cayangate	19,685	1957	G. Hauser, B. Huhn, T. Achilles	356
Mariposa	19,096	1957	G. Hauser, B. Huhn, T. Achilles	356
Caracol	18,869	1957	G. Hauser, B. Huhn, T. Achilles	356

Nudo de Apolobamba

Chaupi Orco	19,830	1958	[German party]	
Palomani Grande	19,686			
Salluyo	19,686			
Angelico	19,358			
Fiorroccia	19,358			

Bolivia
Cord. Quimsacruz/ Cochabamba

Jachakukukollo	19,521	1911	T. Herzog, C. Seelig	
Cerro Immaculado	18,619	1911	T. Herzog, C. Seelig	
Aguilar (Carnival)	18.044	1911	T. Herzog, C. Seelig	
Chancapina	17,634	1904	H. Hoek	
Pireo	17,388	1911	T. Herzog, C. Seelig	
Incachaca	17,158	1910	T. Herzog, R. Bock	
Tunari	17,073	1903	H. Hoek, G. Steinmann	
Trinidad	17,060	1911	T. Herzog, C. Seelig	
Cometa	17,060	1911	T. Herzog, C. Seelig	
Anaroya	16,896	1904	H. Hoek, G. Steinmann	

Cord. Occidental

Sajama	21,426	1939	J. Prem, P. Ghiglione, W. Kühm	
Parinacota	20,767	1928	J. Prem	
Huallatiri	19,970	1926	F. Ahlfeld	
Tacora	19,645	1904	H. Hoek	
Ollague	19,258	1888	H. Berger	

Cord. Real

Illimani	21,201	1898	W. M. Conway, *A. Macquignaz, L. Pellisier*	179
—North Peak		1950	H. Ertl, G. Schröder	
Anchohuma) Sorata	21,082	1919	A. Schulze, R. Dienst	
Illampu)	20,830	1928	E. Hein, A. Horeschowsky, H. Hörtnagel, H. Pfann	
Haukana	20,502	1919	A. Schulze, R. Dienst	
Chearoco	20,102	1928	German party (Hein, Pfann, Troll, Ahlfeld,	
			Horeschowsky, Hörtnagel)	
Caca Aca (Huayna Potosi)	19,996	1919	A. Schulze, R. Dienst	

Chachacomani	19,927	1947	F. Buchholtz, F. Fritz	
Yoka de Anchohuma	19,873	1966	A. G. Smythe, R. Hall, D. H. Challis	
Pico Norte	19.784	1928	E. Hein & party	
Kunotawa	19,622	1966	D. H. Challis, A. G. Smythe	
Casiri Este	19,510	1966	M. Birchall, R. Winfield, R. Hall	
Kimsakolyo	19,332	1966	A. G. Smythe, R. Hall, D. H. Challis	
Arichiri	19,300	1964	E. Cotter, H. Jacobs, D. Mackay	
Casiri	19,121	1928	E. Hein & party	
Casiri Aguja	19,000	1964	E. Cotter, H. Jacobs, D. Mackay	
Ch'amakawa	18,922	1966	M. Birchall, R. Winfield, R. Hall	
Casiri Norte	18,900	1964	E. Cotter, H. Jacobs, D. Mackay	
Llaulini	18,701	1928	E. Hein & party	
San Pablo	18,634	1966	R. Hall, R. Winfield	
Triangulo	18,609	1966	A. G. Smythe, D. H. Challis	
Condoriri	18,556	1941	W. Kühm probably	
Mesket'anta	18,463	1966	M. Birchall, R. Winfield, R. Hall	
Makatanya	18,433	1966	R. Winfield, R. Hall	
Pico de Linea	18,400	1966	A. G. Smythe, D. H. Challis	
Taparacu	18,400	1964	H. Jacobs, D. Mackay, M. Nelson	
Vinohuara	18,372	1928	E. Hein & party	
El Yunque	18,372	1915	A. Schulze, R. Dienst	
Vilujo	18,372	1928	E. Hein & party	
Haltatawa	18,370	1966	D. H. Challis, A. G. Smythe	
Tiquimani(East)	18,209	1963	[South African party]	**335**

Puna de Atacama

Ojos del Salado	22,590	1937	Szczepanski, J. Wojsznis
Llullaillaco	22,058	1952	B. Gonzalez & party
Tres Cruzes	21,720	1937	S. Osiecki, W. Pariski
Incahuasi	21,656	1859	E. Flint
Nacimiento	21,302	1937	W. Pariski
Nevado Bonete	21,130	1913	W. Penck
Colorado (Fatima)	20.013	1895	R. Hauthal
Nev. del Chani	19,882	1901	Hofsten, Mercado, Fries
Socompa	19,787	1905	F. Reichert
San Francisco	19,701	1913	W. Penck
Licancabur	19,455	1884	S. Titchoca
C. de la Aguada	19,009	1904	F. Reichert

Argentina-Chile
Aconcagua Region

Aconcagua	22,835	1897	*M. Zurbriggen*	**180 262 273**
				502. 948
Pissis	22.242	1937	S. Osiecki	
Mercedario	21,883	1934	A. Karpinsky	
Tupungato	21,490	1897	S. Vines, *M. Zurbriggen*	**273 948**
Nev. del Acay	20,790	1914		
Marmolejo	20,013	1928	A. Maass, S. Krückel, Sattler	
Nev. Juncal	19,880	1911	R. Helbling, F. Reichert, D. Beiza	
C. San Franzisco	19,759	1931	A. Maass	
Nev. de Pinqueñes	19,741	1933	J. Lüders, O. Pfenninger	
Cerro Polleras	19,518	1908	F. Reichert	
San Jose	19,292	1931	S. Krückel, O. Pfenninger	
C. del Plata	19,183	1925	F. Peters	
Tupungatito	18,503	1897	L. Risopatron	
Clavillo de				
Aconquija	18,208	1883	R. Hauthal	
Nev. del Plomo	17,814	1896	G. Brandt, Luck	
Tolosa	17,618	1903	C. & N. de Meyendorff	
Catedral	17,421	1897	E. A. Fitzgerald	**273**
Maipu	17,355	1883	P. Güssfeldt	
Cadillal	17,388	1884	P. Leon	
Meson Alto	17,345	1929	A. Maass, O. Pfenninger, S. Krückel, Conrads, Wolf	
C. Rio Blanco	17,152	1908	F. Reichert	
C. Altar	17,132	1929	J. Lüders, O. Pfenninger, S. Kruckel.	

Lakes District

Lanin	12,388	1897	R. Hauthal [1933: E.S.G. de la Motte]

Tronador	11,253	1934	G. Claussen	
Osorno	8,728	1948	J. Renous	
Puntiagudo	8,182	1937	R. Roth	

Patagonia

San Valentin	12,716	1958	[German party]	
C. Mariano Moreno	11,500	1958	W. Bonatti & party	88
Fitzroy	11,057	1952	G. Magnone, L. Terray	39, 802
Cerro Torre	10,280	1959	C. Maestri, T. Egger	88, 354
Aig. Poincenot	10,120	1962	D. D. Whillans, F. Cochrane	893
Towers of Paine	9,941	1963	C. Bonington, D. D. Whillans	893
Cerro Huemel	9,023	1916	A. Kölliker, F. Kühn	

Tierra del Fuego

Darwin	8,760	1962	E. E. Shipton & party	
Sarmiento	7,546	1956	C. Mauri, C. Maffei	180. 705
Cerro Cotorra	4,954	1933	G. Fester	

General references:
[397], [703], [757]   See also A. J. Vol. 60, p77.

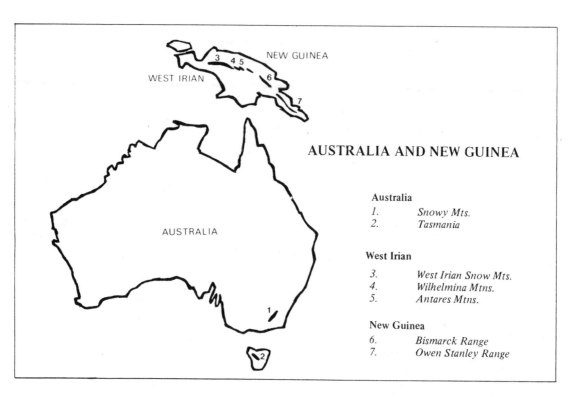

AUSTRALIA AND NEW GUINEA

Australia
1.   *Snowy Mts.*
2.   *Tasmania*

West Irian
3.   *West Irian Snow Mts.*
4.   *Wilhelmina Mtns.*
5.   *Antares Mtns.*

New Guinea
6.   *Bismarck Range*
7.   *Owen Stanley Range*

AUSTRALIA AND NEW GUINEA

Name of Peak	Height (Feet)	Details of first recorded ascent Date	Names of Party, etc.	References to Books
Australia				
Snowy Mountains				
Kosciusko	7,316	1840	Count Strzelecki	
Townsend	7,249		R. von Lendenfeld	
Twynam	7,207			526
Carruther's Peak	7,042			
Northcote	6,791			

Tasmania

Ben Lomond	5,160		
Barn Bluff	5,115		
Cradle Mountain	5,069	1914	F. & J. Malcher
Frenchman's Cap			
Olympus		1835	G. Frankland
Anne		1929	V. C. Smith & party

West Irian
Snow Mountains

Carstenz Pyramid	16,500	1962	H. Harrer, R. P. Temple, R. Kippax, B. Huizenga	
Ngapalu	16,400	1936	D. Colijn & party	
Idenburg Top	15,360	1962	R. P. Temple	
East Carstenz Top				
Wollaston Peak				
Sunday Peak		1962	H. Harrer	348 799
Colijn Peak				
Dozy Peak				
Wissel Peak				

Wilhelmina Mtns

Trikora (Wilhelmina)	15,584	1912	Dutch party

Antares Mtns

Juliana	15,420	1959	De Wijn, Escher, Verstappen, Tissing, Ter Laag	113

Australian
New Guinea
Bismarck Range

Wilhelm	14,786

Owen Stanley Range

Victoria	13,363	1889	Sir Wm MacGregor & party
Albert Edward	13,200		

General references: [129], **Appendix VI**

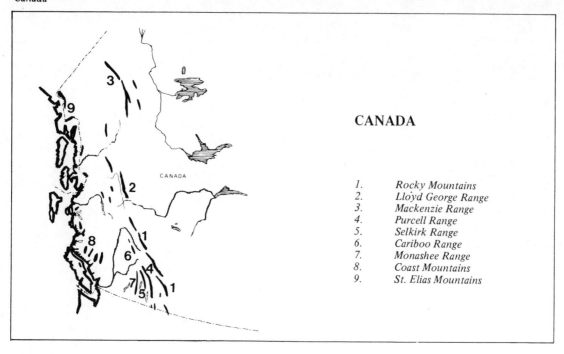

CANADA

1. *Rocky Mountains*
2. *Lloyd George Range*
3. *Mackenzie Range*
4. *Purcell Range*
5. *Selkirk Range*
6. *Cariboo Range*
7. *Monashee Range*
8. *Coast Mountains*
9. *St. Elias Mountains*

CANADA

Note: The mountains of the Canadian Rockies are grouped according to Palmer & Thorington's climber's guide. The groups are listed from south to north.

Name of Peak	Height (Feet)	Date	Details of first recorded ascent Names of Party, etc.	References to Books
Rocky Mountains				
Group 2				
Tornado	10,169	1915	[Boundary Commission]	
Group 3				
Joffre	11,274	1919	J. W. A. Hickson, *E. Feuz Jr.*	
Nivelle	10,620	1928	J. W. A. Hickson, *E. Feuz Jr.*	
Group 4				
Sir Douglas	11,174	1919	J. W. A. Hickson, *E. Feuz Jr.*	
French	10,610	1921	H. S. Hall Jr, M. Morton Jr, *E. Feuz Jr.*	
Group 5				
King George	11,226	1919	V. A. Fynn, *R. Aemmer*	
Queen Mary	10,600	1922	C. F. Hoogeboon. F. N. Wateman, *R. Aemmer*	
Prince Edward	10,590	1929	Miss K. Gardiner, *W. Feuz*	
Prince Henry	10,560	1929	Miss K. Gardiner, *W. Feuz*	
Prince Albert	10,530	1928	Misses C. & M. Crosby, Miss H. Pillsbury C. A. Willard, *R. Aemmer*	
Group 6				
Assiniboine	11,870	1901	J. Outram, *C. Bohren C. Häsler*	**460 592 744 769**
Lunette Peak	11,150	1901	J. Outram, *C. Bohren, C. Häsler*	**592**
Eon	10,860	1921	W. E. Stone	411
Aye	10,640	1934	H. S. Crosby, *R. Aemmer*	
Group 7				
Ball	10,865	1904	J. D. Patterson, *C. Kaufmann, H. Kaufmann*	
Storm Mtn	10,372	1889	W. S. Drewry, A. St. Cyr	
Stanley Peak	10,351	1901	E. Whymper & guides	

Group 8

Galatea	10,600	1930	Miss K. Gardiner, *E. Feuz*		
Longheed	10,190	1889	W. S. Drewry, A. St. Cyr		

Group 9

Bonnet Mtn	10,662	1927	Oertele, *W. Feuz*		
—South Peak	10,400	1890	A. St. Cyr		
Aylmer	10,375	1889	J. J. McArthur		

Group 10

Temple	11,636	1894	W. D. Wilcox, S. E. S. Allen, L. F. Frissell	**905**		
Hungabee	11,457	1903	H. C. Parker, *C. & H. Kaufmann*	744		
Victoria	11,365	1897	J. N. Collie, C. E. Fay, A. Michael, *P. Sarbach*	**170**	744	**769**
—North Peak	11,160	1900	J. Outram, W. Outram, J. H. Scattergood A. Clarke, *Zurfluh*	**592**		
Deltaform	11,235	1903	A. Eggers, H. C. Parker, *C. & H. Kaufmann*			
Lefroy	11,230	1897	J. N. Collie, H. B. Dixon, C. E. Fay, C. L. Noyes A. Michael H. C. Parker, C. S. Thompson J. Vanderlip, *P. Sarbach*	**170,769**		
Huber	11,051	1903	E. Tewes, *C. Bohren, C. Kaufmann*			
Biddle	10,888	1903	H. C. Parker, A. Eggers, *C. & H. Kaufmann*			
Glacier Peak	10,831	1909	V. A. Fynn, C. R. Hart, C. A. Richardson L. C. Wilson			
Allen	10,830	1904	Miss G. E. Benham, *C. Kaufmann*			
Ringrose Peak	10,765	1909	V. A. Fynn, E. F. Pilkington			
Tuzo	10,658	1906	Miss H. L. Tuzo, *C. Kaufmann*			
Fay	10,622	1904	Miss G. E. Benham, *C. Kaufmann*			
Neptuak	10,617	1902	J. N. Collie, H. Woolley, H. E. M. Stutfield, G. M. Weed, *C. Kaufmann*	**769**		
Stephen	10,495	1887	J. J. McArthur, T. Riley			
Cathedral Mt	10,464	1901	J. Outram, J. Bossonney, *C. Klucker*	**592**		
Popes Peak	10,376	1905	L. S. Amery. *C. Kaufmann*	**27**		
Aberdeen	10,350	1894	S. E. S. Allen, L. F. Frissell, W. D . Wilcox	**905**		
Odaray	10,165	1887	J. J. McArthur			
Owen	10,128	1892	J. J. McArthur			
Cathedral Crags	10,083	1900	J. & W. Outram, *C. Häsler*	**592**		
Whyte	9,786	1901	*C. Kaufmann, C. Klucker, J. Pollinger*			
Whymper	9,331	1901	E. Whymper & guides			

Group 11

Vaux	10,891	1901	C. E. Fay J. Outram, J. H. Scattergood *C. Häsler*	**592**	
Chancellor Peak	10,761	1901	J. Outram, J. H. Scattergood, G. M. Weed *C. Häsler* [preceded by incomplete ascent by C. E. Fay, J. Outram et al]	**592**	
Goodsir	11,686	1903	C . E. Fay, J. Outram, J. H. Scattergood G. M. Weed, *C. Häsler* [preceded by incomplete ascent in 1901]	**592**	
Allan Peak	10,627	1933	Miss K. Gardiner, Miss L. Gest, *W. Feuz C. Häsler*		
Foster Peak	10,511	1933	Miss K. Gardiner, K. Jones *W. Feuz*		

Group 12

Howse Peak	10.800	1902	H. Woolley, H. E. M. Stutfield, J. N. Collie G. M. Weed, *C. Kaufmann*	**769**	
Balfour	10,741	1898	C. S. Thompson, C. L. Noyes, G. M. Weed	411	**769**
Chepren Peak	10,715	1913	J. W. A. Hickson, *E. Feuz*		
Des Poilus	10,371	1901	E. Whymper, J. Outram, *C. Kaufmann, C. Kain J. Pollinger*	**592**	
Gordon	10,346	1897	C. E. Fay, J. N. Collie, H. B. Dixon, C. S. Thompson, A. Michael, C. L. Noyes, H. C. Parker, G. P. Baker, *P. Sarbach*	**769**	
Daly	10,342	1903	J. H. Batcheller, C. E. Fay, E. Tewes *C. Bohren, C. Häsler*		
Collie	10,325	1901	E. Whymper, J. Outram, *C. Kaufmann C. Klucker, J. Pollinger*	**592**	
President	10,297	1901	J. Outram, *C. Kaufmann, J. Pollinger*	**592**	

Sarbach	10,260	1897	J. N. Collie G. P. Baker, *P. Sarbach*	769
Thompson	10,119	1898	J. N. Collie, H. Woolley 'H. E. M. Stutfield	769
Vice-President	10,059	1901	J. Outram, *C. Kaufmann, J. Pollinger*	592
Marpole	9,832	1901	E. Whymper & guides	
Kiwetinok Peak	9,522	1901	J. Outram, *C. Kaufmann, J. Pollinger*	592
Kerr	9,394	1901	E. Whymper & guides	
Isolated Peak	9,234	1901	J. Outram, E. Whymper. J. Bossonney	
			C. Kaufmann C. Klucker J. Pollinger	592

Group 13

Hector	11,135	1895	P. S. Abbot, C. E. Fay, C. S. Thompson	
Cataract Peak	10,935	1930	J. W. A. Hickson, *E. Feuz*	
St. Bride	10,875	1910	J. W. A. Hickson, *E. Feuz, E. Feuz Jr.*	
Douglas	10,615	1907	L. M. Earle, *E. Feuz, G. Feuz*	

Group 14

Willingdon	11,044	1919	[Topographical Survey]	
Harris	10,825	1919	[Topographical Survey]	

Group 16

Barnard	10,955	1922	H. Palmer, J. M. Thorington, *E. Feuz Jr.*	807
Freshfield	10,945	1902	H. Woolley, H. E. M. Stutfield, G . M. Weed,	
			J. N. Collie, J. Outram, *C. Kaufmann,*	
			H. Kaufmann	769, 807
Mummery	10,918	1906	I. T. Burr, S. Cabot, W. R. Peabody,	
			R. Walcott, *G. Feuz, C. Kaufmann*	170
Bulyea	10,900	1910	J. E. C. Eaton, *H. Burgener*	
Walker	10,835	1910	J. E. C. Eaton, B. Otto, *H. Burgener*	
Pilkington	10,830	1910	J. E. C. Eaton, B. Otto, *H. Burgener*	
Solitaire	10,800	1926	M. M. Strumia, *E. Feuz Jr.*	
Nanga Parbat	10,780	1922	H. Palmer, J. M. Thorington, *E. Feuz Jr.*	807
Prior Peak	10,750	1937	E. Cromwell, E. Cromwell Jr, Miss G.	
			Engelhard, F. S. North, J. M. Thorington	
Dent	10,720	1910	J. E. C. Eaton, B. Otto, *H. Burgener*	
Trutch	10,690	1922	H. Palmer, J. M. Thorington, *E. Feuz Jr.*	807

Group 17

Forbes	11,902	1902	J. Outram, H. E. M. Stutfield, H. Woolley,	
			J. N. Collie, G. M. Weed, *C. & H. Kaufmann*	592, 769
Lyell (Peak 2)	11,495	1902	J. Outram, *C. Kaufmann*	592, 769
—Peak 1	11,370	1926	A. J. Ostheimer, M. M. Strumia, J. M. Thorington,	
			E. Feuz Jr.	
—Peak 3	11,495	1926	A. J. Ostheimer, M. M. Strumia, J. M. Thorington,	
			E. Feuz Jr.	
—Peak 4	11,260	1927	D. Duncan, T. Lynes, J. Simpson, *E. Feuz*	
—Peak 5	11,150	1926	A. J. Ostheimer, M. M. Strumia, J. M. Thorington,	
			E. Feuz Jr.	
Alexandra	11,214	1902	J. Outram, *C. Kaufmann*	592
Queens Peak	10,990	?		
Amery	10,940	1929	L. S. Amery, B. Meredith, *E. Feuz Jr.*	28
Spring Rice	10,745	1923	J. W. A. Hickson, *E. Feuz Jr.*	
Fresnoy	10,730	1902	J. Outram, *C. Kaufmann*	592
Outram	10,670	1924	F. V. Field, W. O. Field, L. Harris, *J. Biner,*	
			E. Feuz	
Farbus	10,550	1937	E. R. Gibson ,S. B. Hendricks	
Mons Peak	10,114	1902	J. Outram, *C. Kaufmann*	592

Group 18

Cline	11,027	1927	J. H. Barnes, A. Castle, A. Castle Jr,	
			J. Simpson, *R. Aemmer*	
Murchison	10,936	1902	H. E. M. Stutfield, G. M. Weed, J. N. Collie,	
			H. Kaufmann	769
Stewart	10,871	1902	A. P. & L. Q. Coleman [incomplete ascent]	168
Cirrus Mtn	10,685	1939	C. B. Sissons, J. Sissons	
Wilson	10,631	1902	J. Outram, *C. Kaufmann*	592
Observation Peak	10,214	1895	W. Peyton, W. D. Wilcox	905

Group 19

Columbia	12,294	1902	J. Outram, *C. Kaufmann*	170, 592, 769, 807

North Twin	12,085	1923	W. S. Ladd, J. M. Thorington, *C. Kain*	415, 807
Alberta	11,874	1925	Y. Maki, 5 companions & guides	413, 744
South Twin	11,675	1924	F. V. & W. O. Field, L. Harris, *J. Biner,*	
			E. Feuz Jr.	
Bryce	11,507	1902	J. Outram, *C. Kaufmann*	28, 592, 769
Kitchener	11,500	1927	A. J. Ostheimer, *H. Fuhrer*	
Athabaska	11,452	1898	J. N. Collie, H. Woolley	170, 769, 807
King Edward	11,400	1924	J. W. A. Hickson, H. Palmer, *C. Kain*	415
Snow Dome	11,340	1898	J. N. Collie, H. E. M. Stutfield, H. Woolley	744, 769
Stutfield	11,320	1927	A. J. Ostheimer, *H. Fuhrer*	
Woolley	11,170	1925	Y. Maki, 5 companions & 3 guides	
Diadem Peak	11,060	1898	J. N. Collie, H. Woolley, H. E. M. Stutfield	769
Saskatchewan	10,964	1923	J. M. Thorington, W. S. Ladd, *C. Kain*	415, 807

Group 20

Dais Mtn	10,612	1927	A. J. Ostheimer, *H. Fuhrer*	
Chaba Peak	10,540	1928	E. Schoeller, J. Rähni	

Group 21

Clemenceau (Pyramid)	12,001	1923	H. B. Schwab, H. S. Hall, D. B. Durand,	
			W. D. Harris	
Tsar	11,232	1927	A. J. Ostheimer, *H. Fuhrer, J. Weber*	
Tusk Peak	10,960	1927	J. DeLaittre, W. R. Maclaurin, A. J. Ostheimer,	
			H. Fuhrer	
Bras Croche	10,781	1927	A. J. Ostheimer, *H. Fuhrer*	
Apex Peak	10,600	1922	A. Carpe, H. S. Hall Jr.	
Ghost Mtn	10,512	1927	A. J. Ostheimer, *H. Fuhrer*	
Brouillard	10,500	1892	A. P. & L. Q. Coleman, L. B. Stewart	168

Group 22

Brazeau	11,380	1923	A. Carpe, W. D. Harris, H. Palmer	168
Sunwapta Peak	10,833	1906	J. Simpson	
Warren	10,800	1928	W. R. Hainsworth, M. M. Strumia	
Henry MacLeod	10,600	1923	A. Carpe, W. D. Harris, H. Palmer	
Unwin	10,550	1923	A. Carpe, W. D. Harris, H. Palmer	

Group 23

Fryatt	11,026	1926	J. W. A. Hickson, H. Palmer, *H. Fuhrer*	
Scott	10,826	1928	W. R. Hainsworth, J. G. Hillhouse, M. M. Strumia,	
			J. M. Thorington	
Catacombs	10,800	1927	W. R. Maclaurin, A. J. Ostheimer, *H. Fuhrer,*	
			J. Weber	
Hooker	10,782	1924	J. M. Thorington, A. J. Ostheimer, M. M. Strumia,	
			C. Kain	415, 807
Serenity	10,573	1920	A. Carpe, W. D. Harris, H. Palmer	
Oates	10,220	1924	A. J. Ostheimer, M. M. Strumia, J. M. Thorington,	
			C. Kain	415, 807

Group 24

Edith Cavell	11,033	1915	E. W. D. Holway, A. J. Gilmour	597

Group 25

Simon Peak	10,899	1924	A. J. Ostheimer, M. M. Strumia, J. M. Thorington,	
			C. Kain	415, 807
Geikie	10,854	1924	V. A. Fynn, M. D. Geddes, C. G. Wates	
Bennington Peak	10,726	1926	R. B. H. Bibby, J. H. Hoag, N. W. S. Vecchia	
McDonell Peak	10,700	1919	A. Carpe, R. H. Chapman, H. Palmer	
Casemate Mtn	10,160	1928	D. L. Busk, J. E. Johnson, *H. Fuhrer*	138

Group 26

Robson	12,972	1913	A. H. MacCarthy, W. W. Foster, *C. Kain*	168, 411, 415
				695, 744, 807
Resplendent	11,240	1911	B. Harmon, *C. Kain*	415, 807
Helmet	11,160	1928	Miss G. Engelhard, *H. Fuhrer*	
Dome	10,098	1908	A. P. & L. Q. Coleman, G. B. Kinney, J. Yates	168

Group 27

Whitehorn Mtn	11,130	1911	*C. Kain*	415

Canada

Phillips	10,660	1910	J. N. Collie, A. L. Mumm, F. Stephens, G. Swain, J. Yates, *M. Inderbinen*	
Longstaff	10,440	1916	A. J. Gilmour, E. W. D. Holway, H. Palmer	597

Group 28

Chown	10,930	1924	G. Hargreaves, W. B. Putnam	
Bess	10,550	1911	J. N. Collie, A. L. Mumm, J. Yates, *M. Inderbinen*	

Group 29

Sir Alexander	10,900	1929	Miss H. I. Buck, A. J. Gilmour, N. D. Waffe	

Rocky Mountains
(Northern extensions)

Lloyd George Range

Lloyd George	9,800	1947		
Glendower	9,750	1947		
Criccieth	9,400			
Crosby	8,700			
Grey Peak	8,100			
Cloudmaker Mtn	8,100	1947	F. S. Smythe	744
Dryas Peak	7,900			
Columbine Peak				
Chesterfield				
Hardesty				

Mackenzie Range

Sir James McBrien	9,049			
Keele Peak	8,500			
Hunt				
Dome Peak				397
Sidney Dobson				
Ida				

Interior Ranges
British Columbia

Purcell Range

Farnham	11,342	1914	A. H. MacCarthy	460
Bugaboo Group				
—Howser Spires	11,150	1916	*C. Kain*	415, 460 810
—Snowpatch Spire		1940		
—Bugaboo Spire		1916	*C. Kain*, Mr. & Mrs. MacCarthy, J. Vincent	415

Selkirk Range

Sir Sanford	11,590	1912	E. W. D. Holway, H. Palmer, *R. Aemmer, E. Feuz*	595
Jumbo Mtn	11,217			
Dawson	11,123	1899	C. E. Fay, H. C. Parker	
Wheeler	11,023	1902	A. O. Wheeler & party	
Selwyn	11,013	1890	H. Forster, H. Topham	
Adamant Mtn	10,980	1912	E. W. D. Holway, H. Palmer	595
Austerity	10,960	1911	F. K. Butters, E. W. D. Holway, H. Palmer	595
Turret Peak	10,910			
Grand Mtn	10,842	1910	E. W. D. Holway, H. Palmer	595
Sir Donald	10,818	1890	E. Huber, C. Sulzer, H. Cooper	769
Findlay	10,780			
Nelson Peak	10,772			
Augustine	10,762	1909	F. K. Butters, E. W. D. Holway, H. Palmer	595
Sugarloaf	10,732	1890	H. Forster, E. Huber, H. W. Topham	
Cyprian	10,712	1908	F. K. Butters, E. W. D. Holway, H. Palmer	595
Gothics (Pioneer)	10,660	1910	F. K. Butters, E. W. D. Holway, H. Palmer	595
Beaver Mtn	10,644	1913	E. W. D. Holway	595
Hamill Peak	10,640			
Iconoclast Mtn	10,630			
Kilpatrick	10,624	1909	F. K. Butters, E. W. D. Holway, H. Palmer	595
Blackfriars	10,580			
Fox	10,572	1890	H. W. Topham	
Duncan	10,548	1913	E. W. D. Holway	595
Toby	10,537			

Rogers	10,525	1896	P. S. Abbot, G. T. Little, C. S. Thompson	
Swiss Peak	10,515	1890	C. Sulzer	
Purity	10,457	1890	H. Forster, E. Huber, H. W. Topham	
The Footstool	10,410	1910	F. K. Butters, E. W. D. Holway, H. Palmer	**595**
Sorcerer Mtn	10,387	1904	H. Peterson	
Coppercrown Mtn	10,218			
Moloch	10,195			
Bonney	10,194	1888	W. S. Green, H. Swanzy	**328**
Hermit	10,194	1904	A. M. Gordon, S. H. Gray, J. C. Herdman	
Albert Peak	10,008	1909	R. R. Copeland, H. Siegfried	
Holway	10,002	1911	F. K. Butters, E. W. D. Holway, H. Palmer	**595**
Carnes Mtn	10,000	1910	M. P. Bridgland & party	
Swanzy Peak	c. 10,000	1900	S. Spencer, A. Michael	769

Cariboo Range

Sir Wilfred Laurier	11,750	1923	A. Carpe, Chamberlin	
Sir John Abbott	11,250			
Sir John Thompson	11,250			397
Sir Mackenzie Bowell	11,000			
Stanley Baldwin	10,900			

Monashee Range
(Gold Range)

Monashee	10,650	1952	Hendricks, Hubbart, Wexler	
Albreda Peak	10,000	1928	A. Carpe, Chamberlin	397
Hallam Peak	10,560			
Begbie	8,962			

Coast Mountains
British Columbia

Waddington	13,177	1936	W. House, F. Wiessner	**413, 556, 695, 877**
Serra Peaks	12,800			
Tiedemann	12,559		H. S. Hall, S. Hendricks, R. Gibson	
Combatant	12,400	1933	H. S. Hall	**556**
Asperity	12,300			
Bell	11,800			
Monarch Mtn	11,712	1935	H. S. Hall	**556**
Munday	11,500			**556**
Geddes	11,000			**556**
Remote	11,000			
Queen Bess	10,700			
Goodhope	10,670	1922	R. P. Bishop	
Razorback	10,667	1932	H. S. Hall	
Monmouth	10,470			
Ratz	10,290			
Gilbert	10,200			
Grenville	10,200			
Taseko	10,057	1922	R. P. Bishop	
Tatlow	10,050	1922	R. P. Bishop	
Saugstad	10,000			

St. Elias Mountains
(See **ALASKA**)

General references:
[397], [413], [425], [596], Appendix VI

Name of Peak	Height (Feet)	Details of first recorded ascent		References to Books
		Date	Names of Party, etc.	
Elbruz	18,482	1874	A. W. Moore. F. C. Grove, H. Walke, F. Gardiner, *P. Knubel*	231, 336
−East Peak	18,407	1868	D. W. Freshfield, A. W. Moore, C. C. Tucker, *F. Devouassoud*	285
Shkhara	17,064	1888	J. G. Cockin	396
−West Peak	16,592	1903	T. G. Longstaff, L. W. Rolleston	460
Dykh-tau	17,055	1888	A. F. Mummery, *H. Zurfluh*	396, 555
Koshtan-tau	16,881	1889	H. Woolley	
Dzhangi-tau	16,572	1903	R. Helbling, F. Reichert, A. Schulze, A Weber	396
−East Peak	16,530	1888	J. G. Cockin	
Kazbek	16,559	1868	D. W. Freshfield, A. W. Moore, C. C. Tucker	285
Katuin-tau	16,356	1888	H. W. Holder, H. Woolley	
Mishirgi	16,169	1934	L. Saladin, W. Frei, O. Furrer, H. Graf	
−East Peak	16,136	1889	H. Woolley	
Gestola	15,946	1886	C. T. Dent, W. F. Donkin, *A. Burgener, B. Andenmatten*	
Tetnuld	15,923	1887	D. W. Freshfield	
Gimarai Khokh	15,672	1891	G. Merzbacher	
Ushba	15,454	1903	A. Schulze, R. Helbling, F. Reichert, O. Schuster, A. Weber	396, 402
−North Peak	15,422	1888	J. G. Cockin	
Ullu-Auz-Bashi	15,370	1889	V. Sella, E. Sella	
Tikhtengen	15,125	1903	T. G. Longstaff, L. W. Rolleston	460
Maily Khokh	15,157	1892	N. de Poggenpohl	
Tuituin-Bashi	14,929	1933	Gache, Lagarde, Montcel, Valluet	
Ailama	14,840	1889	H. Woolley	
Sugan	14,731	1896	V. Sella, E. Gallo	
−South Peak	14,731	1909	Mme H. Kuntze	
Suatisi Khokh	14,675	1910	W. Fischer, G. Kuhfahl, O. Schuster	
Dongus-Orun	14,661	1891	G. Merzbacher, L. Purtscheller	
−SE Peak	14,575	1888	W. F. Donkin, H. Fox	
Tepli (Central)	14,510	1896	V. Sella, E. Gallo	
Kaltber	14,462	1910	W. Fischer, O. Schuster	
Nakhashbita	14,410	1909	Mme H. Kuntze	
Lyalver	14,372	1903	A. Schulze	
Shau Khokh	14,340	1911	W. Fischer, O. Schuster	
Burdjula	14,295	1890	J. G. Cockin, H. W. Holder	
Adyrsu Bashi	14,278	1896	J. G. Cockin, H. W. Holder, H. Woolley	
Saluinan-Bashi	14,267	1888	H. W. Holder, J. G. Cockin	
Ukiu	14,259	1887	D. W. Freshfield	
Shkhelda	14,174	1903	R. Helbling, F. Reichert, A. Schulze, A. Weber	
Bzhedukh	14,013	1903	L. Distel, G. Leuchs, H. Pfann	

General reference:
[288] − Exploration of the Caucasus by D. W. Freshfield.

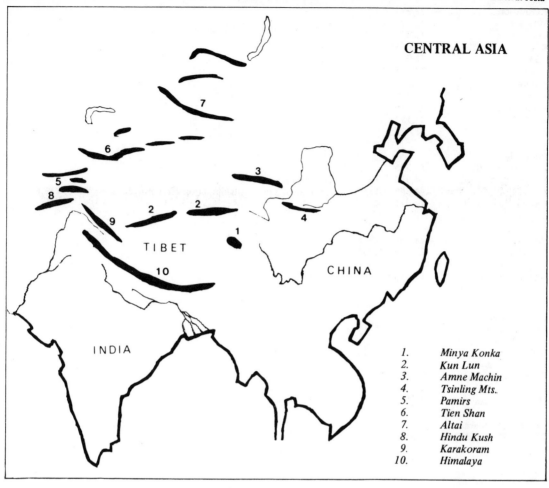

CENTRAL ASIA

Name of Peak	Height (Feet)	Details of first recorded ascent		References to Books
		Date	Names of Party, etc.	
Ta Hsueh Shan				
Minya Konka	24,892	1932	R. L. Burdsall, T. Moore	**134**
Kun Lun				
(Arka Tagh)				
Ulugh Muztagh I	25,340			
Ulugh Muztagh II	24,150			
Ulugh Muztagh III	24,115			
Bokalikh Tagh	25,328			
(Amne Machin)				
Amne Machin Peak	23,490	1960	Chinese party	**612**
(Tsinling Mtns)				
Tai Pai Shan	13,474			
Pamirs				
(Trans-Alai)				
Kommunismus (Garmo, Stalin)	24,590	1933	E. M. Abolakov	**116, 665, 710**
Lenin (Kaufmann)	23,406	1928	E. Allwein, E. Schneider, K. Wien	
Korjenevskoi	23,310	1953	Guschtschin, Golofist, Korsun, Prokudajew	

Central Asia

Revolution	22,924			
Moscow	22,260			
October	22,244			
Karl Marx	22,068			
Fikker	22,041			
Dzerzhinsky	22,025			
Garmo	21,637			
Engels	21,359			
Leningrad	21,349			
Abalakov	21,152			
Pravda	21,018			

(Sinkiang)

Kungur Tagh (II)	25,325			
Kungur Tjube Tagh	24,919	1956	Sino-Russian party	
Muztagh Ata	24,757	1956	Sino-Russian party [incomplete ascent 1947]	699, 819, 935
Chakragil	22,071			

Tien Shan

Pik Pobeda	24,406	1956	V. Abalakov & party	706
Khan Tengri	22,949	1931	M. T. Pogrebezki, F. Sauberer, B. Tjurin	
Bogdo Ola				
—Turpanat Tagh	17,946			699, 819

Altai
(Katun Range)

Gora Beluhka	15,157	1914	B. V. & M. V. Tronov	831
—West Peak	14,563			
Willer's Peak		1903	S. Turner	831

(Taban Bogdo Ola)

Kuitun	14,291
Monho Hayrhan	14,311

General references:
[129], [515], [612], [685], [858].

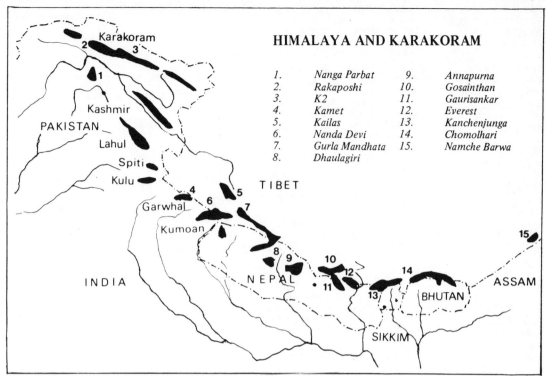

HIMALAYA AND KARAKORAM

1.	*Nanga Parbat*	*9.*	*Annapurna*
2.	*Rakaposhi*	*10.*	*Gosainthan*
3.	*K2*	*11.*	*Gaurisankar*
4.	*Kamet*	*12.*	*Everest*
5.	*Kailas*	*13.*	*Kanchenjunga*
6.	*Nanda Devi*	*14.*	*Chomolhari*
7.	*Gurla Mandhata*	*15.*	*Namche Barwa*
8.	*Dhaulagiri*		

HIMALAYA

Name of Peak	Height (Feet)	Details of first recorded ascent Date	Names of Party, etc.	References to Books
Kashmir				
Nanga Parbat	26,660	1953	H. Buhl	**67, 69, 71, 131 170, 364, 429**
−Rakiot Peak	23,196	1932	P. Aschenbrenner, H. Kunigk	429
Nun(Ser)	23,410	1953	Mme C. Kogan, P. Vittoz	**406, 617, 867 928**
Kun(Mer)	23,219	1913	L. Borelli, M. Piacenza, *J. Gaspard, Ali Rahin & another*	867, **928**
Pinnacle Peak	22,737	1906	Mrs. Workman	**928**
White Needle	21,650			
Agyasol	20,340			
Shiwje-ka-Pahar	19,700			
Haramoukh	16,904	1899	E. F. Neve, G. Millais	
Kuku, Spiti, Lahul				
Central Peak	21,620	1961	J. Scarr, B. Spark	684
Mulkila	21,380	1939	F. Kolb, L. Krenek, R. Johnson	433
White Sail Peak	21,148	1941	J. O. M. Roberts	325
Guan Neida	20,680			
Indrasan	20,410	1962	[Japanese party]	325
Gangstang Peak	20,218	1945	[Italian prisoners of war]	
Lion	20,100	1961	J. Scarr, B. Spark	**684**
Shilla	20,050			
Cathedral Peak	20,000	1956	E. Gregory	
Mukar Beh	19,910	1968	J. Ashburner, *Wangyal*	325
Deo Tibba	19,687	1952	C. & J. Graaf, K. Berrill	230, 325
Garhwal-Kumaon				
Nanda Devi	25,645	1936	N. E. Odell, H. W. Tilman	**411, 696, 815**
−East Summit	24,391	1939	J. Bujak, M. J. Klarner	

Kamet	25,443	1931	F. S. Smythe, E. E. Shipton, R. L. Holdsworth, *Lewa*	508, 553, 729
Abi Gamin	24,130	1950	G. Chevalley, R. Dittert, A. Tissieres	
Mana Peak	23,862	1937	F. S. Smythe	734
Mukut Parbat	23,761	1951	H. E. Riddiford, E. M. Cotter	
Chaukamba	23,412	1952	L. George, V. Russenberger	
Trisul	23,360	1907	T. G. Longstaff, *A. & H. Brocherel, Kharbir*	460, 553
Satopanth	23,213	1947	A. Sutter, R. Dittert, A. Roch, A. Graven	
Tirsuli (East)	23,210	1966	S. Chakravarty, N. Mallik, *N. Tashi, Dorji*	
Dunagiri	23,183	1939	A. Roch, F. Steuri, D. Zogg	734
Panch Chuli	22,650	1950	W. H. Murray, T. Weir	560, 880
Nilkanta	21,640			406, 734
Uja Tirche	20,350	1950	W. H. Murray, T. Weir	560, 880
Changabang		1974		95

Nepal

Everest	29,028	1953	E. P. Hillary, *Tensing Norgay*	See SUBJECT INDEX
Lhotse	27,923	1956	E. Reiss, F. Luchsinger	240
−Lhotse Shar	27,504	1970	[Austrian party]	
Makalu	27,825	1955	J. Couzy, L. Terray	279, 313, 371 550, 802, 872
−Makalu II	25,066	1954	J. Franco, L. Terray, *Gyalgen, P. Norbu*	
Dhaulagiri	26,795	1960	K. Diemberger, P. Diener, E. Forrer, A. Schelbert, *Nyima Dorji, Nawan Dorji*	214, 241, 353
−Dhaulagiri II	25,429	1971	[Austrian party]	
−Dhaulagiri III	25,312	1973	[German party]	
−Dhaulagiri IV	25,133		[Unclimbed]	
−Dhaulagiri V	24,992			
Manaslu	26,760	1956	[Japanese party]	792
Cho Oyu	26,750	1954	H. Tichy, S. Jöchler, *Pasang Dawa*	346, 369, 438 812
−Ngojumba Ri I	25,611			
−Ngojumba Ri II	25,086	1965	N. Uemara, *Pemba Tenzing*	
Annapurna	26,504	1950	M. Herzog, L. Lachenal	91, 366
−Annapurna II	26,041	1960	R. Grant, C. Bonington, *Ang Nyima*	90, 324
−Annapurna III	24,860	1961	M. S. Kohli, *Sonam Gyatso, Sonam Girmi*	431
−Annapurna IV	24,688	1955	H. Biller, H. Steinmetz, J. Wellenkamp	
Gyachung Kang	25,990	1964	Y. Kato, K. Sakaizawa, *Pasang Phutar III*	
Nuptse	25,850	1961	D. P. Davis, *Tashi*	90
Himalchuli	25,801	1960	M. Harada, H. Tanabe	
Peak 29 (Dakura)	25,705	1970	[Japanese party]	
Chomo Lönzo	25,640	1954	J. Couzy, L. Terray	792
Fang Annapurna	25,089			
Kangchungtse	25,066	1954		
Gangapurna	24,457	1965	G. Hauser, L. Greissl, E. Reismüller, H. Köllensperger, *Ang Temba, Phu Dorji*	
Ganesh Peak	24,299	1955	R. Lambert E. Gauchat, Mme C. Kogan	
Churen Himal	24,184	1970	[Japanese party]	
Chamlang I	24,012	1962	S. Anma, *Pasang Phutar III*	
Putha Hiunchuli	23,750	1954	J. O. M. Roberts, *Ang Nyima*	
Baruntse	23,688	1954	G. Harrow, C. Todd	370
Modi Peak	23,682	1954	S. Uyeo	
Khartaphu	23,640	1935	E. E. Shipton, E. Kempson, C. Warren	
Sharphu	23,622	1963	[Japanese party]	
Menlungtse	23,560			
Chamar	23,545	1953	M. Bishop, *Namgyl*	654
Pumori	23,442	1962	E. Forrer, G. Lenser, U. Hurlemann	
Gaurisankar	23,440			325, 438, 893
Glacier Dome	23,433	1964	N. Nishimura	
Lönpo Gang	23,240	1962	T. Morita, K. Yasuhisa	
Api	23,399	1960	K. Hirabayashi, *Gyaltsen Norbu*	
Kellas Rock Peak	23,180	1935	E. E. Shipton, H. W. Tilman, E. H. L. Wigram	
Manaslu (North)	23,130	1964	A. J. Driessen, J. de Lint, H. Schreibl, *Nima Tenzing, Ila Tsering*	
Saipal	23,079	1963	K. Hirabayashi, *Pasang Phutar III*	
Nilgiri (North)	23,072	1962		
Kharta Changri	23,071	1935	E. Kempson, C. Warren	
Nupchu	23,059	1962	T. Tsubaki, *Chotale*	

Kang Guru	22,996	1955	H. Steinmetz, J. Wellenkamp, Lubbichler	
Machapuchare	22,958	1957	W. Noyce [incomplete ascent]	**579**
Dorje Lakpa	22,929			
Ama Dablam	22,494	1961	B. C. Bishop	**313, 371, 539** **872**
Kangtega	22,340	1963	J. Wilson, M. Gill, D. Dornan, T. Frost	**313, 372**
Phurbi Chyachu	21,844			
Langtang II	21,592	1963	P. Taylor	**797**
Taweche	21,463	1963	J. Wilson, M. Gill [incomplete ascent]	**313, 372**
Lha Shamma	21,035	1962	J. Scarr, B. Spark	**684**
Gyalgen Peak	21,000	1955	M. Jackson, B. Stark	**407**
Kagmara I	19,560	1962	D. Evans, D. Gravina, N. Smith, P. Wood	**684**
−Kagmara II	18,500	1962	D. Gravina, P. Wood	**684**
−Kagmara III	18,700	1962	J. Scarr, D. Evans, N. Smith, B. Spark	**684**
Triangle Peak	19,340	1962	J. Scarr, D. Evans, B. Spark	**684**

Sikkim

Kanchenjunga	28,208	1955	G. C. Band, J. Brown	**66, 116, 249** **289. 728, 826**
−Kanchenjunga II	28,146	1973		
−Kangbachen Peak	25,782			
−Zemu	25,526			
Jannu	25,294	1962	R. Desmaison, R. Paragot, P. Keller, *Gyaltsen Mikchung*	**280**
Jongsong Peak	24,518	1930	H. Hoerlin, E. Schneider	**728**
−Domo	24,416	1930	G. O. Dyrenfurth	
Tent Peak	24,162	1939	E. Grob, H. Paidar, L. Schmaderer	
Talung Peak	24,112	1964	F. Lindner, *Tensing Nyinda*	
Kabru	24,076	1935	C. R. Cooke [disputed ascent 1883]	323
Sharpu	23,622	1963		
Nepal Peak	23,557	1939	E. Grob, H. Paidar, L. Schmaderer	
−Central	23,500	1936	A. Göttner, K. Wien	
−SW Peak	23,443	1930	E. Schneider	
Pauhunri	23,385	1910	A. M. Kellas, Sonam & another	
Langpo Peak	22,815	1909	A. M. Kellas	
Siniolchu	22,600	1936	K. Wien, A. Göttner	**67**
Kangchenjau	22,603	1912	A. M. Kellas	
Chomiomo	22,430	1910	A. M. Kellas	
Sentinel Peak	21,290	1910	A. M. Kellas	

Bhutan

Khula Kangri	24,784			
Kangar Pünzum	24,740			
Chutte Kang	24,541			
Chomolhari	24,000	1937	F. S. Chapman, *Pasang Dawa*	**146** ⎱ **763, 872**
Taka Khan	23,950			
Gyu Khan	23,622			
Masa Khan	23,507			

Assam

Kangdu	23,260			
Nayegi Kansang	23,120			**816**
Chiumo	22,760			
Gori Chen	21,450			

Tibet

Shisha Pangma	26,291	1964	Hsu Ching & 9 other Chinese	**612**
Namche Barwa	25,445			
Gurla Mandhata	25,355			
Phola Gangchen	25,135			
Shahkangsha	25,132			**362, 460, 820**
Nangpai Gosum	24,120			
Palung Tse	24,102			
Gyala Peri	23,460			
Kailas	22,028			

General references:
[105], [337], [503], [801]

HINDU KUSH

Name of Peak	Height (Feet)	Date	Details of first recorded ascent — Names of Party, etc.	References to Books
Tirich Mir	25,290	1950	P. Kvernberg	563
—East Peak	25,233	1964	R. Höibakk, A. Opdal	
—West I	24,564	1967	J. Cervinka, I. Galfy, V. Smida, I. Urbanovic	
—West IV	24,075	1967	K. Diemberger, D. Proske	214
Noshaq	24,580	1960	G. Iwatsabo, T. Sakai	
—East	24,540	1963	G. Gruber, R. Pischinger	
—West	23,688	1963	G. Gruber, M. Hofpointer, S. Jungmaier, H. Pilz, R. Pischinger, M. Schober, G. Werner	
Istor-o-Nal	24,290	1955	J. E. Murphy, T. E, Mutch	
—North	23,754	1967	K. Lapuch, M. Oberegger, M. Friedwagner	
Saraghrar	24,110	1959	F. Alletto, P. Consiglio, G. Castelli, B. Pinelli	494
—South	23,973	1967	[Japanese party]	
Darban Zom	23,688	1965	U. Kössler, M. Schmuck	
Koh-i-Nadershan	23,375	1970	[Yugoslav party]	
Udren Zom	23,321	1964	G. Gruber, R. Pischinger	
Shingeik Zom	23,291	1966	K. Holch, I. Trübswetter	
Schachaur	23,242	1964	G. Gruber, R. Pischinger	
Nobaisum Zom	23,196	1967	K. Diemberger, K. Lapuch	214
Koh-i-Langar	23,166	1964	O. Huber	
Akher Chioh	23,022	1966	H. Schell, R. Göschl	
Langar	23,019	1964	O. Huber	
Urgend	23,019	1963	A. Strickler, S. Burkhardt, M. Eiselin, H. Ryf, V. Wyss	
Koh-i-Tez	23,016	1962	J. Krajski, W. Olech, A. Pachalski	
Mir Samir	19,880			567
[Bashgal Valley]				824

General references:
[105], [214], [503]

JAPAN AND SOUTH-EAST ASIA

Name of Peak	Height (Feet)	Date	Details of first recorded ascent — Names of Party, etc.	References to Books
Japan				
Northern Alps				
Oku-Hotaka	10,466			
—Kite-Hotaka	10,171			
—Karasa	10,181			869, 885, 886
—Mae-Hotaka	10,138			
Yarigatake	10,428			
Tsurugi	9,851			
Southern Alps				
Kita dake	10,472			
Ai-no-take	10,464			869, 885, 886
Akaishi	10,237			
Ontake	10,049			
Fujiyama	12,388	[c.800]	Ascended by monks	
Taiwan (Formosa)				
Yu Shan (Morrison)	13,113	1896	Dr. S. Honda & Japanese officials	
Hsueh Shan	12,743			869
Ta Pa Chien Shan	11,722			

General references:
[129], [422], [757]

KARAKORAM

Name of Peak	Height (Feet)	Date	Names of Party, etc.	References to Books
K2	28,250	1954	A. Compagnoni, L. Lacedelli	65, 88, **212, 266** **385, 615**
Gasherbrum	26,470	1958	P. K. Schoening, A. J. Kaufman	**247**
—Gasherbrum II	26,360	1956	F. Moravec, S. Larch, H. Willenpart	
—Gasherbrum III	26,090			
—Gasherbrum IV	26,000	1958	W. Bonatti, C. Mauri	88, **493**
Broad Peak	26,400	1957	M. Schmuck, F. Wintersteller, H. Buhl, K. Diemberger	**214**
Disteghil Sar	25,868	1960	G. Stärker, D. Marchart	
Khiangyang Kish	25,760	1971	[Polish party]	
Masherbrum	25,660	1960	G. I. Bell, W. Unsoeld	867, 893
Rakaposhi	25,550	1958	M. E. B. Banks, T. W. Patey	**53, 55**
Hunza Kunji I	25,540	1959		
Kanjut Sar	25,460	1959	C. Pelissier	
Saltoro Kangri I	25,400	1962	A. Saito, Y. Takamura, R. Bashir	867
Batura Mustagh II	25,361			
Austria Peak	25,349	1956	Ratay, Reiss, Weiler	
Trivor	25,329	1960	C. W. F. Noyce, J. Sadler	**581, 893**
Saser Kangri I	25,170	1970		
Chogolisa	25,110	1958	M. Fujihira, K. Hirai	214, **266**
Shispare (Batura)	25,000			
Skyank Kangri	24,750			266
Mamostong	24,690			
Pumar Kish	24,581			
K12	24,503	1960		
Teram Kangri I	24,489			
Malubiting West	24,451	1971	H. Schindlbacher, H. Sturm, H. Schell, K. Pirker	
Sia Kangri	24,350	1934	H. Ertl, A. Höcht	
—West	24,130	1934	G. O. & H. Dyrenfurth, H. Ertl, A. Höcht	
Skil Brum	24,345	1957	M. Schmuck, F. Wintersteller	
Haramosh	24,299	1958	H. Roiss, S. Pauer, F. Mandl	58
Mount Ghent	24,280	1961	W. Axt	
Momhil Sar	24,090	1964	R. Pischinger, H. Schell, H. Schindlbacher, L. Schlömmer, R. Widerhofer	
Baltoro Kangri III	23,989	1963	M. Kono, T. Shibata, K. Fujimoto, S. Shima	
Batura Muztagh	23,950	1954	D. Meyer, M. Schliessler	
Muztagh Tower	23,872	1956	J. Brown, I. M. Davis	116, 605
Diran (Minapin)	23,862	1968	[Austrian party]	
Baltoro Kangri E.	23,820	1934	J. Belaieff, P. Ghiglione, A. Roch	
Depak Peak	23,457	1960	M. Anderl, E. Senn	
Yengutz Har	23,056	1955	R. Diepen, E. Reinhardt, J. Tietze	792

General references:
[105], [214], [503]

NEW ZEALAND

Name of Peak Southern Alps	Height (Feet)	Date	Names of Party, etc.	References to Books
Cook (Aorangi)	12,349	1894	T. C. Fyfe, J. Clarke, G. Graham [incomplete ascent 1882]	**228, 272, 327** **832, 920, 948**
Tasman	11,475	1895	E. A. Fitzgerald, *M. Zurbriggen, J. Clarke*	**228, 272, 948**
Dampier	11,287	1912	Miss Du Faur, *P. Graham, C. Milne*	**228, 322**
Silberhorn	10,757	1895	E. A. Fitzgerald, *M. Zurbriggen, J. Clarke*	**272, 948**
Lendenfeld	10,450	1907	E. Teichelmann, H. E. Newton, R. S. Low, *Graham*	
David's Dome	10,443	1906	H. E. Newton, R. S. Low, *Graham*	
Malte Brun	10,421	1894	T. C. Fyfe	603
Torres	10,376	1907	E. Teichelmann, H. E. Newton, R. S. Low, *Graham*	
Teichelmann	10,370	1929		

Sefton	10,354	1895	E. A. Fitzgerald, *M. Zurbriggen*	228, 272, 948
Haast	10,294	1907	E. Teichelmann, H. E. Newton, R. S. Low, *Graham*	
Elie de Beaumont	10,200	1906	Sillem, *P. Graham*	322, 603
Haidinger	10,178	1895	E. A. Fitzgerald, *M. Zurbriggen, J. Clarke*	272, 948
Douglas Peak	10,107	1907	E. Teichelmann, H. E. Newton, R. S. Low, *Graham*	
La Perouse	10,101	1906	E. Teichelmann, H. E. Newton, R. S. Low, *Graham*	
Minarets	10,058	1893	M. Ross, T. C. Fyfe	667

Westland

D'Archiac	9,279	1910	J. Dennistoun, L. M. Earle, J. Clarke	603
Arrowsmith	9,171	1912	H. F. Wright, J. P. Murphy	603
Evans	8,612	1934	J. D. Pascoe & 2 others	603
Rolleston	7,453	1912		603

South Westland

Aspiring	9,957	1909	B. Head, J. M. Clarke, *A. Graham*	311, 627
Earnslaw	9,250			312
Tutoko	9,042	1924	S. Turner, *P. Graham*	322, 833
Hooker	8,644	1928	S. Turner, C. Turner	603
Darran Mtns				313

North Island

Ruapehu	9,175	1879	G. Beetham, J. P. Maxwell	73
Egmont	8,260	1839	E. Dieffenbach, J. Hebberley	70
Ngauruhoe	7,515	1839	J. C. Bidwill	73, 832
Tongariro	6,458			73

General references:
[322], [603]

NORWAY

Name of Peak	Height (Feet)	Details of first recorded ascent		References to Books
		Date	Names of Party, etc.	
Jotunheimen				
Galdhøpiggen	8,100	1850	L. Arnesen, S. Flotten, S. Sulheim	
Glittertind	8,100	1842	H. N. Wergeland, H. Sletten	
Skagastøltind	7,890	1876	W. C. Slingsby	712
Styggedalstind	7,831	1883	C. Hall, M. Soggemoen	
Skarstind	7,786	1884	O. Kristiansen, S. Thor, S. Wleugel	
Gjertvasstind	7,717	1876	W. C. Slingsby, E. Mohn, K. Lykken	712
Centraltind	7,700	1885	C. Hall, T. Sulheim, M. Soggemoen	
Knutsholstind	7,677	1875	J. T. Heftye, K. Løkken	
Vestre Memerutind	7,513	1874	A. Dewhurst, J. T. Heftye, W. C. Slingsby, R. Alfsen	712
Visbretind	7,332	1881	W. C. Slingsby, J. Vigdal	712
Romsdal				
Kvanndalstind	5,824	1885	C. Hopkinson, W. C. Slingsby, L. Jensen	712
Romsdalhorn	5,102	1827	C. Hoel, H. Bjermeland	
Trolltind (Wall)				692
Sunnmore				588, 712
Arctic Norway				
Lofoten Isles				170, 712, 881
Lyngen Peninsula				450, 712, 772 881

General references:
[605], [629], Appendix VI

Name of Peak	Height (Feet)	Date	Details of first recorded ascent Names of Party, etc.	References to Books
Greenland				
Gunnbjornsfeld	12,139	1935	L. R. Wager	
Forel	11,024	1938	[Swiss party]	
Ejnar Mikkelsen	10,700	1970	A. Ross, G. Williams, N. Robinson, P. Lewis	
Petermann Peak	9,650	1929	[Cambridge party]	
Dansketinde	9,170	1954	J. Haller, W. Diehl	
Mt. Gog	8,740	1933	N. E. Odell & Mrs. Odell	
Nathorst Peak	7,700	1933	N. E. Odell, W. A. Wood	
Sulugssuguta	7,350			147, 340, 460
Payer Peak	7,000	1870	J. Payer & 2 others	
Nalumassortoq	6,560			
Kilertinguit	6,430	1872	E. Whymper	
Teufelschloss	4,300	1933	N. E. Odell, W. A. Wood	
Sadlen	3,970	1909	De Quervain	
Hjortetakken	3,870	1909	De Quervain	
Spitsbergen (Svalbard Isles)				
Newton	5,676	1900	A. Vassilev & party	177, 178, 460
Terrier		1905	[Austrian party]	585
Iceland				
Hvannadalshnuker	6,952	1891	F. W. Howell & 2 Icelanders	20
Jan Mayen Island				
Beerenberg	7,472	1921	P. L. Mercanton, T. C. Lethbridge, J. M. Wordie	674
Baffin Island				
Tete Blanche	7,074	1953		
Asgard	6,600	1953	H. Weber, J. Marmet, Röthlisberger, Schwarzenbach	692
Antarctica				
Ellsworth Mtns				
Vinson Massif	16,860	1966		
Tyree	16,290	1967	10 members of A.A.C. expedition,	
Shinn	15,748	1966	Dec. 1966–Jan. 1967. [See article in	
Gardner	15,381	1966	*National Geographic Magazine*, Vol.	
Ostenso	13,710	1967	131, no. 6 June 1967.]	
[Other ranges]				
Kirkpatrick	14,860			
Markham	14,270			
Bell	14,200			
Sidley	13,850			
Fridtjof Nansen	13,700	1962	W. W. Herberts, K. Pain	
Erebus	13,350	1908	T. W. E. David & party	
Lister	13,000	1962	J. Wilson, B. Gunn	
Sabine	13,000			
Huggins	12,100	1958	B. Gunn, R. Brooke	
Terror	11,400	1959	B. Alexander, J. Wilson, M. White	
Herschel	10,942	1967	M. Gill, B. Jenkinson	313
Discovery	9,090	1959	J. Harrison, H. J. Harrington, B. Fitzgerald	
Harmsworth	9,090	1957	B. Gunn, G. Warren, A. Heine	
South Georgia				
Allardyce Range				790
Paget	9,625	1964	S. H. Down, T. J. Lynch, J. R. Chester	790
Heard Island				
Big Ben (Mawson)	9,002	1965	R. P. Temple, G. M. Budd, J. R. Crick, W. M. M. Deacock, C. K. Putt	800
Kerguelen Isles				
Ross	6,430			

General references:
[757], [792], [801]

Name of Peak	Height (Feet)	Details of first recorded ascent Date	Names of Party, etc.	References to Books
Pic de Nethou	11,168	1842	A. de Franqueville, P. de Tchihatcheff	
Pic de Posets	11,073	1856	Halkett	
Pic de Milieu	11,044			
Mont Perdu	11,007	1802	Ramond de Carbonnières	
Cylindre	10,899			
Vignemale	10,820	1838	Prince de Moscowa [Or possibly 1834: Miss Anne Lister.]	
Pic de Marbore	10,673			
Pic Perdighero	10,564	1860?	C. Packe [1st recorded ascent]	
Pic Russell	10,489			
Pic Long	10,483			
Pic Cambiel	10,410			
Pic Badet	10,378			
Pic du Port d'Oo	10,335			
Pic de la Munia	10,334		C. Packe	594, 638, 758
Taillon	10,322			
Balaitous	10,318	1825	[Officers of the Etat-Major. Charles Packe, 1864.]	
Pic de Litayrolles	10,316			
Pic d'Estats	10,302			
Pic de Crabioules	10,230			
Pic Albe	10,230			
Tuc de Maupas	10,203			
Pic Intermediare	10,184			
Pic d'Enfer	10,112	1867	H. Russell-Killough	
Pic Astazou	10,105			
Pic de Montcalm	10,105			
Pic de Boum	10,039			
Pic Quarrat	10,036			
Pic d'Eriste	10,024			
Los Encantados		1902	H. Brulle, D'Astorg	258

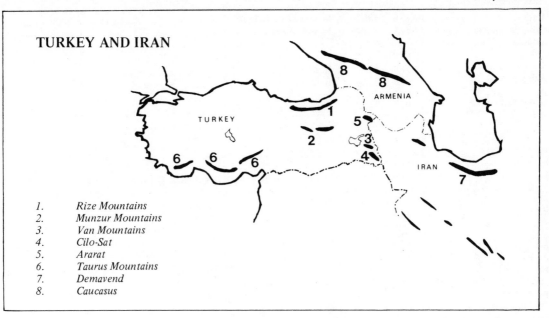

TURKEY AND IRAN

ARMENIA

TURKEY

IRAN

1. *Rize Mountains*
2. *Munzur Mountains*
3. *Van Mountains*
4. *Cilo-Sat*
5. *Ararat*
6. *Taurus Mountains*
7. *Demavend*
8. *Caucasus*

TURKEY AND IRAN

Name of Peak	Height (Feet)	Date	Details of first recorded ascent — Names of Party, etc.	References to Books
Turkey				
Rize Mountains				
Kackar Dag	12,917			
Kackar Tepe	11,975			
Kirklar Dag	11,348			374
Vercenik Dag	12,175			
Güngörmez Dag	11,585			
Aiguille Point	11,320	1963	R. Fedden	
Munzur Mountains				
Munzur Dag	10,460			
Van Mountains				
Baset Dag	12,300			
Arnas Dag	11,645			
Artos Dag	11,400			
Cilo-Sat				
Gelyasin (Resko)	13,681			**408**
Suppa Durak	13,320			
Hendevade	12,500			
Maunsells Peak	12,361			
Mazan	12,221			
Ararat	16,916	1829	J. J. F. W. von Parrot	**128, 285, 564, 599**
—Little Ararat	12,877			
Suphan Dag	14,547			
Kandil Dag	12,841			
Taurus Mountains				
Erciyas Dagi	12,850			
Demirkazik (Kaldi)	12,251			32, **242**
Bulgar Dag	11,680			
Iran				
Demavend	18,603	1836	W. T. Thomson	

United States of America

Alam Kuh	15,880	1902	Bornmüller Brothers
Takht-i-Suleiman	15,154	1936	H. Bobek & party
Zard Kuh	c. 14,000		
Kuh-i-Dena	c. 14,000		
Kuh-i-Savalan	c. 14,000	1934	H. Bobek & party
Kuh-i-Taftan	13,268		

General references:
[32], [129], [374]

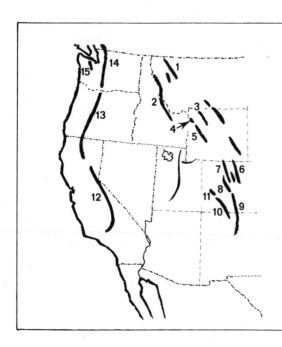

WESTERN UNITED STATES

ROCKY MOUNTAINS
1. Lewis Range
2. Bitterroot Range
3. Absaroka Range
4. Teton Range
5. Wind River Range
6. Front Range
7. Park Range
8. Sawatch Range
9. Sangre de Christo/Culebra Ranges
10. San Miguel/San Juan Ranges
11. Needle Mountains
12. *SIERRA NEVADA*
13. *CASCADES*
14. *NORTH CASCADES*
15. *OLYMPIC MOUNTAINS*

UNITED STATES OF AMERICA
(Excluding Alaska)

Name of Peak	Height (Feet)	Details of first recorded ascent Date	Names of Party, etc.	References to Books
Rocky Mountains				
Lewis Range				
Cleveland	10,448	1924	[Sierra Club party]	
Beartooth Range				
Granite Peak	12,799	1923	E. Koch, Ferguson, Williams	
Wood	12,661		E. Ikerman	850
Mission Range				
Swan Range				
Absaroka Range				
Francs Peak	13,140		[Surveyors]	
Washakie Needles	12,496	1904	Bannon & party	
Pilot Peak	11,708	1932	H. Mees, R. McKenzie	
Ramshorn Peak	11,625		[Surveyors]	
Index Peak	11,343	1939	G. Haas, J. Makowski, P. Smith	
Abiathar Peak	10,800	1940	P. Smith, G. Haas	
Teton Range				
Grand Teton	13,767	1898	W. Owen, F. Spalding, F. Petersen, J. Shive	
—Owen	12,922	1930	R. Underhill, K. Henderson, F. Fryxell, P. Smith	

−South Teton	12,505	1923	A. R. Ellingwood, E. Davis		
−Teewinot	12,317	1929	F. Fryxell, P. Smith		
−Nez Perce	11,900	1930	F. Fryxell, P. Smith		299,615
−Disappointment	11,616	1925	P. Smith, W. Harvey		
Moran (North)	12,594	1919	L. Jeffers	411	
−South		1922	L. H. Hardy, B. C. Rich, Fr. McNulty		
Thor Peak	12,018	1930	P. Petzoldt, B. Strange		
Buck Mtn	11,923	1898	T. M. Bannon, G. A. Buck		

Wind River Range

Gannett Peak	13,785	1922	A. C. Tate, F. J. Stahlnaker [1833: Capt. Benjamin L. E. Bonneville]
−Fremont Peak	13,730	1878	J. Eccles, *M. Payot* & Hayden Survey party
−Warren	13,720	1924	C. Blaurock, A. R. Ellingwood
−Sacagawea	13,607	1926	A. R. Ellingwood, S. Hart, E. S. Davis, M. E. Warner
−Helen	13,600	1924	C. Blaurock, H. Buhl, A. R. Ellingwood
−Dinwoody Peak	13,400	1922	A. E. Bent, E. P. Jackson, J. Wyman Jr.
Doublet Peak	13,600	1929	H. S. Hall Jr, R. L. M. Underhill, K. A. Henderson
Woodrow Wilson	13,500	1842	J. C. Fremont & party
East Sentinel	13,500	1937	P. Petzoldt, H. K. & E. Hartline
Wind River Peak	13,499	1877	Hayden Survey
Downs Mtn	13,344	1906	[Survey party]
Lizard Head Peak	12,842	1933	Drummond

Colorado
[Principal references]
23, 130, 145
317, 352, 821

Medicine Bow/
   Front Ranges

Grays Peak	14,274			
Torreys Peak	14,264			
Evans	14,260			
Longs Peak	14,255	1868	J. W. Powell, Byers	138, 145, 565
Bierstadt	14,046			
Hagues Peak	13,562			145
North Arahapo	13,506			
James Peak	13,260			
Clark Peak	12,965			
Richtofen	12,953			
Ptarmigan	12,480			
Lone Eagle Peak	11,900			

Park/Ten/Mile/
   Mosquito Ranges

Lincoln	14,284		
Quandary Peak	14,256		
Bross	14,169		
Democrat	14,142		
Pikes Peak	14,110	1820	E. James & 2 others
Sherman	14,037		
Zirkel	12,200		

Sawatch Range

Elbert	14,431	1874	H. W. Stuckle
Massive	14,418	1874	H. Gannett
Harvard	14,417		
La Plata Peak	14,337		
Antero	14,245		
Shavano	14,179		
Princeton	14,177		
Yale	14,172		
Belford	14,152		
Oxford	14,146		
Columbia	14,084		
Grizzly	14,000		
Tabeguache	14,000		
Holy Cross, Mt. of	13,996		

Elk Mountains

Castle Peak	14,259			
South Maroon Peak	14,126			
Capitol Peak	14,100		Hayden Survey	
Snowmans Mtn	14,077			338
North Maroon Peak	14,000			
Pyramid Peak	14,000		P. Hagerman	
Sopris	13,823			
Hagerman Peak	13,600			

Sangre de Christo/ Culebra Ranges

Sierra Blanca	14,363		
Crestone Peak	14,291	1916	A. R. Ellingwood, Miss E. S. Davis
Crestone Needle	14,191		
Old Baldy	14,125		
Kit Carson Peak	14,100		
Culebra Peak	14,069		
Humboldt Peak	14,044		
Little Bear	14,040		
West Spanish Peak	13,623		
Trinchera	13,546		
Greenhorn Mtn	12,334		

San Miguel/San Juan Ranges

Uncompaghre Peak	14,306		
Wilson	14,250		
El Diente	14,200	1890	P. W. Thomas
Sneffels	14,170		
San Luis Peak	14,146		
Redcloud Peak	14,047		
Stewart Peak	14,032		
Wilson Peak	14,026		
Wetterhorn Peak	14,017		
Sunshine Peak	14,015		
Handies Peak	14,013		
Rio Grande Pyramid	13,827		
Arrow Peak	13,803		
La Garita Peak	13,725		
Hesperus Peak	13,225		
Bennett Peak	13,189		
Lizard Head	13,156	1920	A. R. Ellingwood, J. B. Hoag
Engineer Mtn	12,972		
Mesa Peak	12,955		
Lone Cone	12,761		
Bowers Peak	12,300		
Chimney	11,785		

Needle Mtns

Windom Mtn	14,091		
Eolus	14,086		
Sunlight Peak	14,060		
Pigeon Peak	13,961		
Monitor Peak	13,703		
Index	13,400	1937	H. L. McClintock, T. M. Griffiths, F. McClintock

Sierra Nevada (Sequoia Nat. Park)

Whitney	14,495	1873	A. H. Johnson, C. D. Begole, J. Lucas	420, 889
Williamson	14,384	1884	W. L. Hunter, C. Mulholland	411
Russell	14,190	1926	N. Clyde	165
Langley	14,042	1871	C. King, P. Pinson	
Muir	14,025	?	[Unknown]	
Tyndall	14,025	1864	C. King, R. D. Cotter	420
Barnard	14,003	1892	J. & W. Hunter, C. Mulholland	
Le Conte	13,960	1935	N. Clyde	165
Mallory	13,870	1925	N. Clyde	165

Irvine	13,790	1925	N. Clyde	**165**
Carillon	13,572	1925	N. Clyde	**165**

(Kings Canyon)

North Palisade	14,254	1903	J. N. Le Conte, J. K. Moffitt, J. S. Hutchinson	
Sill	14,162	1903	J. N. Le Conte, J. K. Moffitt, R. D. Pike, J. S. Hutchinson	
Split Mtn	14,058	1902	J. N. & H. E. Le Conte, C. M. Lindley	
Middle Palisade	14,049	1921	F. P. Farquhar, A. F. Hall	
Thunderbolt Peak	14,040	1931	N. Clyde, R. L. Underhill, B. Robinson, F. P. Farquhar, G. Dawson, L. Clark, J. Eichorn	**165**
Agassiz	13,891	1925	N. Clyde	**165**
Winchell	13,768	1923	H. C. Mansfield, J. N. Newell, W. B. Putnam	
Brewer	13,577	1864	W. H. Brewer, C. F. Hoffman	
North Guard	13,304	1925	N. Clyde	**165**
Deerhorn Mtn	13,275	1927	N. Clyde	**165**
Temple Crag	13,016	1909	[Survey party]	
Clarence King	12,909	1896	B. C. Brown	
Gardiner	12,907	1896	J. N. Le Conte, B. C. Brown	

(San Joaquin area)

Humphreys	13,972	1904	E. C. & J. S. Hutchinson
Darwin	13,841	1908	E. C. Andrews, W. D. Johnson
Morgan (South)	13,739	1870	Wheeler Survey
Abbott	13,736	1908	J. S. Hutchinson, J. N. Le Conte, D. McDuffie
Bear Creek Spire	13,705	1923	H. F. Ulrichs
Haeckel	13,435	1920	W. L. Huber & party
Mills	13,352	1908	J. S. Hutchinson, J. N. Le Conte, D. McDuffie

(Yosemite)

Ritter	13,156	1872	J. Muir	
Lyell	13,090	1871	J. B. Tileston	
Dana	13,050	1863	W. H. Brewer, C. F. Hoffman	**420, 670, 896**
Excelsior Mtn	12,440	1931	H. Sloan	**911**
Clark	11,506	1866	C. King, J. T. Gardiner	
Half Dome		1875	G. Anderson	

Cascades

Rainier	14,410	1870	H. Stevens, P. B. van Trump	**510, 531, 909**
Shasta	14,162	1854	E. D. Pearce	**420**
Adams	12,307	1854	Shaw, Aiken, Allen	**910**
Hood	11,234	1857	H. L. Pittock, L. Chittenden, T. A. Wood, W. Cornell [incomplete ascent 1854]	**910**
Jefferson	10,495			
Lassen Peak	10,457			
Three Sisters	10,354			
—North Peak	10,058			
—Middle Peak	10,053			
Washington	7,794			

North Cascades

Baker	10,778	1868	E. T. Coleman, Stratton	
Glacier Peak	10,541			
St. Helens	9,677	1853	T. Dryer & 3 others	**910**
Stuart	9,415			**72**
Fernow	9,249			
Goode Mtn	9,200	1936	Bauer, Hossack, MacGowan & 2 others	
Forbidden Peak	8,815	1940	L. Anderson, J. Crooks, D. Lind, F. & H. Beckey	

Olympic Mountains

Olympus	7,954		
Constance	7,777		
Anderson	7,321		
Tom	7,150		**924, 925**
Carrie	7,020		
Meany			
Boulder Rock	7,000		

General references:
[129], [254], [411], [413], Appendix VI

Scafell, Miterdale and Eskdale, Lake District, England

AUTHOR INDEX

ABNEY, Sir William de Wyveleslie (1843–1921)
British chemist and scientist, who contributed to
the development of photographic chemistry, about
which he wrote several books. See [197].

ABRAHAM Ashley Perry (1876–1951)
Professional photographer and mountaineer. Together with his brother George Abraham (qv) he
was largely responsible for the development and
popularization of rock-climbing in the English
Lake District and other parts of the British Isles.

* 1. **Rock-climbing in Skye**
  London: Longmans, 1908. xxiv, 330p, 31 plates;
  ill, map (in pocket); 24cm
  Part of a classic trilogy, the others being [2] &
  [414].

ABRAHAM George Dixon (1872–1965)
Professional photographer and mountaineer. He
pioneered many rock-climbs in the Lake District,
often in the company of his brother and O. G.
Jones (qv). Also active in North Wales, Skye and
the Alps.

* 2. **Rock-climbing in North Wales**
  By George and Ashley Abraham
  Keswick: G. P. Abraham, 1906. xxii, 394p, 30
  plates; 24cm
  Part of a classic trilogy, the others being [1] &
  [414].

* 3. **The complete mountaineer**
  London: Methuen,
  1907. xvi, 493p, 75 plates; 23cm
  1908. 2nd ed. [imp]
  1923. 3rd ed. revised
  Virtually a distillation of all his writings: an
  omnibus work.

* 4. **British mountain climbs**
  London: Mills & Boon,
  1909. xvi, 448p, 18 plates; 18cm. Some early
  copies were box-bound.
  1923. 2nd ed.   ⎫
  1932. 3rd ed.   ⎪
  1937. 4th ed.   ⎬ Reprints
  1945. 5th ed.   ⎪
  1948. 6th ed.   ⎭
  Intended as a guidebook but readable as a history.

5. **Mountain adventures at home and abroad**
   London: Methuen, 1910. x, 308p, 26 plates; 23cm
   Personal and other adventures.

6. **Swiss mountain climbs**
   London: Mills & Boon, 1911. xvi, 423p, 24 plates;
   18cm. Some early copies were box-bound.
   Similar to [4] but has not stood the test of time.

7. **On Alpine heights and British crags**
   London: Methuen, 1919. xii, 308p, 24 plates;
   23cm
   Climbing reminiscences and other topics.

8. **First steps to climbing**
   London: Mills & Boon, 1923. 126p [122], 24
   plates; 19cm
   Instructional.

9. **Modern mountaineering**
   London: Methuen,
   1933. x, 198p, 16 plates; 20cm
   1945. 2nd ed.

1948. 3rd ed. revised
Instructional.

ADAMS, Ansel
See: [549].

[**ADAMS**, William Henry Davenport.]
Author of numerous nineteenth century children's
books.

10. **Alpine adventure: or, Narratives of travel and
    research in the Alps**
    By the author of 'The Mediterranean Illustrated',
    'The Arctic World' etc.
    London: Nelson,
    1878. 237p; ill; 18cm
    1881. Revised ed. entitled **Alpine climbing**

11. **Alpine climbing: narratives of recent ascents of
    Mont Blanc, the Matterhorn, the Jungfrau, and
    other lofty summits of the Alps**
    By the author of . . .
    London: Nelson, 1881. viii, 237p [229]; ill; 17cm.
    Revised ed. of **Alpine Adventure**. Copies seen
    bound in red or blue.

12. **Mountains and mountain climbing: records of
    adventure and enterprise among the famous moun-
    tains of the world**
    By the author of . . .
    London: Nelson, 1883. 415p; ill; 20cm

ADAMS-REILLY, Anthony Miles William (1836–85)
Irish mountaineer, painter and amateur cartographer,
who prepared the first reliable map of the Mont Blanc
area. See [22] He also collaborated in the writing
of a biography of J. D. Forbes (qv).

AHLUWALIA, Hari Pal Singh
13. **Higher than Everest: memoirs of a mountaineer**
    Delhi; London: Vikaś,
    1973. ix, 188p; ill, map, ports; 23cm
    1973. Reprinted
    1974. 2nd revised ed.
    1975. 3rd reprint
    1976. Adapted for children as **Climbing Everest**

14. **Climbing Everest**
    Delhi; London: Vikas, 1976. 72p, 4 plates; 21cm

AIREY, Alan F.
15. **Irish hill days**
    Manchester: Open Air Pub., [1937]. 47p, fold.
    map; 18cm

AITKEN, Samuel
* 16. **Among the Alps: a narrative of personal experiences**
  Illustrations by Vittorio Sella.
  Northwood, Middx: S. Aitken, [1900]. xvi, 119p,
  73 plates; 27 x 37cm
  Sella's photographs are the attraction in this
  otherwise obscure work.

ALACK, Frank
New Zealand mountain guide, born in Tyrol, who
climbed between the wars.

17. **Guide aspiring**
Edited by J. Halket Millar.
Auckland: Oswald-Sealy, [1966]. 229p, 8 plates;
23cm
Climbing autobiography.

Alpina Americana
See under: American Alpine Club.

ALPINE CLUB, Members of
The publications of the Alpine Club are discussed
in Part I. **Peaks, passes and glaciers** (Series I & II)
are commonly regarded as the cornerstone of any
mountaineering collection.

* 18. **Peaks, passes and glaciers: a series of excursions by members of the Alpine Club**
Edited by John Ball.
London: Longmans,
1859. xvi, 516p, 9 maps, 8 col. plates; ill; 22cm
1859. 2nd ed., 3rd ed., and 4th ed. with
corrections and different vignette on title-page.
1860. 5th ed. Traveller's 'Knapsack' edition,
xvi, 328p; 18cm.

Notes:
The first edition may be distinguished from the
others in having a different vignette on the
title-page, 23 woodcuts in place of 24 later, the gilt
illustration on the front cover narrow (44mm) and
the slope at 60° instead of 45° on the others.
The contents are indexed in the Index to the
Alpine Journal, Vol. I-XV, edited by F. A.
Wallroth.

19. **Narratives selected from 'Peaks, passes and glaciers'**
Edited with introduction and notes by George
Wherry.
Cambridge: University Press, 1910. [6], 156p,
maps; 18cm
6 chapters from Series I.

* 20. **Peaks, passes and glaciers: being excursions by members of the Alpine Club**
Second Series. Edited by Edward Shirley Kennedy.
London: Longmans,
1862. 2v. xiv, 445p, 8 fold. maps, 5 plates;
22cm; viii, 541p, 6 fold. maps, 7 plates; 22cm

Note:
The contents are indexed in the Index to the
Alpine Journal, Vol. I-XV, edited by F. A.
Wallroth.

21. **Peaks, passes and glaciers**
Selected and annotated by E. H. Blakeney.
London: Dent, 1926. xxxxviii, 317p; 18cm
Everyman's Library selection from Series I & II.

22. **Peaks, passes and glaciers: by members of the Alpine Club**
Third series. Edited by A. E. Field and Sydney
Spencer.
London: Methuen, 1932. xii, 307p, 16 plates;
23cm. Bound with or without gilt block on front
cover.
Selection from Volumes I-V of the Alpine
Journal.

AMENT, Pat
Leading American rock-climber.

* 23. **High over Boulder**
By . . . and Cleveland McCarty.
Boulder: Pruett, 1970

* 24. **Swaramandal**
Boulder: Vitaar Pub., 1973. 132p; ill;
Personalities in modern American rock-climbing.

* 25. **Master of rock**
[To be published June, 1977. 200p; ill; 18 x
26cm]
Biography of John Gill.

AMERICAN ALPINE CLUB

* 26. **Alpina Americana**
No. 1 **The High Sierra of California** by J. N. Le
Conte. 1907.
No. 2 **The Canadian Rocky Mountains** by C. E.
Fay. 1911. 19p, maps, plates; 35cm
No. 3 **Mountain exploration in Alaska** by A. H.
Brooks. 1914. 22p, map, plates.
Three short monographs.

AMERY, Leopold Charles Maurice Stennett
(1873-1955)
Leading British politician, writer and mountaineer.
A. C. President 1944-46. A virgin peak in Canada,
Mount Amery, was named after him and he
subsequently made the first ascent in 1929.

27. **Days of fresh air: being reminiscences of outdoor life**
London: Jarrolds, 1939. 320p, 47 plates; ill, port;
22cm

28. **In the rain and the sun: a sequel to 'Days of fresh air'**
London: Hutchinson, 1946. 251p, 33 plates
(1 col.); 22cm

AMES, Edward Levi (1832-92)
Barrister and country gentleman. Original A. C.
member. See [18].

ANDERSON, Eustace (1819-1889)
British soldier and mountaineer. Original A. C.
member. See also [18].

29. **Chamouni and Mont Blanc: a visit to the valley and an ascent of the mountain in the autumn of 1855**
London: Cornish, 1856. vi, 113p, 2 col. plates; 18cm
Late example of the pre-'Golden Age' type of
book.

ANDERSON, J.

* 30. **The book of the White Mountains**
By . . . and S. Morse.
New York: Minton Balch, 1930.
Eastern United States.

[ANONYMOUS]

31. **The peasants of Chamouni: containing an attempt to reach the summit of Mont Blanc, and a delineation of the scenery among the Alps**
London: Baldwin, Cradock & Joy,
1823. 164p, col. plate; 32mo
1826. 2nd ed.
The book which inspired Albert Smith (qv):
includes the story of the Hamel accident.

ASHENDEN (pseud. Sidney Edward Payn Nowill)

32. **The mountains of my life: journeys in Turkey and the Alps**
London: Blackwood, 1954. xii, 212p, 28 plates; 25cm
Climbing reminiscences.

ASSOCIATION OF BRITISH MEMBERS OF THE SWISS ALPINE CLUB

Clinton Dent (qv) was the first President of the Association, 1909-12. The Britannia Hut is the only mountain club hut in the Alps built entirely from money raised by British climbers.

33. **Inauguration of the Cabane Britannia, on the Klein Allalinhorne, Saas Fee, August 17th, 1912: and obituary notices and portrait of Clinton Dent**
London: A.B.M.S.A.C., 1913. [2], 54p, 14 plates (incl. facsim, port); 22cm

34. **The technique of alpine mountaineering**
Publication of the Uto Section of the S.A.C. English edition adapted by members of the . . . Translated by E. A. M. Wedderburn.
[London: A.B.M.S.A.C., 1935]. 74p; ill; 16cm
From the original: **Technique of alpinism** by Emile Kern (Uto Section, 1929).

35. **Mountaineering handbook: a complete and practical guide for beginner or expert**
Published for the . . .
London: Paternoster Press, 1950. 168p; ill; 19cm
From the original: **Bergsteigen** edited by Emile Kern (S.A.C. [1943?]).

ATKINS, Henry Martin (c. 1818–42)

36. **Ascent to the summit of Mont Blanc, on the 22nd and 23rd August, 1837**
NOT PUBLISHED
London: Calkin and Budd, 1838. 51p, 6 plates; 23cm. [Reissued in 1842 with an account of his funeral]
Atkins made the twenty-fourth ascent of Mont Blanc.

AUDEN, Wystan Hugh (1907–73)
Poet and dramatist.

37. **The ascent of F.6: a tragedy in two acts**
By . . . and Christopher Isherwood.
London: Faber,
    1936. 123p [121]; 23cm
    1937. 2nd ed.
    1937. Reprinted.
Undistinguished satirical verse drama, first performed 26 February 1937, at the Mercury Theatre, London.

AULDJO, John (1805–86)

* 38. **Narrative of an ascent to the summit of Mont Blanc, on the 8th and 9th August, 1827**
London: Ptd. for Longmans,
    1828. xii, 120p, map, 20 plates (incl. facsim); 33cm
    1830. 2nd ed. xii, 148p, 3 maps (col), 19 plates; ill, facsim; 22cm. The title varies, i.e. 'on the eighth and ninth'.
    1856. 3rd ed. xii, 119p, ill; 18cm
    1867. 4th ed.

AZEMA, Marc Antonin

* 39. **The conquest of Fitzroy**
By . . . Translated by Katherine Chorley and Nea Morin.
London: Deutsch, 1957. 237p, 12 plates; ill, maps, ports; 22cm
From the original: **La conquête du Fitzroy** (Paris: Flammarion, 1954).

BADÉ, William Frederic

See under: John Muir

BAKER, Ernest Albert

Contemporary of the Abraham brothers (qv), with whom he climbed on occasions. His published works include **On foot in the Highlands** (Maclehose, 1932). See also [142].

* 40. **Moors, crags and caves of the High Peak and the neighbourhood**
Manchester: Heywood, [1903]. 207p, 2 maps, plates; 22cm

* 41. **The voice of the mountains**
Edited by . . . and Francis E. Ross
London: Routledge,
    [1905]. xxii, 294p; 17cm
    1906. 1st reprint with corrections
    1913. 3rd reprint.
A well-known anthology.

42. **The Highlands with rope and rucksack**
London: Witherby, 1923. 253p, 19 plates; 23cm

43. **The British highlands with rope and rucksack**
London: Witherby, 1933. 236p, 11 plates; 22cm
Wakefield: E. P. Ltd., 1973. Facsim reprint with new introduction by A. H. Griffin.

BAKER, George Percival (1856–1951)

Wealthy English climber, whose expeditions included Ararat, the Caucasus and the Canadian Rockies, where he climbed with Collie (qv).

44. **Mountaineering memories of the past**
London: Privately printed by Spottiswoode, Ballantyne, 1942. 38p, 4 plates (incl. ports); 22cm
London: Privately printed, 1951. 62p, 11 plates; 22cm
Chiefly material derived from his articles in the **Alpine Journal.**

BALCH, Edwin Swift
American and A.A.C. founder member.

45. **Mount McKinley and mountain climbers' proofs**
Philadelphia: Campion, 1914. 142p; 27cm
An abortive attempt to resolve the conflicting claims to the first ascent, using Dr. Cook's false evidence.

BALL, John (1818–89)
Lawyer, politician, mountaineer and botanist. First A. C. President. He produced the first comprehensive mountain traveller's guide to the Alps, the standard work until the appearance of the Conway-Coolidge climbers' guidebooks. **See also** [18] & [381].

*†46. **The Alpine Guide**
This was published in two guises, i.e. in three

volumes, and as a ten-part set. The original three volumes are:

General Introduction and the Western Alps (1863)
Central Alps (1864)
Eastern Alps (1868)

In subsequent editions the **General Introduction** was published separately from the **Western Alps**.

The ten-part set, which consists of the three volume edition broken down by chapters into regional guidebooks, first appeared in 1873.

47. **Introduction to the 'Alpine Guide'**
London: Longmans,
  1863. Included in 'Western Alps'
  1864. First appearance as separate publication.
  1873. cxxxp; 18cm
  1875.
  1899. New edition prepared on behalf of the Alpine Club by W. A. B. Coolidge, entitled **Hints and notes practical and scientific for travellers in the Alps being a revision of the general introduction to the 'Alpine Guide'.** clxivp; 18cm

48. **Hints and notes practical and scientific for travellers in the Alps**
See: Introduction to the 'Alpine Guide'.

49. **Western Alps**
London: Longmans,
  1863. cxliv, 377p
  1866. 2nd ed.
  1870. 3rd ed. xxiv, 404p
  1873. Reprint
  1898. New edition reconstructed and revised on behalf of the Alpine Club by W. A. B. Coolidge. lii, 612p; 19cm

50. **Central Alps**
London: Longmans,
  1864. xx, 502p
  1866. 2nd ed.
  1870. xx, 521p
  1873. Reprint
  1876. Reprint
  1882. Reprint
  1907. Part I of revised edition: general editor A. V. Valentine-Richards. xxviii, 326p
  1911. Part II of revised edition: general editor George Broke. xx, 432p.

51. **Eastern Alps**
London: Longmans,
  1868. xxiv, 639p, 8 maps; 18cm
  1869. New ed.
  1870. xxiv, 602p, [639?]
  1874. New ed. xxiv, 639p
  1879. xxiv, 639p.

52. **The Alpine Guide in ten parts**

South-western Alps
London: Longmans, 1873, [4], 180p, 6 maps; 18cm

Pennine Alps
London: Longmans,
  1873. [4], 181 − 378p, 4 maps; 18cm
  1875. New ed.
  1878. New ed.

Bernese Alps
London: Longmans,
  1873. [4], 144p, 3 maps; 18cm
  1875. New ed.

North Switzerland
London: Longmans, 1873. [4], 145−244p, 2 maps; 18cm

The Pass of St. Gotthards
London: Longmans, 1873. [4], 245−346p, 2 maps; 18cm

East Switzerland
London: Longmans,
  1873. [2], 347−489p, 5 maps; 18cm
  1876.

North Tyrol, Bavarian and Salzburg Alps
London: Longmans, 1873. [4], 138p, 3 maps; 18cm

Central Tyrol
London: Longmans,
  1873. [2], 139−314p, 3 maps; 18cm
  1878. New ed.

Styrian, Carnic and Julian Alps
London: Longmans,
  1873. 315 − 398p & 530 − 602p, 3 maps; 18cm
  1876. New ed.

South Tyrol and Venetian or Dolomite Alps
London: Longmans,
  1873. [2], 399−529p; 18cm
  1876. New ed. 399−534p.

BAND, George C. (b. 1931)
British mountaineer and member of several Himalayan expeditions − Everest, 1953; Rakaposhi, 1954; and Kanchenjunga, 1955, which he climbed with Joe Brown (qv). **See also [396]**.

53. **Road to Rakaposhi**
London: Hodder, 1955. 192p, 31 plates; maps, ports; 21cm

BANKS, Michael Edward Borg (b. 1922)
Marine commando, writer, photographer and mountaineer. Leader of the successful 1958 expedition to Rakaposhi, which he climbed with Tom Patey (qv). His published works include **High Arctic** (Dent, 1957) and **Greenland** (1974).

54. **Commando climber**
London: Dent, 1955. xiv, 240p, 17 plates (incl. col. port); 22cm
London: Burke, 1961. Abridged ed. entitled **Snow commando**.
Climbing memoirs.

55. **Rakaposhi**
London: Secker & Warburg, 1959. 238p, 19 plates (1 col); ill, ports; 23cm

56. **Snow commando**
Illustrated by Robin Collomb.
London: Burke, 1961. 192p, 8 plates; ill, map; 21cm. Children's edition of **Commando climber**.

BARFORD, John Edward Quintus (1914−47)
Engineer and mountaineer. A.C. member. Killed in the Alps.

* 57. **Climbing in Britain**
Edited by . . .
Harmonsworth: Penguin.

1946. 160p, 16 plates; ill; 18cm. [Pelican paperback]
1947. Reprinted.

This book was prepared at the instigation of the newly formed B.M.C. and marks the start of the post-war surge of interest. Instructional.

BARKER, Ralph
Journalist, whose published works include **One man's jungle** (Chatto & Windus, 1975), a biography of F. Spencer Chapman (qv).

* 58. **The last blue mountain**
London: Chatto & Windus, 1959. 212p, 23 plates; 23cm
New York: Doubleday, 1960.

This account of the ill-fated 1957 Haramosh expedition was prepared from expedition diaries and discussions with the survivors.

BARROW, John (1808–98)
Soldier, climber and A.C. member.

59. **Expeditions on the glaciers: including an ascent of Mont Blanc, Monte Rosa, Col du Geant, and Mont Buet, by a private of the Thirty-eight Artists, and member of the Alpine Club**
London: E. & F. N. Spon, 1864. [6], 122p, plate; 20cm

60. **Mountain ascents in Westmoreland and Cumberland Cumberland**
London: Sampson Low, 1886. viii, 208p, fold. map, 2 plates; 20cm

The delights of hill-walking in Victorian England.

BARRY, Martin (1802–55)
Scottish Quaker doctor, who made the twenty-first ascent of Mont Blanc.

61. **Ascent to the summit of Mont Blanc, 16th–18th of 9th month (SEPT'), 1834**
London: [H. Teape for the author, 1835]. 40p, 2 plates; 23cm. Title pages vary, 'Septr' being either in small letters or capitals.
Edinburgh: Blackwood, 1836. ii viii, 119p, 2 col. plates; 24cm. Variation of title, viz: **Ascent to the summit of Mont Blanc in 1834.** This edition revised and presented as two lectures.

BASTERFIELD, George

62. **Songs of a cragsman**
Published by G. R. Speaker for the Fell and Rock Climbing Club of the English Lake District (London Section), 1930. 27p; 26cm

63. **Songs of a cragsman: twelve songs of the hills**
Words and music by ... Musical editor, Oliver Knapton.
Barrow-in-Furness: Geo Basterfield, 1935. 27p; 26cm

64. **Mountain lure**
Kendal: Titus Wilson, 1947. [12], 166p, 6 plates (incl. port); 22cm
Essays and verses.

BATES, Robert G. Hicks
American mountaineer. Member of the 1938 and 1953 K.2 expeditions. **See also [385].**

* 65. **Five miles high: the story of an attack on the second highest mountain in the world, by members of the first American Karakoram expedition**
[By ... and others]
New York: Dodd Meade, 1939. xvi–381p
London: Hale, 1940. 319p, 31 plates (incl. ports); 22cm

BAUER, Paul (b. 1896)
German lawyer and mountaineer. Leader of pre-war German expeditions to Kanchenjunga and Nanga Parbat.

* 66. **Himalayan campaign: the German attack on Kanchenjunga, the second [sic] highest mountain in the world**
Translated [from the German] by Sumner Austin.
Oxford: Blackwell,
1937. xviii, 180p, 64 plates; maps, ports; 23cm
1937. 2nd imp.
From the originals: **Im Kampf um den Himalaja** (Munich: Knorr & Hirth, 1931); and **Um den Kantsch** (Munich: Knorr & Hirth, 1933).

* 67. **Himalayan quest: the German expeditions to Siniolchum and Nanga Parbat**
Edited by ... Translated from the German by E. G. Hall.
London: Nicholson & Watson, 1938. xxvi, 150p, 96 plates; maps, ports; 26cm
From the original: **Auf Kundfahrt in Himalaja** (Munich: Knorr & Hirth, 1937).

68. **Kanchenjunga challenge**
London: Kimber, 1955. 202p, 12 plates; 24cm
From the original: **Kampf um den Himalaja** (Munich: Knorr & Hirth, 1952).
Chiefly a rewrite of [66].

69. **The siege of Nanga Parbat 1856–1953**
Translated from the German by R. W. Rickmers.
London: Hart-Davis, 1956. 211p, 21 plates; facsim, ports; 22cm
From the original: **Das Ringen um den Nanga Parbat** (Munich: Süddeutscher Verlag, 1955).

BAUGHAN, Blanche Edith

70. **Mt. Egmont**
Auckland: Whitcombe & Tombs, 1929. 75p; ill; 17cm
A volcano on North Island, New Zealand.

BECHTOLD, Fritz

71. **Nanga Parbat adventure: a Himalayan expedition**
Translated from the German of ... by H. E. G. Tyndale.
London: Murray, 1935. xx, 93p, 80 plates; maps, ports; 26cm [Reprinted 1935, 1938?]

From the original: **Deutsche am Nanga Parbat** (Munich: Bruckmann, 1935).

BECKEY, Fred W. (b. 1923)
Leading American mountaineer, particularly associated with exploration in the Cascades.

* 72. **Challenge of the North Cascades**
Seattle: Mountaineers, 1969. 280p; ill.

BEETHAM, Bentley (1886–1963)
English schoolmaster and mountaineer, who made many new rock-climbs in the English Lake District. See [573].

[BEETHAM, George]

73. **The first ascent of Mount Ruapehu, New Zealand, and a holiday jaunt to Mounts Ruapehu, Tongariro and Ngauruhoe**
London: Privately printed by Harrison & Sons, 1926. 40p, 2 plates 22cm

BELL, James Horst Brunnerman (1896–1976)
Scottish climber, prominent in Scottish mountaineering from 1920s.
Editor of S.M.C. Journal for many years.

74. **British hills and mountains**
By ... , E. F. Bozman and J. Fairfax Blakeborough.
London: Batsford,
1940. viii, 67 plates (3 col); ill, maps; 22cm
1943. 2nd ed. [imp]
1950. 3rd ed. revised.
A general survey.

* 75. **A progress in mountaineering: Scottish hills to Alpine peaks**
London: Oliver & Boyd, 1950. xii, 424p, 24 plates; ill, maps; 22cm
Mixture of instruction and reminiscence. He stresses the importance of Scottish winter climbing as preparation for the Alps.

BENSON, Claude Ernest (–1932)

76. **Crag and hound in Lakeland**
London: Hurst & Blackett, 1902. xvi, 313p; ill; 23cm
[2nd ed. with different illustrations?]
Mixture of rock-climbing and fox-hunting.

* 77. **British mountaineering**
London: Routledge, 1909. xii, 224p; ill; 19cm.
Two versions of this edition have been seen:
(i) dark green patterned cloth; gilt-blocked design on front cover; gilt-blocked spine; rounded corners; 4pp. advertisements at end.
(ii) light green plain cloth; cover illustration and lettering in black; less blocking on spine and lacking the word 'Illustrated'; square corners; no advertisement leaves.
London: Routledge, 1914. 2nd ed. revised.

78. **Mountaineering ventures**
London: T. C. & E. C. Jack, [1928]. 224p; ill; 21cm
The Matterhorn story, etc. retold.

BENUZZI, Felice (b 1910)
Italian diplomat.

* 79. **No picnic on Mount Kenya**
London: Kimber,
1952. x, 231p [221], 2 plates (incl. port); 23cm
1952. 2nd, 3rd & 4th editions [impressions]
1953. 5th ed. [imp]
1955. Kimber pocket ed. (paperback)
London: Longman, 1960. Concise ed. ix, 181p;

17cm
London: Kimber, 1974. New ed.
Three prisoners of war make a remarkable attempt to climb Mount Kenya, with only makeshift equipment and hoarded rations.

BERE, Rennie M.
Mountaineer, Director of Uganda National Parks.

* 80. **The way to the Mountains of the Moon**
London: Barker, 1966. xvi, 147p, 16 plates; ill, maps; 23cm
A naturalist's account of climbing in Africa.

BERNHARD, Oscar
Swiss doctor and surgeon.

* 81. **First aid to the injured, with special reference to accidents occurring in the mountains: a handbook for guides, climbers and travellers**
Translated from the German by Michael G. Foster.
Samaden: Tanner, 1896. viii, 136p; ill; 18cm
London: Fisher Unwin, 1900. 2nd ed.
The first book dealing with mountain accidents.

BERNSTEIN, Jeremy
American Professor of Physics, New York University.

82. **Ascent: of the invention of mountain climbing and its practice**
New York: Random House, 1965. x, 124p; ill.

BHATTACHARJYA, Bidypati

83. **Mountain sickness**
Bristol: John Wright, 1964. 58p; ill; 22cm
Baltimore: Williams & Wilkins, 1964. 58p.
Summarizes our knowledge of the physiology of mountain sickness.

BICKNELL, Peter
British architect and mountaineer. A.C. member. He held the record for the traverse of the Cuillin ridge in Skye for many years. See also [532].

* 84. **British hills and mountains**
London: Collins, 1947. 48p, 8 col. plates; 23 b/w ill; 23cm
'Britain in Pictures' Series. Interesting collection of artists' impressions of British hills from the eighteenth century onwards.

BLACKSHAW, Alan (b. 1933)
British administrator and mountaineer; one of the leading post-war British alpinists.

* 85. **Mountaineering from hill walking to alpine climbing**
Harmondsworth: Penguin,
1965. 542p; ill; 18cm. Paperback
1968. Revised ed.
London: Kaye & Ward, 1968. Hardback ed.
Harmondsworth: Penguin.
1970. 3rd ed. revised
1973. Revised
1975. Revised.
This is the standard manual of instruction in use and is approved by the B.M.C. and M.C. of S.

BLACKSTONE, Frederic Elliott (1830 – 1892)
A.C. Member See [20].

BLAKENEY, Edward Henry
See also [21].

86. **Alpine poems**
Winchester: Printed at the author's private press, 1929. 60 numbered copies.

BLANCHET, Emile Robert (1877–1943)
Swiss pianist and mountaineer, who accomplished many difficult Alpine climbs: see his **Hors des chemins battus** (1932). See [757].

BOELL, Jacques
French mountaineer and novelist.

87. **High heaven**
Translated from the French by Dilys Owen
London: Elek, 1947. 126p [128], 32 plates; ill, maps; 22cm
From the original: **Cimes d'Oisans: Récits de courses en Dauphiné** (Paris: Flammarion, 1937).
Climbing in the Dauphiné Alps.

BONATTI, Walter (b. 1930)
Exceptional Italian guide and mountaineer of the modern era. His solo ascent of the south-west pillar of the Dru in 1955 is one of the most remarkable achievements in mountaineering.

* 88. **On the heights**
Translated from the Italian by Lovett F. Edwards.
London: Hart-Davis, 1964. 248p, 16 plates (incl. ports); 23cm
From the original: **Le mie montagne** (Bologna: Zanichelli, 1962).
Climbing autobiography.

* 89. **The great days**
Translated [from the Italian] by Geoffrey Sutton.
London: Gollancz, 1974. 189p, 32 plates; 23cm
From the original: **I giorni grandi** (Milan: Mondadori, 1971).
Continuation of [88].

BONINGTON, Christian John Storey (b. 1934)
Professional mountaineer, who made the first British ascent of the Eigerwand. Leader of recent Himalayan expeditions of great severity.

* 90. **I chose to climb**
London: Gollancz,
1966. 208p, 40 plates (incl. ports); 23cm
1966. 2nd imp.
1969. 3rd imp.
1973. 4th imp.
London: Arrow Books, 1975. Paperback ed.
Autobiography.

* 91. **Annapurna South Face**
London: Cassell, 1971. x, 334p, 48 col. plates (incl. ports); 24cm
New York: McGraw. 1971.
H'worth: Penguin, 1973. Paperback ed.

92. **Everest South-west Face**
London: Hodder, 1973. 352p, fold. map, 56 plates (incl. 24 col); ill, ports; 24cm
New York: Stein & Day, 1973. 352p. Published as **The ultimate challenge**

H'worth: Penguin, 1975. Paperback ed.
Unsuccessful attempt.

93. **The ultimate challenge: the hardest way up the highest mountain in the world**
New York : Stein & Day, 1973. 352p. U.S.A. edition of **Everest South-west Face**

* 94. **The next horizon: Autobiography II**
London: Gollancz, 1973. 304p, 56 plates (incl. 8 col); ill, ports; 24cm
London: Arrow Books, 1975. Paperback ed.
Continuation of [90].

95. **Changabang**
By . . . & M. Boysen, A. Hankinson, D. Haston, B. Sandhu, D. Scott.
London: Heinemann, 1975. [x], 118p, 4 col. plates; ill, ports; 26cm
First ascent of this difficult peak in Garhwal Himalaya

* 96. **Everest the hard way**
London: Hodder, 1976. 239p, 80 col. plates (incl. ports); 27cm
London, Hutchinson, 1977, Arrow Paperback.
Success on the South-west Face.

BONNEY, Thomas George (1833 – 1923)
Clergyman, mountaineer, geologist and writer. A.C. President 1881-3. He travelled and climbed extensively in the Alps for over fifty years. His later books were concerned more with natural history and geology. He collaborated with Elijah Walton (qv) in a series of illustrated folios. See also [20] & [868].

* 97. **Outline sketches in the high Alps of Dauphiné**
London: Longmans, 1865. xvi, 52p, map, 14 plates; 26cm

* 98. **The alpine regions of Switzerland and the neighbouring countries: a pedestrian's notes on their physical features, scenery and natural history**
With illustrations by Edward Whymper.
Cambridge: Deighton Bell, 1868. xvi, 351p, 5 plates; ill; 22cm

* 99. **The building of the Alps**
London: Fisher Unwin,
1912. 384p, 32 plates; ill; 23 cm,
1913. 2nd imp.

BORCHERS, Philipp
German mountaineer, who took part in important expeditions to the Pamirs and the Peruvian Andes. See [757].

BORTHWICK, Alistair
Scottish journalist and climber. Chronicler of many exploits of the Creagh Dhu Club, well known for their tough approach to climbing.

*100. **Always a little further**
London: Faber, 1939. 276p; 21cm
Stirling: Mackay, 1947. New [2nd] ed. 221p.
Glasgow: T. Smith, 1969. viii, 221p.
Climbing reminiscences.

BOURRIT, Marc-Theodore (1739 – 1819)
Painter, traveller and writer, who failed in his attempts to climb Mont Blanc. He wrote several

books on Alpine glaciers and travel, most of which are not available in English.

101. A relation of a journey to the glaciers in the Dutchy of Savoy
Translated from the French of . . . by Cha. & Fred Davy.
Norwich: R. Beatniffe,
    1775. xxi, 264p; 19cm
    1776. 2nd ed. 52, xxii, 268p [Also published in London by G. Robinson,]
Dublin: R. Cross, 1776. xx, [8], xviii, 222p; 16cm
From the original: **Description des Glacières . . . du Duché de Savoie** (Geneva, 1773).

BOWIE, Mick

***102. The Hermitage years**
Wellington: Reed, 1969. 196p, 16 plates (incl. group ports); 22cm
Biography of well-known Mount Cook guide by Nan Bowie.

BOWMAN, W. E.

* **103. The ascent of Rum Doodle**
London: Parrish, 1956. 141p [139,] 16 plates; 21 cm
Fiction: satirizes run of the mill expedition books.

BOZMAN, Ernest Franklin (1895–1968)
Publisher and A.C. member. **See also [74] & Appendix IV**

 104. Mountain essays by famous climbers
Edited by . . .
London: Dent,
    1928. vi, 256p; 16cm
    1933. Revised ed. with additional extract from Smythe's **Kamet conquered**.
Anthology in the Kings Treasuries of Literature series.

BRAHAM, Trevor
British mountaineer with thirty years' experience of exploring and climbing throughout the Himalaya, Karakoram and Hindu Kush.

***105. Himalayan odyssey**
London: Allen & Unwin, 1974. 243p [241], 24 plates; ill; maps. ports; 25 cm
Well-written and authoritative climbing memoirs.

BRASHER, Christopher
See [396].

BREWER, William H.
American surveyor, who worked with Josiah Whitney (qv) and Clarence King (qv).

***106. Up and down California in 1860–1864: the journal of William H. Brewer**
Edited by Francis P. Farquhar.
New Haven: Yale Univ. Press. 1930.601p.
Berkeley: Univ. Calif. Press. 1950.

***107. Rocky Mountain letters, 1869**
Edited by E. B. Rogers
Denver: Colorado Mountain Club, 1930.
Journal of an early geological expedition to the Colorado Rockies.

BRIDGE, L. D. ['Bill']

108. Mountain search and rescue in New Zealand
New Zealand: Fed. M.C. of N.Z., 1961. 225p, 8 plates; ill, maps; 19cm. A much enlarged version of **Mountain search and rescue organisations** published in 1948 by the Tararua Tramping Club.

BRIGGS, Raymond

109. First up Everest
Illustrations by . . . . Text by Showell Styles.
London Hamilton, 1969. [40p]; ill (some col), ports; 21cm
Written for children.

BRINTON, William
Doctor and A.C. member. **See [20]**.

BROCKEDON, William (1787–1854)
Writer, painter, traveller and inventor. He made his first tour in 1824 for the purpose of investigating Hannibal's route and later assisted in the preparation of Murray's Swiss guidebook. In the course of his researches he traversed the Alps fifty-eight times, crossing more than forty different passes.

***110. Illustrations of the passes of the Alps**
London: the author, 1828–9. 2v. 109 plates. [Various sizes; see below.]
London: Bohn, [1877]. 2v. 109 plates; 28cm
Originally published during 1827–9 in twelve parts. The following editions were offered for sale by the author:

Imperial 8vo	@ 10 guineas
Royal 4to proofs	@ 15 guineas
Royal 4to proofs on India paper	@ 20 guineas
Imperial 4to, before the letters	@ 30 guineas
Ditto, with etchings	@ 40 guineas
Colombier folio, with etchings	@ 60 guineas

Published in book form, 2v. folio or quarto, 1828–9. The original drawings were all by Brockedon and were sold in 1837 for 500 guineas.

***111. Journals of excursions in the Alps: the Pennine, Graian, Cottian, Rhetian, Lepontian and Bernese**
London: James Duncan,
    1833. xvi, 376p, fold. map; 21cm
    1845. 3rd ed.
Account of his travels in 1824 and 1825.

BROKE, Horatio George (1861–1932)
British diplomat, later clergyman. A.C. member. He climbed extensively in the Alps. Edited part of Ball's **Alpine Guide**. [50].

112. With sack and stock in Alaska
London: Longmans, 1891. xii, 158p, 2 col. maps; 20cm
Attempt on Mt. St. Elias in 1888.

BRONGERSMA, Leo Daniel
Dutch leader of chiefly scientific expedition to the eastern mountains of the Nassau Range, New Guinea.

113. To the mountains of the stars
By . . . and G. F. Venema. Translated from the Dutch by Alan G. Readett.
London: Hodder, 1962. xvi, 318p. [302], 48 plates (incl. 24 col); ill, maps, ports; 23 cm
From the original: **Het witte Hart van Nieuw-Guinea** (Amsterdam: Scheltens & Giltay, 1960).

BROOKS, Alfred Hulse
American geologist. See [26].

BROUGHTON, Geoffrey

114. **Climbing Everest**
An anthology selected and edited by . . . from the writings of the climbers themselves. Illustrated by W. Heaton Cooper and Howard Somervell.
London: O.U.P., 1960. 149p; ill; 20cm

BROWER, David Ross
American rock-climber and conservationist. One of the party who made the first ascent of Shiprock, New Mexico in 1939.

115. **Manual of ski mountaineering**
Edited by . . .
Berkeley: Univ. Calif. Press,
   1942. 135p, plate
   1946. 2nd ed. 201p
Sierra Club,
   1962. Revised ed.

BROWN, Frederic Augustus Yeats (1837–1925)
English alpinist, who made several new ascents with F. F. Tuckett (qv), and other major Alpine expeditions. See [22].

BROWN, Joe (b. 1930)
World-renowned English rock-climber, who led the resurgence of British rock-climbing in the 1950s, often in partnership with Don Whillans (qv), pioneering many new climbs of exceptional severity. He has also made some notable ascents in the Alps, together with first ascents of Kanchenjunga and the Muztagh Tower.

*116. **The hard years: an autobiography**
London: Gollancz,
   1967. 256p, 33 plates (incl. ports); 23cm
   1967. 2nd imp.
   1969. 3rd imp.
   1972. 4th imp.
H'worth: Penguin,
   1975. Paperback ed.

BROWN, Thomas Graham (1882–1965)
British scientist, climber and mountain historian. Starting late in life, he climbed extensively in the Alps and also further afield. The planning and execution of three new routes on the Brenva face of Mont Blanc most notable among his many achievements. See also [757].

*117. **Brenva**
London: Dent, 1944. xvi, 228p, map, 73 plates; 22cm

118. **The Alpine Annual 1950: adapted from the 1949 numbers of the Alpine Journal**
Edited by . . .
London: Dent, 1950. xii, 255p, 29 plates (1 col); facsims, ports; 23cm

119. **The Alpine Annual: 2; adapted from the 1950 numbers of the Alpine Journal**
Edited by . . .
London: Dent, 1951. viii, 282p, 29 plates (1 col); ill, port; 23cm

*†120. **The first ascent of Mont Blanc**

Published on the occasion of the Centenary of the Alpine Club
By . . . and Sir Gavin De Beer.
London: O.U.P., 1957. x, 460p, 16 plates; facsims, maps, ports; 23cm
Scholarly examination of the controversy surrounding the first ascent.

BROWNE, Belmore (1880–1954)
American artist, explorer and mountaineer, who helped to expose the fraudulent claims of Dr. F. A. Cook (qv).

*121. **The conquest of Mount McKinley: the story of three expeditions through the Alaskan wilderness to Mount McKinley, North America's highest and most inaccessible mountain**
Appendix by Herschel C. Parker.
New York: Putnam, 1913. xviii, 381p, fold. map, 64 plates (1 col); 23cm
Boston: Houghton, Mifflin, 1956. 2nd ed. xxxii, 381p.

BRUCE, Hon. Charles Granville (1866–1939)
Soldier, mountaineer and Himalayan explorer. A.C. President 1923–5. He accompanied Conway (qv) in the Karakoram, and Mummery on Nanga Parbat, later leading the 1922 and 1924 Everest expeditions. See also [573].

*122. **Twenty years in the Himalaya**
London: Arnold, 1910. xvi, 335p, col. map, 29 plates; 21cm

*123. **Kulu and Lahoul**
London: Arnold, 1914. xii, 308p, map, 24 plates; 23cm

*124. **The assault on Mount Everest 1922**
By . . . and other members of the expedition.
London: Arnold, 1923. xii, 339p, 2 fold. maps, 33 plates (incl. ports); 26cm

*125. **Himalayan wanderer**
London: Maclehose, 1934. [8], 309p, 16 plates (incl. port); 23cm

BRUNNING, Carl K.
Journalist

126. **Rock-climbing and mountaineering**
Diagrams drawn by R. G. Twentyman.
Manchester: Open Air Pub., [1936]. 108p; ill; 19cm
London: Faber, 1946. New ed. 87p.
Instructional.

BRYANT, Leslie Vickery ['Dan'] (1905–57)
New Zealand mountaineer. He climbed extensively in New Zealand, Switzerland, Canada and the Himalaya, accompanying Shipton (qv) on the 1935 Everest reconnaissance.

127. **New Zealanders and Everest**
Wellington: Reed, 1953. 48p; ill, ports; 22cm

BRYCE, James, Viscount Bryce (1838–1922)
First Viscount, historian and statesman. A.C. President 1899–1901. Mount Bryce in the Canadian Rockies is named after him. His books show alert observation and wide interests. **Memories of**

travel (Macmillan, 1923) includes some climbing reminiscences, particularly the Tatras with Leslie Stephen (qv).

128. **Transcaucasia and Ararat: being notes of a vacation tour in the autumn of 1876**
London: Macmillan,
    1877. x [xiv], 420p, col. map, plate; 20cm
    1877. 2nd ed. [imp].
    1878. 3rd ed. [imp].
    1896. 4th ed. revised.
Includes the third ascent of Ararat.

BUELER, William M.
American mountaineer, widely travelled, particularly in North America, Europe and Asia.

*129. **Mountains of the world: a handbook for climbers and hikers**
Rutland, Vermont: Tuttle, 1970. 279p; 43 maps (some fold.); 18cm
London: Prentice-Hall Int., 1970. 279p; 43 maps (some fold.); 18cm
Concise and informative guide to routes and areas.

*130. **Roof of the Rockies: a history of mountaineering in Colorado**
Boulder: Pruett, 1974. 200p, maps

BUHL, Hermann (1924–57)
Austrian mountaineer, who accomplished many very severe Alpine climbs. His solo ascent of Nanga Parbat, from the final camp, is one of the most outstanding feats in climbing history. He fell to his death on Chogolisa, while descending with Kurt Diemberger (qv).

*131. **Nanga Parbat pilgrimage**
Translated [from the German] by Hugh Merrick.
London: Hodder, 1956. 360p, 17 plates (incl. ports); 23cm
New York: Dutton, 1956. Published as **Lonely challenge**
From the original: **Achttausend drüben und drunter** (Munich: Nymphenburger, 1954).

132. **Lonely challenge**
New York: Dutton, 1956. 318p; ill, map; 22cm.
U.S.A. edition of **Nanga Parbat pilgrimage**.

BUNTING, James

133. **Climbing**
London: Macmillan, 1973. 92p [88]; ill, map, ports; 23cm
Leisure Guide series.

BUNBURY, E. H.
See [18].

BURDSALL, Richard Lloyd (1895–1953)
American civil engineer and mountaineer, who took part in the 1938 American K.2 expedition.
See also [65].

*134. **Men against the clouds: the conquest of Minya Konka**
By ... and Arthur B. Emmons 3rd. With contributions by Terris Moore and Jack Theodore Young.
New York: Harper, 1935) xvi, 292p, 31 plates; ill,
London: Lane, 1935 .) map, ports; 23cm

BURLINGHAM, Frederick

135. **How to become an alpinist**
By ... *(The man who cinematographed the Matterhorn)*
London: Werner Laurie, 1914. xii, 218p, 32 plates (incl. ports); 20cm. Bound in red or blue cloth.
Good selection of photographs of early climbers.

BURMAN, Jose

*136. **A peak to climb: the story of South African mountaineering**
Published under the auspices of the Mountain Club of South Africa.
Cape Town: C. Struik, 1966. xii, 175p, plates; ill, maps; 24cm. Limited edition of 1200 numbered copies, of which the first 75 are leather bound deluxe.

BURNABY, Mrs. Fred
See: Mrs. Le Blond.

BURPEE, Laurence Johnston

137. **Among the Canadian Alps**
London; New York: Lane, 1915. 239p, 6 maps, 35 plates; 23cm
Well-illustrated travel book: the mountaineering sections are culled from various sources.

BUSK, Sir Douglas Laird (b. 1906)
British diplomat and mountaineer.

138. **The delectable mountains**
Sketches by Bridget Busk.
London: Hodder,
    1946. xii, 274p, 4 fold. maps, 37 plates (incl. port); 23cm
    1947. 2nd ed.
Climbing reminiscences.

*139. **The fountain of the sun: unfinished journeys in Ethiopia and the Ruwenzori**
London: Parrish, 1957. 240p, 33 plates; ill, maps, ports; 23cm
Travels in Ethiopia and climbing on Ruwenzori, with an appendix on the mountains of Ethiopia.

BUXTON, Edward North (1840–1924)
Brewer. A.C. member. He took part in several important Alpine first ascents. See [20].

BUXTON, Sir Thomas Fowell (1837–1916)
See [20].

BYNE, Eric (1911–69)
British climber, who made a major contribution to Peak District climbers' guidebooks.

*140. **High peak: the story of walking and climbing in the Peak District**
By ... and Geoffrey Sutton
London: Secker & Warburg, 1966. 256p, 25 plates (incl. facsims, ports); 23cm
He highlights the contribution made by gritstone training to post-war achievements in rock-climbing.

CANADIAN PACIFIC RAILWAY

141. **Mountaineering in the Canadian Alps**
?: C.P.R., 1901, 10p; ill; obl. 8vo.
One example of the publicity material that
Whymper helped to produce.

CARR, Glyn (pseud. Showell Styles)
His detective fiction written under this pseudonym. Creator of the amateur detective, actor-
manager Sir Abercrombie Lewker. The stories
involve climbing situations. Many titles: see **Appendix IV.**

CARR, Herbert Reginald Culling
Schoolmaster. Prominent in Welsh climbing in
1920s and author of the first C.C. guidebook to
Snowdon and the Beddgelert district.

*142. **The mountains of Snowdonia: in history, the
sciences, literature and sport**
[By ... and others]
Edited by ... and George A. Lister
London: John Lane Bodley Head, 1925. xx, 405p,
6 fold. maps (some col), 29 plates (some col);
23cm
Crosby Lockwood, 1948. 2nd ed. revised xiv,
312p.

CASEWIT, Curtis W.

143. **The mountaineering handbook, an invitation to
climbing**
By ... and Dick Pownall.
Philadelphia: Lippincott, 1968. 222p; ill;

CENTRAL COUNCIL OF PHYSICAL RECREATION

144. **Safety on mountains**
By the staff of Plas y Brenin, the Snowdonia
National Recreation Centre. Illustrated by Gordon
F. Mansell.
London: C.C.P.R.,
1961. Reprinted. 41p; ill; 16cm
1962. 3rd ed. 40p; ill; 15cm

CHAPIN, Frederick H.
American climber.

*145. **Mountaineering in Colorado: the peaks about Estes
Park**
Boston: Appalachian M.C.,
1889.
1890. 2nd ed. xii [xvi], 168p [156], 11 plates;
20cm
London: Sampson Low,
1890. Same as 2nd U.S.A. edition.

CHAPMAN, Frederick Spencer (1907–71)
British schoolmaster, traveller and mountaineer. He
led an adventurous life but is best known for his
ascent of Chomolhari. **One man's jungle** (Chatto &
Windus, 1975) is a biography of Chapman, written
by Ralph Barker (qv).

146. **Helvellyn to Himalaya: including an account of the
first ascent of Chomolhari**
London: Chatto & Windus, 1940. xvi, 285p, 48
plates (incl. ports) 23cm Also published under the
title **Memoirs of a mountaineer** with another of his
books, **Lhasa, the holy city.**

*147. **Northern Lights: the official account of the British
Arctic air-route expedition 1930–1931**
London: Chatto & Windus,
1932.
1932. 2nd imp.
1933. 3rd imp.
1934. 4th ptg (1st cheap ed.) xvi, 264p, map,
32 plates; 26cm

CHURCHILL, George Cheetham (1822–1906)
Solicitor, scientist and Alpine traveller. A.C.
member. See [309].

CLARK, Ronald William (b. 1916)
Journalist, writer and mountain historian.

*148. **The splendid hills: the life and photographs of
Vittorio Sella 1859–1943**
London: Phoenix, 1948. xii, 35p, 118 plates; 30cm

*149. **The early Alpine guides**
London: Phoenix, 1949. 208p, 32 plates (incl.
ports); 22cm

*150. **The Victorian mountaineers**
London: Batsford, 1953. 232p; ill, ports; 23cm

151. **Come climbing with me**
Illustrated by T. K. Beck.
London: Muller, 1955. 160p; ill; 19cm
Written for children.

152. **A picture history of mountaineering**
London: Hulton Press, 1956. 154p (chiefly ill. incl.
facsims, ports); 29cm

153. **Great moments in mountaineering**
Illustrated by Thomas K. Beck.
London: Phoenix, 1956. 128p; ill; 19cm
Written for children.

154. **Six great mountaineers**
London: Hamilton, 1956. 203p, 6 plates (ports);
19cm
Written for children.

*155. **Mountaineering in Britain: a history from the
earliest times to the present day**
By ... and Edward C. Pyatt.
London: Phoenix, 1957. 288p, 73 plates (incl.
ports); 25cm

156. **The true book about mountaineering**
Illustrated by F. Stocks May.
London: Muller, [1957]. 143p; ill; 20cm
Written for children.

*157. **An eccentric in the Alps: the story of the Rev.
W.A.B. Coolidge**
London: Museum Press, 1959. 224p, 17 plates
(incl. facsim, ports); 23cm

*158. **The day the rope broke: the story of a great
Victorian tragedy**
London: Secker & Warburg, 1965. 221p, 4 plates;
23cm
Examination of the Matterhorn disaster.

159 **The Alps**
London: Weidenfield & Nicolson, 1973. 288p; ill
(some col), ports; 26cm
General survey.

160. **Men, myths and mountains**
London: Weidenfeld & Nicolson, 1977. 304p; ill; 26cm. [First published in U.S.A.].

CLARK, Simon

161. **The Puma's claw**
London: Hutchinson, 1959. 223p, 17 plates (1 col); ill, maps, group port; 22cm
Cambridge Andean expedition to Pumasillo.

CLEARE, John S. (b. 1936)
British climber and outstanding mountain photographer, who has worked on most of the television rock-climbing spectaculars filmed in Britain. **See** also [745] & Appendix V.

*162. **Sea cliff climbing in Britain**
By ... and Robin Collomb.
London: Constable, 1973. 189p; ill, maps; 25cm

163. **Mountains**
London: Macmillan, 1975. 256p; ill (some col), maps, ports (some col); 24cm [Also in paper back.]
Highlights of world mountaineering and mountaineers.

CLISSOLD, Frederick

164. **Narrative of an ascent to the summit of Mont Blanc, August 18, 1822: with an appendix upon the sensations experienced at great elevations**
London: Rivingtons and Cochran, 1823. [4], 56p; 22cm
The fifteenth ascent.

CLYDE, Norman (1885–1972)
American schoolmaster, turned mountaineer and guide, who made more than 100 first ascents in the Sierra Nevada, mostly alone.

*165. **Norman Clyde of the Sierra Nevada**
By ..., with foreward by Francis Farquhar, prologue by Jules Eichorn, and a long letter by Smoke Blanchard.
San Francisco: Scrimshaw Press, 1971. 180p.

CLYDESDALE, Marquess of Douglas and

166. **The pilots' book of Everest**
By ... and D. F. M'Intyre.
Edinburgh: Wm Hodge & Co., 1936. xvi, 209p, 4 maps, 33 plates (incl. ports); 24cm
1933 aerial survey expedition.

COLE, Mrs. Henry Warwick

*167 **A lady's tour round Monte Rosa: with visits to the Italian valleys of Anzasca, Mantalone, Camasco, Sesia, Lys, Challant, Aosta, and Cogne, in a series of excursions in the years 1850–56–58**
London: Longmans, 1859. xii, 402p; ill, col. map, 4 col. plates; 22cm

COLEMAN, Arthur Philemon (1852–1939)
Canadian scientist and explorer. Active in 1880s.

*168. **The Canadian Rockies: new and old trails**
Toronto: Frowde, 1911.
London: Fisher Unwin, 1911. 384p, 4 maps (some col. & fold); 31 plates; 23cm
One of the most interesting accounts of Canadian mountain exploration and climbing.

COLEMAN, Edmund Thomas (c. 1823–92)
Artist and mountaineer. Original A.C. member. He climbed in the Alps and Cascades.

169. **Scenes from the snowfields: illustrations of the upper ice world of Mont Blanc**
London: Longmans, 1859. viii, 47p, 12 plates (col); 54cm

COLLIE, John Norman (1859–1942)
Scientist and mountaineer and one of the best-loved figures in British mountaineering. A.C. President 1920–2. Particularly remembered for his pioneer work in Skye and the Canadian Rockies, with Stutfield (qv). He accompanied Mummery to Nanga Parbat in 1895 and his book contains a full account of that unfortunate expedition. **See** also [387] & [769].

*170. **Climbing on the Himalaya and other mountain ranges**
Edinburgh: Douglas, 1902. xii, 315p, 3 fold. maps, 18 plates; 23cm

COLLINS, Francis, Arnold

171. **Mountain climbing**
Toronto: Goodchild, 1923. vi, 314p, 15 plates; 20cm
London: John Long, 1924. vi, 314p, 15 plates; 20cm
Superficial general reference book.

COLLOMB, Robin Gabriel (b. 1930?)
Publisher, writer, mountaineer and artist, with special interest in climbers' guidebooks (mainly Alpine). **See** also [162].

172. **A dictionary of mountaineering**
London: Blackie, 1957. 175p; ill; 20cm

173. **Alpine points of view: or, Contemporary scenes from the Alps, including some observations and opinions of an itinerant alpinist**
London: Spearman, 1961. 239p; ill; 23cm
Alpine experiences; illustrated with his own drawings.

CONDON, T. ,
See [889].

CONWAY, William Martin, Baron Conway of Allington (1856–1937)
Traveller, mountaineer, art connoisseur. A.C. President 1902–4. He undertook important expeditions to the Karakoram, South America and Spitsbergen. Also collaborated with Coolidge (qv) in a series of climbers' guidebooks. Biography: The Conways: a history of three generations (Museum Press, 1966) by Joan Evans. **See** also [189] & [918].

*174. **Zermatt pocket-book: a guide-book to the Pennine Alps, from the Simplon to Arolla; intended for the use of mountaineers**
London: E. Stanford, 1881. [4], 140p; 14 cm
The progenitor of all modern Alpine guidebooks.

*175. **Climbing and exploration in the Karakoram-Himalayas**
Illustrated by A. D. McCormick.
London: Fisher Unwin, 1894. xxviii, 709p; ill,

fold. map; 26cm. Plus supplementary volume of scientific reports and maps. Also limited edition of 150 copies of which 125 were for sale, numbered and signed by Conway & McCormick, with duplicate proofs on Japan silk tissue. 2v. (4v. with reports & maps).

*176. **The Alps from end to end**
With 100 full page illustrations by A. D. Mc-Cormick. [Chapter by W. A. B. Coolidge]
London: Constable,
    1895. xii, 403p, 100 plates; 25cm
    1895. 2nd, 3rd, 4th imp.
    1900. Cheap ed. viii, 300p
    1904, Reprint
    1905, Reprint.
London: Nelson,
    [1910]. Shilling Library series
London: Cape,
    1933. Travellers Library ed.

*177. **The first crossing of Spitsbergen: being an account of an inland journey of exploration and survey, with descriptions of several mountain ascents, . . .etc.**
With contributions by J. W. Gregory, A. Trevor-Battye and E. J. Garwood.
London: Dent, 1897. xii, 371p, 8 col. plates; ill, maps, ports; 25cm

178. **With ski and sledge over Arctic glaciers**
London: Dent, 1898. x, 240p, 14 plates; 21cm
Sequel to [177].

*179 **The Bolivian Andes: a record of climbing and exploration in the Cordillera Real in the years 1898 and 1900**
London: Harper, 1901. x, 403p, 55 plates; 23cm

*180. **Aconcagua and Tierra del Fuego: a book of climbing, travel and exploration**
London: Cassell, 1902. xii, 252p, fold. map, 19 plates; 23cm

181. **The Alps**
Described by . . . Painted by A. D. McCormick.
London: A. & C. Black,
    1904. x, 294p, 70 col. plates; 23cm. Also large paper edition, limited to 300 numbered copies, signed by the publishers.
    1910. [Cheap ed.] with 23 illus. from photographs by L. Edna Walter. viii, 294p.
    1914.

182. **Mountain memories: pilgrimage of romance**
London: Cassell, 1920 }[x] 282p, 16
New York: Funk & Wagnalls, 1920 } plates; 25cm
London: Cape, 1933. Revised ed. entitled **The autobiography of a mountain climber**

183. **The autobiography of a mountain climber**
London: Cape, 1933. 246p [248]; 17cm. Reissue of **Mountain memories**

COOK, Frederick A.
American doctor and polar explorer. He claimed to have made the first ascent of Mount McKinley but this was later proved to be false.

184. **To the top of the continent: discovery, exploration and adventure in sub-arctic Alaska. The first ascent of Mt. McKinley, 1903–1906**

New York: Doubleday
London: Hodder, 1908. xxiv, 321p, 47 plates (1 col); ill; maps, ports; 24cm

COOLIDGE, William Augustus Brevoort (1850–1926)
American anglo-phile, mountaineer and mountain historian. He climbed extensively in the Alps with his aunt, Meta Brevoort, and his dog 'Tschingel'. He edited the **Alpine Journal** and revised part of Ball's **Alpine Guide**, apart from writing innumerable articles on mountain affairs. His literary style is generally extremely dull but his books are invaluable for detail and accuracy. See also [157], [274], [301], [830] & Appendix I & VI.

185. **Swiss travel and Swiss guide books**
London: Longmans, 1889. xii, 336p; 20 cm

186. **Climbs in the Alps made in the years 1865 to 1900**
London: Privately printed J. E. Francis, [1900]. 23p; 20cm. Limited edition of 100 numbered copies.

*187. **The Alps in nature and history**
By . . . with map, illustrations and diagrams.
London: Methuen 1908. xx, 440p, 8 maps, 20 plates; 23cm
His most readable and useful book.

188. **Alpine studies**
London: Longmans, 1912. xiv, 307p, 16 plates; 24cm

*†189.**Conway and Coolidge's Climbers' Guides**
A set of fifteen volumes covering the western and central Alps only.

Climbers' guide to the central Pennine Alps
By W. M. Conway.
London: Fisher Unwin, 1890. viii, 156p; 13cm

Climbers' guide to the eastern Pennine Alps
By W. M. Conway.
London: Fisher Unwin, 1891. xii, 152p; 13cm

The Lepontine Alps
By W. M. Conway and W. A. B. Coolidge.
London: Fisher Unwin, 1892. xx '06p; 13cm

The central Alps of the Dauphiny
By W. A. B. Coolidge, H. Duhamel and F. Perrin.
London: Fisher Unwin,
    1892. xx, 248p; 13cm
    1905. 2nd ed. revised. 17cm

The chain of Mont Blanc
By Louis Kurz.
London: Fisher Unwin, 1892. xxx, 143p; 13cm

The Adula Alps
By W. A. B. Coolidge.
London: Fisher Unwin, 1893. xx, 192p; 13cm

The mountains of Cogne
By G. Yeld and W. A. B. Coolidge.
London: Fisher Unwin, 1893. xvi, 176p; 13cm

The range of the Tödi
By W. A. B. Coolidge
London: Fisher Unwin, 1894. xxxii, 167p; 13cm

The Bernese Oberland

(i) From the Gemmi to the Mönchjoch
By G. Hasler.
London: Fisher Unwin,
    1902. xviii, 164p; 13cm
    1909. 2nd ed. Part I
    1910. 2nd ed. Part II

(ii) From the Mönchjoch to the Grimsel
By W. A. B. Coolidge
London: Fisher Unwin, 1904. xx, 196p; 13cm

(iii) Dent de Morcles to the Gemmi
By H. Dübi.
London: Fisher Unwin, 1907. xxiv, 136p; 13cm

(iv) Grimsel to the Uri Rothstock
By H. Dübi.
London: Fisher Unwin, 1908. 2v. xxx, 111p: xxiv, 132p; 13cm

The Alps of the Bernina
By E. L. Strutt.
London: Fisher Unwin, 1910. 2v. xxiv, 234p, map: xiv, 232p; 13cm

COPELAND, Fanny S.

190. **Beautiful mountains: in the Jugoslav Alps**
Split: Jugoslav Bureau, [1931]. 120p; ill.

CORBETT, Edmund Victor

191. **Great true mountain stories**
Selected and introduced by . . .
London: Arco,
    1957. x, 213p; 23cm
    1958. Reprinted.
Twenty-four extracts, mainly from books included in this bibliography.

COVERLEY-PRICE, Victor
British diplomat, artist and mountaineer. A.C. member.

192. **An artist among mountains**
With 33 illus. from drawings by the author.
London: Hale, 1957. 231p, 33 plates; 23cm
Climbing reminiscences.

COWELL, John Jermyn (1838–67)
Made the first ascents of the Grand Paradis and other peaks in the eastern Graian Alps. See [20].

COXHEAD, Elizabeth
Journalist, novelist and climber.

*193. **One green bottle**
London: Collins,
    1951
    1955. Reprint
    1955. Fontana paperback
Bath: Chivers,
    1973. Portway reprint.
By far the best climbing novel.

CRABB, Edmund William

194. **The challenge of the summit: stories of mountains and men**
London: Paternoster Press, [1957]. 152p, 16 plates; 19cm

CREW, Peter (b. 1942)
Leading English rock-climber, who has also made a major contribution in the field of Alpine guidebooks. See also [752] & Appendix VI.

195. **Encyclopaedic dictionary of mountaineering**
London: Constable, 1968. 140p; 16 plates; 23cm

CROUCHER, Norman

196. **High hopes**
London: Hodder, 1976. 160p, 8 plates (incl. ports); 21cm
Mountaineering by a physically handicapped person.

CUNNINGHAM, Carus Dunlop (1856–96)
Scottish climber and early advocate of Scottish winter climbing.

*197. **The pioneers of the Alps**
By . . . and Capt. W. de W. Abney.
London: Sampson Low,
    1887. xii, 287p, 24 plates (incl. ports); 33cm.
    Also large paper (41cm) edition of 50 copies numbered and signed by Cunningham.
    1888. 2nd ed. viii, 180p, 22 plates (ports); 30cm
Illustrated with Abney's superb photographic portraits. The second edition is the nicest version.

198 **A facsimile of Christian Almer's 'Führerbuch', 1856–94**
Reproduced under the superintendence of . . . and W. de W. Abney.
With an introduction and a photogravure of Christian Almer.
London: Sampson Low, 1896. [4], xxxii, 261p; facsims; 19cm. Limited edition of 200 copies.
This publication caused a furore in Alpine circles.

DAUDET, Alphonse (1840–97)
French novelist

199. **Tartarin on the Alps**
London: ?,   1885.
London: ?,   1887.
London: Dent,   1902. 368p
From the original: **Tartarin sur les Alpes** (Paris, 1885)
The second of the Tartarin burlesque novels.

DAUNT, Achilles

200. **Crag, glacier and avalanche: narratives of daring and disaster**
London: Nelson 1889. 212p, 12 plates; 18cm

DAVIDSON, Art
American mountaineer.

*201. **Minus 148° : the winter ascent of Mt. McKinley**
New York: W. W. Norton, 1969. 218p; 16 plates; 23cm. Published in U.K. as **The coldest climb**
The most powerful struggle against a mountain since Annapurna.

202. **The coldest climb: the winter ascent of Mt. McKinley**
London: Bodley Head, 1970. [2], 218p, 16 plates

(incl.ports); 23cm. Published in U.S.A. as **Minus 148°**

DAVIDSON, Mavis
See [367].

DAVIES, John Llewelyn (1826–1916)
Clergyman and social reformer. Original A.C. member. See [18].

DAVIES, Joseph Sanger (? – 1900)

203. **Dolomite strongholds: the last untrodden Alpine peaks. An account of ascents of the Croda di Lago, the Little and Great Zinnen, the Cinque Torri, the Fünffingerspitze and the Langkofel.**
With map and illus. by . . .
London: Bell,
  1894. xii, 176p, col. map, 10 plates (2 col); 20cm
  1896. 2nd ed. Smaller format and with different gilt block on front cover.

DE BEER, Sir Gavin Rylands (1899–1792)
Author of several authoritative books on early travellers in the Alps and Switzerland, touching on mountaineering. His published works include **Escape to Switzerland** (Penguin, 1945); **Speaking of Switzerland** (Eyre & Spottiswoode, 1952); and **Alps and elephants: Hannibal's march** (Bles, 1955). See also [120].

*204. **Early travellers in the Alps**
London: Sidgwick & Jackson,
  1930. xx, 204p, 40 plates; ill, facsims, maps; 23cm
  1966. New ed. Paperback

*†205.**Alps and men: pages from forgotten diaries of travellers and tourists in Switzerland**
London: Arnold, 1932. 256p, 16 plates (incl. ports); 23cm

*†206.**Travellers in Switzerland**
Oxford: O.U.P., 1949. xviii, 584p, 23 plates; 23cm
Lists, arranged in chronological, topographical and alphabetical order.

DE LÉPINEY, Jacques and Tom
French climbers, who made many fine climbs in 1920s.

*207. **Climbs on Mont Blanc**
Translated [from the French] by Sydney Spencer.
London: Arnold, 1930. xii, 179p, 16 plates; 22cm
From the original: **Sur les crêtes du Mont Blanc** (Chambéry: Dardel, 1929)

DELVILLE, E.

208. **Description of & guide to Jasper Park**
By . . . and −. Bridgland.
Ottawa: Dept. of Interior, 1917. 97p; ill; 26cm
Canadian Rockies.

DENMAN, Earl L.
Canadian.
209. **Alone to Everest**
London: Collins,
  1954. 255p, 7 plates; ill, maps, port; 22cm
  1956. Fontana paperback
Includes his ascents of the Virunga Mountains.

DENT, Clinton Thomas (1850–1912)
Surgeon, mountaineer and photographer. A.C. President 1887–9. He made the first ascent of the Dru in 1878 and visited the Caucasus four times during the years 1886–95.

*210. **Above the snowline: mountaineering sketches between 1870 and 1880**
With 2 engravings by Edward Whymper and an illustration by Percy MacQuoid.
London: Longman, 1885. xiv, 327p, 3 plates; 20cm

*211. **Mountaineering**
By . . . and others. Ilustrated by H. G. Willink and others.
London: Longman,
  1892. xx, 439p, 13 plates; ill; 20cm. Also large paper ed.
  1892. 2nd ed. [imp].
  1900. 3rd ed. xx, 464p
  1901. Reprint.
An omnibus work in the Badminton Library series: humorous.

DESIO,Ardito (b. 1897)
Italian geologist and mountaineer: leader of numerous expeditions.

*212 **Ascent of K.2: second highest mountain in the world**
Translated [from the Italian] by David Moore.
London: Elek Books, 1955. 239p, 24 plates (incl. ports); 23cm
From the original: **La Conquista del K.2** (Milan: Garzanti, 1954)

DIAS, John

213. **The Everest adventure: story of the second Indian expedition**
Delhi: Min. Inform. & Broadcasting, 1965. 63p [65]. plates (some col); 29cm.
The 1962 attempt.

DIEMBERGER, Kurt (b. 1932)
Leading Austrian mountaineer, who made the first ascent of Broad Peak.

*214. **Summits and secrets**
Translated [from the German] by Hugh Merrick.
London: Allen & Unwin, 1971. 344p, 56 plates; ill, maps, ports; 24cm
Leicester: Cordee, 1976. Reprinted.
Well illustrated autobiography. Includes details of the death of Hermann Buhl on Chogolisa.

DINGLE, Graeme

Leading New Zealand mountaineer and now Director of the Outdoor Pursuits Centre of New Zealand based near Mount Ruapehu. He has made a number of severe climbs in Europe and the Andes, including the first traverse of Yerupaja in 1968.

*214a.**Two against the Alps**
Christchurch: Whitcombe & Tombs, 1972. 153p; ill.
First winter traverse of the Southern Alps of New Zealand in 1971.

*214b. **Wall of shadows: Jannu the New Zealand adventure**
Auckland/London: Hodder, 1976. xiv, 177p, [163], 24 plates (mostly col); 24cm.
Attempt on the very severe North Face.

DISLEY, John
British athlete and mountaineer.

215. **Tackle climbing this way**
Line drawings by Gordon Mansell.
London: S. Paul,
1959. 127p, 17 plates; ill, maps, port; 20cm
1968. New ed.
1977. Revised (soft cover) ed.

DITTERT, René
Swiss mountaineer.

*216. **Forerunners to Everest: the story of the two Swiss expeditions of 1952**
By . . . , Gabriel Chevalley and Raymond Lambert.
English version by Malcolm Barnes.
London: Allen & Unwin, 1954.
New York: Harper, [1954].
London Hamilton, 1956. Panther paperback
From the original: **Avant-Premières a l'Everest**
(Paris: Arthaud, 1953)
These Swiss expeditions paved the way for the British success.

DIXON, Christopher Michael

217. **Rock-climbing**
London: Biblick Pub.,
1958, 48p; ill; 13 x 20cm
1968. 2nd ed.
Wakefield: E.P. Pub.,
1975. New ed. by Dennis Kemp. 32p; ill (some col); 14 x 21cm
'Know the Game' series.

DOCHARTY, William McKnight

218. **A selection of some 900 British and Irish mountain tops**
Compiled and arranged by . . .
Edinburgh: Darien Press for the author, 1954.
124p, 9 fold. plates; 25cm
Lists of mountains. Memento private edition.

219. **Supplement to a selection of some 900 British and Irish mountain tops: and a selection of 1000 tops under 2500 feet**
Compiled and arranged by . . .
Edinburgh: Darien Press for the author, 1962. 2v.
259p, plates; 25cm

DODDERIDGE, M.

220. **Man on the Matterhorn**
Edited by . . . from Edward Whymper's **Scrambles amongst the Alps**
London: Murray, 1940, [8], 135p; ill, map; 17cm

DODSON, J. G.
Politician. A.C. member. See [20]

DOIG, Desmond
See [371].

DOLBIER, M.
221. **Nowhere near Everest**
New York: ?, 1955. 56p; ill;
Amerian version of [321].

DOUGHTY, Joseph Henry (1889–1936)
Schoolmaster, whose example did much to improve the literary qualities of mountaineering club journals.

*222. **Hill-writing of J. H. Doughty**
Collected by H. M. Kelly.
Manchester: Rucksack Club, 1937. xx [xviii], 150p, 2 plates (ports); 22cm

DOUGLAS, John Scott

223. **Summits of adventure: the story of famous mountain climbs and mountain climbers**
London: Muller, 1955. xii, 227p, 16 plates; 21cm
Better than average gloss of world mountaineering.

DOUGLAS, William Orville (b. 1898)
American judge and mountaineer.

224. **Of men and mountains**
New York: Harper, 1950.
London: Gollancz, 1951. xiv, 338p; map (endpaper); 23cm
Outdoor life in the Cascades.

225. **Exploring the Himalaya**
New York: Random House, 1958. 177p; ill; 21cm
Written for children: miscellany or history, peoples and customs.

DOWNER, Arthur Cleveland

226. **Mountaineering ballads**
London: C. Murray, 1905. 47p.

DUDLEY, Ernest
Writer and broadcaster.

*227. **Rangi: highland rescue dog**
London: Harvill Press, 1970. 126p, 16 plates (incl. ports); 22cm
Rangi was the first search dog trained by Hamish MacInnes (qv).

DU FAUR, Freda
Australian mountaineer, who made many notable climbs during the years 1909–13; particularly the first traverse of the summit ridge of Mount Cook.

*228. **The conquest of Mount Cook and other climbs: an account of four seasons' mountaineering on the Southern Alps of New Zealand.**
London: Allen & Unwin,
1915. 250p, 40 plates; 27cm
1937. 2nd ed. xv, 230p; ill; 25cm

DUNN, Robert

*229. **The shameless diary of an explorer**
New York: Outing Pub., 1907. viii, 297p, 2 maps, 11 plates; 18cm
Story of very rough exploration round Mt. McKinley in 1903 with Dr. Cook (qv).

DUNSHEATH, Joyce
English traveller and mountaineer. She has also published **Afghan quest** (Harrap, 1961), an account

of an expedition to the Mir Samir region of the Hindu Kush.

230. Mountains and memsahibs
By the members of the Abinger Himalayan Expedition 1956.
London: Constable, 1958. x, 198p, 9 plates (incl. ports); 22cm

231. Guest of the Soviets: Moscow and the Caucasus 1957
London: Constable, 1959. viii, 183p, map, 7 plates (incl. port); 23cm

DURHAM, William Edward (1857–1921)
Clergyman and mountaineer, who climbed extensively in the Alps. Killed in rock-climbing accident on Tryfan, North Wales.

232. Summer holidays in the Alps 1898–1914
London: Fisher Unwin, 1916. 207p, 48 plates (incl. ports); 28cm

DUTTON, E. A. T.
*233. Kenya Mountain
With an introduction by Hilaire Belloc.
London: Cape,
1929. xvi, 219p, fold. map, 56 plates; 27cm
1930. 2nd ed. revised (minor corrections).
The classic book on Mount Kenya.

DYRENFURTH, Günter Oskar (1886–1975)
German–American mountaineer and geologist. Leader of numerous expeditions, particularly the international attempt on Kanchenjunga in 1930, in which Frank Smythe (qv) took part.

*†234.To the third pole: the history of the high Himalaya
With contributions by Erwin Schneider. Translated from the German by Hugh Merrick.
London: Werner Laurie, 1955. xxx, 233p, 48 plates; 26cm
From the original: **Zum Dritten Pol: Die Achttausender der Erde** (Munich: Nymphenburger, 1952)
History of attempts on the 8000-metre peaks.

ECKENSTEIN, Oscar Johannes Ludwig (1859–1921)
Railway engineer and mountaineer, who climbed with Conway (qv) and Aleister Crowley. He collaborated with August Lorria in producing **The Alpine Portfolio** (1889), a collection of 100 photographs.

235. The Karakorams and Kashmir: an account of a journey
London: Fisher Unwin, 1896. xvi, 253p; 20cm

EDWARDS, Amelia Blandford
*236. Untrodden peaks and unfrequented valleys: a midsummer ramble in the Dolomites
London: Longmans,
1873. xxvi, 385p, fold. map, 8 plates; 24cm
Leipzig: Tauchnitz,
1873. 302p; 23cm
?. ?, 1889.
London: Routledge,
1890. 2nd ed. Pictorial cover
1893. 2nd ed. xxvi, 389p
189–. 3rd ed. 389p, 9 plates; 23cm
nd. 3rd ed.

The various editions are further complicated by the fact that the book was also published under its subsidiary title **Midsummer ramble.**

237. Midsummer ramble in the Dolomites
London: Routledge,
1889. 2nd ed. 389p, map, 9 plates; 24cm
[1890]. 2nd ed. Same as 1890 edition of **Untrodden Peaks** apart from title
nd. 3rd ed. xxvi, 389p. Same as **Untrodden peaks?**
New York: Dutton,
nd. 3rd ed. xxvi, 389p. Same as **Untrodden peaks?**
London: Routledge, 1898. 4th ed.

All the foregoing appear to be the same as **Untrodden peaks and unfrequented valleys** apart from the title.

[EDWARDS, John Menlove (1910–58)]
Psychiatrist and leading British rock-climber in 1930s. Editor of C.C. guidebooks to North Wales.

*238. Samson: the life and writings of Menlove Edwards
Edited, with a biographical memoir, by Geoffrey Sutton and Wilfrid Noyce.
[Stockport: Cloister Press, 1961]. vi[x], 122p, 8 plates (incl. ports); 23cm

EGELER, Cornelis Geoffrey
Dutch mountaineer, who took Lionel Terray (qv) to the Andes as his guide.

239. The untrodden Andes: climbing adventures in the Cordillera Blanca, Peru
by . . . in co-operation with T. de Booy. Translated from the Dutch by W. E. James.
London: Faber, 1955. 203p [201], 32 plates; maps, ports; 22cm
From the original: **Naar onbestegen Andes toppen** (Amsterdam: Scheltens & Giltay, 1953)

EGGLER, Albert
Swiss mountaineer

240. The Everest-Lhotse adventure
By . . . Translated [from the German] by Hugh Merrick.
London: Allen & Unwin, 1957. 224p, 25 plates (1 col); maps, ports; 23cm
From the original: **Gipfel über den Wolken** (Berne: Hallwag, 1956)
Swiss ascent of Everest and first ascent of Lhotse.

EISELIN, Max
Swiss sports writer and mountaineer.

*241. The ascent of Dhaulagiri
Translated from the German by E. Noel Bowman.
London: O.U.P., 1961. xii, 160p, 29 plates (5 col) (incl. ports); 23cm
From the original: **Erfolg am Dhaulagiri** (Zurich: Orell-Füssli, 1960)

ELLIOT, Claude Aurelius (1888–1973)
English schoolmaster and member of Winthrop Young's climbing circle, who would have been a front-rank mountaineer but for an early rock-climbing accident. See [938].

ELWOOD, Harold

242. **The Queen's University expedition to the Taurus, 1969**
Belfast: Queen's Univ. M.C., 1970. 96p, fold. map, ill; 22cm
Includes outlines of previous expeditions and basic information on Turkey and its mountains.

EMMONS, Arthur Brewster 3rd (1910—62)
American mountaineer who took part in pre-war expeditions to Minya Konka and Nanda Devi. See [134].

ENGEL, Claire Eliane (—1977)
French writer, whose work tends to be inaccurate in matters of detail.

243. **A History of mountaineering in the Alps**
London: Allen & Unwin,
1950. 296p, 24 plates; 25cm
1971. Revised and enlarged edition entitled **Mountaineering in the Alps: an historical survey**

244. **They came to the hills**
London: Allen & Unwin, 1952. 276p, 17 plates (incl. facsims, ports); 23cm
Biographical sketches, mostly of nineteenth century climbers.

245. **Mont Blanc**
An anthology compiled by ...
London: Allen & Unwin, 1965. 232p, 48 plates (incl. facsims, ports); 25cm
From the original: **Mont Blanc** (Paris: Editions d'Art et d'Histoire, 1965)

*246. **Mountaineering in the Alps: an historical survey**
London: Allen & Unwin, 1971. 318p, 24 plates (incl. facsims); 24cm. Revised & enlarged edition of **History of mountaineering in the Alps.**

ESCARRA, Jean (1885—1955)
French lawyer and mountaineer.

*247. **Himalayan assault: the French Himalayan expedition 1936**
[By Jean Escarra, Henry de Segogne and others]
Translated [from the French] by Nea E. Morin.
London: Methuen, 1938. xvi, 204p, 48 plates; 23cm
From the original: **Karakoram: Expedition française a l'Himalaya 1936** (Paris: Flammarion, 1938)
Attempt on Gasherbrum I (Hidden Peak).

ETHERTON, P. T.
Soldier and writer, who helped to organize the Houston-Mount Everest expedition in 1933. See [260].

EVANS .Sir Robert Charles S. (b. 1918)
British mountaineer, Principal of University College of North Wales. A.C. President 1968—70. Member of several Himalayan expeditions – Annapurna IV, Cho Oyu, Everest, Kanchenjunga.

*248. **Eye on Everest: a sketch book from the great Everest expedition**
London: Dobson, 1955. 123p; ill; 26cm
A delightful book for children.

*249. **Kanchenjunga: the untrodden peak**
London: Hodder, 1956. xx, 187p, 37 plates (5 col); ill, ports; 23cm. Published in U.S.A. as **Kanchenjunga climbed.**
First ascent.

250. **Kanchenjunga climbed**
U.S.A. edition of **Kanchenjunga: the untrodden peak**

251. **On climbing**
London: Museum Press, 1956. 191p, 32 plates; ill, maps; 24cm
Mixture of instruction and reminiscence.

FARQUHAR, Francis Peloubet
American mountaineer and mountain historian. President of the Sierra Club and editor of their Bulletin. See also [106] and Appendix I.

*252. **Exploration of the Sierra Nevada**
San Francisco: Col. Hist. Soc., 1925. 58p

*253. **Place names of the High Sierra**
San Francisco: Sierra Club, 1926. xii, 128p; 25cm. Edition of 1,000 copies of which 200 were printed on all-rag paper.

*254. **First ascents in the United States, 1642—1900**
San Francisco: Grabhorn Press, 1948. 12p.

*255. **History of the Sierra Nevada**
Berkeley: Univ. Calif. Press, 1966. xiv, 262p; ill, maps;

FARRAR, John Percy (1857—1929)
Soldier, businessman and mountaineer, who was a leading alpinist of his day. President A.C. 1917—19. Many contributions to the **Alpine Journal**.See also [938].

*256. **The first ascent of the Finsterraarhorn: a re-examination**
London: Spottiswoode, 1913. 38p, 3 plates; 21cm. [Reprinted from the **Alpine Journal**].

FAY, Charles Ernest (1846—1931)
American professor, who climbed with Collie (qv). First President of the A.A.C. and one of the advocates of climbing in Canada. See [26].

FEDDEN, Henry Robin Romilly (b. 1908)
Writer and traveller.

*257. **Alpine ski-tour: an account of the High Level Route**
London: Putnam, 1956. 93p, 24 plates; ill, map; 29cm
The classic ski mountaineering route from Chamonix to Zermatt.

*258. **The Enchanted Mountains: a quest in the Pyrenees**
London: Murray, 1962. 124p, 2 maps, 7 plates; 22cm
A search for the little known Los Encantados.

FEDERATED MOUNTAIN CLUBS OF NEW ZEALAND

259. **Safety in the mountains**
Wellington: F.M.C.N.Z., 1963. 5th ed. 120p; ill; 19cm
See also [108].

FELLOWS, Peregrine Forbes Morant (1883–1955)
British airman.

260. **First over Everest: the Houston-Mount Everest expedition 1933**
By . . . [and others]
London: John Lane Bodley Head, 1933. xx, 279p, 49 plates; ill, maps, ports; 25cm
Manchester: Cherry Tree Books, nd. Paperback.

FELLOWS, Sir Charles (1799–1860)
British archeologist, who made the fourteenth ascent of Mont Blanc with William Hawes, adopting a variation of the route, via the Mur de Côte. See also [357].

261. **A narrative of an ascent to the summit of Mont Blanc**
London: Thomas Davison, 1827. viii, 35p, facsim, 12 plates; 30cm. Fifty copies were printed for private circulation; a few have coloured plates.

FERLET, René
French mountaineer.

*262. **Aconcagua: South Face**
By . . . and Guy Poulet. Translated from the French by E. Noel Bowman.
London: Constable, 1956. xii, 209p, 18 plates (incl. ports); 23cm
From the original: **Victoire sur l'Aconcagua** (Paris: Flammarion, 1955)
A very severe climb during which several members of the team were badly frost bitten.

FIENNES, Sir Ranulph Twistleton-Wykeham–(b. 1944)
British soldier, explorer and mountaineer.

263. **Ice-fall in Norway**
London: Hodder, 1972. 160p, 16 plates (incl. ports); 23cm

FIELD, Alfred Ernest (1864–1949)
English mountaineer, who made first ascents in the Lake District with O. G. Jones (qv) and the Abraham brothers (qv). See [22].

FILIPPI, Filippo de (1869–1938)
Italian surgeon, scholar and mountain †raveller. He was the official recorder of the Duke of Abruzzi's famous expeditions, three great landmarks in mountaineering exploration. Filippi led the Italian Himalayan Scientific Expedition 1913–14.

*264. **The ascent of Mount St. Elias (Alaska) by H.R.H. Prince Luigi Amadeo di Savoia, Duke of the Abruzzi**
Narrated by . . . Illustrated by Vittorio Sella and translated [from the Italian] by Signora Linda Villara with the author's supervision.
London: Constable, 1900. xvi, 241p, 2 col. fold. maps, 34 plates (some fold.); 28cm. Also de luxe edition with mounted photographs; 30cm (100 copies on hand-made paper).
From the original: **La Spedizione di S.A.R. il Principe Luigi Amadeo di Savioa, Duca degli Abruzzi, al Monte Sant' Elia (Alaska): 1897** (Milan: Hoepli, 1900).

*265. **Ruwenzori: an account of the expedition of H.R.H. Prince Luigi Amadeo of Savoy, Duke of the Abruzzi**
[Translated from the Italian by Caroline de Filippi]
London: Constable, 1908. xvi, 403p, 5 maps, 32 plates (1 col); 27cm
From the original: **Il Ruwenzori** 2v. (Milan: Hoepli, 1909).

*266. **Karakoram and western Himalaya 1909: an account of the expedition of H.R.H. Prince Luigi Amadeo of Savoy, Duke of the Abruzzi**
By . . . With a preface by H.R.H. the Duke of the Abruzzi. [Translated from the Italian by Caroline de Filippi and H. T. Porter] Illustrations from photographs taken by Vittorio Sella.
London: Constable, 1912. xviii, 469p, 36 plates (2 col); 28cm. Plus portfolio of 18 photo panoramas and 3 maps. Also edition de luxe.
From the original: **La spedizione nel Karakoram e nell'Himalaya occidentale 1909** (Bologna: Zanicheli, 1911).

FINCH, George Ingle (1888–1969)
British scientist and mountaineer, who was on the 1922 Everest expedition. A.C. President 1959–61. See also [124] & [938].

*267. **The making of a mountaineer**
London: Arowsmith, 1924. 340p, 56 plates; 26cm. [Several impressions].

268. **Climbing Mount Everest**
London: G. Philip,
    1930. 72p; ill, map; 18cm
    1931. 2nd ed. [imp]
    1933. 3rd ed. [imp].

FIRSOFF, Valdemar Axel
Author of several books such as **The Cairngorms on foot and ski** (Hale; 1949) and **Arran with camera and sketchbook** (Hale, 1951).

269. **The Tatra Mountains**
[London]: Lindsay Drummond,
    [1942]. 128p; ill, maps; 24cm
    1946. 3rd imp.
Includes chapter on climbing: very little available in English.

FISHER, Joel E.

*270. **Bibliography of American mountain ascents**
A.A.C. Research Fund, 1946. var. pag (see below); 22cm
Comprises:
Canadian mountain ascents (103pp)
Eastern seaboard mountain ascents (16pp)
Mexican, Central and South American mountain ascents (25pp)
United States mountain ascents (except Pacific Coast States and the eastern seaboard) (60pp)
Prepared from mountaineering journals.

FISHER, Marnie

*271. **Expedition Yukon**
Edited by . . .
Nelson (Canada), 1972. 200p; ill; 26cm

Canadian centennial celebration expedition to the St. Elias Mountains in 1967, making many first ascents in the Centennial Range and elsewhere.

FITZGERALD, Edward Arthur (1871 – 1931)

British soldier and mountaineer, who led important expeditions to New Zealand and South America, and accompanied Conway (qv) on parts of his 1894 tour through the Alps. The light-hearted style used in writing about his New Zealand adventures met with much critical disapproval.

*272. **Climbs in the New Zealand Alps: being an account of travel and discovery**
By . . . and with contributions by Sir Martin Conway, Professor T. G. Bonney, C. L. Barrow.
London: Fisher Unwin,
    1896. xvi, 363p, 46 plates; fold. map (pocket); 25cm. Edition of 1000 copies. Also de luxe edition of 60 copies on Japanese paper, numbered and signed.
    1896. 2nd ed. [imp] . Edition of 500 copies.

*273. **The highest Andes: a record of the first ascent of Aconcagua and Tupungato in Argentina and the exploration of the surrounding valleys**
By . . . With chapters by Stuart Vignes and contributions by Prof. Bonney [and others] . With 2 maps by A. E. Lightbody.
London: Methuen, 1899, xvi, 390p, 2 fold. maps, 45 plates (1 fold.); 25cm. Also numbered edition of 60 copies.

FORBES, James David (1809–68)
Scottish scientist and traveller, whose views on the theory of glaciers conflicted with Tyndall's (qv). He made many observations and mountain expeditions in the Alps, Norway and Dauphiné. In 1841 he made the fourth (first British) ascent of the Jungfrau and, in 1842, the first British ascent of a virgin peak, the Stockhorn. Forbes spans the era from de Saussure to Alfred Wills and his books are the first English accounts of systematic Alpine exploration and description of various regions. Biography: **Life and letters of James David Forbes** (Macmillan, 1873) by J. C. Shairp, P. G. Tait and A. M. W. Adams-Reilly.

*274. **Travels through the Alps of Savoy and other parts of the Pennine chain with observations on the phenomena of glaciers**
Edinburgh. A. & C. Black.
    1843. x, 424p, 2 maps, 9 plates (2 col); 27cm
    1845. 2nd ed. revised xvi, 460p
    1855. Abridged edition entitled **The tour of Mont Blanc and of Monte Rosa**
1900. New edition revised and annotated by W.A.B. Coolidge. [Contains all Forbes' Alpine writings.]

275. **The tour of Mont Blanc and of Monte Rosa: being a personal narrative abridged from the Author's 'Travels in the Alps of Savoy'**
Edinburgh: A. & C. Black, 1855. x1, 320p; ill, maps; 17cm

*276. **Norway and its glaciers visited in 1851: followed by journals of excursions in the high Alps of Dauphiné, Berne and Savoy**
Edinburgh: A. & C. Black, 1853. xxiv, 349p, 2 maps (1 fold), 10 col. plates; 26cm

FORSTER, R. W. Elliot
See [18] & [20].

FOSTER, George Edward (1839/40–1906)
Banker and mountaineer, who made a number of first class ascents in the Alps. **See [22].**

FOX, Joseph Hoyland (1832–1915)
Brother-in-law of F. F. Tuckett (qv), whom he accompanied on many Alpine excursions.

277. **Holiday memories**
Wellington, Somerset: Privately printed by L. Tozer & Co., 1908. [6] , 147p; 28cm

FRANCIS, Godfrey Herbert (1927–60)
British mountaineer, killed on Pillar Rock, Lake District.

278. **Mountain climbing**
Diagrams drawn by Erik Thorn.
London: E.U.P.,
    1958. 192p; ill, 8 plates; 18cm
    1964. 2nd ed. 200p
This book in the 'Teach Yourself' series was B.M.C./A.S.C.C. sponsored when originally published but now overtaken by Blackshaw (qv).

FRANCO, Jean
French mountaineer.

*279. **Makalu: 8470 metres (27,790 feet). The highest peak yet conquered by an entire team**
Translated from the French by Denise Morin.
London: Cape, 1957. 256p, 21 plates (1 col); maps, ports; 21cm
From the original: **Makalu** (Paris: Arthaud, 1955).

*280. **At grips with Jannu**
By . . . and Lionel Terray. Translated from the French by Hugh Merrick.
London: Gollancz, 1967. 192p, 48 plates; 23cm
From the original: **Bataille pour le Jannu** (Paris: Gallimard, 1966).
The French ascent of Jannu in 1962 was the most difficult Himalayan climb accomplished at that time.

FRASER, Colin

*281. **The avalanche enigma**
London: Murray, 1966. xvi, 301p; ill, map, 36 plates (incl. facsim); 22cm
Deals with the work of the Swiss Federal Institute for Snow and Avalanche Research: the best English language book on the subject.

FREEMAN, Lewis R.

282. **On the roof of the Rockies: the great Columbia icefield of the Canadian Rockies**
New York: Dodd Mead, 1925.
London: Heinemann, 1926. 270p, 62 plates; 24cm
Photographic surveying expedition.

FRERE, Richard Burchmore

283. **Thoughts of a mountaineer**
London: Oliver & Boyd, 1952. vi, 177p, 8 plates; 19cm
Well-written reminiscences of climbing in Scotland.

FRESHFIELD, Douglas William (1845–1934)
English barrister, mountaineer, writer and poet. A.C. President 1893–5 and editor of the A.J. He was one of the greatest mountain explorers but his name is particularly linked with the Caucasus. He was one of the most scholarly and sensitive of mountain writers and was twice Chairman of the Society of Authors. Also a leading figure in the Royal Geographical Society. His published works include **Quips for cranks** (1923). **See also [211].**

284. **Across country from Thonon to Trent: rambles and scrambles in Switzerland**
London: Spottiswoode, 1865. [8], 135p; 23cm

*285. **Travels in the Central Caucasus and Bashan: including visists to Ararat and Tabeez; and ascents of Kazbek and Elbruz**
London: Longmans, 1869. xvi, 510p, 3 fold. maps, 4 plates (1 col); 22cm

*286. **Italian Alps: sketches in the mountains of Ticino, Lombardy, the Trentino and Venetia**
London: Longmans, 1875. xviii, 385p, 5 fold. maps, 9 plates; 21cm
Oxford: Blackwell, 1937. viii, 246p

287. **A tramp's wallet of Alpine and roadside rhymes**
[By . . .]
London: Elkin Matthews, 1890. xii, 87p; 16cm

*288. **The exploration of the Caucasus**
With illustrations by Vittorio Sella. [Contributions by J. G. Cockin, Maurice de Déchy, H. W. Holder, H. Woolley, T. G. Bonney].
London: Arnold,
1896. 2v. xxiv, 278p, 39 plates: x, 295p, 37 plates; ill, maps, panoramas, ports; 29cm. Also large paper edition in 2v. (33cm)
1902. 2nd ed. 2v. xii, 278p: viii, 296p; ill, maps; 29cm A much less imposing edition than the first Freshfield's masterpiece.

*289. **Round Kanchenjunga: a narrative of mountain travel and exploration**
London: Arnold, 1903. xvi, 373p, 2 fold. maps, 41 plates (1 fold.); 26cm
This dangerous and exhausting circuit of Kanchenjunga was a classic of mountain exploration.

290. **Unto the hills**
London: Arnold, 1914. viii, 120p; 17cm
Poems.

291. **Hannibal once more**
London: Arnold, 1914. [8], 120p, 3 maps, 3 plates; 22cm

*292. **The life of Horace-Bénédict de Saussure**
By . . . with the collaboration of Henry F. Montagnier.
London: Arnold, 1920. xii, 479p, 2 maps, 21 plates (incl. ports); 24cm
This biography of de Saussure gained Freshfield an Honorary Doctorate of Laws from the University of Geneva.

*293. **Below the snow line**
London: Constable, 1923. viii, 270p; 9 maps; 23cm
Climbs in Corsica and the lesser Alps.

FRESHFIELD, Mrs. Henry
Keen Alpine traveller and mother of D. W. Freshfield.

*294. **Alpine byways: or, Light leaves gathered in 1859 and 1860; by a lady**
London: Longmans, 1861. x, 232p, 4 maps, 8 col. plates; 21cm
Classic travel book.

295. **A summer tour in the Grisons and Italian valleys of the Bernina**
London: Longmans, 1862. x, 292p, 2 col. maps, 4 col. plates; 20cm
Not so good as [294].

FRISON-ROCHE, Roger
French writer: author of several novels set in the Mont Blanc range, of which **First on the rope** is the first and best known. **See also [795] & Appendix IV.**

*296. **First on the rope**
A novel by . . .
Translated [from the French] by Janet Adam Smith.
London: Methuen, 1949. xii, 268p; 19cm
From the original: **Premier de cordée** (Paris: Arthaud, 1941).

297. **Mont Blanc and the seven valleys**
By . . . and Pierre Tairraz. Translated [from the French] and adapted by Roland Le Grand with the co-operation of Wilfrid Noyce.
London: Kaye, 1961. 267p; ill, map, ports; 23cm
From the original: **Mont Blanc aux sept vallées** (Paris: Arthaud, 1961)
A general survey.

FRITH, Henry

298. **Ascents and adventures: a record of hardy mountaineering in every quarter of the globe**
London: Routledge, 1884. 320p; ill; 22cm

FRYXELL, Fritiof N.
American geologist and national park ranger, who made many first ascents in the Tetons between the wars.

*299. **The Teton peaks and their ascents**
Wyoming: Crandall Studios, 1932. xiv [xii], 106p, fold. map, 15 plates; 20cm

*300. **The Tetons: interpretations of a mountain landscape**
Berkeley: Univ. Calif. Press,
1938. xiv, 77p, fold. map, 13 plates; 20cm
1953.
Companion volume to [299], dealing with geology.

GANSSER, August
See [362].

[GARDINER, Frederick (1850–1919)]
Liverpool shipowner and mountaineer. Keen advocate of guideless climbing and also of climbing in Britain.

*301. **The Alpine career (1868–1914) of Frederick Gardiner**

Described by his friend, W. A. B. Coolidge.
Grindlewald: privately printed, 1920. 75p, port;
23cm. Limited edition of fifty copies.

GARDNER, Arthur
His published works include **Peaks, lochs and
coasts of the western Highlands** (Witherby, 1942)
and **Britain's mountain heritage** (Batsford, 1942).

*302. **The art and sport of alpine photography**
London: Witherby, 1927. xvi, 224p [208], 150
plates; 23cm

GARDNER, John Dunn (1811–1903)

303. **Ascent and tour of Mont Blanc, and passage of the
Col. du Geant, between Sept 2nd and 7th, 1850**
Chiswick: C. Whittingham, 1851. 61p; 15cm
The thirty-eighth ascent of Mont Blanc.

GEIGER, Hermann

*304. **Alpine pilot**
Translated [from the German] by Alan Tuppen.
London: Cassell, 1956. 104p, 32 plates (incl.
ports); 21cm

GEORGE, Hereford Brooke (1838–1910)
Military historian and mountaineer. First editor of
the A.J. See also [22].

*305. **The Oberland and its glaciers: explored and
illustrated with ice-axe and camera**
With 28 photographic illustrations by Ernest
Edwards.
London: Bennett, 1866. xii [xiv], 243p, map, 11
plates; 28cm
Contains prized examples of early mountain
photographs.

GEORGE, Marian M.

306. **A little journey to Switzerland: for home and
school**
Edited by ...
Chicago: Flanagan, [1902]. 192p
Written for children: includes the first ascents of
Mont Blanc and the Matterhorn.

GERVASUTTI, Giusto (1909–46)
Leading Italian mountaineer, who made many
difficult ascents in the Dolomites and Mont Blanc
range. Killed trying a new route on Mont Blanc du
Tacul.

*307. **Gervasutti's climbs**
Translated [from the Italian] by Nea Morin and
Janet Adam Smith.
London: Hart-Davis, 1957. 201p, 15 plates (incl.
port); 22cm
From the original: **Scarlate nelle Alpi** (Milan:
Garzanti, 1947).

[**GESNER**, Conrad (1516–65)]

*308. **On the admiration of mountains, the prefatory
letter addressed to Jacob Avienus, in Gesner's
pamplet 'On milk and substances prepared from
milk' first printed at Zurich in 1543. A description
of the Riven Mountain, commonly called Pilatus,
addressed to J. Chrysostome Huber, originally**

printed with another work of Gesner's at Zurich in
1555
Translated [from the Latin] by H. B. D. Soulé.
Together with **On Conrad Gesner** and **The mount-
aineering of Theuerdank** by J. Monroe Thorington.
Bibliographical notes by W. Dock and J. Monroe
Thorington.
San Francisco: The Grabhorn Press, 1937. [20],
57p; 8 ill (facsims); 29cm. Limited edition of 325
copies.
Gesner is regarded as one of the forefathers of
mountaineering.

GILBERT, Josiah (1814–92)
Portrait painter and writer. A.C. member. He
travelled in the Alps with G. C. Churchill, with
whom he collaborated again in producing **Knapsack guide to Tirol** (1867).

*309. **The Dolomite Mountains: excursions through
Tyrol, Carinthia, Carniola and Friuli in 1861, 1862
and 1863**
By ... and George Cheetham Churchill. With a
geological chapter and pictorial illustrations from
original drawings on the spot.
London: Longmans, 1864. xx, 576p, 2 fold. maps,
6 col. plates; 22cm
Alpine travel classic.

GILKINSON, W. Scott
New Zealand mountaineer.

310. **Peaks, packs and mountain tracks**
Auckland: Whitcombe & Tombs, 1940, 120p, 8
plates; 18cm

311. **Aspiring New Zealand: the romantic story of the
"Matterhorn of the Southern Alps"**
Christchurch: Whitcombe & Tombs, 1951. 80p, 23
plates; maps; 18cm
Climbing history of Mt. Aspiring.

312. **Earnslaw, monarch of Wakatipu**
Christchurch: Whitcombe & Tombs, 1957.

GILL, Michael (b. 1937)
New Zealand doctor, physiologist and mountaineer. Member of some of Hillary's (qv) expeditions, climbing Ama Dablam, Taweche and Kangtega.

*313. **Mountain midsummer: climbing in four continents**
London: Hodder, 1969. 220p, 48 plates; ill. maps,
ports; 23cm
Climbing memoirs: includes chapters on the Darran
Mountains, New Zealand.

GILLMAN, Peter
Journalist.

314. **Eiger direct**
By ... and Dougal Haston. Photographed by
Christian Bonington.
London: Collins, 1966. 183p, 40 (16 col) plates
(incl. ports); 24cm. U.S.A. edition entitled **Dirett-
issima: the Eiger assault**.

315. **Direttissima: the Eiger assault**
New York: Harper, 1966. 174p, 40 plates. U.S.A.
edition of **Eiger direct**.

GIRDLESTONE, Arthur Gilbert (1842–1908)
Clergyman. Enthusiastic but inept mountaineer, who had a number of lucky escapes. In the opinion of his contemporaries his book did the cause of mountaineering a serious disservice (at that time).

*316. **The high Alps without guides: being a narrative of adventures in Switzerland, together with chapters on the practicability of such mode of mountaineering, and suggestions for its accomplishment**
London: Longmans, 1870. x, 182p, 2 maps, plate; 22cm

GODFREY, Bob
English climber resident in U.S.A. One time Professor of Psychology at Colorado University, he is now a full-time author and photographer.

*317. **Climb!**
By ... and Dudley Chelton.
[To be published for the A.A.C. by Westview Press (Frederick A. Praeger Publishers) June, 1977. 262p; ill; 22cm].
Illustrations and descriptions of the best in Colorado rock-climbing.

GOS, Charles (1885–1949)
Swiss writer and mountaineer, whose climbing career was terminated early by illness. **See also Appendix IV.**

*318. **Alpine tragedy**
Translated from the French by Malcolm Barnes.
London: Allen & Unwin, 1948. x, 282p, 6 maps, 32 plates (incl. ports); 24cm
From the Original: **Tragédies alpestres** (Paris: Editions de France, 1940)
Recounts over twenty well-known Alpine accidents.

GOS, Francois

319. **Zermatt and its valley**
London: Cassell, [1926]. 180p [178], col. fold. map; ill; 25cm
Well illustrated monograph.

320. **Rambles in High Savoy**
Translated [from the French] by Frank Kemp.
London: Longmans, 1927. 169p; ill, col. map, ports; 25cm
From the original: **Les Alpes de la Haute Savoie** (Thonon les Baines: Lib. Pellissier, 1926).

GOSWAMI, S. M.

321. **Everest, is it conquered?**
Calcutta: the author, 1954. xviii, 122p, 2 plates: 19cm
Argues that Hunt's 1953 expedition did not succeed.

GRAHAM, Peter (1878–1961)
New Zealand guide, who climbed with Miss Du Faur (qv). He and his brother Alex were the leading New Zealand guides for over thirty years.

*322. **Peter Graham: mountain guide. An autobiography**
Edited by H. B. Hewitt
Wellington: Reed, 1965.

London: Allen & Unwin,
1965. xiv, 245p, 16 plates (incl. ports); 24cm
Wellington: Reed, 1973. 2nd imp.

GRAHAM, William Woodman (c. 1859–?)
He was the first to visit the Himalaya for pleasure mountaineering. His claim to have climbed Kabru in 1883 has never been disproved.

323. **Climbing the Himalaya**
London: Isbister, 1887. In From the Equator to the Pole, pp54–131; ill; 8vo. [This is apparently a reprint of the article in 'Good Words', with a few sentences omitted]

GRANT, Richard Henry
Royal Marine Officer and mountaineer.

324. **Annapurna II**
London: Kimber, 1961. xii, 192p [180], 8 plates; 23cm
First ascent.

GRAY, Dennis Dillon (b. 1935)
Professional mountaineer and first General Secretary of the B.M.C.

*325. **Rope boy**
London: Gollancz, 1970. 320p, 27 plates (incl. ports); 23cm
Climbing autobiography.

[GREAT BRITAIN, Royal Air Force]

326. **Mountain rescue handbook**
London: H.M.S.O.,
1952.
1968. 178p; ill; 22cm
1972. 3rd ed. 152p

GREEN, William Spotswood (1847–1919)
Irish clergyman and civil servant. His uncompleted ascent of Mount Cook in 1882 marks the start of high alpine climbing in New Zealand. He was also one of the first climbers in Canada, where he made the first ascent of Mount Bonney in the Selkirks in 1888.

*327. **The high alps of New Zealand: or, A trip to the glaciers of the antipodes with an ascent of Mount Cook**
London: Macmillan, 1883. xvi [xiv], 350p, 2 maps (1 col); 20cm

*328. **Among the Selkirk glaciers: being the account of a rough survey in the Rocky Mountains region of British Columbia**
London: Macmillan, 1890. xvi [xiv], 251p, fold. map, 9 plates; 20cm

GREENBANK, Anthony
Writer and broadcaster. His published works include **Climbing, canoeing, skiing and caving** (Elliot, 1964) and **A book of survival** (Wolfe, 1967).

329. **Instructions in rock-climbing**
London: Museum Press, 1963. 159p, 8 plates; ill; 23cm

330. **Instructions in mountaineering**
London: Museum Press, 1967. 125p, 8 plates; ill; 23cm

331. **Enjoy your rock-climbing**
London: Pelham 1976. 150p, 8 plates; ill; 23cm

GREGORY, Alfred (b. 1913)
Photographer, lecturer and mountaineer, who has taken part in various Himalayan and other high altitude expeditions, including Everest in 1953.

332. **The picture of Everest: a book of full-colour reproductions of photographs of the Everest scene**
Chosen and explained by . . .
London: Hodder, 1954. [96p] , 43 col. ill; 28cm

GRIBBLE, Francis Henry
Journalist.

*333. **The early mountaineers**
London: Fisher Unwin, 1899. xiv, 338p, 48 plates (incl. facsims); 23cm
Authoritative record of pre-'Golden Age' mountaineering.

334. **The story of Alpine climbing**
London: Newnes, 1904. 180p, 20 plates; 15cm
London: Hodder, nd [c. 1912] Revised and enlarged edition.
Good little summary.

GRIFFIN, Margaret

335. **Tiquimani**
Stellenbosch: Kosmo Pub., 1965. 164p, 13 plates (1 col); 22cm
Account of the 1963 South African expedition to the Cordillera Real, Bolivia.

GROVE, Florence Crauford (1838–1902)
English mountaineer and one of the ablest climbers of his day. A.C. President 1884–6. He led the condemnation of guideless climbing in the 1870s, against Girdlestone (qv). See also [22].

*336. **'The frosty Caucasus': an account of a walk through part of the range and of an ascent of Elbruz in the summer of 1874**
With illustrations engraved by Ed. Whymper from photographs taken during the journey by H. Walker.
London: Longmans, 1875. x, 341p, fold. map, 6 plates; 20cm. The first issue was bound in blue cloth. The second issue, with errata slip, was bound in decorative (reindeer & sled) grey cloth or plain green cloth.

GURUNG, Harka Bahadur

*337. **Annapurna to Dhaulagiri: a decade of mountaineering in Nepal Himalaya, 1950–1960**
Katmandu: Nepal Dept. of Inform., 1968. xiv, 122p; ill (some col), map; 22cm
Summarizes about 100 expeditions.

HAGERMAN, Percy
One of the first Americans to climb solely for pleasure.

338. **Notes on mountaineering in the Elk Mountains of Colorado, 1908–1910**
? : ?, 1912.
Denver: Colorado M.C., 1956.

HALL, Richard Watson

339. **The art of mountain tramping: practical hints for both walker and scrambler among the British peaks**
London: Witherby, 1932. 191p, 4 plates; ill; 23cm
Sports & Pastimes series.

HALL, William Edward (1835–95)
Barrister and traveller, who made several important first ascents in the Alps. See [22].

HALLWORTH, Rodney
Journalist.

340. **The last flowers on earth**
Maidstone: Angley Books, 1966. 167p, 9 plates (incl. group port); 21cm
Account of the ill-fated Royal Navy East Greenland mountaineering expedition to Schweizerland.

HAMILTON, Helen

341. **Mountain madness**
London: Collins, 1922. x, 274p, 11 plates; 19cm
Climbing reminiscences around Chamonix.

HANKINSON, Alan
Journalist, television newsman and mountaineer. See also [95].

*342. **The first tigers: the early history of rock-climbing in the Lake District**
London: Dent, 1972. xviii, 196p, 16 plates (incl. ports); 23cm
Covers the period from the earliest eighteenth century records up to 1914.

*343. **Camera on the crags: a portfolio of early rock climbing photographs by the Abraham Brothers**
Selected and written by . . .
London: Heinemann, 1975. [vi], 42p, 96 plates (incl. ports); 29cm

HARDING, Warren
American civil engineer and leading rock-climber.

*344. **Downward bound: a mad guide to rock-climbing**
By Warren 'Batso' Harding. With illustrations by Beryl 'Beasto' Knath
Englewood Cliffs, N.J.:
Prentice Hall, 1975. 204p; ill;

HARDY, John Frederick
Original A.C. member. He climbed in the Alps and Norway, and enjoyed guideless climbing. See [18] & [20].

HARPER, Arthur Paul (1865–1955)
New Zealander, who made several first ascents and did much exploration and survey work in 1890s with Charles Douglas and C. E. Mannering (qv). He also wrote **Memories of mountains and men** (Christchurch: Simpson & Williams, 1946).

*345. **Pioneer work in the Alps of New Zealand: a record of the first exploration of the chief glaciers and ranges of the Southern Alps**
London: Fisher Unwin, 1896. xvi, 336p, map, 39 plates; 23cm [20 copies on Japan paper in British Museum]

HARPER, Stephen
Journalist.

346. **Ladykiller Peak: a lone man's story of twelve women on a killer mountain**
London: World Distributors, 1965. 124p; 18cm.
'Consul' paperback.

He followed this all women expedition to Cho Oyu, when Claude Kogan was killed.

HARRER, Heinrich
Austrian mountaineer, who took part in the first ascent of the Eigerwand. He escaped from internment in India and later wrote **Seven years in Tibet** (Hart-Davis, 1953), his best-known book outside mountaineering circles.

*347. **The White Spider: the history of the Eiger's North Face**
Translated from the German by Hugh Merrick.
London: Hart-Davis,
1959. 240p, 41 plates (incl. ports); 24cm
1965. 2nd ed. revised with ten additional chapters by Harrer and Kurt Maix.
1976. 3rd ed. revised
[Numerous impressions overall.]

From the original: **Die Weisse Spinne** (Berlin: Ullstein, 1958)
The second edition ends with the first feminine ascent in September 1964.

348. **I come from the Stone Age**
Translated from the German by Edward Fitzgerald.
London: Hart-Davis, 1964. 256p, 32 plates (16 col); ill, ports; 24cm
From the original: **Ich komme aus der Steinzeit** (Berlin: Ullstein, 1963)
Includes climbing all the Carstenz peaks (New Guinea).

HARRIS, George W.

349. **The Mount Cook alpine region**
By . . . and Graeme Hasler.
Wellington: Reed, 1971. 224p; ill (some col); 29cm. Cover title **A land apart**
Chiefly photographs.

HARRIS, Walter B.

350. **Tafilet: the narrative of a journey of exploration in the Atlas mountains and the oases of the north-west Sahara**
Illustrated by Maurice Romberg.
London: Blackwood, 1895. xiv, 386p, 2 maps (1 fold), 8 plates; 22cm

HARRISON, Frederic (1831–1923)
Lawyer, philosopher and writer. President of the English Positivist Committee, 1880–1905. Original A.C. member.

351. **My alpine jubilee 1851–1907**
London: Smith Elder, 1908. x, 141p, port; 20cm
Nostalgic letters and essays.

HART, Henry Chicester (1847–1908)
Irish explorer, who collaborated with Haskett Smith (qv) in the production of the first British rock-climbing guidebook. Hart's portion of this guidebook has been reissued recently: see [726].

HART, John L. Jerome

*352. **Fourteen thousand feet: a history of the naming and early ascents of the high Colorado peaks**
Denver: Colorado M.C.,
1925.
1932. Revised edition with **A climber's guide to the high Colorado peaks** by Elinor Eppich Kingery. 71p, plates; 23cm
1972.

HARVARD, Andrew

353. **Mountain of storms: the American expeditions to Dhaulagiri 1969 and 1973**
By . . . and Todd Thompson.
New York: New York Univ. Press, 1974. 210p; ill;

HASTON, Dougal (1940–77)
Scottish professional mountaineer, who played a prominent role in several very severe climbs, including a winter ascent of the Eigerwand and the South-west Face of Everest. Killed in an avalanche.
See also [95] & [314].

*354. **In high places**
London: Cassell,
1972. [8], 168p, 16 plates (incl. group port); 23cm
1973. 2nd & 3rd imp.
Hutchinson,
1974. Arrow paperback.
Climbing autobiography.

*355. **The Eiger**
London: Cassell, 1974. [10], 170p, 16 plates (incl. ports); 23cm
The modern history of the Eiger-wand.

HAUSER, Günter

356. **White mountain and tawny plain**
Translated from the German by Richard Rickett.
London: Allen & Unwin, 1961. 224p, 15 plates; ill, maps, ports; 23cm
From the original: **Ihr Herren Berge** (Stuttgart: Engelhornverlag, 1959)
Climbing in the Peruvian Cordilleras Blanca and Vilcanota.

HAWES, Sir Benjamin (1797–1862)
British politician.

357. **A narrative of an ascent to the summit of Mont Blanc, made during the summer of 1827 by Mr. William Hawes and Mr. Charles Fellows**
By . . . [from material supplied by his brother William.]
London: printed for Benjamin Hawes by Arthur Taylor, 1828. 35p, plate; 25cm
Variations: Some copies have a plate depicting heights; others a plate of de Saussure's ascent.
Some copies have more variations overall, viz:
Slightly larger; title finishing at '1827'; insertion of 'junior', i.e. 'printed for Benjamin Hawes junior'.
These copies appear to have the plate of heights.

HAWKINS, Francis Vaughan (1833–1908)
Barrister and original A.C. member. He assisted Tyndall (qv) in his early glacier experiments. **See** [18].

[HAYES, Geoff]
See under: RUSSELL, Jean

HAZARD, Joseph F.

358. **Snow sentinels of the Pacific North-west**
Seattle: Lowmans & Hanford, 1932. 249p; ill;
History of principal peaks in Cascades and Olympic
Mountains.

HECKEL, Vilem
Czechoslovak photographer and mountaineer.

359. **Climbing in the Caucasus**
Text by Josef Styrsa.
London: Spring Books, [1958]. 208p, plates
(some col); 28cm
Photo album.

HECKMAIR, Anderl (b. 1906)
Leading German climber of the pre-war era;
professional guide. He took part in the first ascent
of the Eigerwand.

*360. **My life as a mountaineer**
Translated [from the German] by Geoffrey
Sutton.
London: Gollancz, 1975. 224p, 16 plates (incl.
ports); 23cm
From the original: **Mein Leben als Bergsteiger**
(Munich: Nymphenburger, 1972).

'HEDERATUS'

*361. **Cambridge night climbing**
London: Chatto & Windus, 1970. 95p, 32 plates;
23cm
Wall and roof climbing is a traditional Cambridge
sport.

HEIM, Arnold

*362. **The throne of the gods: an account of the first
Swiss expedition to the Himalayas**
By ... and August Gansser. Translated [from the
German] by Eden and Cedar Paul.
London: Macmillan, 1939. xxvi, 236p, 120 plates
(incl. ports); fold. map (end pocket); 24cm
From the original: **Thron der Götter** (Zurich:
Morgarten, 1938)
Superbly illustrated account of chiefly geological
expedition, which explored the area around Kailas
in Tibet.

HEINE, Arnold J.
New Zealand mountaineer who has taken part in
several Antarctic expeditions.

362a..**Mountaincraft manual**
Wellington: National Mountains Safety Council of
New Zealand, 1971. 170p; ill;
Includes specific sections on New Zealand
conditions.

HENDERSON, Kenneth Atwood
American banker and mountaineer, who climbed
with Underhill and Fryxell (qv).

*363. **The (American Alpine Club's) handbook
of American mountaineering**
Edited by ...
New York: A.A.C., 1941. 179p; ill

Boston: Houghton Mifflin, 1942. [8], 239p; ill;
19cm
Comprehensive instruction manual for U.S. Army.

HERLIGKOFFER, Karl Maria
German mountaineer and leader of Himalayan
expeditions.

*364. **Nanga Parbat: incorporting the official report of
the expedition of 1953**
Translated and additional material supplied by
Eleanor Brockett and Anton Ehrenzweig.
London: Elek, 1954. 254p, 54 (9 col) plates (incl.
ports); 23cm
New York: Knopf, 1954. 260p, U.S.A. edition
entitled **The Killer Mountain**
London: Hamilton, 1956. Panther paperback ed.
From the original: **Nanga Parbat 1953** (Munich:
Lehmanns, 1954)
Summarizes the earlier attempts leading to the first
ascent.

365. **The Killer Mountain, Nanga Parbat**
New York: Knopf, 1954. 260p. U.S.A. edition of
Nanga Parbat.

HERZOG, Maurice (b. 1919)
French politician and mountaineer. Leader of the
successful Annapurna expedition, suffering severe
frostbite during descent. Later French Minister for
Sport.

*366. **Annapurna: conquest of the first 8000-metre peak
(26,493 feet)**
Translated from the French by Nea Morin and
Janet Adam Smith.
London: Cape, 1952. 288pm maps (1 col. fold), 28
plates (3 col., some ports); 21cm. [Several im-
pressions].
New York: Dutton, 1952.
London: Collins, 1956. Fontana paperback.
Bath: Cedric Chivers, 1974. New ed. 288p
One of the great landmarks in mountaineering.

HEWITT, L. Rodney

367. **The mountains of New Zealand**
By ... and Mavis Davidson.
Wellington: Reed, 1954. 128p; ill, map; 26cm
London: Phoenix House, 1954.
Chiefly illustrations with supporting text.

HIEBELER, Toni
German journalist, publisher and mountaineer.

*368. **North face in winter: the first winter climb of the
Eiger's north face March 1961**
Introduced and translated [from the German] by
Hugh Merrick.
London: Barrie and Rockcliff, 1962. 121p, 15
plates (incl. ports); 23cm
From the original: **Im Banne der Spinne** (Munich:
Bassermann'sche Verlag, 1961).

HILLARY, Sir Edmund Percival (b. 1919)
New Zealand mountaineer, who made the first
ascent of Everest. Leader of several New Zealand
Himalayan expeditions. His published works include **No latitude for error** (Hodder, 1961), which
deals with his part in the Trans-Antarctica expedition.

*369. **High adventure**
London: Hodder, 1955. 225p, 33 plates (1 col); ill, maps, ports; 21cm
New York: Dutton, 1955. 256p, maps, 31 plates; 21cm
London: Hodder,
   1955. 2nd imp.
   1958. Paperback ed.
Chiefly about his climbs on Everest.

370. **East of Everest: an account of the New Zealand Alpine Club Himalayan expedition to the Barun Valley in 1954**
By . . . and George Lowe.
London: Hodder, 1956. 71p, 3 maps, 48 plates (incl. ports); 25cm
New York: Dutton, 1956.

*371. **High in the thin cold air**
By . . . and Desmond Doig.
New York: Doubleday, 1962. x, 254p; ill, maps; 24cm
London: Hodder, 1963. 287p, 31 plates (incl. ports); 22cm
Search for the yeti and an attempt on Makalu.

*372. **Schoolhouse in the clouds**
London: Hodder, 1964. xii, 180p, 32 col. plates; 22cm
H'worth: Penguin, 1968. Paperback ed.
Includes ascents of Kangtega and Taweche.

*373. **Nothing venture, nothing win**
London: Hodder, 1975. xiv, 319p, [305] 32 (8 col) plates (incl. ports); 25cm
London: Coronet, 1977. Paperback ed.
Autobiography.

HILLS, Denis Cecil

374. **My travels in Turkey**
London: Allen & Unwin, 1964. 252p [250], 25 plates (1 col); ill, maps, ports; 22cm
Includes climbing in various parts of Turkey.

HINCHLIFF, Thomas Woodbine (1825–82)
Barrister, botanist and traveller. A.C. member and President 1875–7. His book and his personality were decisive influences on contemporary mountaineering. See also [18].

*375. **Summer months among the Alps: with the ascent of Monte Rosa**
London: Longmans, 1857. xviii, 312p, 3 maps (col, fold) 4 plates; 21cm

HINDLEY, Geoffrey

376. **The roof of the world**
London: Aldus, 1971. 191p; ill (some col), col. facsim, maps (chiefly col), ports (some col); 27cm
Aldus Encyclopaedia of Discovery and Invention.

HIRST, John

377. **Songs of the mountaineers**
Collected and edited by . . . for the Rucksack Club.
Manchester: Rucksack Club, [1922]. [8], 124p; 18cm

HOARE, Robert John

378. **The high peaks**
[By . . .] Illustrated by Carlo Alexander.
London: Ginn, [1966]. 80p; ill, maps; 20cm
Written for children.

HODGKINSON, George Christopher (1816–80)
Clergyman, who climbed with Hudson (qv). See [20].

HOEK, Henry William (1878–1951)
Swiss geologist and author of books on mountains and skiing. A.C. member. See [757].

HOHLE, Per

379. **The mountain world of Norway**
Oslo: Dreyers Forlag, 1956.
London: Stanford, 1957.
Chiefly a photo album.

HOLLAND, C. F.
See [142].

HOLLAND, E. T.
See [20].

HOLMES, Peter

380. **Mountains and a monastery**
London: Bles, 1958. 191p, 8 plates; ill, maps; 22cm
First ascents in Spiti at the head of the Ratang Nulla.

HOOKER, Sir Joseph Dalton (1817–1911)
English botanist and traveller, whose journeys included expeditions to Antarctica, the northern frontiers of India and the Morocco Atlas. His published works include the well-known **Himalayan Journals.**

*381. **Journal of a tour in Marocco and the Great Atlas**
By . . . and John Ball. With an appendix . . . by George Maw.
London: Macmillan, 1878. xvi, 499p, fold. maps, 8 plates (1 fold); 23cm
Comprehensive account of the vegetation and geology, and of climbs in the Atlas.

HORIZON

382. **Mountain conquest**
By the editors of 'Horizon' magazine. Author: Eric Shipton in consultation with Bradford Washburn.
New York: American Heritage Pub. Co., 1966.
London: Cassell, 1967. 153p [151]; ill (some col), facsims, maps, ports; 27cm
Survey of world mountaineering.

HORNBEIN, Thomas Frederick (b. 1930)
American doctor and mountaineer, who made the first traverse of Everest; one of the finest Himalayan climbs of the 1960s.

*383. **Everest: the west ridge**
San Francisco: Sierra Club, 1965. ⎫ 201p; 89 col. ill;
London: Allen & Unwin, 1966. ⎬ 35cm
San Francisco: Sierra Club, 1966. 160p; ill (col); 24cm
Ballantine Books, 1968. Reprinted in small format.

London: Allen & Unwin, 1971. Revised edition, 181p; ill; 22cm
One of the superb Sierra Club Exhibit Format series.

HORNBY, Emily

384. **Mountaineering records**
[By] E. H. [Compiled by M. L. Hornby]
Liverpool: Thompson, 1907. viii, 352p; 23cm
Record of ascents 1873–95 by a leading woman climber of her generation.

HORNBY, James John
Clergyman, who climbed extensively in the Alps in 1860s. **See [22].**

HOUSE, William P.
Amerian mountaineer, who made the first ascent of Mt. Waddington with Fritz Wiessner. **See [65].**

HOUSTON, Charles S. (b. 1913)
American medical professor and mountaineer, who led two expeditions to K.2 and who also climbed in the Himalaya with Tilman (qv). **See also [65].**

* 385. **K.2: the savage mountain**
By . . . and Robert Bates.
New York: McGraw-Hill, 1954. 334p; ill, map; 21cm
London: Collins, 1955. 192p, 24 plates; 22cm
Unsuccessful attempt: the whole party were nearly swept away on descent.

HOWARD, Eliot
See **[22].**

HOWARD, William (1793–1834)
The ninth ascent of Mont Blanc and the first by Americans. Howard's companion, Dr. Jeremiah Van Rensselaar, also wrote an account of their climb.

386. **A narrative of a journey to the summit of Mont Blanc, made in July 1819**
Baltimore: Fielding Lucas, 1821. [6], 49p, plate; 17cm

HOWARD-BURY, Charles Kenneth (1883–1963)
Army officer, who led the first Everest expedition.

*387. **Mount Everest: the reconnaissance, 1921**
By . . . and other members of the Mount Everest expedition.
London: Arnold, 1922. xii, 356p, 3 fold. maps, 33 plates (incl. ports); 26cm. Also large paper edition, numbered and limited to 200 copies, with fourteen extra plates.

HUDSON, Charles (1828–65)
Clergyman and leading amateur mountaineer of his day. He made the first ascent of the highest point of Monte Rosa and the first guideless ascent of Mont Blanc. Killed in the Matterhorn disaster. See also [20]

*388. **Where there's a will there's a way: an ascent of Mont Blanc by a new route and without guides**
By . . . and Edward Shirley Kennedy.
London: Longmans,

1856. xvi, 95p, col. map, plate; 21cm
1856. 2nd ed. with accounts of two ascents of Monte Rosa. xvi, 114p, col. map, plate; 21cm

HUF, Hans

389. **English mountaineers: A. Wills, J. Tyndall, E. Whymper, C. Dent, A. F. Mummery**
Herausgegeben von . . .
Bamberg: C. C. Buchners Verlag, 1926. 88p; ill; 19cm
English reader for German schools.

HUMBLE, Benjamin Hutchison (– 1977)
Scottish mountaineer, active in the mountain rescue movement. He also wrote **Tramping in Skye** (Grant & Murray, 1933).

390. **Songs for climbers**
Edited by . . . and W. M. McClellan.
Glasgow: Wm McClellan, 1938. 30p; 22cm

391. **On Scottish hills**
London: Chapman & Hall, 1946. 128p; ill, maps; 26cm
Illustrations with supporting text.

*392. **The Cuillin of Skye**
London: Hale, 1952. xvi, 144p, 49 plates; facsims, maps; 26cm
The principal book on the history of climbing in Skye.

HUNT, Henry Cecil John, Baron Hunt of Llanvair Waterdine (b. 1910)
Soldier, administrator and mountaineer. He climbed in the Himalaya pre-war and led the 1953 Everest expedition. A.C. President 1956–8. The 'father figure' of post-war British mountaineering. **See also [659].**

*393. **The ascent of Everest**
[Sketches by Charles Evans]
London: Hodder, 1953. xx, 300p, 56 plates (8 col); ill, ports; 23cm [Several imp.]
New York: Dutton, 1954. U.S.A. edition entitled **Conquest of Everest**
London: Univ. London Press, 1954. Abridged edition for children. Senior version 160pp; junior version 96pp
London: Tandem, 1973. xii, 300p 'Great Venture' series.

394. **The conquest of Everest**
New York: Dutton, 1954. U.S.A. edition of **Ascent of Everest.**

395. **Our Everest adventure: the pictorial history from Kathmandu to the summit**
Leicester: Brockhampton Press, 1954. 128p; ill, ports; 25cm
Chiefly previously unpublished photographs: companion volume to: [393].

*396. **The Red Snows: an account of the British Caucasus expedition 1958**
By . . . and Christopher Brasher.
London: Hutchinson, 1960. 176p, 17 (1 col) plates (incl. ports); 22cm

HUXLEY, Anthony J.

*397. **Standard encyclopaedia of the world's mountains**
Edited by . . .
London: Weidenfeld & Nicolson, 1962. 383p, 16 col. plates; ill, maps; 24cm
Useful reference work, subject to minor inaccuracies.

INGRAM, John Anthony

398. **Fellcraft: some advice for fell-walkers**
London: S. Paul,
1964. 140p, 12 plates; 19cm
1968. 2nd ed.
Instructional.

IRVING, Robert Lock Graham (1877–1969)
Schoolmaster, writer and mountaineer, who took a number of pupils climbing in the Alps, the most famous being Mallory (qv). He also wrote a short item, **The mountains shall bring peace** (Oxford: Blackwell, 1947).

*399. **The romance of mountaineering**
London: Dent,
1935. xiv, 320p, 36 plates; 24cm
1935. 2nd imp.
1946. 3rd imp.
Traces the development of mountaineering.

*400. **The mountain way: an anthology in prose and verse**
Collected by . . .
London: Dent, 1938. xxii, 656p; 20cm
The standard anthology.

401. **The Alps**
London: Batsford, 1939. viii, 120p, 81 (1 col) plates; 22cm
New York: Scribners, 1940.
London: Batsford,
1942. 2nd ed.
1947. 3rd ed.
General description.

402. **Ten great mountains**
London: Dent,
1940. xii, 213p, 15 plates; 23cm
1942. Reprint
1947. Reprint
Includes Snowdon, Ben Nevis, Ushba, Mt. Logan.

*403. **A history of British mountaineering**
London: Batsford, 1955. xvi, 240p, 31 plates (incl. facsims, ports); 23cm

IRWIN, William Robert

404. **Challenge: an anthology of the literature of mountaineering**
Edited by . . .
New York: Columbia Univ. Press, 1950. xx, 444p; 23cm

ISHERWOOD, Christopher William Bradshaw (b. 1904)
English novelist. See [37].

IZZARD, Ralph William Burdick
Journalist and Daily Mail correspondent covering the 1953 Everest expedition. His published works include **The Abominable Snowman adventure** (Hodder, 1955).

405. **The innocent on Everest**
New York: Dutton, 1954. 319p; ill;
London: Hodder, 1955. 256p, 31 plates (incl. ports); 21cm

JACKSON, John Angelo
Mountain school instructor

*406. **More than mountains**
London: Harrap, 1955. 213p, 29 plates (1 col); ill, 4 maps, music; 22cm
A record of mountaineering and wild life in the Himalaya.

JACKSON, Monica

407. **Tents in the clouds: the first women's Himalayan expedition**
By . . . and Elizabeth Stark
London: Collins, 1956. 255p, 5 maps, 24 plates (incl. ports); 22cm

*408. **The Turkish time machine**
London: Hodder, 1966. 159p, map, 8 plates; 21cm
Climbing on the Cilo-Sat mountains of south-east Turkey.

JACOMB, Frederick William (c. 1828–93)
He played a large part in establishing the High Level ski route from Chamonix to Zermatt. See [20].

JAMES, Ronald (b. 1933)
British mountain guide and educationalist in outdoor pursuits.

409. **Rock face: techniques of rock-climbing**
London: B.B.C., 1974. 118p; ill; 20cm
Text accompanying television series.

JAVELLE, Jean Marie Ferdinand Émile (1847–83) (1847–83)
French writer, schoolmaster and climber, who lived in Switzerland. He climbed extensively in the Alps. His poor narrative style was imitated by Swiss, and later by French, writers.

410. **Alpine memories**
With a biographical and literary notice by Eugène Rambert.
Translated from the French and with an introduction by W. H. Chesson.
London: Fisher Unwin, 1899. viii, 444p, 4 plates (incl. facsim, port) 21cm
From the original: **Souvenirs d'un Alpiniste** (Lausanne: Payot, 1886.)

JEFFERS, Le Roy (1878–1926)
American librarian and mountaineer: killed in aeroplane crash. See also Appendix I.

*411 **The call of the mountains: rambles among the mountains and canyons of the United States and Canada**
New York: Dodd Meade, 1922. xviii, 282p, 65 plates (1 col); 24cm
London: Fisher Unwin, 1923. xvi, 282p, plates; 25cm
He made the first ascent (solo) of Mt. Moran in the

Tetons.

JERSTAD, Luther G.
American climber, mountain guide and speech instructor: member of 1963 American expedition to Everest. **See [478].**

JONES, Anthony S. G.

412. **Some thoughts on the organisation of mountain search and rescue operations**
By ..., Hon. Chairman, Ogwen Valley Mountain Rescue Organisation.
With Notes on mountain rescue first aid by Dr. Ieuan W. Jones.
[Bangor] : First published (by O.V.M.R.O.) June, 1973. 90p; ill; 21cm
1973. Reprint.

JONES, Christopher
English mountaineer, resident in U.S.A.

*†413. **Climbing in North America**
Berkeley: Pub. for A.A.C. by Univ. Calif. Press, 1976. xii, 392p; ill; 23cm
History of climbing in North America.

JONES, Ieuan W.
See [412].

JONES, Owen Glynne H. (1867–99)
Leading English rock-climber in 1890s, who climbed with the Abraham brothers (qv). Killed on the Dent Blanche.

*414. **Rock-climbing in the English Lake District**
London: Longmans,
    1897. xxvi, 284p, 39 plates; 24cm
Keswick: Abraham,
    1900. 2nd ed. lxiv, 322p. With a memoir [of O. G. Jones by W. M. Cook] and portrait of the author ... and an appendix [of new climbs] by G. & A. Abraham.
    1911. 3rd ed. lxiv, 384p. [Appendix II added (p317–79) by G. & A. Abraham].
Manchester: E.J. Morten,
    1973. Facsim reprint of 2nd ed.
The first part of a trilogy completed by the Abraham brothers (qv) after Jones' death: a great classic.

KAIN, Conrad (1883–1934)
Austrian guide employed by the Alpine Club of Canada. He guided the first ascent of Mt. Robson in 1913.

*415. **Where the clouds can go**
Edited, with additional chapters by J. Monroe Thorington.
New York: A.A.C., 1935. xxiv, 456p, 19 plates (incl. port); 24cm
Boston: C. T. Branford, 1954. Reprint. [London: Bailey & Swinfen].

KARR, Heywood W. Seton
Naval officer, who made the first reconnaissance of Mount St. Elias in 1886.

416. **Shores and alps of Alaska**
London: Sampson Low, 1887. xvi, 248p; ill, 3 maps (2 col); 23cm

[KEARSLEY, G.]
See [500].

KEENLYSIDE, F.

417. **Peaks and pioneers: the story of mountaineering**
London: Elek, 1975. 248p; ill (some col), facsims (1 col), maps, ports (some col); 31cm

KEMP, Dennis
See [217].

KENNEDY, Edward Shirley (1817–98)
English mountaineer and adventurer, who accompanied Hudson (qv) in numerous guideless ascents. He was active in the formation of the A.C., later President 1861–3. **See [18], [20] & [22].**

KENNEDY, Thomas Stuart (1841–94)
All-round athlete and sportsman, who made a number of notable Alpine climbs. **See [22].**

KENNETT, John

418. **The story of Annapurna**
Retold and adapted by ... from Maurice Herzog's **Annapurna**
Bombay: Blackie, 1955. 72p; ill;

KILGOUR, William T.

*419. **Twenty years on Ben Nevis: being a brief account of the life, work and experiences of the observers at the highest meteorological station in the British Isles**
Paisley: A. Gardner,
    [1905]. iv, 154p, map, 32 plates; 20cm
    1906. 2nd ed. iv, 173p

KING, Clarence (1842–1901)
American geologist and mountaineer. He was a member of the 1864 California survey team when he made his famous ascent of Mount Tyndall in the Sierra Nevada. His book is the great mountain classic of the U.S.A. Biography: **Clarence King** (New York: Macmillan, 1958) by Thurman Wilkins.

*420. **Mountaineering in the Sierra Nevada**
Boston: J. R. Osgood,
    1872. 292p; 21cm. Green or maroon cloth; t.e.g.; gilt lettering. Some variations of title page. Also large paper copies for presentation by the author.
London: Sampson Low,
    1872. vi, 292p; 22cm. Brown cloth, gilt blocked (saddlebags & guns)
    1872. viii, 292p; 20cm. Reset and slightly smaller format. Frontispiece in some copies. Green cloth, gilt blocked (peaks & eagle on spine).
Boston: J. R. Osgood,
    1874. '4th' ed. viii, 308p, 2 col. fold. maps; 20cm. With additional chapter on Mt. Whitney.
London: Sampson Low,
    1874. New ed. No preface, otherwise as '4th' ed.

? Reprint ('5th' ed) without change.
Boston: Ticknor,
  1886, Reprint ('6th' ed) without change
  ? Reprint ('7th' ed) without change
  ? Reprint ('8th' ed) without change
  nd. c. 1888, Reprint ('9th' ed) without change.
New York: Scribners,
  1902. xiv, 378p; 20cm. Entirely reset.
London: Fisher Unwin,
  1903. Reprint. ('3rd ed'?) xi, 378p
  1907. Reprint?
New York: Scribners,
  1923.
New York: W. Norton,
  1935. Edited by Francis P. Farquhar.
  1946, Reset on lighter-weight paper. Bound
  blue cloth.
London: A. & C. Black,
  1947. 320p, 8 plates (incl. port); 22cm. Edited
  and with a preface by Francis P. Farquhar. First
  [sic] English edition. 1000 copies.
Univ. Nebraska Press,
  1970. Reprint of 1872 edition.

KING, Edward J.
See [877].

KING, Samuel William (1821–68)
Clergyman, traveller, entomologist, geologist. He
was an enthusiastic mountaineer and travelled
frequently, usually accompanied by his wife. He
died and is buried at Pontresina.

421. **The Italian valleys of the Pennine Alps: a tour
through all the romantic and less-frequented 'vals'
of northern Piedmont, from the Tarentaise to the
Gries**
London: Murray, 1858. x, 558p, 3 fold. maps, 10
plates; 22cm

KINGDON-WARD Frank (1885–1958)
English botanist and explorer: one of the greatest
plant hunters.

*422. **Burma's icy mountains**
London: Cape, 1949. 287p, 2 fold. maps, 16 plates;
21cm
The story of two expeditions, 1937–9, into
Burma's 20,000' mountains.

KIRKPATRICK, William Trench (1858–1941)

423. **Alpine days and nights**
By ... with a paper by the late R. Philip Hope and
a foreword by Col. E. L. Strutt.
London: Allen & Unwin, 1932. 198p [196], 12
plates (incl. port); 21cm
Collection of articles first published in the A. J.
during the years 1900–31, relating to his climbs
with R. P. Hope.

KIRKUS, Colin F. (1910–42)
English climber, who dominated Welsh rock-
climbing with J. Menlove Edwards (qv) in 1930s.
Cousin of Wilfrid Noyce (qv). Killed in the war.

*424. **"Let's go climbing!"**
London: Nelson,
  1941. viii, 208p [200] 15 plates; ill, map; 21cm
  1946. Reprint
  1960. 3–200p; 19cm. Nelson Juniors series.

KITSON, John Hawthorne (1843–99)
See [22].

KLUCKER, Christian (1853–1928)
Swiss guide from the Bernina Alps. He was on the
first ascent of the Peuterey Arête of Mont Blanc
and made many climbs with Norman-Neruda (qv).
He accompanied Whymper to the Canadian
Rockies in 1901.

*425. **Adventures of an alpine guide**
Translated from the third German edition by
Erwin and Pleasaunce von Gaisberg. Edited and
with additional chapters by H. E. G. Tyndale.
London: Murray, 1932. xiv, 329p, 16 plates (incl.
ports); 23cm
From the original: **Erinnerungen eines Bergführers.**
Edited by Ernst Jenny (Zurich: Rentsch, 1930).

KNOOP, Faith Yingling

426. **A world explorer: Sir Edmund Hillary**
Champaign, Ill: Garrard, 1970. Published in U.K.
under title **Sir Edmund Hillary**

427. **Sir Edmund Hillary**
By ... Illustrated by William Hutchinson.
London: F. Watts, [1974]. 96, [4]p; ill (col),
maps, ports; 22cm. Previously published as **A
world explorer**

KNOWLES, Archibald Campbell

428. **Adventures in the Alps**
London: Skeffington, 1913. xii, 176p, 15 plates;
18cm

KNOWLTON, Elizabeth
American mountaineer, who made some first
ascents in the Andes. She accompanied the Nanga
Parbat expedition as press reporter. She has also
written a biography of Fanny Bullock Workman
(qv) for the publication **Notable American Women.**
See also [795].

*429. **The naked mountain**
New York: Putnam, 1933. [12], 335p, 24 plates
(incl. ports); 24cm
Account of the 1932 German-American expedition, the first since Mummery's attempt in
1895.

KOGAN, Claude
French mountaineer, wife of Georges Kogan. She
climbed in the Andes and the Himalaya. Killed on
Cho Oyu. See [346] & [438].

KOGAN, Georges
French mountaineer.

430. **The ascent of Alpamayo: an account of the
Franco-Belgian expedition to the Cordillera Blanca
in the high Andes**
By ... and Nicole Leininger. Translated [from the
French] by Peter E. Thompson.
London: Harrap, 1954. 134p, 32 plates (1 col);
maps; 21cm
From the original: **Cordillère Blanche** (Paris:
Arthaud, 1952).

KOHLI, M. S.

431. **Last of the Annapurnas**
Delhi: Min. Inform. & Broadcasting, 1962. 143p;
ill, map, plates (some col. incl. ports); 23cm
Ascent of Annapurna III.

432. **Nine atop Everest: story of the Indian ascent**
Bombay: Orient Longmans, 1969. xxviii, 384p, 56
plates (16 col); ill, ports; 25cm

KOLB, Fritz

433. **Himalaya venture**
Translated [from the German] by Laurence Wilson.
London: Lutterworth Press, 1959. 148p, 3 maps,
15 plates; 22cm
From the original: **Einzelgänger im Himalaya**
(Munich: Bruckmann, 1957)
Lightweight climbing and exploration, in 1939 and
1946, in Lahul and Padar, by two Austrians who
were interned in India.

KUGY, Julius (1858–1944)
Austrian mountaineer, who achieved almost legendary distinction during his lifetime. He was
particularly knowledgeable about the Julian Alps.

*434. **Alpine pilgrimage**
Translated [from the German] by H. E. G. Tyn-
dale.
London: Murray, 1934. xxiv, 374p, 21 plates (incl.
ports); 23cm
From the original: **Aus dem Leben eines Berg-
steigers** (Munich: Rother, 1925)
One of the most fascinating of Alpine books.

435. **Son of the mountains: the life of an alpine guide**
Translated [from the German] by H. E. G. Tyndale.
London: Nelson, 1938. 200p, 9 plates (incl. port);
21cm
From the original: **Anton Oitzinger: ein Berg-
führerleben** (Graz: Verlag Leykam, 1925)
Biography of Anton Oitzinger, Kugy's friend and
guide.

KUMAR, N.

436. **Nilakanta: story of the Indian expedition of 1961**
Indian Govt. Pub. Div., 1965. xvi, 140p; ill, map;
22cm
Garhwal Himalaya.

LACHAPELLE, Edward R.

437. **ABC of avalanche safety**
? : Highlander Pub. Co., 1961.

LAMBERT, Raymond
Swiss guide, who made a heroic attempt to gain
Everest's south summit in 1952. **See also [216].**

*438. **White fury: Gaurisankar and Cho Oyu**
By . . . and Claude Kogan. Translated [from the
French] by Showell Styles.
London: Hurst & Blackett, 1956. 176p, 15 plates
(incl. ports); 22cm
From the original: **Record à l'Himalaya** (Paris:
France-Empire, 1955).

LANE, Ferdinand Cole.

439. **The story of mountains**
New York: Doubleday, 1950. xxiv, 448p, plates;
26cm
Unsatisfactory survey of the mountain world and
mountaineering.

LANGMUIR, Eric
Scottish mountain school instructor.

440. **Mountain leadership: the official handbook of the
Mountain Leadership Training Boards of Great
Britain**
Edinburgh: Scottish Council of Physical Re-
creation, [1969] 89p; ill; 24cm

LANGUEPIN, Jean-Jaques
French film photographer and mountaineer.

441. **To kiss high heaven**
Translated from the French by Mervyn Savill.
London: Kimber, 1956. 199p, 7 plates; 22cm
From the original: **Himalaya, passion cruelle** (Paris:
Flammarion, 1955)
Expedition to Nanda Devi in 1951, when the
summit pair disappeared.

LARDEN, Walter (1855–1919)
Well-known English alpinist, schoolmaster and
Naval instructor. His published works include
Argentine plains and Andine glaciers (Fisher
Unwin, 1911) and **Inscriptions from Swiss chalets**
(O.U.P., 1913). **See also Appendix VI.**

*442. **Recollections of an old mountaineer**
London: Arnold, 1910. xvi, 320p, 17 plates; 24cm
Climbing memoirs.

LATROBE, Charles Joseph (1801–75)
Traveller and Governor of Australia. He was a
pioneer of guideless climbing, making numerous
ascents and crossings of passes hitherto unexplored
by Englishmen, during the years 1824–30. His
published works include **The rambler in North
America, 1832–33** 2v. (London, 1835).

443. **The alpenstock: or, Sketches of Swiss scenery and
manners, MDCCCXXV–MDCCCXXVI**
London: Seeley & Burnside,
(829. x, 388p, 3 plates; 23cm
[1839] . 2nd ed. x [vi] , 366p, plates; 17cm
Variations seen or noted:
  (i) 3 plates; grey binding, uncut
  (ii) 4 plates & vignette; crimson cloth, a.e.g.
  (iii) 7 steel engravings & 3 woodcuts; no roman
dates on title page; mauve binding, blind stamped,
gilt decoration on front, a.e.g. Probably a late
issue.

444. **The pedestrian: a summer's ramble in the Tyrol
and some of the adjoining provinces**
? : ? 1832.

LE BLOND, Elizabeth Alice Frances (1861–1934)
(Née Hawkins-Whitshead)
(She also wrote under her other married
names – Mrs. Fred Burnaby, Mrs. Main).
Wealthy society woman, who originally went to
Switzerland for health reasons. She climbed exten-
sively in the Alps and later in Norway. She was the

first President of the Ladies Alpine Club, 1907.
She also wrote **The story of an Alpine winter** (Bell,
1907), a semi-factual tale, and **Day in, day out**
(Lane Bodley Head, 1928), which is autobiographical.

*445. **The high Alps in winter: or, Mountaineering in
search of health**
London: Sampson Low, 1883. xx, 204p, 2 maps (1
fold), 5 plates; 18cm

446. **High life and towers of silence**
By the author of 'The high alps in winter'
London: Sampson Low, 1886. xii, 195p, 7 plates
(incl. port); 19cm

447. **My home in the Alps**
London: Sampson Low, 1892. viii, 131p; 20cm

448. **True tales of mountain adventure for non-climbers
young and old**
London: Fisher Unwin,
1903. xviii, 299p, 36 plates (incl. ports); 22cm
1903. 2nd imp.
1906. 3rd imp.
London: Nelson,
1915. Shilling Library series
1916. Shilling Library series.

449. **Adventures on the roof of the world**
London:Fisher Unwin, 1904 } xvi, 333p, 32 plates;
New York: Dutton, 1904 } 22cm
London: Fisher Unwin, 1907.
London: Nelson, [1916]. Shilling Library series.

*450. **Mountaineering in the land of the midnight sun**
London: Fisher Unwin, 1908. xii, 304p, map, 64
plates; 23cm
First ascents in the Lyngen Peninsula.

LECONTE, Joseph Nisbet (1870–1950)
American mountaineer and A.A.C. founder mem-
ber. Professor of Geology, University of California.
A fine mountain photographer. See also [26].

451. **A journal of ramblings through the High Sierra of
California by the University Excursion Party [in
1870]**
San Francisco: Francis & Valentine, 1875. 103p, 9
plates; 22cm. About 100 copies made for members
of the party.
San Francisco: Sierra Club, 1930. xvi, 154p, 5
plates; ill, facsim, port; 22cm. Edition of 1500
copies. Includes bibliographical notes of various
editions and articles by the author.

John Muir (qv) accompanied this glacier fact-
finding expedition.

LEE, Frank Harold

452. **The lure of the hills: an anthology**
Selected by . . .
London: Harrap, 1928. 253p; 18cm

LEFEBURE, Molly

*453. **Scratch & Co.: the great cat expedition**
By . . . With drawings by A. Wainwright.
London: Gollancz, 1968. 158p; ill; 21cm
Delightful children's fiction: may be compared
with [103].

LEININGER, Nicole
See [430].

LE MESURIER, W. H.

454. **An impromptu ascent of Mont Blanc**
London: Elliot Stock, 1882. 76p, map, 7 plates;
22cm

LEONARD, Richard M.
American climber, who was the first to study
belaying techniques in rock-climbing, including the
concept of dynamic belaying.

*455. **Belaying the leader**
By . . . and Arnold Wesler.
San Francisco: Sierra Club, 1947. [Reprinted from
Sierra Club Bulletin 31 (7) (Dec. 1946): 68?]

LEWIN, Walter Henry

456. **Climbs**
London: the author, distributed by W. H. Smith &
Sons, 1932. xviii, 226p, 16 plates (incl. port);
23cm. Limited edition of 250 numbered and
signed copies.
Climbing reminiscences.

LIEBENBERG, Doyle P.
South African climber who made a number of
pioneer ascents in the Drakensberg in 1930s.

*457. **The Drakensberg of Natal**
Cape Town: Bulpin, 1972. x, 178p, maps, 24 (8
col) plates; 25cm
Includes climbing and list of recorded climbs.

LISTER, George Anslow (1879–1952)
See [142].

LIVANI, Masao

458. **Encyclopaedia of the world's mountains**
Edited by . . .
? : ?, 1971.

LONGLAND, Sir John [Jack] Laurence (b. 1905)
Educationalist, broadcaster and mountaineer.
Member of the 1933 Everest expedition and a
leading rock-climber. See [659].

LONGSTAFF, Tom George (1875–1964)
Doctor, naturalist and mountain explorer. A.C.
President 1947–9. He was a pioneer of the light
expedition. He climbed in most of the mountain
areas of the northern hemisphere and was the first
to ascend a 7,000 metre peak in the Himalaya. See
also [124], [757] & [938].

459. **Mountain sickness and its probable cause**
London: Spottiswoode, 1906. 56p; 22cm
Written as a graduation thesis.

*†460.**This my voyage**
London: Murray,
1950. [xii], 324p, 23 plates; ill, maps, ports,
23cm
1951. Reprint
Climbing memoirs.

LOVELOCK, James

461. **Climbing**
With a chapter on artificial climbing by Trevor Jones.
London: Batsford, 1971. 185p, 16 plates; 23cm
Instructional.

LOWE, W. George
New Zealand climber and explorer.

462. **Because it is there**
London: Cassell, 1959. viii, 216p; ill, maps, plates; 22cm
New York: St. Martins Press, 1961. Published under title **From Everest–to the South Pole**
Chiefly about his Antarctic experiences.

463. **From Everest–to the South Pole**
New York: St. Martins Press, 1961. viii, 216p.
U.S.A. edition of **Because it is there.**

LUCKHOFF, C. A.

*464. **Table Mountain: our national heritage after three hundred years**
Cape Town: A. A. Balkema, 1951. 152p, 125 plates (4 col); ill, ports; 28cm
Lavish monograph with sections on geology, flora and climbing.

LUKAN, Karl

465. **The Alps**
With descriptive essays by . . .
By Wilfrid Noyce and . . . Translated from the German by Margaret Shenfield.
London: Thames & Hudson,
    1961. 312p; 5 maps, 230 plates; 28cm
    1963. Revised ed.
From the original: **Die Alpen von Mont Ventoux zum Kahlenberg** (Vienna: Schroll, 1959)
Wilfrid Noyce's contribution is chiefly introductory.

466. **The Alps and alpinism**
Edited by . . . Translated [from the German] by Hugh Merrick.
London: Thames & Hudson, 1968. 200p; ill, facsims, plates (some col. incl. ports); 29cm
Based on: **Der Alpinismus in Bildern** by Alfred Steinitzer, (Munich: R. Piper & Co., 1913).

467. **Mountain adventures**
London: Collins, 1972. 128p; ill (chiefly col), col. maps, ports (some col); 26cm

LUNN, Sir Arnold Henry Moore (1888–1974)
Writer, skier and champion of Anglo-Swiss friendship. He wrote many books on Switzerland and skiing, mostly with a mountaineering flavour. His published works include **The Bernese Oberland** (Eyre & Spottiswoode, 1958); **Zermatt and the Valais** (Hollis & Carter, 1955); **Mountain jubilee** (Eyre & Spottiswoode, 1943); and **Unkilled for so long** (Allen & Unwin, 1968), which is autobiographical.

*468. **Oxford mountaineering essays**
Edited by . . .
London: Arnold, 1912. xii, 237p; 20cm

*469. **The Englishman in the Alps: being a collection of English prose and poetry relating to the Alps**
Edited by . . .
London: O.U.P.,
    1913. xx, 294p; 18cm
    1927. 2nd ed. xx, 300p; 18cm

470. **The Alps**
London: Williams & Norgate, 1914. 256p; 17cm
New York: 1914 [Published as **The exploration of the Alps?**].

471. **The mountains of youth**
London: O.U.P., 1925. [8], 192p, 20 plates; 22 cm
London: Eyre & Spottiswoode, 1949. 2nd ed. xvi, 192p

472. **A history of skiing**
London: O.U.P., 1927. xvi, 492p, 24 plates (incl. ports), 22cm
Includes winter mountaineering.

473. **Mountains of memory**
London: Hollis & Carter, 1948. xii, 248p, plates (incl. ports); 23cm

*474. **A century of mountaineering 1857–1957**
London: Allen & Unwin, 1957. [iv], 263p, 24 (8 col) plates; 25cm
A very good survey.

475. **The Swiss and their mountains: a study of the influence of mountains on man**
London: Allen & Unwin, 1963. 167p, 24 plates (some col. incl. ports); 23cm

476. **Matterhorn centenary**
London: Allen & Unwin, 1965. 144p, 25 plates (incl. facsims, ports); 22cm
100 years of climbing on the Matterhorn.

LYMAN, Tom

477. **The field book of mountaineering and rock-climbing**
By . . . with Bill Riviere.
New York: Winchester Press, 1975. [8], 213p, ill; 24cm

McCALLUM, John D.

478. **Everest diary: based on the personal diary of Lute Jerstad, one of the first five Americans to climb Everest**
Chicago: Follett Pub., 1966. vi, 213p; ill; 22cm

McCARTY, Cleveland
See [23].

McCORMICK, Arthur David (1860–1943)
Artist, who accompanied Conway (qv) on several expeditions and illustrated his books. He also illustrated other mountaineering books.

479. **An artist in the Himalayas**
London: Fisher Unwin, 1895. xii, 306p; ill, map, plate; 23cm

MACDONALD, Reginald John Somerled (1840–76)
Civil servant and keen alpinist of the 'Golden Age'.
See [22].

MACINNES, Hamish
Professional mountaineer: leader of the Glencoe
Mountain Rescue Team. **See also Apendix V.**

480. **Climbing**
Edinburgh: Scottish Y.H.A., 1963. 86p; ill; 18cm
Stirling: Scottish Y.H.A., 1964. 84p [80]; ill;
19cm
A guide to mountaineering and mountain rescue.

481. **International mountain rescue handbook**
London: Constable, 1972. 218p; ill; 23cm

*482. **Call-out**
London: Hodder, 1973. 190p, 16 plates (incl.
ports); 23cm [Several impressions]
H'worth: Penguin, 1977. Paperback ed.
The work of the Glencoe Mountain Rescue Team.

*483. **Climb to the Lost World**
London: Hodder, 1974. 224p, 32 (8 col) plates
(incl. ports); 23cm
H'worth: Penguin, 1976. Paperback ed.
Climbing the Great Prow of Roraima, Guyana.

M'INTYRE, D. F.
See [166].

MACINTYRE, Neil

484. **Attack on Everest**
London: Methuen, 1936. viii, 172p; 20cm
Poor summary of various attempts.

McMORRIN, Ian
See [584].

McMORRIS, William Bruce

485. **The real book of mountaineering**
Illustrated by Albert Orbaan.
New York: Doubleday, 1958.
London: Dobson, 1961. 192p; ill; 21cm. Revised
ed.
Written for children: inaccurate.

McNEIL, Fred H.

486. **Wy' East 'The Mountain'**
Portland, Ore: Metropolitan Press, 1937.
A chronicle of Mount Hood, Cascades.

MAEDER, Herbert (b. 1930)
Swiss photographer-journalist and mountaineer.

*487. **The mountains of Switzerland: the adventure of
the high Alps**
Edited, with photographs and commentary, by . . .
Translated [from the German] by Hendrik P. B.
Betlem.
London: Allen & Unwin, 1968. 288p; ill (some
col); 30cm
From the original: **Die Berge der Schweiz** (Olten:
Walter Verlag, 1967)
Includes sections on geology, flora and fauna.
Heavily illustrated with supporting text.

488. **The lure of the mountains**
Edited and selection of photos by . . .
London: Elsevier-Phaidon, 1975. [6], 138p; col.
ill; 30cm
New York: T. Y. Crowell, 1975
From the original: **Lockende Berge** (Zurich:
Silva-Verlag, 1971)
Elaborate anthology comprising nine extracts from
well-known authors, e.g. Whymper.

MAGNONE, Guido
French mountaineer, who made many notable
ascents, including Fitzroy and Makalu.

*489. **West face**
Translated from the French by J. F. Burke.
London: Museum Press, 1955. 166p, 13 plates
(incl. ports); 23cm
From the original: **La Face W des Drus** (Paris:
Amiot-Dumont, 1953)
First ascent of the west face of the Dru.

MAIN, Mrs.
See: LE BLOND, Elizabeth

MALARTIC, Yves
French journalist.

490. **Tenzing of Everest**
Translated [from the French] by J. B. Heller.
London: Kimber, 1954. 285p; ill;
From the original: **La conquête de l'Everest par le
Sherpa Tensing** (Paris: Scorpion, 1953)
An inaccurate and ill-informed account.

MALLORY, George Herbert Leigh (1886–1924)
English schoolmaster. He climbed in Britain and
the Alps but rose to fame as a member of the early
Everest expeditions, disappearing without trace in
1924. See [124] & [387].

MANDOLF, Henry Ikarus (1897–1972)
American.

491. **Basic mountaineering**
Edited by . . .
San Diego, Calif: Sierra Club, 1961. 112p; ill;

MANNERING, George Edward (1862–1947)
New Zealand mountaineer, who was responsible
for much exploration and survey work in the
1890s in the Mount Cook area. Co-founder of the
New Zealand Alpine Club with A. P. Harper (qv).
He also wrote **Eighty years in New Zealand** (1943).

*492. **With axe and rope in the New Zealand alps**
London: Longmans, 1891. xii, 139p, map, 17
plates; 24cm

MANNING, Harvey
See [761].

MARAINI, Fosco (b. 1912)
Italian writer, mountaineer, scholar, connoisseur.
His published works include **Secret Tibet** (Hutchinson, 1952). His books rank high for the quality of
the writing and illustrations.

*†493. **Karakoram: the ascent of Gasherbrum IV**
Translated from the Italian by James Cadell.
New York: Viking Press, 1961. 320p, 80 (40 col) plates; ill, maps, ports; 24cm
From the original: **Gasherbrum 4°** (Bari: Leonardo da Vinci, 1959).

*†494. **Where four worlds meet: Hindu Kush 1959**
Translated from the Italian by Peter Green.
London: Hamish Hamilton, 1964. xii, 290p, 100 (16.col) plates; col. fold. maps, ports; 24cm
[U.S.A.]: Harcourt Brace, 1964.

From the original: **Paropàmiso** (Bari: Leonardo da Vinci, 1963)
Ascent of Saraghrar.

MARCH, William
Mountaineering instructor.

495. **Improvised rescue techniques**
Edinburgh: Jacobean Press, (printed by) 1974. [ix], 94p; ill; 21cm. Cover title reads **Improvised techniques in mountain rescue.**
Self-help for rock-climbers.

*496. **Modern snow and ice techniques**
Manchester: Cicerone Press, 1973. 66p, 7 plates; ill; 16cm [Reprinted 1974. 1975. 1976. 1977.]

*497. **Modern rope techniques in mountaineering: incorporating 'Improvised techniques in mountain rescue'**
Manchester: Cicerone Press, 1976. 127p; ill; 17cm [Reprinted 1977.]

MARINER, Wastl

*498. **Mountain rescue techniques**
Drawings by Fritz and Gert Ebster. First aid instructions by Hans Heinz Seidel. Revised by and translated from the German by O. T. Trott & K. G. Beam.
Innsbruck: Austrian Alpine Club, 1963. 200p; ill; 21cm

MARSHALL, Howard
Writer and broadcaster.

499. **Men against Everest.**
London: Country Life, 1954. 64p, 17 plates (incl. ports); 23cm
The Everest story up to the first ascent.

MARTEL, Pierre-Guillaume (1701/2–61)
Swiss instrument-maker. See [922].

M[ARTYN], T[homas] (1735–1825)
Botanist. He toured the Continent in the years 1778–80.

500. **Sketch of a tour through Swisserland: with an accurate map**
London: G. Kearsley,
   1787. 98p; map; 18cm. Bound with **an appendix, containing catalogues of paintings ... in different parts of Italy.** This has its own title page and is separately paginated.
   1788. An appendix to the **Sketch of a tour through Swisserland, containing a short account of an expedition to the summit of Mont Blanc,**
by M. de Saussure of Geneva, in August last: Paginated 99–127.
   1788. 2nd edition. Original book plus supplement. 131p; 18cm. The main title-page is altered to: **Sketch of a tour through Swisserland: with an accurate map. A new edition, to which is added a short account of an expedition to the summit of Mont Blanc, by M. de Saussure, of Geneva.**
   The title-page of the supplement reads: **A short account of an expedition to the summit of Mont Blanc, by M. de Saussure of Geneva, in August last; in order to ascertain the height of that celebrated mountain, the loftiest point of the three ancient continents, and to make a variety of observations and experiments on the form and structure of the mountain, the state of the air, with many other curious particulars.**

MASON, Alfred Edward Woodley (1865–1948)
English novelist and A.C. member. Climbing episodes and themes are used in some of his stories.

*501. **Running water**
London: Hodder, 1907. viii, 355p; 20cm. [Various impressions/editions.]
Well-known story involving the Brenva ice-ridge.

MASON, Gene

502. **Minus three**
Englewood Cliffs, N. J.: Prentice-Hall, 1970. 190p; ill (col);
Account of his ascents of McKinley, Aconcagua and Kilimanjaro.

MASON, Sir Kenneth (1887–1976)
Formerly Superintendent of the Survey of India and subsequently Professor of Geography at Oxford University.

*503. **Abode of snow: a history of Himalayan exploration and mountaineering**
London: Hart-Davis, 1955. xii, 372p, maps, 20 plates (incl. ports); 23cm
New York: Dutton, 1955.
Authoritative source of reference to the historical and geographical background to the entire Himalayan range, with a remarkably concise and comprehensive history of Himalayan exploration.

MATHEWS, Charles Edward (1834–1905)
Solicitor. Original A.C. member and President 1878–80. He climbed regularly in the Alps. See also [22] & [211].

*†504. **The annals of Mont Blanc: a monograph**
London: Fisher Unwin, 1898. xxiv [xxii] 368p facsims, fold. map, 28 plates (incl. ports); 23cm. Also extra illustrated edition containing additional five plates and map.

MATHEWS, William Jr. (1828–1901)
Land agent and surveyor. A.C. member and President 1869–71. See [18] & [20].

MAY, W. G.

505. **Mountain search and rescue techniques**
Boulder, Col: Rocky Mountain Rescue Group, 1973. 324p.

MAYHEW, Henry & Athol

506. **Mont Blanc: a comedy in three acts**
First produced at the Theatre Royal, Haymarket,
Whit Monday, May 25, 1874.
London: privately printed, 1874. 61p; 8vo.

MAZEAUD, Pierre (b. 1929)
French lawyer, politician and mountaineer, who
was with Bonatti (qv) on the Central Pillar of
Frêney.

*507. **Naked before the mountain**
Translated [from the French] by Geoffrey Sutton
London: Gollancz, 1974. 256p, 24 plates (incl
ports); 23cm
From the original: **Montagne pour un homme nu**
(Paris: Arthaud, 1971) First published in Germany
under the title **Schritte himmelwärts** (Heering-
Verlag, 1968).
Climbing memoirs.

MEADE, Charles Francis (b. 1881)
Himalayan explorer, who attempted Kamet three
times between 1910–13. **See also [757].**

*508. **Approach to the hills**
London: Murray,
     1940. [x], 265p, 2 maps, 16 plates (incl.
     ports); 23cm
     1941. Reprint
     1948. Albermarle Library ed.
Some Alpine stories and his own Himalayan
experiences.

*509. **High mountains**
London: Harvill Press, 1954, 136p, 11 plates;
22cm
Examines the question of mountains and nature
mysticism.

MEANY, Edmond Stephen (1862–1935)
Professor of History, University of Washington.
President of the Mountaineers Club. His published
works include a book of poems and songs
Mountain camp fires (Seattle: Lowman & Hanford,
1911).

510 **Mount Rainier: a record of exploration**
Edited by . . .
New York: Macmillan, 1916. xii, 325p, 17 plates
(chiefly ports); 23cm
Extracts from the accounts of explorers,
1792–1914.

MELDRUM, Kim

*511. **Artificial climbing walls**
By . . . and Brian Royle
London: Pelham, 1970. 69p, 12 plates; ill; 23cm
Their design and use.

MENDENHALL, Ruth & John

512. **Introduction to rock and mountain climbing**
By Ruth and John Mendenhall: illustrated by
Vivian Mendenhall.
Harrisburg, Pa: Stackpole Books, 1969. 192p.

MERRICK, Hugh (pseud. H. A. Meyer)
Writer and translator of numerous mountain

books. His published works include **Rambles in the
Alps** (Country Life, 1951) and **The Alps in colour**
(Constable, 1970). **See also Appendix IV.**

513. **Savoy episode**
London: Hale, 1946. x, 192p [182], 32 plates;
22cm
Pre-war holiday rambles in the Graian Alps: nicely
illustrated.

514. **The perpetual hills: a personal anthology of
mountains**
London: Newnes, 1964. 247p, 32 plates; 26cm

MERZBACHER, Gottfried (1846–1926)
German climber and explorer, who was active in
the Dolomites. He later visited the Caucasus and
ranges of central Asia.

*515. **The central Tian-Shan Mountains, 1902–1903**
Published under the authority of the Royal
Geographical Society.
London: Murray, 1905. x, 294p, fold. map, 18
plates; 23cm

MESSNER, Reinhold (b. 1944)
Leading Austrian mountaineer.

*516. **The seventh grade: most extreme climbing**
London: Kaye & Ward, 1974. 160p, 4 col. plates;
21cm
New York: O.U.P., 1974. 160p
From the original: **Der 7 Grad** (Munich: BLV
Verlag, 1973).

MEYER, Hans
German explorer, who also visited the Andes of
Ecuador.

*517. **Across East African glaciers: an account of the first
ascent of Kilimanjaro**
Translated from the German by E. H. S. Calder.
London: Geo. Philip, 1891. xx, 404p, 3 col. maps,
21 (1 col) plates; 26cm
From the original: **Ostafrikanische Gletscher-
fahrten: Forschungsreisen im Kilimandscharo-
Gebiet** (Leipzig, 1890)
First ascent of Kibo peak: a most handsome
volume.

MILLS, Ernest James Edward (1926–62)
British soldier and mountaineer.

518. **Airborne to the mountains**
London: Jenkins, 1961. 202p, 32 plates; 23cm
New York: A. S. Barnes, 1961. 212p
Army expedition to Mt. McKinley region.

MILLMAN, Arthur (–1912)
See [20].

MILNE, Lorus Johnson

519. **The mountains**
By . . . and Margery Milne, and the editors of
Time-Life Books.
     1963
Amsterdam: Time-Life International,
     1963.
     1970. 192p; ill (some col); 28cm
Time-Life Nature Library.

MILNE, Malcolm

520. **The book of modern mountaineering**
Edited by . . .
London: Barker, 1968. 304p; ill (some col), ports (some col); 30cm
Contributions by many well-known climbers.

MILNER, Cyril Douglas
Businessman, mountaineer and photographer.

*†521.**Mountain photography: its art and techniques in Britain and abroad**
London: Focal Press,
  1945. 238p; ill; 25cm
  1946. Reprinted.

*522. **Rock for climbing**
London: Chapman & Hall, 1950. viii, 128p; ill; 26cm
Photographs of many classic routes, with supporting text.

*523. **The Dolomites**
London: Hale, 1951. xiv, 105p, 97 plates; maps; 26cm
Well illustrated survey of this important region.

*524. **Mont Blanc and the Aiguilles**
London: Hale, 1955. xvi, 176p, 65 (1 col) plates; ill, maps; 24cm
Well illustrated survey of climbing in this important region.

525. **All about taking pictures in the hills with your camera**
London: Focal Press, 1955. 56p, 16 plates; 16cm

MITCHELL, Elyne
Australian writer and skier.

*526. **Australia's alps**
Sydney: Angus & Robertson, 1946. xii, 185p, 52 plates; maps; 25cm
The Snowy Mountains: the main attraction is high mountain skiing.

MOFFAT, Gwen
Professional mountain guide and writer, including detective fiction with climbing settings. **See Appendix IV.**

*527. **Space below my feet**
London: Hodder, 1961. 286p, 7 plates (incl. port); 21cm
H'worth: Penguin, 1976. Paperback
Autobiography.

*528. **Two Star Red: a book about R.A.F. [Royal Air Force] mountain rescue**
London: Hodder, 1964. xviii, 206p, maps, 16 plates (incl. ports); 21cm
A history of the teams in Britain, and elsewhere.

529. **On my home ground**
London: Hodder, 1968. 256p, 15 plates (incl. ports); 23cm
Autobiography: sequel to [527].

530. **Survival count**
London: Gollancz, 1972. 175p, 8 plates; 23cm
Autobiography: sequel to [529].

MOLENAAR, Dee (b. 1918)
American mountaineer and member of the 1953 expedition to K.2.

*531. **The challenge of Rainier: a record of the explorations and ascents, triumphs and tragedies on the Northwest's greatest mountain**
Seattle: The Mountaineers, 1971. xx, 332p; ill; 26cm

MOLONY, Eileen

532. **Portraits of mountains**
Edited by . . .
London: Dobson, 1950. 117p, 12 plates; 23cm
Essays on British mountains by well-known climbers.

MONKHOUSE, Frank

533. **Climber and fellwalker in Lakeland**
By . . . and Joe Williams.
Newton Abbot: David & Charles, [1972]. 214p, maps, 17 plates; 23cm
Good general survey.

MONTAGNIER, Henry Fairbanks (1877–1933)
American. Specialist on the history of Alpine exploration. **See [292] and Appendix I.**

MONTAGUE, Charles Edward (1867–1928)
English writer and journalist. Some of his novels and stories include mountaineering situations, the most famous being **In Hanging Garden Gully**, which is usually quoted in full in mountaineering anthologies: **see [400]. See also [795].**

MOON, Kenneth

534. **Man of Everest: the story of Sir Edmund Hillary**
London: Lutterworth Press, 1962. 96p, 1 col. plate (port); 19cm
Written for children.

MOORE, Adolphus Warburton (1841–87)
Senior British civil servant. He made extensive Alpine tours in the years 1860–81, notably with Whymper and Horace Walker in 1864, and was a member of the party which made the first ascent of the Brenva ice-ridge on Mont Blanc. In 1868 he visited the Caucasus with Freshfield (qv). The A.C. hold his later unpublished diaries, parts of which were incorporated into the 1902 edition, including his account of the Brenva climb. **See also [22].**

*535. **The Alps in 1864: a private journal**
[Privately printed], 1867. x, 360p, 10 maps; 24cm. 100 copies only.
Edinburgh: David Douglas, 1902. xxxvi, 444p, 22 plates; ill, 10 maps, port; 26cm. Edited by A. B. W. Kennedy.
Oxford: Blackwell, 1939. 2v. Edited by E. H. Stevens.

MOORE, Terris (b. 1908)
American mountaineer, who made the first ascent of Minya Konka in 1932 with Burdsall (qv).

*536. **Mount McKinley: the pioneer climbs**
College: Univ. Alaska Press, 1967. xvi, 202p, col. plate; ill, maps, ports; 24cm

MORDECAI, D.

537. **The Himalaya: an illustrated summary of the world's highest mountain ranges**
Calcutta: Daw Sen, 1966. 28p, 30 plates (incl. ports); 18 x 31cm
Annotated list of 569 peaks over 20,000' in Himalaya, Karakoram and Hindu Kush.

MORIN, Micheline (1899–1972)
Well-known French alpinist and exponent of 'manless' climbing. See her book **Encordées** (Paris, 1937). Sister-in-law of Nea Morin (qv).

538. **Everest – from the first attempt to the final victory**
London: Harrap, 1955 } 205p; ill some col).
New York: John Day, 1955 } 10 maps, 21cm
From the original: **Everest, du premier assaut à la victoire** (Paris: Arthaud, 1953).

MORIN, Nea E. (b. 1905) (née Barnard)
English mountaineer and one of the leaders in the development of women's climbing. She has also translated several mountaineering books into English.

*539. **A woman's reach: mountaineering memoirs**
London: Eyre & Spottiswoode, 1968
New York: Dodd Meade, 1968
Includes a list of first feminine ascents.

MORRIS, James Humphry [Jan] (b. 1927)
British writer and journalist.

*540. **Coronation Everest**
London: Faber
1958. 146p, [144], 8 plates (incl. port); 23cm
1963. School edition.
Well-written story of the first ascent told by the 'Times' correspondent, who relayed the news to Britain on the eve of Coronation Day.

MORSE, S.
See [30].

MOULD, Daphne Desirée Charlotte Pochin

541. **The mountains of Ireland**
London: Batsford, 1955. 160p [157], 32 plates; 23cm
General survey.

Mountain climbing (Out of Door Library)
See under: WILSON, E. L.

Mountaineering (Lonsdale Library)
See under: SPENCER, S.

Mountaineering in China
See under: PEOPLE'S PHYSICAL CULTURE PUBLISHING HOUSE

Mountaineering in South Africa
See under: SOUTH AFRICAN RAILWAYS

MOUNTAINEERS [CLUB]

*542. **Mountaineering: the freedom of the hills**
Seattle: Mountaineers,
1960. 430p; ill
1967. 2nd ed. Edited by Harvey Manning.
1974. 3rd ed. xvi, 478p; ill; 23cm
Comprehensive instruction manual.

543. **Medicine for mountaineering**
Edited by J. A. Wilkerson.
Seattle: Mountaineers,
1967.
1969. 309p
Expedition handbook.

MOUNTAIN RESCUE COMMITTEE

544. **Mountain rescue [and cave rescue]**
Issued by the Mountain Rescue Committee.
Cheadle Hume, Stockport: M.R.C.,
1957. 42p; ill, 2 maps; 18cm
1958. Revised. This and subsequent editions entitled **Mountain rescue and cave rescue.**
1962. 56p, [Revised regularly.]
Includes first aid and details of British rescue facilities.

Mountain World
See under: SWISS FOUNDATION FOR ALPINE RESEARCH

MUIR, John (1838–1914)
Scottish-born naturalist, writer and explorer, who emigrated to the U.S.A. in early boyhood. He visited Alaska and the Arctic and was very active in California. Founder and President of the Sierra Club: also a founder member of the A.A.C. He exercised considerable influence over American concepts of mountains. As an ardent lover of all natural scenes, animals and open-air life, he was largely responsible for the establishment of Yosemite and other areas as national parks. He also wrote **Our National Parks** (Boston: Houghton Mifflin, 1903).
Biographies:
The life and letters of John Muir, 2vol. (Boston: Houghton Mifflin, 1923–4) by William Frederic Badè; **Son of the wilderness: the life of John Muir** (New York: Knopf, 1945) by L. M. Wolfe (qv). See also Appendix VI.

*545. **The mountains of California**
New York: The Century Co. 1894.
London: Fisher Unwin, 1894
1911. 9th ed.
Boston: Houghton Mifflin 1917,
2vols
New York: Doubleday, 1961.

*546. **My first summer in the Sierra**
Boston: Houghton Mifflin, 1911 } x, 354p, 12
London: Constable, 1911 } plates 21 cm.
[Several editions.]

547. **Travels in Alaska**
Boston: Houghton Mifflin, 1916 xii, 328p; 12 plates, 21cm. [Prepared for publication by Marion R. Parsons.]

548. **Steep trails**
Edited by William Frederick Badè
Boston: Houghton Mifflin, 1918. xii, 392p, 12 plates; 22cm

*549. **Yosemite and the Sierra Nevada**
Selected writings of John Muir and 64 photographs by Ansel Adams.
Boston: Houghton Mifflin, 1948.

MULGREW, Peter D.

*550. **No place for men**
Wellington: Reed, 1964. 199p, 24 plates (incl. ports); 23cm
London: Nicholas Vane, 1965. 1st ed. reprinted
New York: Doubleday, 1965. Published under title
I hold the heights
An account of Hillary's 1960 expedition to Makalu, experimenting with the effects of high altitude climbing without oxygen. The author was severely crippled with frostbite.

551. **I hold the heights**
New York: Doubleday, 1965. U.S.A. edition of **No place for men**

MULLER, Edwin Jr. (1892–1963)
American writer: editor of *Reader's Digest*.

552. **They climbed the Alps**
London: Cape, 1930. [10], 217p, 16 plates; 22cm
Résumé of various classic nineteenth century ascents.

MUMM, Arnold Louis (1859–1927)
British publisher and mountaineer, who explored in the Himalaya and Canadian Rockies. **See also** **[938].**

*553. **Five months in the Himalaya: a record of mountain travel in Garhwal and Kashmir**
London: Arnold, 1909. xvi, 263p, 28 (4 fold) plates; 2 fold. maps; ill, group port; 26cm

*†554. **The Alpine Club Register 1857–63**
London: Arnold,
    1923. viii, 391; 23cm
    1925. Vol. 2 (1864–76). viii, 375p; 23cm
    1928. Vol. 3 (1877–90). viii, 352p; 23cm
The A.C. have typescripts of projected volumes covering the years 1891–95 and 1896–1901.
An invaluable reference source: the dates refer to year of election to the Alpine Club.

MUMMERY, Albert Frederick (1855–95)
English businessman and mountaineer. Expert rock-climber and alpinist, who made many important climbs in the Mont Blanc region. He led an expedition to Nanga Parbat in 1895, accompanied by Collie (qv) and Bruce (qv), and disappeared whilst reconnoitring.

*555. **My climbs in the Alps and Caucasus**
London: Fisher Unwin,
    1895. xii, 360p, 11 plates (some col); 28cm.
    Also edition on Japan paper – 24 numbered and signed copies of which only 20 were for sale.
New York: Scribners,
    1895.
London: Fisher Unwin,
    1895. 2nd/3rd imp.
    1908. 2nd ed.[4th imp] With an introduction by Mrs. Mummery and an appreciation by J. A. Hobson. Portrait of author substituted for picture of Aiguille Verte.
London: Nelson,
    [1913] Edition with introduction and appreciation as 1908 ed.
Oxford: Blackwell,
    1936. Edited by H. E. G. Tyndale, with introduction by M. Mummery.
Lawrence, Mass: Quarterman Pub,
    1974. Facsim. reprint of 2nd ed.[imp.] 1895.

MUNDAY, Walter Alfred Don
Canadian mountaineer, who, with his wife, discovered Mt. Waddington in 1925 and spent nearly ten years trying to climb it.

*556. **The unknown mountain**
London: Hodder, 1948. xx, 268p, fold. map, 31 plates; 23cm
Seattle: Mountaineers, 1975, 268p.

MUNDELL, Frank

557. **Stories of alpine adventure**
London: Sunday School Union, [1898]. 158p; ill, plates, ports; 19cm

MURRAY, William Hutchison (b. 1913)
Scottish mountaineer and writer. Prominent in Scottish rock and winter climbing in the 1930s, accomplishing many new severe routes. He has also written general guides to the Highlands of Scotland and several novels. **See also [532] & [843].**

*558. **Mountaineering in Scotland**
London: Dent,
    1947. xii, 252p, 32 plates; 22cm
    1962. xii, 252p
    ? . Aldine paperback.

*559. **Undiscovered Scotland: climbs on rock, snow, and ice**
Maps and diagrams by Robert Anderson.
London: Dent,
    1951. viii, 232p. 24 plates. 22cm
    1954.

560. **The Scottish Himalayan Expedition**
11 maps and diagrams by Robert Anderson.
London: Dent, 1951. xiv, 282p, 36 plates (4 col); ill, maps, ports; 22cm **See also [880].**

561. **The story of Everest**
Maps and diagrams by Robert Anderson.
London: Dent,
    1953. ix, 193p, 23 plates; 23cm
    1953. 2nd ed.[imp]
    1953. 3rd ed. x, 198p
    1953. 4th ed. x, 218p
    1953. New ed. x, 230p
History of attempts up to first ascent.

562. **The craft of climbing**
By . . . and J. E. B. Wright.
London: Kaye, 1964. 77p, 16 plates; 23cm

[NAESS, Arne]

*563. **Tirich Mir**
By members of the Norweigan Himalayan expedition.
Translated [from the Norwegian] by Sölvi and Richard Batison.
London: Hodder, 1952. 192p, 39 plates (incl. ports); 23cm
From the original: **Tirich Mir Til Topps: den Norske Himalaia-Ekspedisjonen** (Oslo: Gyldendal, 1950)
First major ascent in the Hindu Kush.

NAVARRA, Fernand

564. **The forbidden mountain**
Translated from the French by Michel Legat.
London: Macdonald, 1956. x, 176p [166], 2 maps,
15 plates; 23cm
From the original: **L'expédition au Mont Ararat**
(Bordeaux: Biere, 1953)
Ascent of Ararat in search of Noah's Ark.

NESBIT, Paul W.

*565. **Longs Peak: its story and a guide for climbing it**
Colorado Springs: Out West Ptg Co.,
1946. 47p; ill;
1963.
1966. 5th ed. 65p.

NEVE, Arthur
Medical missionary and mountaineer. His published
works include **Picturesque Kashmir** (Sands, 1900).

566. **Thirty years in Kashmir**
London: Arnold, 1913. viii, 316p, 17 plates; 23cm
Holiday expeditions to Nun Kun, Nanga Parbat etc.

NEWBY, George Eric (b. 1919)
English writer and traveller.

*567. **A short walk in the Hindu Kush**
London: Secker & Warburg, 1958. 247p, fold.
map, 25 plates (incl. ports); 22cm
London: Arrow Books, 1961.
London: Hodder, 1972. Reprinted from 1st ed.
London: Pan Books, 1974. Paperback.
Two non-mountaineers attempt 19,880' Mir Samir
in north-east Afghanistan and explore the remote
region of Nuristan.

NICHOLS, Robert Cradock (1824–92)
A.C. member, who made a number of first ascents
in the Graian Alps. **See [20]**.

NICHOLS, Starr Hoyt

568. **Monte Rosa: the epic of an alp**
Boston: Houghton Mifflin, 1883. 148p
Epic poem.

NOCK, Peter W. W.

569. **Rock-climbing**
London: W. & G. Foyle, 1963. 96p, 4 plates; 19cm
Foyles Handbooks for Sportsmen series.

NOEL, John Baptist Lucius

*570. **Through Tibet to Everest**
London: Arnold, 1927. 302p, 20 plates (incl.
facsim, ports); 22cm
Boston: Little, Brown, 1927. U.S.A. edition
entitled **Story of Everest**
London: Arnold, 1931. Kingfisher Library ed.
An account of the first three attempts on Everest
by the photographer to the 1922 and 1924
expeditions.

571. **Story of Everest**
Boston: Little, Brown, 1927. U.S.A. edition of
Through Tibet to Everest

NORMAN-NERUDA, Ludwig (1864–98)
English mountaineer and one of the leading
climbers of his day. Some of his climbs are still
highly regarded. He was taken ill and died during a
climb.

*572. **The climbs of Norman-Neruda**
Edited, and with an account of his last climb, by
May Norman-Neruda.
London: Fisher Unwin, 1899. xii, 335p, 30 plates
(incl. ports); 23cm

NORTON, Edward Felix (1884–1954)
Soldier: grandson of Sir Alfred Wills (qv). He led
the Everest expedition in 1924, when he
climbed to a height of about 28,100' without
oxygen.

*573. **The fight for Everest: 1924**
By . . . and other members of the expedition.
London: Arnold, 1925. xii, 372p, fold. map, 32 (8
col) plates (incl. ports); 26cm

NOWILL, Sidney Edward Payn
See under: ASHENDEN

NOYCE, Cuthbert Wilfrid Frank (1917–62)
Schoolmaster, writer and mountaineer. One of the
best British writer-mountaineers. Member of the
1953 Everest expedition. He was killed climbing in
the Pamirs; **see [710]**. In addition to his own
numerous works he was involved (as author or
editor) with many others, including some of the
C.C. guides to North Wales. His expedition books
are among the best of their kind. He also wrote
The springs of adventure (Murray, 1958). **See also
[238], [465], [532], [630], [659], [943], &
Appendix VI.**

*574. **Mountains and men**
London: Bles,
1947. 160p, 4 maps, 17 plates; 25cm
1954. 2nd ed. with revised preface.
Climbing autobiography.

*575. **Scholar mountaineers: pioneers of Parnassus**
With wood engravings by R. Taylor.
London: Dobson, 1950. 164p, 12 plates; 22cm
Essays on the effect of mountains on various
historical figures.

*576. **South Col: one man's adventure on the ascent of
Everest, 1953**
Line drawings and end-papers by A. J. Veilhan
with the co-operation of the author.
London: Heinemann, 1954. xx, 303p, 52 (4 col)
plates (incl. ports); 22cm
New York: Sloane, 1955.
London: Heinemann, 1956. Abridged ed. New
Windmill series.
One of the best of the many Everest books.

577. **Everest is climbed**
By . . . and R. Taylor.
H'worth: Penguin, 1954. 31p; ill; 19 x 23cm.
Puffin Picture book.
Written for children.

578. **The gods are angry**
London: Heinemann, 1957. 198p
Cleveland: World Pub., 1958. 214p
Mountaineering novel set in the Himalaya.

579. **Climbing the Fish's Tail**
London: Heinemann, 1958. xiv, 150p, 25 plates
(incl. ports); 21cm
Ascent of Machapuchare, Nepal Himalaya.

*580. **Poems**
London: Heinemann, 1960. 98p; 23cm

*581. **To the unknown mountain: ascent of an unexplored twenty-five thousander [Trivor] in the
Karakoram**
London: Heinemann, 1962. xii, 183p, 13 plates
(incl. ports); 22cm

582. **They survived: a study of the will to live**
London: Heinemann, 1962. xiv, 202p, 12 plates;
ill, ports; 22cm
Includes mountaineering examples.

583. **The climber's fireside book**
Compiled by . . .
London: Heinemann, 1964. xvi, 268p, 16 plates
(incl. facsims); 22cm
Anthology, which follows the development of
mountaineering.

*584. **World atlas of mountaineering**
Edited by . . . and Ian McMorrin.
London: Nelson, 1969. 224p, 48 plates; ill (some
col), 32 maps (some col); 28cm

NUNLIST, Hugo
Swiss mountaineer.

*585. **Spitsbergen: the story of the 1962 Swiss-
Spitsbergen expedition**
Translated from the German by Oliver Coburn.
London: Kaye, 1966. 191p, 24 plates; ill, maps;
24cm
From the original: **Spitzbergen** (Zurich: Orell
Fussli, 1963)
The pleasures and drawbacks of modern mountain-
eering in Spitsbergen are well described.

ODELL, Noel Ewart
British mountaineer and Everest climber, who also
climbed in Canada and the Arctic. **See [573]**.

OLIVER, William Dudley

586. **Crags and craters: rambles in the island of Réunion**
London: Longmans, 1896. xiv, 213p, fold. map;
ill; 20cm
Includes climbs on Piton des Neiges, Salazes etc.

OLSEN, John [Jack] Edward
Journalist.

*587. **The climb up to Hell**
London:Gollancz, 1962. 191p, 16 plates (incl. ports);
22cm
Rescue of Corti from the Eigerwand in 1957. **See
also [709]**.

OPPENHEIM, Edwin Camillo (1868–1941)

588. **New climbs in Norway: an account of some ascents
in the Sondmore district**
Illustrated by A. D. McCormick.
London: Fisher Unwin, 1898. x, 257p, plate; ill;
21cm

589. **The reverberate hills**
London: Constable, 1914. viii, 56p; 20cm
Poems.

OPPENHEIMER, Lehmann J. (1868–1916)
Artist and climber, killed in first World War. He
encouraged his fellow-climbers in many new climbs
and is best remembered for his pioneer work on
the Buttermere crags and for his book.

*590. **The heart of Lakeland**
London: Sheratt & Hughes, 1908. [xiv], 196p, 38
plates; 24cm [in blue or red cloth.]

ORLOB, Helen

591. **Mountain rescues**
New York: Nelson, 1963. 176p; ill;
Semi-factual accounts of rescues; written for
children.

ORMEROD, Alick
See [893].

ORMSBY, John (1829–95)
He explored the Atlas Mountains and mountains in
Spain at a time when they were virtually unknown.
See [20].

OUTRAM, Sir James Bt (1864–1925)
Clergyman, who made the first ascents of Mounts
Assiniboine, Columbia and Forbes, and other peaks
in the Canadian Rockies in opposition to Collie's
party: see [769].

*592. **In the heart of the Canadian Rockies**
London: Macmillan, 1905. xiv, 466p, 3 maps (1
fold); ill; 23cm

OXLEY, T. Louis

593. **Jacques Balmat: or, The first ascent of Mont Blanc,
a true story**
[Translated from the French from a narrative by
Venance Payot].
London: Kerby and Endean, 1881. 38p; 19cm

PACKE, Charles Jr. (1826–96)
Barrister, botanist, cartographer and mountaineer,
who was largely responsible for opening up the
Pyrenees as a climbing district. His guidebook
remained the standard work until the turn of the
century. He also wrote **The spirit of travel**
(Chapman & Hall, 1857). See also [20].

*594. **A guide to the Pyrenees: especially intended for
the use of mountaineers**
London: Longmans,
   1862. xvi, 130p, 3 maps (2 col), 2 plates; 17cm
   1867. 2nd ed. Rewritten and enlarged.

PALMER, Howard (1883–1944)
American lawyer, businessman and mountaineer.

*595. **Mountaineering and exploration in the Selkirks: a
record of pioneer work among the Canadian alps,
1908–1912**

New York: Putman, 1914, xxviii, 439p. maps (col.
& fold), 139 plates; 24cm
The principal work on the Selkirk range.

*596. **A climber's guide to the Rocky Mountains of Canada**
By . . . and J. Monroe Thorington.
New York: Putnam, 1921.
Philadelphia: A.A.C.,
1930. 2nd ed.
1940. 3rd ed. 299p. 300 copies only
1953.
1966. 6th ed.
The standard guide to the Rockies. The first edition drew attention to the challenge of the then unclimbed Mt. Alberta.

*597. **Edward W. D. Holway: a pioneer of the Canadian alps**
Minneapolis: Univ. Minnesota Press, 1931. xiv, 81p, map, 7 plates; 21cm
Holway and Palmer made many first ascents in the Selkirks.

PALMER, William Thomas
Author of numerous topographical works concerning the British Isles, including many about the Lake District, such as **Odd corners in English Lakeland** (Skeffington, 1913).

598. **The complete hillwalker, rock climber and cave explorer**
London: Pitman, 1934. xii, 219p; ill; 22cm

PARKER, Elizabeth [Mrs. H. J. Parker]
See [888].

PARROT, J. J. Friedrich von

599. **Journey to Ararat**
Translated [from the German] by W. D. Cooley.
London: Longmans, [1845]. viii, 375p, fold. map; ill; 23cm

From the original: **Reise zum Ararat** 2v. (Berlin: Haude & Spenner, 1834).
The first ascent of Ararat.

PASCOE, John Dobrée
New Zealand mountaineer. His published works include a photo-album **The mountains, the bush and the sea** (Whitcomb & Tombs, 1950) and **Exploration New Zealand** (Reed, 1972).

*†600. **Unclimbed New Zealand: alpine travel in the Canterbury and Westland Ranges, Southern Alps**
London: Allen & Unwin,
1939. 238p, 50 plates; ill, maps, ports; 23cm
1950. 2nd ed. 244p
1954. 3rd imp.
Climbing memoirs.

*601. **Land uplifted high**
Christchurch: Whitcomb & Tombs, 1952. [12], 235p, 4 maps, 17 plates; 22cm
Sequel to [600].

602. **Mr. Explorer Douglas**
Edited by . . .
Wellington: Reed, 1957. viii, 331p, facsim, 4 maps, plates; 23cm

Douglas was a Westland explorer, who worked with A. P. Harper (qv) and C. E. Mannering (qv).

*†603. **Great days in New Zealand mountaineering: the rock and the snow**
Wellington: Reed, 1958. 199p, 16 plates; 22cm
[London: Bailey & Swinfen]
Historical survey.

PATERSON, M.

604. **Mountaineering below the snow-line: or, The solitary pedestrian in Snowdonia and elsewhere**
With etchings by Mackaness.
London: Redway, 1886. viii, 397p, 4 plates; 19cm
Hillwalking in the British Isles and Norway.

PATEY, Thomas Walton (1932–70)
Scottish doctor, humorist and mountaineer, who made the first ascents of the Muztagh Tower and Rakaposhi. He was killed in a climbing accident.

*605. **One man's mountains: essays and verses**
London: Gollancz, 1971. 287p, 23 plates (incl. ports); 23cm [Several impressions]
Includes accounts of television rock-climbs and 'The ballad of Joe Brown'.

PAULCKE, Wilhelm (? –1949)
German climber and pioneer ski-mountaineer. He revised Zsigmondy's book and enlarged it, i.e. the 4th/5th edition. This went through subsequent editions up to the 9th edition (1933). In 1969 the publishers, Rudolf Rother of Munich, asked Helmut Dumler to undertake a new compilation.

*606. **Hazards in mountaineering**
By . . ./ and Helmut Dumler.
Translated from the German by E. Noel Bowman.
London: Kaye & Ward, 1973. 161p; ill (2 col); 21cm
Based on: **Die Gefahren der Alpen** By Emil Zsigmondy (Leipzig: Baldamus, 1885).

PAUSE, Walter

607. **Salute the mountains: the hundred best walks in the Alps**
Translated [from the German] by Ruth Michaelis-Jena and Arthur Ratcliffe.
London: Harrap, 1962. 211p; ill, maps; 26cm
From the original: **Bergheil: die 100 schönsten Bergwanderungen in den Alpen** (Munich: BLV Verlag, 1958).

PEACOCKE, Thomas Arthur Hardy

608. **Mountaineering**
London: A. & C. Black,
1941. viii, 212p, 8 plates; 19cm
1943. 2nd ed.
1953. 3rd ed.
1954.
Instructional.

PEARSE, Reginald O.
South African schoolmaster and climber with thirty years' experience of the Drakensberg.

*†609. **Barrier of spears: drama of the Drakensberg**

[By] ... Illustrated by Malcolm L. Pearse.
[Cape Town]: Howard Timmins, 1973. xii [xxiv], 304p, 20 col. plates; 29cm

Lavish monograph, which includes some climbing history and list of first ascents.

PECK, Annie Smith
American university professor, who made the first ascent of Huascaran. A.A.C. founder member. She also wrote a general travel book about South America.

*610. **A search for the apex of America**
New York: ?, 1911.
London: Fisher Unwin, 1912. xx, 370p, 64 plates; ill, map, ports; 24cm. Published as **High mountain climbing in Peru and Bolivia**.
Includes Illampu, El Misti, Huascaran.

611. **High mountain climbing in Peru and Bolivia: a search for the apex of America, including the conquest of Huascaran**
London: Fisher Unwin, 1912. xx, 370p, 64 plates; ill, map, ports; 24cm. U.K. edition of **Search for the apex of America**.

PEOPLE'S PHYSICAL CULTURE PUBLISHING HOUSE

*612. **Mountaineering in China**
Compiled by the People's Physical Publishing House.
Peking: Foreign Languages Press, 1965. [98p]; ill, ports; 17cm
Includes Minya Konka, Everest, Amne Machin, Shisha Pangma: chiefly pictorial.

PERCIVAL, Walter

613. **Mountain memories**
London: Jacey, 1962. [4], 120p; 22cm
Alpine climbing reminiscences.

PERRY, Alex. W.

614. **Welsh mountaineering**
London: Upcott Gill, 1896. 172p; maps; 15cm

PETZOLDT, Patricia

615. **On top of the world: my adventures with my mountain-climbing husband**
New York: Crowell, 1953. viii, 248p; ill; 21cm
London: Collins, 1954. 254p, 8 plates; 21cm
London: Hamilton, 1956. Panther paperback
Biography of Paul Petzoldt, Grand Teton guide and member of the 1938 American K.2 expedition.

PHILLIPS, Francis (1830–98)
Barrister.

616. **A reading party in Switzerland: with an account of the ascent of Mont Blanc on the 12th and 13th of August 1851**
Manchester: Simms and Dinham, 1851. [4], 49p; 17cm
He made the 40th ascent, with Albert Smith (qv).

PIERRE, Bernard (b. 1920?)
French mountaineer, who climbed in the Alps,

Britain, Africa, Peru, Iran and the Himalaya.

617. **A mountain called Nun Kun**
Translated from the French by Nea Morin and Janet Adam Smith.
London: Hodder, 1955. 189p, 16 plates; 21cm
From the original: **Une montagne nommée Nun Kun** (Paris: Amiot-Dumont, 1954).

PIGEON, Anna
With her sister Ellen she made numerous Alpine expeditions, including the fourth crossing of the Sesiajoch in 1869.

618. **Peaks and passes**
By ... and Ellen Abbot.
London: Griffith, Farran, Okeden, & Welsh, 1885. 31p; 17cm. Printed for private circulation.
Dates and times of ascents only.

PILKINGTON, Charles (1850–1918)
With his brother Lawrence he made many first guideless ascents in the Alps. He was among the first to climb in Skye, Sgurr Thearlaich being so named in his honour. See [211].

PILKINGTON, Lawrence

619. **An Alpine valley and other poems**
Wood-engravings by Margaret Pilkington.
London: Longmans, 1924. [6], 72p; ill; 23cm

620. **The hills of peace, and other poems**
London: Longmans, 1930. 47p; 20cm

PILLEY, Dorothy
Leading British woman alpinist between the wars.
See also [532].

*621. **Climbing days**
By ... (Mrs. I. A. Richards)
London: Bell, 1935. xiv, 352p, 64 plates (incl. ports); 23cm
London: Secker & Warburg, 1965. 2nd ed. with additional material 'Retrospection'.
One of the classics of mountaineering literature.

PIUS XI, Pope [Achille Ratti] (1857–1939)

*622. **Climbs on alpine peaks**
By Abate Achille Ratti, mountaineer (now Pope Pius XI).
Translated [from the Italian] by J. E. C. Eaton.
London: Fisher Unwin,
    1923. 136p, 16 plates (incl. ports); 23cm
    1925. 2nd imp.
London: E. Benn,
    1929. Essex Library edition, xxx, 128p; 17cm

PLATT, William

623. **The joy of mountains**
London: Bell, 1921. 80p, 16 plates; 18cm
Child's introduction to mountains and climbing: includes the Mont Blanc and Matterhorn stories.

PLUNKET, The Hon. Frederica Louisa Edith

624. **Here and there among the Alps**
London: Longmans, 1875. viii, 195p; 20cm
Account of her Alpine rambles, written to en-

courage other young ladies.

POLLOCK, Sir Frederick
See [211].

PORTER, Edward C.
American. **See also Appendix I.**

625. **Mountaineering: essays on safety and technique**
Edited by . . .
? : ?, 1959.

PORTER, Harold Edward L. (1886–1973)
English climber, who was active in New Zealand, and who also climbed with Mallory (qv). See [757].

POUCHER, William Arthur (b. 1891)
English photographer and mountaineer, who has published numerous books of his photographs of the mountain areas of Britain, with his own accompanying text.

*626. **The magic of Skye**
London: Chapman & Hall, 1949. 223p; ill; 29cm
A favourite example of his work.
Other similar volumes include:
(i) Published by Chapman & Hall – **Lakeland through the lens** (1940); **Snowdonia through the lens** (1941); **Lakeland holiday** (1942); **Snowdon holiday** (1943; **Scotland through the lens** (1943); **Lakeland journey** (1945); **Highland holiday** (1945); **Peak panorama** (1946); **A camera in the Cairngorms** (1947); **Over Lakeland fells** (1948); **Lakeland scrapbook** (1950).
(ii) Published by Country Life – **Escape to the hills** (1943; **The backbone of England** (1946); **Wanderings in Wales** (1949); **The magic of the Dolomites** (1951); **The north-west Highlands** (1954); **Climbing with a camera** (1963).

POULET, Guy
See [262].

POWELL, Paul Sidney

627. **Men aspiring**
Wellington: Reed, 1967. 183p; ill, maps, plates; 25cm
Climbing in the Southern Alps and on Mt. Aspiring.

628. **Just where do you think you've been?**
Wellington: Reed, 1970. 211p, 6 maps, 16 plates; 24cm
Climbing reminiscences.

POWNALL, D.
See [143].

PRAG, Per

*629. **Mountain holidays in Norway**
Compiled by . . .
Oslo: Norway Travel Assoc., [1963]. 200p; ill; 21cm
Basically a guidebook, but includes details of first ascents and general information.

PYATT, Edward Charles
British writer and mountaineer. In addition to his own books he has written many articles on climbing, and edited guidebooks. **See also [155].**

*630. **British crags and climbers**
An anthology chosen by . . . and Wilfrid Noyce.
London: Dobson, 1952. 235p, 16 plates; 22cm
Extracts, mainly from club journals, chosen to illustrate the development of mountaineering in Britain.

631. **Where to climb in the British Isles**
London: Faber, 1960. 287p, maps, 17 plates; 19cm
A useful catalogue of crags.

*632. **The boys' book of mountains and mountaineering**
By E. C. and M. E. Pyatt.
London: Burke, 1963. 144p; ill, facsims, maps; 26cm
Interesting illustrations.

633. **Mountains of Britain**
London: Batsford, 1966. 216p, 11 maps, 30 plates; 23cm
General description of the mountains and the development of climbing on them.

*†634. **A climber in the West Country**
Newton Abbott: David & Charles, 1968. 204p, 2 maps, 16 plates (incl. ports); 23cm

635. **Climbing and walking in south-east England**
Newton Abbott: David & Charles, 1970.

PYE, Sir David Randall (1886–1960)
British scientist and mountaineer, who climbed with Mallory in Skye; he also made the first ascent of 'Crack of Doom' on Sron na Ciche.

*636. **George Leigh Mallory: a memoir**
London: O.U.P., 1927. [12], 183p, 6 plates (incl. ports); 21cm

RAEBURN, Harold (1865–1926)
Scottish mountaineer, typical of the new spirit of Scottish mountaineering at the turn of the century. He was an outstanding Alpine climber and also visited Norway and the Caucasus. **See also [938].**

*637. **Mountaineering art**
London: Fisher Unwin, 1920. xii, 274p, 29 plates; 20cm
Instructional.

RAMOND de CARBONNIÈRES, Baron Louis-Francois-Elizabeth (1762–1827)
Important mountaineering pioneer, who explored the Pyrenees and made the first ascent of Mont Perdu in 1802. **See also [333].**

*638. **Travels in the Pyrenees: containing a description of the principal summits, passes and vallies**
Translated from the French of M. Ramond by F. Gold.
London: Longman, 1813. viii, 324p; 24cm

RAMSAY, Sir Andrew Crombie (1814–91)
Geologist and climber, who was active in the glacier controversy. See [18].

RÉBUFFAT, Gaston (b. 1921)
French mountaineer and guide; photographer, film-maker and lecturer. He was a member of the 1950 Annapurna expedition.

*639. **Starlight and storm: the ascent of six great north faces of the Alps**
Translated [from the French] by Wilfrid Noyce and Sir John Hunt.
London: Dent, 1956. xxii, 122p, 37 plates (incl. ports); 23cm
London: Kaye & Ward, 1968. New ed.
From the original: **Etoiles et tempêtes** (Paris: Arthaud, 1954)
Accounts of his own ascents.

640. **Mont Blanc to Everest**
Text translated [from the French] by Geoffrey Sutton: captions by Wilfrid Noyce.
London: Thames & Hudson, 1956. 158p, 77 (8 col) plates (2 fold); 26cm
From the original: **Du Mont Blanc à l'Himalaya** (Paris: Arthaud, 1955)
Chiefly pictorial, tracing Rébuffat's climbing career.

*641. **On snow and rock**
Translated from the French by Eleanor Brockett with technical assistance from J. E. B. Wright.
London: Kaye, 1963. 191p, ill, ports, col. plates; 24cm
London: Vane, 1965. 208p; ill; 24cm
London: Kaye & Ward, 1971, Revised and reissued under title **On ice and snow and rock**
From the original: **Neige et roc** (Paris: Hachette, 1959)
Lavishly illustrated book of instruction by a master of the art.

*642. **Between heaven and earth**
By ... and Pierre Tairraz: translated from the French by Eleanor Brockett.
London: Vane, 1965. 183p [181]; ill (some col); 24cm
London: Kaye & Ward, 1970. Revised ed.
From the original: **Entre terre et ciel** (Paris: Arthaud, 1962).

643. **Men and the Matterhorn**
Translated from the French by Eleanor Brockett.
London: Vane, 1967. 222p; ill (some col); 25cm
New York: O.U.P., 1967.
London: Kaye & Ward, 1973. Revised ed. 27cm
From the original: **Cervin, cime exemplaire** (Paris: Hachette, 1965).

644. **On ice and snow and rock**
Translated from the French by Patrick Evans.
London: Kaye & Ward, 1971. 191p [190] ill (some col), ports; 29cm
New York: O.U.P., 1971.
From the original: **Glace, neige et roc** (Paris: Hachette, 1970); revised edition of **Neige et roc.**

*645. **The Mont Blanc massif: the 100 finest routes**
Translated from the French by Jane and Colin Taylor.
London: Kaye & Ward, 1975. 239p; ill (some col); 27cm
New York: O.U.P., 1975.

Lavishly illustrated with route maps and descriptions.

RENDU, Louis, Bishop of Annecy

646. **Theory of the glaciers of Savoy**
Translated [from the French] by Alfred Wills, to which are added the original memoir and supplementary articles by P. G. Tait and John Ruskin. Edited with introductory remarks by George Forbes.
London: Macmillan, 1874. viii, 216p; map; 22cm
From the original: **Théorie des glaciers de la Savoie** (Chambéry, 1840.

REY, Guido (1861–1935).
Wealthy Italian mountaineer, with a great passion for the Matterhorn, particularly the Furggen Ridge, which he finally overcame with the aid of a ladder.

*647. **The Matterhorn**
With an introduction by Edmondo de Amicis. Translated from the Italian by J. E. C. Eaton. With ... plates and ... drawings by Ed. Rubino.
London: Fisher Unwin,
    1907. 336p, 35 col. plates (incl. ports); 27cm.
    Also 15 copies on Japan paper, numbered and signed by the publisher.
    1908. 2nd ed.
    1913. 3rd ed.
Oxford: Blackwell,
    1946. Revised and with two additional chapters by R. L. G. Irving.
    1949. Reprinted.
From the original: **Il Monte Cervino** (Milan: Hoepli, 1904)
The principal book on the early history of the Matterhorn.

*648. **Peaks and precipices: scrambles in the Dolomites and Savoy**
Translated from the Italian by J. E. C. Eaton.
London: Fisher Unwin, 1914. 238p, 48 plates; 27cm
New York: Dodd Meade, 1914.

RICHARD, Colette

649. **Climbing blind**
Translated [from the French] by Norman Dale.
London: Hodder, 1966. 159p, 4 plates; 21cm
From the original: **Des cimes aux cavernes** (Mulhouse: Ed Salvator, 1965)
The climbing and caving experiences of a blind girl.

RICHMOND, William Kenneth

650. **Climber's testament**
London: Redman, 1950. 8, 246p, 36 plates; 23cm
Reflections on climbing.

RICKMERS, Willi Rickmer (1873–1965)
German mountaineer, explorer and skier, who made important expeditions to the Caucasus and Pamirs. His published works include **Ski-ing for beginners and mountaineers** (Fisher Unwin, 1910). See [757].

RIVIERE, Bill
See [477].

ROBBINS, Leonard Harman

651. **Mountains and men**
New York: Dodd Meade, 1931. xvi, 324p, 20 plates; 20cm
Tales of great mountain ascents.

ROBBINS, Royal
Leading American mountaineer, who has accomplished many extreme climbs in Yosemite Valley. See also [890].

*652. **Basic rockcraft**
Glendale, Calif: La Siesta, 1971, 71p; ill; 22cm

*653. **Advanced rockcraft**
Glendale, Calif: La Siesta, 1973. 96p; ill; 22cm

ROBERTS, A. R.

654. **Himalayan holiday: an account of the New Zealand Himalayan expedition 1953**
Christchurch: Whitcomb & Tombs, 1954. 44p; ill, map; 21cm
First ascent of Chamar.

ROBERTS, David S. (b. 1943)
American mountaineer.

655. **The mountain of my fear**
New York: Vanguard Press, 1968. 157p
London: Souvenir Press, 1969. 157p, 16 plates; ill, maps, ports; 23cm
West face of Mt. Huntingdon, Alaska.

656. **Deborah: a wilderness narrative**
New York: Vanguard Press, 1970. 188p
East Ridge of Deborah, Alaska.

ROBERTS, Dennis

657. **I'll climb Mount Everest alone: the story of Maurice Wilson**
London: Hale, 1957. 158p, 17 plates; ill, facsims, ports; 23cm
Ill-fated solo attempt by non-mountaineer in 1934.

ROBERTSON, David

*658. **George Mallory**
London: Faber, 1969, 279p, 17 plates (incl. ports); 23cm
Over-elaborate biography.

ROBERTSON, Max
Broadcaster.

659. **Mountain panorama: a book of winter sports and climbing**
Edited by . . .
London: Parrish, 1955. 128p; ill, facsims, ports; 24cm
Includes contributions by Hunt, Lunn and Noyce.

ROBINSON, Anthony Melland (1907–50)

660. **Alpine roundabout**
London: Chapman & Hall, 1947. x, 214p, 8 (1 col) plates; 23cm
Climbing reminiscences.

ROCH, André
One of the great Swiss mountaineers of the inter-war period, who made the first ascent of the north face of the Aiguille de Triolet. He climbed in the Himalaya in 1939 and 1947 and was a member of the 1952 Everest expedition.

661. **On Rock and ice: mountaineering in photographs**
London: Black, 1947. xvip, 87 plates; 25cm

*662. **Climbs of my youth**
London: Lindsay Drummond, 1949. 160p, 17· plates; 22cm
From the original: **Les conquêtes de ma jeunesse** (Neuchatel: Attinger, 1943).

663. **Everest 1952**
Edited by Marcel Kurz.
London: Allen & Unwin, 1953. 100 photos.
From the original: **Everest 1952 (Photo Album)** (Paris: Jeheber, 1952)
Photo-album of the first Swiss attempt in 1952.

ROGET, F. F.
Swiss academic, who was outstanding among the pioneers of ski-mountaineering. His published works include **Altitude and health** (Constable, 1919)

*664. **Ski-runs in the high Alps**
Illustrations by L. M. Crisp.
London: Fisher Unwin, 1913. 25 (1 col) plates; 23cm
The principal book in English.

ROMM, Michael D.

*665. **The ascent of Mount Stalin**
Translated [from the Russian] by Alec Brown.
London: Lawrence & Wishart, 1936. xii, 270p, 32 plates (incl. ports); 23cm

ROSCOE, Donald Thomas
Mountaineering instructor.

*666. **Mountaineering: a manual for teachers & instructors**
London: Faber, 1976. [x], 181p, 8 plates; 23cm

ROSS, Francis Edward
See [41].

ROSS, Malcolm (1864–1930)
Journalist and founder member of the New Zealand Alpine Club. See also [938].

*667. **A climber in New Zealand**
London: Arnold, 1914. xx, 316p, 24 plates; 23cm
Chiefly Mt. Cook area.

ROSSIT, Edward A.

668. **Northwest mountaineering**
Caldwell, Idaho: Caxton, 1965. 206p; ill;
Unsatisfactory book on technique and climbing in north-west U.S.A.

ROTH, Abraham

669. **The Doldenhorn and Weisse Frau, ascended for the first time by Abraham Roth, and Edmund von Fellenburg.**
Coblenz: K. Baedaker, 1863. [6], 82p; map (col) plates (col); 22cm

ROWELL, Galen A.
American big wall climber.

*670 **Vertical world of Yosemite**
Berkeley: Wilderness Press, 1974. xiv, 208p; ill; 29cm
Illustrated and with articles on climbs by leading climbers.

RUDGE, E. C. W.

671. **Mountain days near home**
Illustrated with photographs by the author, and drawings by his wife.
Wellingborough: W. D. Wharton, 1941. viii, 75p; ill; 22cm
Climbing in Britain.

RUSK, C. E.

672. **Tales of a western mountaineer: a record of mountain experiences on the Pacific Coast**
Boston: Houghton Mifflin, 1924. xiv, 309p, 31 plates; 20cm
Cascades.

RUSKIN, John (1819–1900)
Writer, critic and mountain lover. His qualification for election to the Alpine Club in 1869 was 'Volume IV of **Modern Painters** ('Of mountain beauty')', references to which occur frequently in the older literature of mountaineering. **See also** [575] & [646].

RUSSELL, Jean (b. 1939)

673. **Climb if you will: a commentary on Geoff Hayes and his club, the Oread Mountaineering Club**
Compiled and edited by Jean Russell in association with Jack Ashcroft
Ashbourne: M. J. Russell, [1974]. xiv, 222p; ill, ports; 23cm
Geoff Hayes was killed in a rock-climbing accident in the Lake District.

RUSSELL, R. Scott

*674. **Mountain prospect**
London: Chatto & Windus, 1946. xvi, 248p, 7 maps, 47 plates; 22cm
Climbing memoirs.

RUTTLEDGE, Hugh L. (1884–1961)
Indian administrator, who led the 1933 and 1936 Everest expeditions.

*675. **Everest 1933**
London: Hodder, 1934. xvi, 390p, 3 fold. maps, 59 plates (incl. ports); 27cm [4 impressions]
New York: McBride, 1935. U.S.A. edition **Attack on Everest** xx, 339p
London: Hodder,
    1936. Adventure Books. xx, 299p; ill; 23cm
    1938. Black Jacket ed.
    1943. Black Jacket ed.

676. **Attack on Everest**
New York: McBride, 1935. xx, 339p, U.S.A. edition of **Everest 1933.**

*677. **Everest: the unfinished adventure**
London: Hodder, 1937. [16], 295p, 2 fold. maps, 63 plates (incl. ports); 27cm

SACK, John
Journalist and non-climbing member of American student expedition.

*678. **The Butcher (The ascent of Yerupaja)**
New York: Reinhart, 1952. 213p
London: Jenkins, 1954. Published in U.K. as **The Ascent of Yerupaja.**

679. **The ascent of Yerupaja**
London: Jenkins, 1954. 191p, 9 plates (incl. ports); 20cm. U.K. edition of **The Butcher**

SALT, Henry Stephen
Writer.

680. **On Cambrian and Cumbrian hills: pilgrimages to Snowdon and Scawfell**
London: Fifield,
    1908. 128p, 2 plates; 18cm
    1911. Reissued in paper covers
London: Daniel,
    1922. Revised ed. 124p
A plea for conservation.

SANDEMAN, R. G.

681. **A mountaineer's journal**
[Carmarthen: Druid Press], 1948. 168p [169], 14 plates; 23cm
Climbing in Scotland.

SANUKI, Matao

682. **The Alps**
By . . . and Keiichi Yamada.
London: Ward Lock, 1970. 146p; ill (some col), maps; 19cm
This Beautiful World series.

SAYRE, Woodrow Wilson (b. 1919)
American professor of philosophy: grandson of President Wilson.

*683. **Four against Everest**
New Jersey: Prentice-Hall, 1964. 259p; ill, maps; 24cm
London: Arthur Barker, [1964]. 251p; ill, ports; 24cm
Englewood Cliffs: Prentice-Hall, 1968. Paperback ed.
Attempt in 1962 by the North Col route by an unauthorized party, without porters.

SCARR, Josephine

684. **Four miles high**
London: Gollancz, 1966. 188p, 33 plates (incl. ports); 22cm
Account of two women's expeditions to the Himalaya (Kulu and Jagdula Himal).

SCHNEIDER, Erwin
See [234].

SCHOMBERG, Reginald Charles Francis
Soldier and explorer. His published works include **Between the Oxus and the Indus** (Hopkinson, 1935).

*685. **Peaks and plains of central Asia**
London: Hopkinson, 1933. 288p, 8 col. plates
(incl. ports); 23cm
Tien Shan and Bogdo Ola.

*686. **Unknown Karakoram**
London: Hopkinson, 1936. viii, 244p [236], fold.
map (end pocket), 23 plates (incl. ports); 23cm
Exploring north of the main range.

687. **Kafirs and glaciers: travels in Chitral**
London: Hopkinson, 1938. 287p, fold. map, 25 (1
col) plates (incl. ports); 23cm

SCHUSTER, Claud, Baron Schuster (1869–1956)
British mountaineer and skier. A.C. President
1938–40. His books convey his joy in the
mountains better than most.

*688. **Peaks and pleasant pastures**
Oxford: Clarendon Press, 1911. 227p, 5 maps;
24cm

*689. **Men, women and mountains: days in the Alps and Pyrenees**
London: Nicholson & Watson,
    1931. xvi, 143p, 13 plates (incl. ports); 25cm
    1931. 2nd imp.

*690. **Postscript to adventure**
London: Eyre & Spottiswoode, 1950. 214p, 9
plates (1 col); 23cm
Papers read before the Alpine Club, et al.

SCHWEITZER, Edward
See [20].

SCOTT, Douglas Keith (b. 1941)
British mountaineer, with reputation for severe, big
wall climbs, including the south-west face of
Everest. **See also [95].**

691. **The Midlands Hindu Kush expedition, 1967: report**
By . . . and W. Cheverst
Nottingham: Nottingham C.C., [1968]. 62p, 41
plates (3 fold); ill, maps, ports; 25cm

*692. **Big wall climbing**
London: Kaye & Ward, 1974. xii, 348p; ill, ports;
21cm
History of climbing in the Dolomites, Yosemite
etc.

SELIGMAN, Gerald Abraham
British scientist and A.C. member.

*693. **Snow structures and ski-fields**
London: Macmillan, 1936. xii, 567p; ill; 23cm
Brussels: Adam, 1962. 555p; ill; 23cm
The principal work on the subject.

SELLA, Vittorio (1859–1943)
Distinguished Italian climber and explorer,
renowned for his mountain photographs. See [16]
& [148].

SERRAILLIER, Ian

694. **Everest climbed**
Illustrated by Leonard Rossman.
Oxford: Geoffrey Cumberlege, O.U.P., 1955. viii,

60p; ill; 20cm
A narrative poem.

SETON-KARR, Heywood W.
See under: KARR, H. W. S.

SHERMAN, Paddy (b. 1928)
Welsh mountaineer and journalist, resident in
Vancouver since 1952, who has climbed many
Canadian peaks.

*695. **Cloud walkers: six climbs on major Canadian peaks**
Maps by John A. Hall.
London: Macmillan, 1966. [12], 161p, 16 plates;
ill, maps; 23cm
Mts. Fairweather, Logan, Waddington, Slesse, Robson and Howson.

SHIPTON, Eric Earle (1907–77)
British mountaineer and leading mountain explorer
of the twentieth century. A.C. President 1965–7.
He took part in five Everest expeditions but is best
known for his private light-weight expeditions,
often with Tilman (qv).

*696. **Nanda Devi**
With drawings in the text by Bip Pares.
London: Hodder,
    1936. xvi, 310p, 27 plates; 23cm
    1939. Black Jacket ed.
One of the greatest pieces of mountain exploration.

*697. **Blank on the map**
London: Hodder, 1938. xviii, 299p, 3 maps (1 col.
fold), 36 plates; 23cm
Exploring the Karakoram, north of the main range.

*698. **Upon that mountain**
London: Hodder,
    1943. 222p, 31 plates; 21cm
    1947.
London: Pan Books,
    1956. Paperback ed.
Climbing memoirs.

*699. **Mountains of Tartary**
London: Hodder, [1951]. 224p, 23 plates; 23cm
Includes Muztagh Ata and Bogdo Ola.

*700. **The Mount Everest Reconnaissance Expedition 1951**
London: Hodder, 1952. 128p; ill, ports; 27cm

701. **The true book about Everest**
Illustrated by F. Stocks.
London: Muller, 1955. 142p; ill; 19cm
New Jersey: Prentice-Hall, 1956. Published as **Men against Everest**

702. **Men against Everest**
New Jersey: Prentice-Hall, 1956. 161p; ill, map;
21cm. U.S.A. edition of **The true book about Everest.**
Written for children.

*703. **Land of tempest: travels in Patagonia 1958–62**
London: Hodder,
    1963. 224p, 17 plates (1 col); ill, maps, ports;
    23cm
    1963. 2nd imp.

Mountain conquest
See under: HORIZON

*704. **That untravelled world: an autobiography**
Line illustrations by Biro.
London: Hodder,
    1969. 286p, 16 plates; ill, maps, ports; 23cm
    1970. 2nd imp.
    1977. Reprinted.

*705. **Tierra del fuego—the fatal lodestone**
London: Chas. Knight, 1973. 175p; ill, maps;
Chiefly a historical account but includes his
exploration of Cordillera Darwin and Mount
Burney.

SIMONOV, Yevgeny

*706. **Conquering the Celestial Mountains**
Translated from the Russian by G. Ivanov-
Mumjiev.
Moscow: Foreign Languages Pub. House, 1958.
130p, 31 plates (incl. ports); 20cm
From the original: **Na Pik Pobeda**
Tien Shan – first ascent of Muztagh Ata. **See also**
[935].

SINGH, Gyan
Indian soldier and leader of first all-Indian attempt
on Everest.

707. **Lure of Everest: story of the first Indian expedition**
Dehli: Min Inform. & Broadcast., 1961. xiv, 41 plates
(1 col); ill, ports; 22cm

SINIGAGLIA, Leone (c. 1870–1944)
Italian musician and mountaineer. He died in tragic
circumstances, a victim of the war.

*708. **Climbing reminiscences of the Dolomites**
With an introduction by Edmund J. Garwood.
Translated [from the Italian] by Mary Alice Vialls.
London: Fisher Unwin, 1896. xxiv, 224p, fold.
map, 39 plates (incl. ports); 26cm. Also 30 copies
on Japan paper. [Cover title, **Climbing in the
Dolomites**].

SKOCZYLAS, Adam

709. **Stefano, we shall come tomorrow**
London: Poets' and Painters' Press, 1962. 35p, 10
plates; 24cm
Death of Longhi on the Eigerwand: **see also** [587].

SLESSER, C. G. Malcolm (b. 1926)
Scottish mountaineer.

*710. **Red Peak: a personal account of the British-Soviet
Pamir Expedition 1962**
London: Hodder, 1964. 256p, 20 plates (4 col);
23cm
Wilfrid Noyce (qv) was killed on this expedition.

711. **The Andes are prickly**
London: Gollancz, 1966. 254p, 29 plates (incl.
ports); 23cm
Climbing in the Peruvian Cordilleras Huayhuash
and Veronica de Urubamba.

SLINGSBY. William Cecil (1849–1929)
British mountaineer and the 'father' of Norwegian
mountaineering. He also climbed in the Alps and in
the British Isles. **See also** [938].

*712. **Norway: the northern playground. Sketches of
climbing and mountain exploration in Norway
between 1872 and 1903**
Edinburgh: Douglas, 1904. xx, 425p; ill, 9 maps,
plates; 23cm
Oxford: Blackwell, 1941. xxviii, 227p.

SMEETON, Miles

713. **A taste of the hills**
London: Hart-Davis, 1961. 207p; ill, map; 22cm
Climbing reminiscences

SMITH, Albert Richard (1816–60)
English writer, with a passion for Mont Blanc.
After his ascent in 1851 he produced an illustrated
lecture based on his experiences. This ran for six
years and made him a rich man. Biography: **The
Baron of Piccadilly** (Bles, 1967) by R. Fitzsimons.
See also Appendix III.

714. **Mont Blanc**
London: Printed for private circulation, 1852. 88p;
18cm. [Reprinted, with additions, from 'Blackwood's Magazine', January 1852, Vol. 71,
pp35–55].

*715. **The story of Mont Blanc**
London: Bogue,
    1853. xii, 219p, plate; 21cm. The plate is
    coloured or plain.
New York: Putnam,
    1853. x, 208p, plate; 20cm
London: Bogue,
    1854. 2nd ed. x, 208p
    1854. 2nd ed. enlarged, xvi, 299p; ill; 18cm
London: Kent,
    1857. Reprint (Kent was Bogue's successor)
    1860. Reprinted with new title-page
Reading: West Col,
    1974. Facsimile of 1853 edition.

716. **The story of Mont Blanc, and a Diary to China and
back**
Privately printed, 1860, xvi, 299p, 60p; 17cm.
Reprint of 1854 enlarged edition, bound with
another story. This version has a new title-page and
reprinted dedication. On the title-page (recto)
there are two photographs of handbills of the two
lectures and (verso) two photographs of Albert
Smith and of the exterior of the Egyptian Hall. On
the dedication page are two photo portraits.
Memorial edition.

717. **A boy's ascent of Mont Blanc: written by himself**
London: Houlston & Wright, [1859]. Fictional
variation. In the **Boy's Birthday Book** . . . by Mrs.
S. C. Hall et al. pp9–145.
London: Maxwell, [1870]. Reissued with slightly
altered title-page.

718. **Mont Blanc**
By . . . with a memoir of the author by Edmund
Yates.
London: Ward Lock,
    nd [1860]. xxxvi, 299p, plate; 17cm. Bound in
    pictorial boards.

London: Ward Lock, & Tyler,
nd [1860]. xxxvi, 299p, plate; 17cm. Bound in cloth, blind and gilt stamped.
nd [1860]. Reprint entitled **A boy's ascent of Mont Blanc.** Altered title-page. Bound in cloth, blind and gilt stamped.
There are two plates used in these editions: a glacier scene; and a woodland hill cottage.

719. **A boy's ascent of Mont Blanc**
By ... with a memoir of the author by Edmund Yates.
London: Ward Lock & Tyler, nd [1860]. Reprint of [718].

SMITH, B. Webster

720. **Pioneers of mountaineering**
London: Blackie, [1933]. 224p, 8 plates; 20cm
Children's book.

SMITH, George Alan

721. **Introduction to mountaineering**
New York: Barnes,
1957.
London: Yoseloff,
1960. xiv, 128p, plate; ill; 26cm
1967. New & revised ed. xiv, 134p.

722. **The armchair mountaineer: a gathering of wit, wisdom and idolatry**
Edited by ... and Carol D. Smith.
New York: Pitman, 1968. xvi, 361p; ill (some col), ports; 26cm

SMITH, Janet Adam
Well-known English alpinist, who climbed between the wars. See also [532].

723. **Mountain holidays**
London: Dent,
1946. xii, 194p, 2 maps, 32 plates; 22cm
1946. Reprinted.

SMITH, Phil D.

724. **Knots for mountaineering**
Twenty-nine Palms, Calif: ?, 1953.
Well illustrated.

SMITH, Walter Parry Haskett (1859–1946)
Lawyer, gentleman of leisure: founder of British rock-climbing, initiated by his solo ascent of Napes Needle in 1886.

*725. **Climbing in the British Isles**
[Vol] 1: England, by ...
With twenty-three illustrations by Ellis Carr.
London: Longmans, 1894. xii, 162p; ill; 16cm

[Vol] 2: Wales and Ireland by H. C. Hart.
With thirty-one illustrations by Ellis Carr.
London: Longmans, 1895. viii, 197p; ill; 16cm
The first guidebook to British rock-climbing: Part III (Scotland) was planned but never executed.

726. **Climbing in the British Isles: Ireland**
By H. C. Hart.
Dublin: Privately printed, [1974]. Facsimile reprint of the second part of [Vol] 2 of Haskett Smith's guidebook.

SMYTHE, Francis [Frank] Sydney (1900–49)
British writer, photographer and mountaineer, who climbed extensively in the Alps and also made several important Himalayan expeditions, including the first ascent of Kamet.

727. **Climbs and ski-runs: mountaineering and ski-ing in the Alps, Great Britain and Corsica**
Edinburgh, Blackwood,
1929. xx, 307p, 61 plates; 23cm
[Several impressions]
London: A. & C. Black,
1957. New ed. xii, 197p.

*728. **The Kanchenjunga adventure**
London: Gollancz, 1930. 464p, 48 plates; ill, ports; 24cm
[Numerous editions/impressions]
Unsuccessful international expedition.

729. **Kamet conquered**
London: Gollancz, 1932. xvi, 420p, fold. map, 50 plates (incl. ports); 24cm
[Various editions/reprints]
London: Hodder, 1947. Uniform edition.

730. **An Alpine journey**
London: Gollancz, 1934. 351p, fold. map, 48 plates; 24cm
London: Hodder, 1940. Black Jacket edition.

*731. **The spirit of the hills**
London: Hodder,
1935. xiv, 308p, 36 plates; 23cm
1937. Black Jacket edition
1946. Uniform edition.

*732. **Over Tyrolese hills**
London: Hodder,
1936. xvi, 292p, map, 36 plates; 23cm
1937. 3rd ed.
1938. Black Jacket ed.

*733. **Camp Six: an account of the 1933 Mount Everest expedition**
London: Hodder,
1937. xii, 307p, 36 plates (incl. ports); 23cm
1938. Black Jacket ed. [also 1941].
London: Black,
1956. New ed. xii, 219p.

*734. **The valley of flowers**
London: Hodder,
1938. xiv, 322p, fold. map, 16 col. plates; 23cm Also a limited edition of 250 numbered copies signed by the author.
1947. Uniform ed.
Garhwal Himalaya and the Bhyundar Valley.

735. **Mountaineering holiday**
London: Hodder,
1940. xiv, 229p, map, 24 plates; 23cm
1941. Black Jacket ed. [also 1943]
1950. Uniform ed. xiv, 229p.

*736. **Edward Whymper**
London: Hodder, 1940. xiv, 330p, 2 fold. maps, 24 plates; ill, facsims, ports; 23cm

737. **The adventures of a mountaineer**
London: Dent,
1940. viii, 228p, 17 plates (incl. ports); 23cm
1945.

*738. The mountain vision
　　London: Hodder,
　　　　1941. xii, 308p, 16 plates; 23cm
　　　　1946. Uniform ed.

739. Over Welsh hills
　　London: Black,
　　　　1941. 101p [103] ; 51 ill; 28 cm
　　　　1942. Reprinted
　　A photo-album.
　　Similar publications include:
　　　　Published by Black – The mountain scene
　　　　(1937); Peaks and valleys (1938); Camera in the
　　　　hills (1939); My Alpine album (1940); Alpine
　　　　ways (1942); Snow on the hills (1946); Swiss
　　　　winter (1948); Rocky Mountains (1948).
　　　　Published by Parrish – Mountains in colour
　　　　(1949).

740. British mountaineers
　　London: Collins,
　　　　1942. 48p, 8 col. plates; ill, ports; 23cm
　　　　1946. Reprinted
　　Bahamas: Britain in Pictures Publishers, nd. Re-
　　print (or original?)
　　Britain in Pictures series.

741. Secret mission
　　London: Hodder, 1942. 256p; [254], 19cm
　　Fiction. Set in Himalaya.

742. Again Switzerland
　　London: Hodder,
　　　　1947. viii, 248p, 33 plates (1 col); 23cm
　　　　1952.

743. The mountain top: an illustrated anthology from
　　the prose and pictures of Frank S. Smythe.
　　London: St. Hugh's Press, 1947. 45p; ill; 16cm

*744. Climbs in the Canadian Rockies
　　London: Hodder, 1950. x, 260p, 34 (2 col) plates
　　(incl. group port); 23cm
　　New York: Norton, nd.

SMYTHE, Anthony G.

*745. Rock climbers in action in Snowdonia
　　Written by ... Illustrated by John Cleare. Cap-
　　tions/descriptions and layout by Robin G.
　　Collomb.
　　London: Secker & Warburg, 1966. 127p, 32 plates;
　　25cm
　　Superbly illustrated account of the climbs and
　　personalities.

SNAITH, Stanley

746. At grips with Everest
　　London: Percy Press,
　　　　1937. xvi, 240p, 8 plates; 20cm
　　　　1945. 2nd ed. xii, 164p
　　Written for children.

747. Alpine adventure
　　London: Percy Press,
　　　　1944. vi, 153p, 8 plates; 20cm
　　　　1946. Reprinted
　　Written for children.

748. The mountain challenge
　　London: Percy Press, 1952. x, 158p, 8 plates;
　　19cm

SNEYD-KYNNERSLEY, E. M.

*749. A snail's wooing: the story of an Alpine courtship
　　London: Macmillan, 1910.
　　Fiction: climbing around Zermatt. Favourite pre-
　　war holiday reading.

SNYDER, Howard H.

750. The hall of the mountain king
　　New York: Chas. Scribners, 1973. 207p; ill;
　　Disaster on Mt. McKinley in 1967.

SOMERVELL, Theodore Howard (1890–1975)
English doctor and mountaineer. A.C. President
1962–4. He was a member of the 1922 and 1924
Everest expeditions. See also [124] & [573].

*751. After Everest: the experiences of a mountaineer
　　and medical missionary
　　London: Hodder,
　　　　1936. xiv, 339p, fold. map, 22 plates (incl.
　　　　port); 23cm
　　　　1938. Black Jacket ed. [also 1947, 1950]

SOPER, N. Jack (b. 1934)
British geologist and mountaineer.

*752. The Black Cliff: the history of rock-climbing on
　　Clogwyn du'r Arddu
　　By ..., Ken Wilson and Peter Crew. Based on the
　　original research of Rodney Wilson.
　　London: Kaye & Ward, 1971. 158p; ill, ports;
　　22cm

SOUTH AFRICAN RAILWAYS

753. Mountaineering in South Africa
　　[Compiled by W. C. West.]
　　Issued by the General Manager, South African
　　Railways, in co-operation with the members of the
　　Mountain Club of South Africa.
　　Johannesburg: South African Railways, 1914. 62p
　　ill, maps, plates; 22cm
　　Covers the Cape Mountains and the Drakensberg.

754. The Drakensberg National Park: South Africa's
　　mountain playground
　　[Cape Town] South African Railways, 1937. 32p;
　　ill;

SPEAKER, G. R.
See [757].

SPECTORSKY, Auguste C.

*755. The book of the mountains: being a collection
　　of writings about the mountains in all of their
　　aspects
　　Edited by ...
　　New York: Appleton-Century-Crofts, 1955. 492p; ill;
　　Good reference book

SPEER, Stanhope T.

756. On the physiological phenomena of the mountain
　　sickness, as experienced in the ascent of the higher
　　Alps
　　Lincoln-cum-Fields: T. Richards, 1853. 51p; 19cm

SPENCER, Sydney (1862–1950)
British mountaineer, who climbed in the Alps and also made some first ascents in Canada. **See also [22] & [938].**

*757. **Mountaineering**
By . . . (editor) and others.
London: Seeley Service, [1934]. 383p, maps, 55 plates; 23cm
Lonsdale Library series: an omnibus work.

SPENDER, Harold

*†758.**Through the High Pyrenees**
With illustrations and supplementary sections by H. Llewellyn Smith.
London: Innes, 1898. xii, 370p, 5 maps (1 fold), 31 plates; 24cm

*759. **In praise of Switzerland: being the Alps in prose and verse**
London: Constable, 1912. xvi, 291p; 23cm

SPRING, Bob and Ira
American mountain photographers.

*760. **High adventure**
By . . . Text by Norma and Patricia Spring.
Seattle: Superior Pub., 1951. 128p; ill;
Outstanding photographs of the mountains of the Pacific north-west.

*761. **High worlds of the mountain climber**
Photographs by . . . Text by Harvey Manning.
Seattle: Superior Pub., 1959. 142p
Introduction to the mountains of western U.S.A.

STEAD, Richard
His published works include **Adventures on the high mountains** (Seeley, 1908).

762. **Daring deeds of great mountaineers**
London: Seeley Service, [1920?].
Written for children.

STEELE, Peter R. C. (b. 1935)
British doctor and mountaineer, who was a member of the international expedition on Everest in 1971.

*763. **Two and two halves to Bhutan: a family journey in the Himalayas**
London: Hodder, 1970. 191p, 16 plates; 23cm
An account of his family's travels, with a little climbing on the side.

*764. **Doctor on Everest**
Line drawings by Phoebe Bullock.
London: Hodder, 1972. 222p, 24 plates (incl. ports); 23cm
A personal and professional eye-view.

765. **Medical care for mountain climbers**
Line drawings by Phoebe Bullock.
London: Heinemann, 1976. xii, 220p; ill; 19cm
Expedition handbook.

STEPHEN, Sir Leslie (1832–1904)
British writer and mountaineer: one of the most famous personalities in mountaineering. His book is as famous as Whymper's 'Scrambles'. Biographies: **The life and letters of Leslie Stephen** (Duck-worth, 1906) by F. W. Maitland; and **Leslie Stephen: his thought and character in relation to his time** (1951) by N. G. Annan. **See also [20] & [575].**

*766. **The playground of Europe**
London: Longmans,
1871. xii, 321p, 3 plates; 20cm
1894. Enlarged ed.
1895. Reprinted
1899. Reissued in the Silver Library series. xiv, 339p. 3 plates; 19cm
1901. Reprinted (and in 1904, 1907, 1910, 1924)
Oxford: Blackwell,
1936. Edited by H. E. G. Tyndale.
Stephen varied the contents in different editions: the first edition is hardly the best. None of the editions contains all his mountain writings.

STEVEN, Campbell

*767. **The island hills**
London: Hurst & Blackett, 1955. 190p, 23 plates; 23cm
Walks and scrambles on most of Scotland's island hills.

STRUTT, Edward Lisle (1874–1948)
British soldier and mountaineer. A.C. member and President 1935–7. Editor of the A.J. See [189].

STUCK, Hudson
American mountaineer, Archdeacon of the Yukon.

*768. **The ascent of Denali (Mount McKinley): a narrative of the first complete ascent of the highest peak in North America**
New York: Chas. Scribner, 1914. xx, 188p, fold. map, 34 plates (incl. ports); 22cm
London: Bickers, 1914. Identical apart from cover, which is red, gilt lettered; whereas the American one is blue, with different lettering and a picture.

STUTFIELD, Hugh Edward Millington (1858–1929)
Traveller, climber and hunter.

*769. **Climbs & exploration in the Canadian Rockies**
By . . . and J. Norman Collie.
London: Longmans, 1903. xii, 343p, fold. map, 52 plates; 23cm
One of the classics of Canadian mountain exploration and climbing.

STYLES, Frank Showell
British writer and mountaineer, who also writes detective stories under the pseudonym Glyn Carr. **See also [109] & Appendix IV, VI.**

770. **A climber in Wales**
By . . . (S.S. of the Birmingham Post)
Birmingham: Cornish Brothers, [1948]. 85p, 21 plates; 22cm
Climbing reminiscences: reprinted from the Birmingham Post.

*771. **The mountaineer's week-end book**
London: Seeley Service,
[1950]. 408p; ill; 19cm
1960. Revised ed.

Compendium of songs, stories, information and verses.

*772. **Mountains of the midnight sun**
London: Hurst & Blackett, 1954. 208p, 14 plates 22cm
Climbing on the Lyngen Peninsula, northern Norway.

*773. **The moated mountain**
London: Hurst & Blackett, 1955. 255p, 21 (1 col) plates (incl. ports); 22cm
Attempt on Baudha, Manaslu district, Nepal.

774. **Introduction to mountaineering**
London: Seeley Service, nd. 159p, 8 plates, ill, 22cm
[Published in 1954 or 1955]
Beaufort Library series: instructional.

775. **Getting to know mountains**
By ... Edited by Jack Cox.
London: Newnes, 1958. 160p, 8 plates; 19cm
Instructional.

776. **How mountains are climbed**
London: Routledge, 1958. xii, 158p, 8 plates; 19cm
Instructional.

777. **Look at mountains**
Illustrated by Derek Williams.
London: Hamilton, 1962. 95p; ill, maps, ports; 20cm
Written for children.

778. **Modern mountaineering**
London: Faber, 1964. 189p, 8 plates; 23cm

*779. **Blue remembered hills**
London: Faber, 1965. 189p [187], plates; ill, map; 21cm
Climbing reminiscences.

780. **The foundations of climbing**
London: S. Paul, 1966. 142p [144], 12 plates; 22cm
London: Arrow, 1967. Reissued as **The Arrow book of climbing**

781. **The Arrow book of climbing**
London: Arrow Books, 1967. 192p, 8 plates; 18cm. Previously published as **The foundations of climbing.**

782. **Rock and rope**
London: Faber, 1967. 174p, 8 plates; 21cm

783. **On top of the world: an illustrated history of mountaineering and mountaineers**
London: Hamilton, 1967. xx, 278p, 32 col. plates; ill, facsims, maps, ports; 26cm.

784. **Mallory of Everest**
London: Hamilton, 1967. 157p, 4 maps, 10 plates (incl. ports); 23cm

785. **Men and mountaineering: an anthology of writings by climbers**
Edited by ...
London: Hamilton, 1968. 207p; 23cm
Comprises chapters from books included in this bibliography.

786. **The climber's bedside book**
London: Faber, 1968. 256p; 21cm

787. **First on the summits**
With diagrams by R. B. Evans.
London: Gollancz, 1970. 157p, 12 plates; ill, maps, ports; 23cm
The stories of various first ascents.

788. **The mountains of North Wales**
London: Gollancz, 1973. 175p, map, 20 plates; 23cm

SUTTON, Geoffrey J. S. (b. 1930)
British schoolmaster, writer and mountaineer, who has also translated several mountaineering books into English. See also [140], [238] & [943].

789. **Artificial aids in mountaineering**
Published under the auspices of the Mountaineering Association.
London: Kaye & Ward, 1962. 64p; ill; 19cm

SUTTON, George

790. **Glacier Island: the official account of the British South Georgia Expedition 1954—55**
London: Chatto & Windus, 1957.
Expedition to the Antarctic with climbing as the prime objective, making first ascents in the Allardyce Range.

SWISS FOUNDATION FOR ALPINE RESEARCH

791. **The first ten years: Swiss Foundation for Alpine Research**
Zurich: S.F.A.R., 1951. 48p, 10 plates; ill, map; 20cm

792. **Mountain World**
London: [published for] The Swiss Foundation for Alpine Research [by] Allen & Unwin, 1953. 220p, plates; ill, maps; 25cm. Edited by Marcel Kurz.
Lavishly produced volume of chiefly topical articles of mountaineering interest.
Similar volumes covering the years up to 1969 as follows: 1953, 1954, 1955, 1956/7, 1958/9, 1960/1, 1962/3, 1964/5, 1966/7, 1968/9. From 1955 onwards the English version was produced by Malcolm Barnes.

793. **Everest: the Swiss Everest expeditions**
London: Hodder, 1954. xvi, [28p], 144 (8 col) plates (incl. ports); 28cm Photo-album of the 1952 expeditions: introduced by Othmar Gurtner.

SYMINGTON, Noel Howard
See: WHIPPLESNAITH

SYNGE, Patrick M.
He led a British Museum party to Ruwenzori in 1934—5.

*794. **Mountains of the Moon: an expedition to the equatorial mountains of Africa**
London: Lindsay Drummond, 1937. xxiv, 221p, 2 maps, 93 (2 col) plates; 23cm
Includes much useful botanical information.

TAIRRAZ, Pierre
See [297] & [642].

TALBOT, Daniel

*795. **A treasury of mountaineering stories**
Edited by . . .
London: Peter Davies, 1955. x, 282p; 21cm
Volume of chiefly fictional tales by Frison-Roche,
C. E. Montague, James Ramsay Ullman and others.

TARBUCK, Kenneth

796. **Nylon rope and climbing safety**
Edinburgh: British Ropes, [1960]. 35p; ill; 13cm.
[Two versions seen.]
Dynamic belaying: the Tarbuck Knot is now
obsolete.

TAYLOR, Peter (b. 1921)

797. **Coopers Creek to Langtang II**
London: Angus & Robertson, 1965. 239p, 24
plates; 23cm
One-man expedition to the Himalaya.

TEJADA-FLORES, Lito

*798. **Wilderness skiing**
By . . . and Allen Steck.
San Francisco: Sierra Club, 1972. 310p
Ski-mountaineering manual: replaces the outdated
[115].

TEMPLE, R. Philip (b. 1939)
English mountaineer, resident in New Zealand. He
also visited New Guinea with Heinrich Harrer: see
[348].

*799. **Nawok! The New Zealand expedition to New
Guinea's highest mountains**
London: Dent, 1962. xiv, 189p, 13 (1 col) plates
(incl. ports); 23cm

*800. **The sea and the snow: the South Indian Ocean
expedition to Heard Island**
Melbourne: Cassell Australia, 1966. [xii], 188p, 16
plates (incl. ports); 22cm
Ascent of Big Ben.

*801. **The world at their feet: the story of New Zealand
mountaineers in the great ranges of the world**
Christchurch: Whitcomb & Tombs, 1969. 250p, 4
maps, 28 (4 col) plates (incl. ports); 25cm

TERRAY, Lionel (1921–65)
French mountaineer, who made many notable
climbs – Eigerwand, Fitroy, Annapurna, Makalu,
Jannu. He also climbed in Peru with Egeler (qv).
He was killed in a climbing accident.

*802. **Conquistadors of the useless: from the Alps to
Annapurna**
Translated [from the French] by Geoffrey Sutton.
London: Gollancz, 1963. 351p, maps, 84 plates
(incl. ports); 23cm
New York: Doubleday, 1964. Published as **The
borders of the impossible**
From the original: **Les conquérants de l'inutile**
(Paris: Gallimard, 1961)
Climbing autobiography.

803. **The borders of the impossible: from the Alps to
Annapurna**
New York: Doubleday, 1964. 350p, U.S.A. edition
of **Conquistadors of the useless**

THOMAS, Lowell
American writer and broadcaster.

*804. **Lowell Thomas' book of the high mountains**
New York: Messner, 1964. 512p; ill; 24cm
Well illustrated summary of all aspects of the
mountains and climbing.

THOMAS, Wynford Vaughan
British broadcaster. See [659].

THOMPSON, Dorothy E. (1888–1961)
Noted British alpinist between the wars. Her book
was written as a tribute to a great guide, who also
climbed with Dorothy Pilley (qv).

*805. **Climbing with Joseph Georges**
Kendal: Titus Wilson, 1962. [xii], 159p, 13 plates
(incl. ports); 22cm

THOMPSON, Todd
See [353].

THOMSON, Joseph

806. **Travels in the Atlas and southern Morocco: a
narrative of exploration**
London: Geo. Philip, 1889. xviii, 488p, 2 fold.
maps, 31 plates; 20cm
Contains descriptions of mountain scenery, views
etc., including ascents of Irghalsor, Gadal and
Yaurirf.

THORINGTON, James Monroe (b. 1894)
American mountaineer and mountain historian,
who climbed extensively in Canada and the Alps.
See also [308], [596] & Appendix I, VI.

*807. **The glittering mountains of Canada: a record of
exploration and pioneer ascents in the Canadian
Rockies 1914–1924**
Philadelphia: Lea, 1925. xxii, 310p, 65 plates; ill,
maps, ports; 23cm

*808. **Mont Blanc sideshow: the life and times of Albert
Smith**
Philadelphia: Winston, 1934. xvi, 255p, 19 plates
(incl. facsims, ports); 23cm

*809. **A survey of early American ascents in the Alps in
the nineteenth century**
New York: A.A.C., 1943. viii, 83p; ill, facsims,
ports; 23cm

*†810.**The Purcell Range of British Columbia**
New York: A.A.C., 1946. [12], 152p; ill, maps (1
in end-pocket); 24cm

THWAITES, Reuben Gold

811. **A brief history of Rocky Mountain exploration,
with especial reference to the expedition of Lewis
and Clark**
New York: D. Appleton, 1904. xiv, 276p; map, 7
plates (incl. ports); 19cm

TICHY, Herbert
Austrian mountaineer, whose expedition to Cho
Oyu was one of the smallest ever to succeed on a
major Himalayan peak.

*812. **Cho Oyu: by favour of the gods**
Translated [from the German] by Basil Creighton.
London: Methuen, 1957. 196p, 36 plates (4 col);
23cm
From the original: **Cho Oyu: Gnade der Götter**
(Vienna: Ullstein, 1955).

*813. **Himalaya**
Translated [from the German] by Richard Rickett
and David Streatfeild
New York: Putnam, 1970
London: Hale, 1971. 175p; ill (some col); 29cm
Lavishly illustrated account of various aspects of
the Himalaya.

TILMAN Harold William (1898–1978)
British explorer and mountaineer, who led the
1938 Everest expedition and undertook many
expeditions with Shipton (qv). Latterly he has
concentrated on ocean sailing and several of his
books, such as 'Mischief' in Patagonia (C.U.P.
1957) deal with his travels in the southern
hemisphere. See also [800].

*814. **Snow on the equator**
London: Bell, 1937. xii, 265p, 20 plates; 23cm
Climbing memoirs.

*815. **The ascent of Nanda Devi**
Cambridge: C.U.P.,
1937. xiv, 235p, 2 maps (1 fold), 35 plates
(incl. group ports); 23cm
1949. Guild paperback.

816. **When men and mountains meet**
Cambridge C.U.P., 1946. x, 232p, maps, 36 plates;
23cm
Exploring in Assam: includes wartime experiences.

817. **Mount Everest 1938**
Cambridge C.U.P., 1948. x, 160p, 2 maps, 36
plates (incl. group ports); 23cm

*818. **Two mountains and a river**
London C.U.P., 1949. xii, 233p, 37 plates; 22cm
Rakaposhi, Mustagh Ata and River Oxus.

*819. **China to Chitral**
Cambridge: C.U.P., 1951. xii, 124p, 69 plates;
24cm
Includes Mustagh Ata and Bogdo Ola.

*820. **Nepal Himalaya**
Cambridge, C.U.P., 1952. xii, 272p, 40 plates;
23cm
Exploring in the Langtang and Annapurna Himal.

TOLL, Roger W.

*821. **Mountaineering in the Rocky Mountain National
Park**
By . . . and Robert Sterling Yard. Compiled from
the records of the Colorado Mountain Club.
Washington [D.C.]: U.S. Dept. Int., Govt. Ptg.
Office, 1919. 106p, plates; ill, map; 23cm

822. **The mountain peaks of Colorado . . . elevations
and topographic details**
Denver: Colorado M.C., 1923. 59p; 23cm
Chiefly orography: contains list of named peaks.

TOWNSEND, J. H.

823. **The two climbers, a cry from the Alps: a true story**
London: Partridge, [1904]. 32p
Account of an accident to the author's brother on
the Dent de Jaman in 1864.

TRANTER, Philip N. L. (1939–66)
Scottish civil engineer and mountaineer, killed in a
road accident. This book, which recounts the
climbs of a 4-man expedition in 1965, was written
by his father from diaries.

*824. **No tigers in the Hindu Kush**
By . . . Edited by Nigel Tranter.
London: Hodder, 1968. 155p [157], 17 (1 col)
plates (incl. ports); 23cm

TROTTER, Coutts
See [22].

TRUFFAUT, Roland (b. 1911)
French architect and mountaineer.

*825. **From Kenya to Kilimanjaro**
London: Hale, 1957. 157p, 24 plates; ill, maps,
ports; 23cm
From the original: **Du Kenya au Kilimanjaro**
(Paris: Fulliard, 1953)
Includes climb of the north face of Mt. Kenya.

TUCKER, John William
British mountaineer: member of the party which
reconnoitred the successful route.

826. **Kanchenjunga**
London: Elek Books, 1955. 224p, 20 plates (incl.
ports); 23cm
London: Hamilton, 1957. Panther paperback
New York: Abelard Schuman, 1966. 224p.

[**TUCKETT**, Elizabeth F.]
Sister of Francis Fox Tuckett, who produced some
delightful Victorian sketchbooks depicting their
Alpine travels.

*827. **How we spent the summer: or, 'A Voyage en
Zigzag' in Switzerland and Tyrol, with some
members of the Alpine Club. From the sketch
book of one of the party.**
London: Longmans,
1864. 2nd ed.
1866. 3rd ed. redrawn, 40p; ill; 26 x 36cm
1874. 6th ed.

*828. **Pictures in Tyrol and elsewhere: from a family
sketchbook**
By the author of 'A voyage en zigzag'
London: Longmans,
1867. 313p
1869. 2nd ed. xii, 313p; ill; 21cm

*829. **Zigzagging amongst Dolomites**
London: Longmans, 1871. [3], 38p; ill; 26 x 36cm

TUCKETT, Francis Fox (1834–1913)
Businessman, traveller and amateur archaeologist.
He climbed extensively in the Alps in the latter
part of the nineteenth century, adopting the
scientific approach to mountain travel. The only
collected edition of his alpine articles is in German:
Hochalpenstudien 2v. (Leipzig, 1873–4). See also
[20].

*830. A pioneer in the high Alps: alpine diaries and letters of F. F. Tuckett 1856–1874.
[Edited by W.A.B. Coolidge]
London: Arnold, 1920. xii, 372p, 8 (2 fold) plates (incl. ports); 23cm

TURNER, Samuel (1869–1929)
British businessman and mountaineer. His bombastic style spoils his books and detracts from his not inconsiderable achievements.

831. **Siberia: a record of travel, climbing and exploration**
London: Fisher Unwin,
1905. xvi, 440p
1911. 2nd ed. 320p, 32 plates (incl. port); 21cm

*832. **My climbing adventures in four continents**
London: Fisher Unwin,
1911. xiv, 283p [269] , 52 plates; 23cm
1913. Cheap ed. xii, 382p; ill; 21cm

*833 **The conquest of the New Zealand Alps**
London: Fisher Unwin, 1922. 292p, 23 plates; 22cm
His later climbs in New Zealand, particularly on Mt. Tutoko.

TUTTON, Alfred Edwin Howard

834. **The natural history of ice and snow: illustrated from the Alps**
London: Kegan Paul,
1927. xvi, 319p, 48 plates; 23cm
1931. Cheap ed.

TYNDALE, Harry Edmund Guise (1888–1948)
British mountaineer: translator and editor of numerous mountaineering publications, including the A.J. **See also [425] & [468]**.

835. **Mountain paths**
London: Eyre & Spottiswoode, 1948. x, 208p; ill, ports; 23cm
Climbing reminiscences.

TYNDALL, John (1820–93)
Irish scientist and mountaineer, who was the chief opponent of Forbes (qv) in the glacier controversy. From a scientific beginning he took more and more to the pleasures of mountaineering, his greatest climb being the first ascent of the Weisshorn. He was also a contender for the first ascent of the Matterhorn. Biography: **The life and work of John Tyndall** (Macmillan, 1945) by A. S. Eve and C. H. Creasey, with a chapter on Tyndall as a mountaineer by Lord Schuster (qv). **See also [18]**.

*836. **The glaciers of the Alps: being a narrative of excursions and ascents, an account of the origin and phenomena of glaciers, and an exposition of the physical principles to which they are related**

London: Murray, 1860. xxii, 444p, 6 plates. ill; 21cm
London: Longmans, 1896. New [2nd] ed. xviii, 445p, 5 plates; ill; 20cm. Prefatory note by Mrs. Tyndall, minor textual corrections and improved index.
London: Routledge, [1905]. New Universal Library ed. xii, 207p; 16cm. Omits Part II

(scientific material).
London: Longmans, 1906. Silver Library ed.
Edited by Mrs. Tyndall.
London: Dent; New York: Dutton

[1906]. Everyman's Library ed. xiv, 274p. Combined with **Mountaineering in 1861**.
1911. Reprinted. Everyman's
1928. Reprinted. Everyman's.

837. **Mountaineering in 1861: a vacation tour**
London: Longmans,
1862. x, 105p, 2 plates; 22cm. Also issued under title **A vacation tour in Switzerland**
1906. Reissued with **Glaciers of the Alps**

838. **A vacation tour in Switzerland**
London: Longmans, [1862], x, 105p, 2 plates; 22cm. Contents the same as **Mountaineering in 1861.**

*839. **Hours of exercise in the Alps**
London: Longmans,
1871. xii, 473p, 7 plates; 21cm
1871. 2nd ed. [imp]
1873. 3rd ed. xiv, 475p
New York: Appleton,
1898. 473p
London: Longmans,
1899. 4th ed. xii, 481p, 7 plates (incl. port); 20cm. With minor textual corrections and an index.
1906. Silver Library ed. Edited by Mrs. Tyndall.

ULLMAN, James Ramsay (1908–71)
American writer and mountaineer. **See also [795] & Appendix IV.**

840. **High conquest: the story of mountaineering**
London: Gollancz, 1942. 320p, 16 plates; 23 cm
London: Collins, 1956. Revised and reissued as **The age of mountaineering**
Good summary, subject to minor inaccuracies.

841. **The White Tower**
Philadelphia: Lippincott,
1945. 479p; 21cm
London: Collins,
1946. 479p; 21cm
1954. Fontana paperback.
1973.
Fiction: set in the Alps.

842. **Kingdom of adventure Everest: a chronicle of Man's assault on the Earth's highest mountain**
Narrated by the participants. With an accompanying text by . . .
New York: Sloane, 1947. 411p, plates; ill, maps; 22cm
London: Collins, 1948. 320p, 25 plates; ill, facsim, maps, ports; 23cm
Passages from various Everest narratives, linked by Ullman's text.

843. **The age of mountaineering**
By . . . with a chapter on British mountains by W. H. Murray.
Philadelphia: Lippincott, 1954. 352p
London: Collins, 1956. 384p, 24 plates; 22cm. Revised edition of **High conquest.**

844. **Tiger of the snows: Tenzing Norgay**
New York: Putnam. 1955. 294p
London: Harrap, 1955. Published in U.K. as **Man of Everest**

*845. **Man of Everest: the autobiography of Tenzing [Norgay]**
Told to . . .
New York: Putnam,
  1955. Published as **Tiger of the snows**
London: Harrap,
  1955. 320p, 36 (4 col) plates (incl. ports); 21cm
  1955. Reprinted
London: Transworld Pub.,
  1957. Corgi paperback
Madras: O.U.P.,
  1958. Abridged edition by W. V. Venkat Ras under title **Tenzing of Everest**
London: Severn House Pub.,
  1975. 320p [318], 32 plates (incl. ports); 21cm
  Spine title: **Sherpa Tenzing, man of Everest.**

846. **Banner in the sky**
Philadelphia: Lippincott,
  1954.
London: Collins,
  1955. 254p; 20cm
  1958. Fontana paperback
  1959. Special edition for children
  1961. Abridged as **Third man on the mountain**
  H'worth: Penguin, 1963. Peacock Books.
  1968. Puffin Books paperback
  ? : ?. 1969. Evergreen edition
Fiction: set in the Alps.

847. **Third man on the mountain**
See: **Banner in the sky**

*848. **Americans on Everest: the official account of the ascent led by Norman G. Dyrenfurth**
By . . . . . and other members of the expedition.
Philadelphia: Lippincott, 1964.
London: Michael Joseph, 1965. xxiv, 429p, 56 (8 col) plates (incl. ports); 25cm

*849. **Straight up: the life and death of John Harlin**
New York: Doubleday, 1968. 287p, 32 plates; **See** See also [314].

UNDERHILL, Miriam (1899–1976) [née O'Brien]
One of the few leading American mountaineers active in the Alps between the wars: contemporary with Dorothy Pilley (qv).

*850. **Give me the hills**
London: Methuen, 1956. 252p, 36 (4 col) plates (incl. ports); 23cm
Riverside, Conn: Chatham Press in assoc. with Appalachian M.C., 1971. 271p
Climbing memoirs: includes climbing in Montana U.S.A.

UNSWORTH, Walter (b. 1928)
Publisher, writer and mountaineer. Most of his books written for children. Author of several other books and climbing guides, such as **The high fells of Lakeland** (Hale, 1972).

851. **The young mountaineer**
London: Hutchinson, 1959. 191p; ill; 20cm

*852. **The English outcrops**
London: Gollancz, 1964. 192p, plates; ill, maps; 22cm

853. **Matterhorn man: being the life and adventures of Edward Whymper**
London: Gollancz, 1965. 127p, 8 plates; 22cm

854. **Tiger in the snow: the life and adventures of A. F. Mummery**
London: Gollancz, 1967. 126p, 8 plates (incl. ports); 23cm

*855. **Because it is there: famous mountaineers, 1840–1940**
London: Gollancz,
  1968. 144p, 8 plates; 23cm
  1973. Reprinted
24 biographical sketches.

856. **The book of rock-climbing**
London: Barker, 1968. 112p; ill; 24cm

857. **North Face: the second conquest of the Alps**
London: Hutchinson, 1969. 160p, 12 plates (incl. ports); 21cm

*858. **Encyclopaedia of mountaineering**
Compiled by . . .
London: Hale, 1975. 272p, 16 plates; ill, maps, ports; 25cm
H'worth: Penguin 1977. Paperback ed.

Excellent reference book, subject to minor inaccuracies.

VALENTINE-RICHARDS, Alfred Valentine (1866–1933)
See [50].

VAN DYKE, John Charles

859. **The mountain: renewed studies in impressions and appearances**
London: Werner Laurie, [1916] xvi, 234p, plate; 19cm
New York: Scribners, 1916.
Essays on mountain beauty.

VERGHESE, B. G.

*860. **Himalayan endeavour**
Edited by . . .
Bombay: Times of India, 1962. xii, 155p, 14 plates; 22cm
Summary of Indian mountaineering: particularly Kamet, Nun, Everest and Annapurna III.

VISSER-HOOFT, Jenny
Wife of Dr. Philips Visser, with whom she carried out four expeditions in the Karakoram in the years 1922–35.

861. **Among the Kara-korum glaciers in 1925**
With contributions by P. C. Visser.
London: Arnold, 1926. xii, 303p, 25 plates; 23cm

WALKER, Horace (1838–1908)
Leading Victorian mountaineer, who climbed in Britain, the Alps and the Caucasus. See [22].

WALKER, James Hubert

862. **Mountain days in the Highlands and Alps**
London: Arnold, 1937. 320p, 64 plates; 23cm
Climbing reminiscences.

863. **On hills of the north**
Edinburgh: Oliver & Boyd, 1948. xvi, 182p, 24 plates; 22cm
Walking through the mountains of Scotland: with geological notes.

*864. **Walking in the Alps**
Edinburgh: Oliver & Boyd, 1951. xii, 274p, 24 plates; ill, maps; 24cm
High level routes and circuits.

WALL, C. W.

865. **Mountaineering in Ireland: for the hill-walker and the rock-climber**
Dublin: Irish Tourist Assoc.,
1939. 88p; ill, map; 18cm
[1944] 2nd ed.
Dublin: Fed. M.C. Ireland/Cordee, 1976.
Rev. by Joss Lynam. 111p; 16m

WALL, David

866. **Rondoy: an expedition to the Peruvian Andes**
London: Murray, 1965. [14], 176p, 24 plates (incl. ports); 23cm
First ascent but two members of the party were killed.

WALLER, James

*867. **The everlasting hills**
London: William Blackwood, 1939. xii, 190p, 64 plates; 23cm
Karakoram – Saltoro Kangri and Masherbrum – with John Hunt.

WALLROTH, Frederick Anthony (1847–1920)
Barrister and A.C. member, who compiled the index to **Peaks, passes and glaciers:see** [18] & [20].

WALTON, Elijah (1832–80)
British artist, who delighted in mountain scenery and atmospheric effects: noted for his truthful rendering of rock structure and mountain form.

*868. **Peaks and valleys of the Alps**
21 chromo-lithographs from drawings by . . . . Descriptive text by T. G. Bonney.
Privately printed, 1867. Subscription edition. Folio.
London: Sampson Low, 1868. Subscription edition reissued, 42p; 21 col. plates 56cm
Other similar volumes (mostly published by Thompson) include:
Flowers from the upper Alps (1869)
The coast of Norway (1871)
Peaks in pen and pencil (1872)
Vignettes: Alpine (1873)
Bernese Oberland (1874)
Welsh scenery (1875)
English Lake scenery (1876)
Alpine flowers (1882)

WALTON, William Howard Murray
Clergyman, missionary.

*869. **Scrambles in Japan and Formosa**
London: Arnold, 1934. 304p, 3 maps. 26 plates; 23cm

WARBURTON, Lloyd E.

*870. **The steepest mountain: the New Zealand Andes expedition, 1960**
Invercargill: Cuthill, 1964. 136p; ill;
Nevado Cayesh, Peru.

WARD, Frank Kingdon
See under: **KINGDON-WARD**, Frank

WARD, Michael Phelps (b. 1925)
British surgeon and mountaineer. He was a member of several Himalayan expeditions – Everest, Ama Dablam, Makalu – and also visited Bhutan. His published works include **Man at high altitude** (1974) and **Mountain medicine: a clinical study of cold and high altitude** (Crosby, Lockwood, Staples, 1975).

*871. **The mountaineer's companion**
Edited by . . .
London: Eyre & Spottiswoode, 1966. 598p, 26 plates (2 col); ill, facsims; 23cm
Anthology containing extracts from numerous books in this bibliography.

*872. **In this short span: a mountaineering memoir**
London: Gollancz, 1972. 304p, 24 plates (incl. ports); 23cm
Climbing memoirs.

WARWICK, Alan Ross

873. **With Whymper in the Alps**
By . . . Illustrated by Henry Toothill.
London: Muller, 1964. 143p, 12 plates; ill, maps port; 19cm
Written for children.

WASHBURN, Henry Bradford Jr. (b. 1910)
American mountaineer: Director, Boston Museum of Science. An authority on Alaskan mountaineering. See also Appendix I.

874. **Among the Alps with Bradford**
New York: Putnam, 1927. xiv, 160p, 42 plates; 20cm
Written for children.

875. **Bradford on Mount Washington**
New York: Putnam, 1928. xii, 123p, 31 plates; 19cm
Written for children.

876. **Bradford on Mount Fairweather**
New York: Putnam, 1930. x, 127p, 3 maps, 30 plates; 19cm
Written for children.

WATSON, Sir Norman, Bart

*877. **Round Mystery Mountain: a ski adventure**
By . . . and Edward J. King.
London: Arnold, 1935. xii, 246p, 33 plates (1 col); 23cm
The first ski crossing of the Coast Range, British Columbia. Mystery Mountain is Mt. Waddington.

WEDDERBURN, Ernest Alexander Maclagan (1912—44)
British mountaineer, killed in the war. **See also** [34].

878. **Alpine climbing on foot and with ski**
Illustrated by Edo Derzaj.
Manchester: Open Air Pubs., [1936]. 118p; ill; 17cm
Manchester: Countrygoer Bks, 1954. x, 131p, 9 plates; ill; maps; 21cm

WEIR, Thomas
Scottish mountaineer, writer, photographer and ornithologist.

*879. **Highland days**
London: Cassell, 1948. xii, 139p, 23 plates; 23cm
Climbing reminiscences.

*880. **The ultimate mountains: an account of four months' mountain exploring in the central Himalaya**
London: Cassell, 1953. x, 98p, 49 plates (incl. ports); 23cm
See also [560].

*881. **Camps and climbs in Arctic Norway**
London: Cassell, 1953. viii, 85p [87], 41 plates; 23cm
The Lofoten district.

882. **East of Katmandu**
Edinburgh: Oliver & Boyd, 1955. [6], 138p, 49 plates (2 col); 23cm

WEST, Lionel F.
British surgeon and climber.

*883. **The climbers' pocket-book: rock climbing accidents with hints on first aid to the injured, some uses of the rope, methods of rescue and transport**
Manchester: Scientific Pub. Co., [1907]. 79p; ill; 16 cm.
The first English crag rescue manual.

WEST, William C.
See [757].

WESTMORLAND, Horace ['Rusty'] (b. 1886)
British soldier and mountaineer, honoured for services to mountain rescue.

884. **Adventures in climbing**
London: Pelham Books, 1964. 124p, 8 plates; ill; 20cm
Part instruction, part reminiscence.

WESTON, Walter (1861—1940)
Clergyman: the 'father' of Japanese mountaineering. **See also** [757].

*885. **Mountaineering and exploration in the Japanese alps**
London: Murray, 1896. xvi, 346p, 2 fold. col. maps, 27 plates (incl. ports); 25cm

*886. **The playground of the Far East**
London: Murray, 1918. xiv, 333p, 2 fold. col. maps, 19 plates; 23cm

WEXLER, Arnold
See [455].

WHEELER, Arthur Oliver (1860—1945)
Canadian government surveyor and one of the leaders of Canadian mountaineering.

887. **The Selkirk Range**
Ottawa: Govt. Print. Bureau, 1905—6. 2v. xviii, 459p, 10 maps, 92 plates (incl. ports); 25cm. [Part II deals with travel and exploration; Part IV deals with mountaineering].

*888. **The Selkirk Mountains: a guide for mountain climbers and pilgrims**
Information by A. O. Wheeler. [Text by Mrs. H. J. Parker].
Winnipeg: Stovel Co., 1912. [8], 199p; ill, maps; 19cm

WHEELOCK, Walt

889. **Climbing Mount Whitney**
By ... and T. Condon. Illustrated by Ruth Daly
Glendale, Calif: La Siesta Press, 1960. 36p; ill, maps

*890. **Ropes, knots and slings for climbers**
By ... Illustrated by Ruth Daly
Glendale, Calif: La Siesta Press, 1967. Revised ed.
1966. 35p; ill
1967. Rev. ed. by ... & Royal Robbins. 70p

WHERRY, George Edward (1852—1928)
Surgeon and mountaineer. **See also** [19].

891. **Alpine notes and the climbing foot**
Cambridge: Macmillan & Bowes, 1896. xvi, 174p, plates; 19cm
One of the curiosities of mountaineering literature.

892. **Notes from a knapsack**
Cambridge: Bowes & Bowes, 1909. xii, 312p; ill, map; 19cm

WHILLANS, Donald Desbrow (b. 1934)
Outstanding British mountaineer, who has made many fine ascents in the Alps, Himalaya and South America. He partnered Joe Brown (qv) in the development of British rock-climbing in the 1950s.

*893. **Don Whillans: portrait of a mountaineer**
By ... and Alick Ormerod.
London: Heinemann,
1971. x, 266p, 16 plates (incl. ports); 23cm
H'worth: Penguin,
1973. Paperback ed. (Also 1976)
Climbing memoirs.

'WHIPPLESNAITH' (pseud. of Noel Howard Symington)

894. **The night climbers of Cambridge**
London: Chatto & Windus,
1937. viii, 184p, 55 plates; 23cm
1937. Reprinted (Also 1952)
Wall and roof climbing is a traditional Cambridge sport.

WHITE, Anne Terry
American writer.

895. **All about mountains and mountaineering**
New York: Random House, [1962]. [viii], 144p ill; 24cm
Written for children: well illustrated.

WHITNEY, Josiah Dwight
American professor and head of the California Survey. Mount Whitney in the Sierra Nevada so named in his honour. Two of his assistants were William Brewer (qv) and Clarence King (qv).

896. **The Yosemite guidebook: a description of the Yosemite Valley and the adjacent region of the Sierra Nevada and of the big trees of California**
Sacramento: Geological Survey of California, 1869. viii, 155p [147], 2 fold. maps (in pockets), 8 plates; 24cm. [Also published by authority of the Legislature (Cambridge, Mass), 1870. Further editions in 1871 & 1874.
Whitney violently (and wrongly) rejected the glacier theories put forward by John Muir (qv).

WHITWELL, Edward Robson (1843–1922)
One of F. F. Tuckett's (qv) climbing companions. See [22].

WHYMPER, Edward (1840–1911)
Wood engraver, writer, lecturer and mountaineer. The central figure in the drama of the first ascent of the Matterhorn, the mountain which first dominated then destroyed him. His book 'Scrambles' is the most famous mountaineering book in the world, and includes among others his climbs in 1864 with A. W. Moore (qv). Whymper's book on the Andes is less well-known but more important scientifically. He provided the illustrations for many nineteenth century mountaineering books. See also [20].

*897. **Scrambles amongst the Alps in the years 1860–69**
London: Murray,
    1871. xx, 432p, 5 fold. maps, 23 plates; 24cm
    1871. 2nd ed. [imp.]
Cleveland: Burrows,
    1871.
Philadelphia: Lippincott,
    1873.
London: Murray,
    1880. 3rd edition, abridged and published as **The ascent of the Matterhorn**
    1893. 4th edition, xx, 468p. Also de luxe edition bound by Zaehnsdorf. [Regarded as the definitive edition . Sold out in 2 weeks.]
Cleveland: Burrows,
    1899. [Bound with another book **Down the Rhine**]
London: Murray,
    1900. 5th ed.
London: Nelson, [1908] Shilling Library series
London: Murray,
    1936. 6th edition. With additional illustrations and material from the author's unpublished diaries. Revised and edited by H. E. G. Tyndale. xxii, 414p
    1948. Reprinted.
    1965. 7th ed.

898. **The ascent of the Matterhorn**
London: Murray, 1880. xxiv, 325p, 2 fold. maps (1 col), 14 plates (incl. ports); 91 ill; 24 cm. 3rd ed. abridged of **Scrambles**

*899. **Travels amongst the great Andes of the equator.**
London: Murray,
    1891–2. xxvi, 456p, 4 maps, 20 plates; ill; 24cm. Plus supplementary volume of scientific material, which was published before the main volume. Also numbered and signed edition in 2v. plus vol. of maps.
New York: ?,
    1892. xxiv, 456p
London: Nelson
    [1911], Shilling Library series
London: Lehmann,
    1949. Chiltern Library ed. 272p
London: Knight,
    1972. xxiv, 214p. Edited and. introduced by Eric Shipton.

900. **Chamonix and the range of Mont Blanc**
A guide by . . .
London: Murray, 1896. xvi, 192p; ill, maps; 19cm. [Reissued annually up to 1911]
Reading: West Col, 1974. Facsimile ed.

901. **The Valley of Zermatt and the Matterhorn**
A guide by . . .
London: Murray, 1897. xiv, 212p; ill, maps; 19cm. [Reissued annually up to 1911]
Reading: West Col, 1974. Facsimile ed.

902. **Episodes from the ascent of the Matterhorn**
By . . . ; illustrated from the author's drawings.
London: Harrap, 1928. 192p; ill; 16cm

WIBBERLEY, Leonard

903. **The epics of Everest**
Illustrated by Genevieve Vaughan-Jackson.
New York: Farrar, Strauss & Young, 1954. 242p; ill;
London: Faber, 1955. 217p [215]; ill; 21cm
Written for children: summary of attempts up to 1953.

WILCOX, Walter Dwight (1869–1949)
American mountaineer and original A.A.C. member. He explored the Canadian Rockies in the 1890s to the north of Kicking Horse Pass, and south to Mt. Assiniboine.

904. **Camping in the Canadian Rockies**
New York: Putnam,
    1896. xiv, 283p, 25 plates; 26cm
    1900. Revised and enlarged edition entitled **The Rockies of Canada**
    1909. 3rd ed. xii, 300p. This edition largely rewritten: photogravures increased from 25 to 38, more than half of them being different from those in the previous edition.

*905. **The Rockies of Canada**
New York: Putnam, 1900. xii, 309p, 42 plates; ill, 2 fold. col. maps (end-pocket); 25cm. Revised edition of **Camping in the Canadian Rockies**

906. **Guide to the Lake Louise District**
New York: Putnam, 1909.

WILLIAMS, Cicely
English climber.

907. **Zermatt saga**
London: Allen & Unwin, 1964. 197p, 9 plates; ill, facsims; 23cm

A history of one of the most important Alpine mountaineering centres.

*908. **Women on the rope: the feminine share in mountain adventure**
London: Allen & Unwin, 1973. 240p, 8 plates (incl. ports); 23cm

WILLIAMS, John Harvey

*909. **The mountain that was "God": being a little book about the great peak which the Indians named "Tacoma" but which is officially called "Rainier".**
Tacoma: published by the author, 1910. 111p; ill (some col); 26cm
New York: Putnam, 1911. 2nd ed. revised & enlarged. 144p; ill (some col), maps, ports; 26cm

*910. **The guardians of the Columbia: Mount Hood, Mount Adams and Mount St. Helens**
Tacoma: Williams, 1912. 144p [142]; ill (some col); 26cm

*911. **Yosemite and its High Sierra**
Tacoma: Williams, 1914. 147p; ill (some col); 26cm
Three matching, finely illustrated and interesting monographs, giving among other things details of climbing history.

WILLIAMS, M. B.
His published works include **Through the heart of the Rockies & Selkirks** (1921), a general guide.

912. **Jasper National Park**
[Ottawa: Dept. Interior], 1928. [6], 176p, 2 fold. maps; ill; 24cm

WILLINK, Henry George (1851–1938)
Amateur artist, who illustrated the Badminton volume on mountaineering with many humorous sketches. See [211].

WILLS, Sir Alfred (1828–1912)
Judge, mountaineer and amateur botanist. Original A.C. member and President 1864–5. His ascent of the Wetterhorn ushered in the 'Golden Age' of mountaineering. See also [18].

*913. **Wanderings among the high Alps**
London: Bentley,
   1856. xx, 384p, 4 col. plates; 20cm
   1858. 2nd ed. revised with additions. xx, 426p
   1863.
Oxford: Blackwell,
   1937.
   1939.

914. **The ascent of Mont Blanc, together with some remarks on glaciers**
London: Privately printed for the author by A. Schulze, 1858. 90p; 16cm

*915. **"The Eagle's Nest" in the valley of Sixt: a summer home among the Alps, together with some excursions among the great glaciers**
[Illustrated with coloured lithographs by his wife]
London: Longmans,
   1860. xx, 327p, 2 fold. maps, 12 col. plates; 21cm
   1860. 2nd ed. [imp,]

WILSON, Claude (1860–1937)
British doctor and mountaineer. A.C. President 1929–31. He climbed extensively in the Alps. See also [757].

*916. **Mountaineering**
With illustrations by Ellis Carr.
London: Bell, 1893. viii, 208p; ill; 17cm. Also 50 copies were printed on handmade paper and were not for sale.
Instructional: a delightful little volume.

917. **An epitome of fifty years' climbing**
Printed for private distribution, 1933. 119p; 22cm. 125 copies only.
Chiefly a list of his climbs.

WILSON, Edward Livingstone

918. **Mountain climbing**
The Out of Door Library.
By . . . , Edwin Lord Weeks, A. F. Jaccaci, Mark Brickell Kerr, William Williams, H. F. B. Lynch, Sir W. Martin Conway.
[New York]: Scribner, 1897. xii, 358p; ill; 21cm.
[Two different bindings seen].

WILSON, Henry Schütz (1824–1902)
Businessman and writer, who climbed in the Alps in the 1870s. A.C. member.

919. **Alpine ascents and adventures: or, Rock and snow sketches**
With two illustrations by Marcus Stone and Edward Whymper.
London: Sampson Low,
   1878. xii, 319p, plate; 19cm
   1878. 2nd ed.

WILSON, James Gilbert (b. 1937)
New Zealand university lecturer, clergyman and mountaineer, who has been on Himalayan and Antarctic expeditions.

*†920 **Aorangi: the story of Mount Cook**
Christchurch: Whitcomb & Tombs, 1968. 253p, 20 plates (4 col); ill, maps, ports; 22cm

WILSON, Ken
Journalist and climber.

*921. **Hard rock: great British rock-climbs**
Compiled by . . . with editorial assistance from Mike and Lucy Pearson. Diagrams by Brian Evans.
London: Hart-Davis, MacGibbon,
   1974. xx, 220p; ill; 29cm
   1975. 2nd imp.
Illustrations, route diagrams and descriptions.

WINDHAM, William (1717–61)
Windham and his friends visited Chamonix in June 1741. They went up to the Montenvers and studied the Mer de Glace. Windham's account is always linked with that of Pierre Martel, who visited Chamonix the following year. Both their original accounts were written in French and circulated in Geneva in manuscript only. A version (still in French) of the two MS narratives, edited by Leonard Boulacre, was published in 'Journal Helvetique', May–June 1743.

*922. An account of the glacieres or ice alps in Savoy, in two letters, one from an English gentleman to his friend at Geneva: the other from Peter Martel, engineer to the said English gntleman [sic] illustrated with a map, and two views of the place etc.
As laid before the Royal Society.
London: Peter Martel, 1744. [MDCCXLIV] 28p [30] , 2 fold. plates (incl. map); 29cm
Ipswich: W. Craighton, 1747. 2nd ed. 34pp.

WINKWORTH, Stephen (1831–86)
See [20].

WOLFE, Linnie Marsh
He also wrote Son of the wilderness: the life of John Muir (New York: Knopf, 1945).

*923. John of the mountains: unpublished journals of John Muir
Edited by . . .
Boston: Houghton Mifflin, 1938. xxiv, 459p 8 plates; 22cm

WOLLASTON, Alexander Frederick Richmond (1875–1930)
Naturalist, geographer and botanist, who explored in Africa, New Guinea and Colombia. His best known book is probably From Ruwenzori to the Congo: a naturalist's journey across Africa (Murray, 1908). See [387] & [938].

WOOD, Robert L.
American geographer, cartographer and mountaineer, with thirty years' experience of exploring the Olympic Mountains. His published works include Trail country: Olympic National Park and Wilderness trails of Olympic National Park.

*924. Across the Olympic Mountains: the Press expedition 1889–90
Seattle: Mountaineers,
    1967. 220p
    1976. 236p
Account of six months winter crossing of a hitherto unknown area.

*†925. Men, mules and mountains
Seattle: Mountaineers, 1976. xx, 507p; ill, maps; 21cm
The first detailed exploration of the Olympic Mountains in 1890 by an expedition led by Lt. Joseph P. O'Neil.

WOOD, Walter A. Jr. (b. 1907)
American geographer and mountaineer, who has climbed in the Alps, Himalaya and Alaska. His history of mountaineering in the St. Elias Mountains is included as an appendix in [271].

WORDIE, Sir James Mann (1889–1962)
Geologist, polar explorer and mountaineer. A.C. member. See [757].

WORKMAN, Fanny Bullock (1859–1924) and William Hunter (1847–1937)
American husband and wife team, who made seven important Himalayan expeditions during the years 1899–1912. A.A.C. founder members. They published accounts of their travels in handsome, well-illustrated volumes. For short biographies of Mrs. Workman see Notable American Women: also On top of the world: five women explorers in Tibet (Paddington Press, 1976) by Luree Miller.

*926. In the ice-world of Himalaya: among the peaks and passes of Ladakh, Nubra, Suru, and Baltistan
London: Fisher Unwin,
    1900. xvi, 204p, 3 col. maps, 67 plates; 23cm
    1901. Cheap ed. being a reprint with the omission of two portraits and route map.

*927. Ice-bound heights of the Mustagh: an account of two seasons of pioneer exploration and high climbing in the Baltistan Himalaya
London: Constable, 1908. xvi, 444p, 2 fold. maps. 7 plates (4 col); ill, ports; 25cm

*928. Peaks and glaciers of Nun Kun: a record of pioneer exploration and mountaineering in the Punjab Himalaya
London: Constable, 1909. xvi, 204p; ill, map; 24cm

*929. The call of the snowy Hispar: a narrative of exploration and mountaineering on the northern frontier of India
With an appendix by Count Dr. Cesare Calciati and Dr. Mathias Koncza.
London: Constable, 1910. xvi, 298p, 2 fold. maps, 86 plates (incl. ports); 25cm

*930. Two summers in the ice-wilds of eastern Karakoram: the exploration of nineteen hundred square miles of mountain and glacier
London: Fisher Unwin, 1917. 296p, 3 maps, 134 plates; 24cm

WRIGHT, Jeremiah Ernest Benjamin (? –1975)
Professional mountaineer, guide and instructor, who founded the Mountaineering Association, a training organization. See also [562].

*931. Mountain days in the Isle of Skye
Edinburgh: Moray Press, 1934. 239p, 63 plates; 23cm

932. The technique of mountaineering: a handbook of established methods
With drawings by W. J. Kidd. Published under the auspices of the Mountaineering Association.
London: Mount. Assoc.,
    1955. 160p, 21 plates; ill; 21cm
London: Nichol. Kaye,
    1955. 144p, 20 plates; ill; 20cm
    1958. 2nd revised ed. 191p
    1964. 3rd revised ed. 192p.

933. Rock-climbing in Britain
London: Kaye for M.A.,
    1958. 142p, maps, 31 plates (incl. ports); 22cm
London: Kaye,
    1958. 142p, maps, 31 plates (incl. ports); 22cm
    1964. Reprinted with revised appendices. 143p.

WYATT, Colin
British ski-jump champion.

934. **The call of the mountains**
London: Thames & Hudson, 1952. 96p, 75 plates; 31cm
Photo-album: a skier's eye-view of the world's mountains.

YANG KE-HSIEN

*935. **The ascent of the Mustagh Ata**
Peking: Foreign Languages Press, 1956. 60p; ill, map; 19cm
First ascent by Russo-Chinese expedition.

YARD, Robert Sterling
See [821].

YATES, Edmund Hodgson (1831–94)
Journalist and novelist. See [718].

YELD, George (1845–1938)
Schoolmaster, mountaineer and editor of the A.J. He was an authority on the Graian Alps and collaborated with Coolidge in the production of one of the Conway-Coolidge climbers' guidebooks. See also [187] & [189].

*936. **Scrambles in the eastern Graians 1878–1897**
London: Fisher Unwin, 1900. xx, 279p fold. map, 20 plates; 21cm

YOUNG, Geoffrey Winthrop (1876–1958)
Writer, poet and mountaineer: one of the best-known figures in mountaineering. His climbing career was severely curtailed by the injuries he sustained in the first world war. He led the development of modern Welsh rock-climbing and was instrumental in the formation of the B.M.C. See also [142] & [757].

*937. **Wall and roof climbing**
By the author of 'The roof-climbers' guide to Trinity'
Eton College: Spotiswoode, 1905. viii, 109p; 23cm
A humorous collection of references in literature to this traditional Cambridge sport.

*938. **Mountain craft**
Edited by . . .
London: Methuen,
    1920. xx, 603p, 10 plates; 23cm
    1928. 2nd ed.
    1934. 3rd ed.
New York: ?,
    1934.
London: Methuen,
    1945. 4th ed. revised, xii, 319p
    1946. 5th ed. [imp]
    1949. 6th ed.
    1949. 7th ed. revised.
The classic of precept and practice.

*939. **On high hills: memories of the Alps**
London: Methuen,
    1927. xvi, 368p, 24 plates (incl. port); 23cm
    1927. 2nd ed.
New York: Dutton,
    1928.
London: Methuen,
    1933. 3rd ed.

1944. 4th ed.
1947. 5th ed. xii, 352p
Accounts of his greatest climbs.

*940. **Collected poems of Geoffrey Winthrop Young**
London: Methuen, 1936. viii, 245p; 23cm
Comprises:
Wind and hill (Smith, Elder, 1909)
Freedom (Smith Elder, 1914)
April and rain (Sidgwick & Jackson, 1923)
Mountain humours

941. **In praise of mountains: an anthology for friends**
Compiled by Eleanor and Geoffrey Winthrop Young.
London: Muller,
    1948. 61p; ill; 14cm
    1951. 2nd imp.

*942. **Mountains with a difference**
London: Eyre & Spottiswoode, 1951. xii, 282p, 12 plates (incl. ports); 22cm
Account of his climbs with an artificial leg after the war.

*943. **Snowdon biography**
By . ., Geoffrey Sutton and Wilfrid Noyce.
Edited by Wilfred Noyce.
London: Dent, 1957. xiv, 194p, 16 plates (incl. ports); 22cm
A history of climbers' involvement with Snowdon.

YOUNG, S. Hall
American missionary in Alaska.

944. **Alaska days with John Muir**
New York: Fleming H. Revell, 1915. 226p [224]. map, 12 plates (incl. port); 20cm

YOUNGHUSBAND, Sir Francis Edward (1863–1942)
British soldier, explorer and mystic, who had considerable knowledge of central Asia. He was a member of the Mount Everest Committee. His published works include **Kashmir** (1909) and **Wonders of the Himalaya** (1924).

*945. **The heart of a continent: a narrative of travels in Manchuria, across the Gobi Desert, through the Himalayas, the Pamirs, and Chitral, 1884–1894**
London: Murray,
    1896.
    1896. 2nd ed. xx, 409p, 4 maps, 18 plates; 24cm
    1898. Abridged ed. entitled **Among the celestials**
    1937. Revised ed. xiv, 243p.

*946. **The epic of Mount Everest**
London: Arnold, 1926. 319p, 16 plates; map, ports; 21cm [Many editions/impressions]
Wakefield: E.P. Pub, 1974. Reprinted.
Summary of the first three expeditions.

*947. **Everest the challenge**
London: Nelson,
    1936. x, 243p, 16 plates; 23cm
    1936. 2nd ed. with an account of the 1936 Everest expedition and future prospects.
    1941. Cheap ed. reprinted three times 1942–4 [Other editions/imp.]
This book deals with the overall appeal of the

Himalaya.

ZURBRIGGEN, Mathias (? −1918)
Alpine guide, who accompanied Conway (qv) to the Karakoram; and Fitzgerald (qv) to New Zealand and the Andes.

*948. **From the Alps to the Andes: being the autobiography of a mountain guide***
[Translated from the Italian by Miss Mary Alice Vialls]
London: Fisher Unwin, 1899. xvi, 269p; ill, ports; 23cm

[ZURCHER, Frédéric]

949. **Mountain adventures in the various countries of the world: selected from the narratives of celebrated travellers**
London: Seeley Jackson, 1869. viii, 320p, 24 plates; 19cm
Based on: **Les ascensions célèbres** Compiled by Frédéric Zurcher and Elie Margollé
Includes stories from Mont Blanc, Pyrenees, Elbruz, Ararat etc.

The Vignettes Hut and Dent Blanche,
Pennine Alps, Switzerland.

APPENDICES

ALPINE CLUB
Catalogue of books in the library of the Alpine Club
London: Alpine Club,
    1880. 36p; 23cm
    1887. 55p; 23cm
Edinburgh: Univ. P.
    1899. 223p; 23cm Edited by Henry Cockburn,
    Librarian: author list with subject index.

BENT, Allen Herbert
A bibliography of the White Mountains
Boston: Pub. for the Appalachian M.C. by Houghton
Mifflin, 1911. viii, 114p; 23cm. [Also a supplement.]

BRIDGE, George
Rock climbing in the British Isles 1894–1970: a bibliography of guidebooks
Reading: West Col, 1971. 40p; ill; 22cm
Lists 303 items, including pamphlets and private press
publications.

CAMPBELL, J. I.
A bibliography of mountains and mountaineering in Africa
Compiled by . . .
Cape Town: School of Librarianship, University of Cape
Town, 1945. [5], 48p; 33cm
Lists 406 items, chiefly articles published in 'Annual of
Mountain Club of South Africa'. One of the bibliograph-
ical series prepared by students studying for the Diploma
in Librarianship.

COOLIDGE, W. A. B.
A list of the writings (not being reviews of books) dating from 1868 to 1912 and relating to the Alps or Switzerland of W. A. B. Coolidge
Grindlewald: Jakober-Peter, 1912. 37p

FARQUHAR, F. P.
A list of publications relating to the mountains of Alaska
By . . . and Mildred P. Ashley
New York: A.A.C., 1934. 37p

Yosemite, the Big Trees and the High Sierra: a selective bibliography
Berkeley: Univ. Calif. Press, 1948. xii, 104p; facsims,
ports; 28cm

The published writings of Francis Peloubet Farquhar
Together with an introduction to 'F.P.F.' by Susanna
Bryant Dakin
San Francisco: privately printed by K. K. Bechtel, 1954.
xii, 17p; 26cm

FELL & ROCK CLIMBING CLUB (of the English Lake District)

Catalogue of the Library
Compiled by Muriel Files
Lancaster: F. & R.C.C., 1972. vi, 81p; 25cm
Classified order with author index.

HIMALAYAN CLUB
Library: classified catalogue of books with alphabetical list of authors
Simla: Himalayan Club, 1936. 69p. Supplements 1936–8.

JEFFERS, Le Roy
Selected list of books on mountaineering
Compiled by . . .
New York: New York Public Library,
    1914. 15p; 15cm
    1916. 46p; 15cm Revised ed.

KAMBARA, Tatsu
Nepal bibliography, 1959
Tokyo: T. Kambara, 1959. 121p; 21cm
Covers Everest and mountaineering

KRAWCZYK, Chess
Mountaineering: a bibliography of books in English to 1974.
Metuchen, N.J.: Scarecrow Press, 1977. xii, 180p; 23cm
Lists 1141 references of all sorts, with short title index
and brief subject index. Numerous errors, omissions
and dubious comments.

LIBRARY ASSOCIATION
Readers' guide to books on mountaineering
London: Library Assoc.
    1962. 27p; 19cm
    1972. 2nd ed. 39p; 19cm
Numerous errors.

MECKLY, Eugene P.
A bibliography of privately printed mountaineering books
[London: Dent, 1951.] In The Alpine Annual: 2; pp.
111–116. Also in the Alpine Journal, Vol. 57.
Compiled from the Alpine Journal, Appalachia, Alpine
Club and Swiss Alpine Club Library catalogues, and
booksellers' catalogues.

MONTAGNIER, H. F.
A bibliography of the ascents of Mont Blanc from 1786–1853
London: Spottiswoode, 1911. 35p; 22cm Reprinted from
the Alpine Journal.

A further contribution to the bibliography of Mont Blanc, 1786–1853
London: Spottiswoode, 1916. 25p, 3 plates (incl. ports);
22cm. Reprinted from the Alpine Journal.

MUMM, A. L.
The Alpine Club Register
London: Arnold, 1923–8, 3v.
Details of all members elected to the Alpine Club from
1857–90, including bibliographical details of all their
published writings.

NATIONAL LIBRARY OF SCOTLAND
Shelf catalogue of the Lloyd collection of [mostly] Alpine books
Boston: G. K. Hall, 1964. vi, 94p; 26cm
Lists 1600 items (many duplications) in several languages
but is extremely laborious to consult.

PORTER, E. C.
Library of mountaineering and exploration and travel: both true and in fiction, history, science, technique, philosophy, art etc.
Chicago: 1959. 74p; 25cm
Lists 750 items.

READ, Brian J.
Mountaineering, the literature in English: a classified bibliography, and an introductory survey
[Unpublished, 1975] Copy of typescript presented to Fell & Rock C.C. Library.

THORINGTON, J. M.
Mountains and mountaineering: a list of the writings (1917–1947) of J. Monroe Thorington
Privately printed, 1947. 12p; 23cm 150 copies only.

Mountains and mountaineering: bibliography of 50 years (1917–67) Alpine writings of J. M. Thorington

WASHBURN, H. B.
Mount McKinley and the Alaska Range in literature: a descriptive bibliography
Boston: Museum of Science, 1951. 88p; 23cm
Lists 264 items.

YAKUSHI, Yoshimi
Catalogue of Himalayan literature
[Tokyo: Y. Yakushi, 1972.] 343p. Edition of 500 copies.
Lists over 2,000 items in various European languages and in Japanese.

YORKSHIRE RAMBLERS' CLUB
Yorkshire Ramblers' Club Library [catalogue], 1959
Compiled by A. B. Craven
Leeds: Y.R.C. & Leeds Public Libraries, 1959. 154p; 25cm

APPENDIX II

Selection of mountaineering club journals published in the English language.

Alpine Journal
London: Alpine Club, 1863–in progress

American Alpine Journal
New York: American Alpine Club, 1930–in progress

Appalachia
Boston: Appalachian M.C., 1882?–in progress.

Ascent
San Francisco: Sierra Club, ?

Canadian Alpine Journal
Vancouver: Alpine Club of Canada, 1907–in progress

Climbers' Club Journal
Climbers' Club,
    1898–1910. Old series
    1912–in progress. New series

Fell & Rock Climbing Club Journal
Fell & Rock C.C., 1907–in progress

Himalayan Journal
Himalayan Club, 1929–in progress

Ladies' Alpine Club Journal/Yearbook
Ladies' Alpine Club,
    1933–57) } Yearbook
    1959–60) }
    1961–   Journal

Mountain Club Annual/Journal
Mountain Club of South Africa, 1892?–in progress.
Variously titled as **Mountain Club Annual, Annual of the M.C. of South Africa, Journal of the M.C. of South Africa.**

Mountaineer
Seattle: Mountaineers, 1907–in progress

New Zealand Alpine Journal
New Zealand Alpine Club, 1921–in progress

Pinnacle Club Journal
Pinnacle Club, 1924–in progress

Scottish Mountaineering Club Journal
Scottish M.C., 1890–in progress

Thrutch
Climbers' Federation of Australia, 1963–in progress

Trail and Timberline
Denver: Colorado M.C., 1918–in progress

A handbook of Mr. Albert Smith's ascent of Mont Blanc
Illustrated by Mr. William Beverley. With twenty-five
outline engravings of the views. First represented at the
Egyptian Hall, Piccadilly, Monday Evening, March 15,
1852.
London:
    1852. 28p; ill;
London: Savill & Edwards,
    1852. [2], 31p; ill; 11 x 19cm
    [1853] 4th ed.
London: Chappell
    [1854]. 29p
London: Pub. for author,
    1856.
Probably six editions in all: the illustrations differ in
number and subjects. The pictures were published by
Madame de Chatelain as colouring books.

**Mr. Albert Smith's ascent of Mont Blanc, Holland and up
the Rhine**
Egyptian Hall, Piccadilly. Every evening (except Satur-
day) at eight o'clock. 8p; ill; 22cm
Lecture programme.

The Mont Blanc room at the Egyptian Hall
Presented, by Mr. Albert Smith, to the ladies in the
gallery, on the occasion of the 1856th representation of
'Mont Blanc', March 1, 1858.
Lithograph.

The new game of the ascent of Mont Blanc
Hamburg: Adler, [c.1853]. Coloured board 16½" x 21".
A sort of Alpine snakes and ladders.

L'echo du Mont Blanc
Polka dedicated to his friend Albert Smith by Jullien.
London: Jullien, [c.1858]. 8p; 34cm
Referred to in the advertisements in the Handbook as
'Les Echos de Mont Blanc Polka, composed by M.
Jullien'. [Also known as the 'Chamonix Polka'?]

The 'Mont Blanc' quadrilles
Composed by J. H. Tully.
London: Charles Jeffreys, Soho Square
Described in the advertisement in the Handbook as
follows; 'The title-page by Brandard is illustrative of the
most interesting portions of the ascent, copied, by favour,
from Mr. Beverley's renowned dioramic views of Mont
Blanc . . . the quadrilles have produced a perfect furore of
delight at all the fashionable soirées dansantes of the
season . . .'

ANDREW, Jim. **Bar-room mountaineers.** Cassell, 1965. (Includes rock-climbing in the Lake District.)

BORDEAUX, Henry. **Footprints beneath the snow.** New York: Duffield, 1913.

BOZMAN, E. F. **'X plus Y':** the story of two unknown quantities. Dent, 1936.

CARR, Glyn. **Death on Milestone Buttress.** Bles, 1951. (Tryfan, North Wales)
Similar titles include: **Youth hostel murders** (1952); **Corpse in the Crevasse** (1952); **Death under Snowdon** (1954); **Corpse at Camp Two** (1955); **Murder of an owl** (1956); **Ice axe murders** (1958); **Swing away climber** (1959); **Lewker in Tyrol** (1967); **Fat man's agony** (1969); **Death of a weirdy: Lewker in Norway; Death finds a foothold; Holiday with murder.**

CLEMENTS, E. H. **High tension.** Hodder, 1959.

COOK, W. Victor. **Anton of the Alps.** Methuen, 1912.

COOPER, E. H. **The Monk wins.** Duckworth, 1900. (Horseracing and mountaineering.)

FORSTER, D. K. **Twin giants.** Hammond, 1952. (Set in Himalaya.)

FRISON-ROCHE, R.
Last crevasse. Methuen, 1952. (Chamonix)
Return to the mountains. Methuen, 1961. (Chamonix)

GARVE, Andrew. **Ascent of D13.** Collins, 1969. (Plane crash in the Russo-Turkish mountains.)

GOS, Charles. **Song of the high hills.** Allen & Unwin, 1949.

HEWITT, D. **Mountain resuce.** Eyre & Spottiswoode, 1950.

HOGG, Garry. **Climbers' glory.** Bodley Head, 1961. (Rock-climbing in North Wales.)

HUNTER, A. **Gently to the summit.** Cassell, 1961.

JOHNSTON, Marjorie.
The mountain speaks. Cassell, 1938. (Alps)
Pilgrim and the phoenix. Hamilton, 1940.

LERNER, L. **A free man.** Chatto, 1968. (Iceland)

MACHARDY, C. **The ice mirror.** Collins, 1971. (Eiger situation)

MCNEILL, John. **Search party.** Hodder, 1959.

MASTERS, John. **Far, far the mountain peak.** Joseph, 1957. (Himalaya)

MASTERSON, W. **Man on a nylon string** W. H. Allen, 1963. (Eiger-type situation.)

MATHIESON, E. **Mountain month.** Hamilton, 1965. (Lake District: written for children.)

MERRICK, Hugh.
Pillar of the sky. Eyre & Spottiswoode, 1941.
The breaking strain. Constable, 1950. (Alps)
Out of the night. Hale, 1957. (Rescue in the Alps)

MOFFAT, Gwen. **Lady with a cool eye.** Gollancz, 1973. (North Wales: thriller)

PETERS, E. **Piper on the mountain.** Collins, 1966.

PURSLOW, R. **Sleep till noonday.** Heinemann, 1964. (Rock-climbing in North Wales.)

RAYMOND, Diana. **The climb.** Cassell, 1962.

ROOKE, D. **Boy on the mountain.** Gollancz, 1969.

STEWART, Cochrane. **Windslab.** Hodder, 1952.

STYLES, Showell.
Shadow Buttress. Faber, 1959.
Snowdon rangers. Faber, 1970. (North Wales: for children)

SUTCLIFFE, Constance. **Our Lady of the ice.** Greening, 1901. (A guide loses his client, then dies trying to save the brother.)

SUTTON, Graham. **Damnation of Mr. Zinkler.** Cape, 1935.

TOWNEND, P. **Man on the end of a rope.** Collins, 1960. (Eiger situation.)

TRACY, Louis. **The silent barrier.** Ward Lock, 1910. (Love, climbing and attempted crime.)

TREVANNIAN. **Eiger sanction.** Heinemann, 1973.

TROYAT, Henri. **The mountain.** 1953. (Plane crash in the Alps)

ULLMAN, J. R. **And not to yield.** Collins, 1970. (Set in Himalaya.)

WARDEN, Gertrude. **The crime in the Alps.** White, 1908. (Booby-trap in a pocket barometer.)

APPENDIX V

Some additions (chiefly since 1970) to 'Rock climbing in the British Isles 1894–1970: a bibliography of Guidebooks' by George Bridge

---

SOUTH-EAST ENGLAND

Recent developments in south-east England
J. V. Smoker & D. G. Fagan
Sandstone C. C., 1963 [3], 22p, 7 plates; 16cm

SOUTH-WEST ENGLAND

Lundy rock climbs
R. D. Moulton
Royal Navy M. C. 1974. 2nd ed. 122p.

Cornwall: West Penwith
R. D. Moulton & T. Thompson
Climbers' Club, 1975.

MIDLANDS

Climbs in Leicestershire
K. S. Vickers
1972.

PEAK DISTRICT, PENNINES, NORTH-WEST ENGLAND, ISLE OF MAN

Chatsworth gritstone area
Eric Byne
Climbers' Club, 1970.

Southern limestone: rock climbs in the Peak
Paul Nunn
Climbers' Club, 1970. 238p; ill; 16cm

Bleaklow area: rock climbs in the Peak
Eric Byne
Climbers' Club, 1971. 2nd ed. 234p; ill; 16cm

Froggatt area
Eric Byne
Climbers' Club, 1973. 2nd ed. 238p; ill; 16cm

Rock climbs – Isle of Man
Geoffrey Gartrell
Manchester: Cicerone Press, [1973]. 50p; ill; maps; 17cm

Kinder area: rock climbs in the Peak
Paul Nunn
Climbers' Club, 1974. 208p; ill; 16cm

Stafford gritstone area
David Salt
Climbers' Club, 1974. 232p; ill; 16cm

Yorkshire gritstone: a rock climbers' guide
M. H. Bebbington
Yorkshire M. C., 1974. 266p

Yorkshire limestone: a rock climbers' guide
Frank Wilkinson
Yorkshire M.C., 1974. 245p

Rock climbing in the Peak District: a photographic guide for rock climbers
P. J. Nunn
London: Constable, 1975. xxii, 304p; ill, maps; 18cm

Stanage area
Brian Griffiths & Alan Wright
Climbers' Club, 1976. 208p; ill; 17cm

Chew Valley area: rock climbs in the Peak
Bob Whittaker
Climbers' Club, 1976. 170; ill; 17cm

NORTH-EAST ENGLAND

Northumberland: a rock climbing guide
N. E. Haighton
Northumberland M.C., 1971. 254p

LAKE DISTRICT

Southern Lake District
R. B. Evans & W. Unsworth
Manchester: Cicerone Press, 1971. 55p; ill; map; 17cm

The western Lake District   Part 1: Diff to Hard Severe
D. N. Greenop
Manchester: Cicerone Press, 1972. 83p; ill, map; 17cm

St. Bees and new climbs in the Lake District
A. G. Cram
Fell & Rock C.C., 1972. 66p

Great Langdale
J. A. Austin & R. Valentine
Fell & Rock C.C. 1973

Scafell group
Micheal Burbage
Fell & Rock C.C., 1974 [14], 201p; plate; ill, map; 16cm

Rock climbing in the lake District
Alan Geoffrey Cram , Chris Eilbeck, Ian Roper
London: Constable, 1975. xiv, 250; ill, maps. 18cm

Dow Crag area
John Robert Martindale
Fell & Rock C.C., 1976. [12], 150p, plate; ill; maps; 16cm

NORTH WALES

Snowdon east
A. J. J. Moulam
Climbers' Club, 1970.

Cwm Glas
P. Crew & I. Roper
Climbers' Club, 1970. 2nd ed.

Cwm Silyn and Cwellyn
Mike Yates & Jim Perrin
Climbers' Club, 1971.

Llanberis area
Peter Crew
1971.

Lliwedd
Harold Drasdo
Climbers' Club, 1972. 3rd ed.

The three cliffs
Pete Hatton
Climbers' Club, 1974. [7], 140p; ill, maps; 16cm

Cwm Idwal
Ken Wilson & Z. Leppert
Climbers' Club, 1974. 3rd ed.

Rock climbing in Wales
Ron James
London: Constable, 1975. xiv, 242p; ill; port, 22cm

Carneddau
Les Holliwell
Climbers' Club, 1975.

Dolgellau area
John Sumner
Reading: West Col, 1975.

Climbs on North Wales limestone
Rowland Edwards
Leicester: Cordee, 1976. 56p; ill, maps; 18cm

SOUTH AND MID-WALES
Central Wales
John Sumner
Reading: West Col,

Rock climbing in Pembrokeshire
Colin Mortlock
Tenby, H. G. Walters, 1974. 160p; maps; 19cm

Gower peninsula (supplement)
J. O. Talbot
Reading: West Col,

SCOTLAND – DISTRICT GUIDES
Islands of Scotland
Norman Tennent
S.M.T., 1971

Southern Uplands
K. M. Andrew & A. A. Thrippleton
S.M.T., 1972

Southern Highlands
Donald Bennet
S.M.T. 1972

Western Highlands
G. Scott Johnstone
S.M.T., 1973

Northern Highlands
Tom Strang
S.M.T., 1975. 2nd ed.

Cairngorms
Adam Watson
S.M.T., 1975. 5th ed.

SCOTLAND – S.M.C./S.M.T. CLIMBERS' GUIDES
Northern Highlands area: Vol II: Torridon etc.
D. G. & R. W. L. Turnbull
S.M.T., 1973

Cairngorms: Vol. I: Loch Avon Horseshoe etc.
W. March
S.M.T., 1973

Cairngorms: Vol. II: Ben Macdhui etc.
G. S. Strange
S.M.T., 1973

Cairngorms : Vol. V.: Creag an Dubh Loch etc.
A. F. Fyffe
S.M.T.,

SCOTLAND – NON S.M.C./S.M.T. GUIDES
Ben Nevis and Glencoe: guide to winter climbs
Ian Clough & Hamish MacInnes
Manchester: Cicerone Press, 1971. Rev. ed. 65p; ill; maps; 17cm

Scottish climbs: a mountaineer's pictorial guide to climbing in Scotland
Hamish MacInnes
London : Constable, 1971. 2v. xx. 223p: xviii, 250p; ill; maps; 17cm

IRELAND
Twelve Bens: hill walker's and rock climber's guide
Joss Lynam
Fed. M.C. Ireland, 1971. 29p

Rock climbs in Donegal
John Forsythe
New Univ. Ulster M.C., [1973].

Wicklow-rock climbs (Glendalough & Luggala)
Pat Redmond
Dublin: Fed. M.C. Ireland, 1973.

Mourne rock-climbs
John Forsythe
Dublin: Fed. M.C. Ireland, 1973.

Dalkey rock-climbs
Stephen Young
Dublin: Fed. M.C. Ireland, 1974

Climbing in the British Isles: Ireland
H. C. Hart
Dublin: Privately printed, [1974]. Facsimile reprint of the second part of [Vol] 2 of Haskett Smith's guidebook.

SEA STACKS
British sea stacks
John Cleare
1974.

Provisional short title catalogue of world guide-books (excluding British Isles)

This list has been compiled as counterpart to George Bridge's bibliography of British guidebooks (see Appendix 1 & V). References are to first editions unless otherwise stated. Items dealt with in the main bibliography are included briefly.

GENERAL

Mountains of the world: a handbook for climbers and hikers
William M. Bueler
London: Prentice-Hall Int., 1970.

ALPS

General

Ball's Alpine Guide
London: Longmans, 1863–8. 3v.

Conway-Coolidge Climbers' Guides
London: Fisher Unwin, 1890–1910. 15v.

Swiss mountain climbs
G. D. Abraham
London: Mills & Boon, 1911

Maritime Alps

Maritime Alps
R. G. Collomb & P. Crew
Reading: West Col, 1968

Dauphiné Alps

Selected climbs in the Dauphiné Alps and Vercours
E. A. Wrangham & J. Brailsford
London: Alpine Club, 1967

Graian Alps

Graians west
R. G. Collomb & P. Crew
Reading: West Col. 1967.

Graians east
R. G. Collomb & P. Crew
Reading: West Col. 1969

Chain of Mont Blanc

Chamonix and the range of Mont Blanc
Edward Whymper
London: Murray, 1896

Selected climbs in the range of Mont Blanc
E. A. Wrangham
London: Allen & Unwin, 1957

Dent du Midi region
West Col, Productions
Reading: West Col, 1967

Selected climbs in the range of Mont Blanc
R. G. Collomb & P. Crew
London: Alpine Club; Reading: West Col. 1967. 2v

Chamonix-Mont Blanc
R. G. Collomb
London: Constable, 1969

Pennine Alps

Zermatt pocket book
W. M. Conway
London: Stanford, 1881

Valley of Zermatt and the Matterhorn
Edward Whymper
London: Murray, 1897

Guide to the walks and climbs around Arolla
Walter Larden
London: S. Chick, 1908

Selected climbs in the Pennine Alps
John Neill
London: Alpine Club, 1962

Selected climbs in the Pennine Alps
R. G. Collomb
London: Alpine Club, 1968. 2v

Zermatt and district
R. G. Collomb
London: Constable, 1969

Pennine Alps east/central
London: Alpine Club; Reading: West Col, 1975. 2v.

Bernese Alps

Walks and excursions in the Valley of Grindlewald
W. A. B. Coolidge
Grindlewald: Luf, 1900

Selected climbs in the Bernese Alps
R.G. Collomb
London: Alpine Club; Reading West Col, 1968

Englehörner and Salbitschijen
J. O. Talbot
Reading: West Col. 1968

Central Switzerland
J. O. Talbot
Reading: West Col, 1969

Bernese Alps west
R. G. Collomb
Reading: West Col, 1970

Lepontine Alps

Mittel Switzerland
Michael Anderson
Reading: West Col, 1974

Bernina Alps

Guide to the climbs in the Upper Engadine
W. J. Gyger
Samaden: Engadin Press, [1930]

Bregaglia west
R. G. Collomb
Reading: West Col, 1967

Bernina Alps
R. G. Collomb & J. O. Talbot
Reading: West Col, 1968

Bregaglia east
R. G. Collomb & P. Crew
Reading: West Col, 1971

Bavarian etc. Alps
Karwendel
Michael Anderson
Reading: West Col, 1971

Kaisergebirge
J. O. Talbot
Reading: West Col. 1971

Ortler, Ötzal and Stubai Alps
Ortler Alps
A. J. Thompson
Reading: West Col, 1968

Ötztal Alps
Walter Unsworth
Reading: West Col, 1969

Stubai Alps
Eric Roberts
Reading: West Col, 1972

Tauern and Zillertal Alps
Glockner region
Eric Roberts
Reading: West Col, 1976

Dolomites
Selected climbs in the Dolomites
Peter Crew
London: Alpine Club, 1963

Dolomite east/west
John Brailsford
London: Alpine Club, 1970. 2v.

REST OF EUROPE
Guide to the Pyrenees
Charles Packe
London: Longmans, 1862

Climbs in the Horungtinder, Norway
Asbjorn Gunneng & Boye Schlytter (Norsk Tindeklub)
Oslo: Grøndahl, 1933

Short guide to the Slovene Alps
F. S. Copeland & M. Debelakova
Ljubljana: Kleinmayr & Bamberg, 1936

Walks and climbs in Malta
Showell Styles
Privately printed, 1944

Rock climbs in Arctic Norway/Jotenheimen/Nordmore/Lofoten/Sunnmore/Romsdal (6 small publications)
London' Norway Travel Assoc., 1953

Mountain holidays in Norway
Per Prag
Oslo: Norway Travel Assoc., [1963]

Selected climbs in Romsdal
Tony Howard
1965

Climbing guide to Gibraltar
A. D. Marsden
Yeovil: Haynes, 1965. 82p. [Published for the Joint Services Mountaineering Assoc.]

Walks and climbs in Romsdal
Tony Howard
Manchester: Cicerone Press, 1970.

Rock climbing in Malta
J. D. Graham
Reading: West Col, 1971.

Staunings Alps – Greenland
Donald J. Bennet
Reading: Gastons Alpine Books & West Col Prodns, 1972

Mountain touring holidays in Norway
Erling Welle-Strand
Oslo: Nortrabooks, 1974

Pyrenees east/west
Arthur Battagel
Reading: Gastons Alpine Books, 1975. 2v.

AFRICA

Table Mountain: some easy climbs to the summit
Cape Town: Cape Peninsula Pub. Assoc., 1914

A mountaineer's paradise: a guide to the mountains of the Worcester district, containing directions for reaching over 80 peaks and brief descriptions of some 200 routes of ascent. [Cape Province]
E. S. Field & E. G. Pells
Cape Town: Mountain Club, n.d.

Table Mountain climbs: a classified list of the routes
Reprinted from the 'Annual of the Mountain Club ot South Africa',
no. 34, 1932.

Table Mountain guide: walks and easy climbs on Table Mountain and Devils Peak, with two contour maps
Cape Town: Stewart Ptg. Co., 1944

Guide-book to Mount Kenya and Kilimanjaro
Ian C. Reid, 1959. Duplicated from typescript.

Some notes on mountaineering in the High Atlas
A. C. Gay, 1968. 17p. Duplicated from typescript.

Mountains of Kenya
Peter Robson
Nairobi: M.C. of Kenya, 1969

Guide book to mount Kenya and Kilimanjaro
John Mitchell
Nairobi: M.C. of Kenya; Reading: West Col, 1971

† **Guide to the Ruwenzori**
H. A. Osmaston & D. Pasteur
Kampala: M.C. of Uganda; Reading: West Col, 1972.

ASIA

Climber's guide to Sonamarg, Kashmir
C. W. F. Noyce
New Dehli: Himalayan Club, 1945

Guide to rock climbing in Hong Kong
D. C. Reur

Rock climbing guide to Hong Kong
J. F. Bunnell

AUSTRALASIA

Southern Alps (Part II) Mount Cook Alpine Region
L. R. Hewitt & M. Davidson
Christchurch: Pegasus Press, 1953

Mount Arapiles
M. Stone & I. Speedie
Melbourne: Victoria C.C., 1965

Rock climbing guide to Victoria
C. Baxter & C. Dewhurst
Melbourne: Victoria C.C., 1967

Rock climbing guide to the Grampians
J. Grandage & R Taylor
Melbourne: Victoria C.C.,

New England tablelands
Univ. New England [Australia] M.C.
Armidale, N.S.W., 1971. 3rd ed.

CANADA

The Selkirk Mountains: a guide for mountain climbers and pilgrims
[Mrs. H. J. Parker] Information by A.O. Wheeler
Winnipeg: Stovel Co., 1912

Northern Cordillera
British Columbia M.C. 1913

Description of and guide to Jasper Park
E. Delville
Ottawa. Dept of Interior, 1917

Climber's guide to the Rocky Mountains of Canada
H. Palmer & J. M. Thorington
New York: Putnam, 1921

Climber's guide to the Interior Ranges of British Columbia
J. M. Thorington
1937

Mountaineering around Montreal
Montreal Section, A.C. of Canada and Le Club de Montagne Canadien.
Point Claire, Que: A.C. of C., 1964.

Climber's guide to the Coastal Range of British Columbia
Richard Culbert
Vancouver: Alpine Club of Canada, 1965

Climber's guide to the Squamish Chief and surrounding area [Vancouver]
Glen Wordsworth
1967

Climber's guide to Yamnuska [East of main Rockies]
Brian Greenwood & Mrs Kallen
1970

UNITED STATES OF AMERICA

Eastern States

Guide to Mt. Washington Range
William H. Pickering
1882

The White Mountains: a guide
Julius H. Ward
1890

White Mountain guide
Appalachian M.C. [c. 1922]

Katahdin guide [Maine]
Appalachian M.C., 1956

Maine mountain guide
Appalachian M.C., 1961

Climber's guide to the Shawangunks
Arthur Gran
New York: A.A.C., 1964

Adirondack mountain guide
Adirondack M.C.

Climber's guide to the Adirondacks
Trudy Healy
1967

Climber's guide to the Quincy Quarries [Boston, Mass]
Crowther & Thompson
1968

Climber's guide to Cathedral and White Horse Ledges
[White Mountains]
Joseph & Karen Cote
Privately Printed, 1969

Monadnock guide
Henry J. Baldwin

Climber's guide to Senaca Rocks [West Virginia]
F. R. Robinson
1971

Shawangunk rock climbs
R. C. Williams
New York: A.A.C., 1972

Pittsburgh area rock climbing guide
Ivan L. Jerak

Rocky Mountains

The Medicine Bow Mountains of Wyoming
F. N. Fryxell
San Francisco, 1926

A climber's guide to the high Colorado peaks
Elinor Eppich Kingery
Denver: Colorado M.C., 1931

The Teton peaks and their ascents [Wyoming]
F. N. Fryxell
Wyoming: Crandall Studios, 1932

Long Peak: its story and a guide for climbing it
[Colorado]
Paul W. Nesbit
1946

Mountain climbing guide to the Grand Tetons
H. Coulter & M. F. McLane
Hanover, N. H.: Dartmouth M.C., 1947

Guide to the Colorado mountains
Robert M. Ormes
Denver: Sage Books, 1952

Climber's guide to the Teton Range
Leigh Ortenburger
San Francisco: Sierra Club, 1956

Climber's guide to Glacier National Park [Montana]
J. Gordon Edwards
1960

† **Guide to the Wyoming mountains and wilderness areas**
O. H. & L. Bonney
1960

Rock climbing guide to the Boulder, Colorado area
David Dornan
Boulder: Outdoors Utd. 1961

Guide to the New Mexico mountains
Herbert E. Ungnade
1965

Field book: the Wind River Range
O. H. & L. Bonney.
Houston, 1968. 2nd rev. ed.

Climber's guide to the Snowy Range of Wyoming
R. G. Jacquot & R. O. Hoff
1970

Guide to the Sandea Mountains [New Mexico]
Lawrence G. Kline
1970

Climber's guide to Rocky Mountain National Park
[Colorado]
Walter W. Fricke Jr
Boulder: Paddock, 1971

Guide to Nevada's Rocky and East Humboldt Mountains
Carmie R. Dafoe Jr
1971

Climber's and hiker's guide to Devil's Lake [North Dakota]
David Smith & Roger Zimmerman

Granite Mountain
D. Lovejoy
Prescott, Arizona: 1973

Sierra Nevada and California
The Yosemite guide-book
J. D. Whitney
Sacramento, 1869

The Yosemite
John Muir
1912

Guide to the John Muir Trail and the High Sierra region
Walter A. Starr Jr
San Francisco: Sierra Club, 1934

Climber's guide to the High Sierra
Hervey Voge
SanFrancisco: Sierra Club, 1956

Climber's guide to Yosemite Valley
Steve Roper
San Francisco: Sierra Club, 1964

Desert peaks guide: Part one
Walter Wheelock
La Siesta Press, 1964. Rev. ed.

Climber's guide to Pinnacles National Monument [California]
Steve Roper
1966

Climber's guide to Tahquitz and Suicide Rocks [California]
Chuck Wilts
1968

Climber's guide to Joshua Tree National Monument
[California]

Cascades and mountains of the North-west
High trails: a guide to the Cascades Crest Trail
Robert H. Wills

Climber's guide to the Cascade and Olympic Mountains of Washington
Fred Beckey
New York: A.A.C., 1949

North Cascades
T. Miller & H Manning
Seattle: Mountaineers, 1964

Routes and rocks: a hiker's guide to the North Cascades from Glacier Peak to Lake Chelan
D. F. Crowder & R. W. Tabor
1966

Climber's guide to Oregon
Nicholas B. Dodge
1968

Routes and rocks in the Mt. Challenger Quadrangle
D. F. Crowder & R. W. Tabor
1968

Climber's guide to the Olympic Mountains
Olympic Mountain Rescue
1972

Cascade alpine guide
Fred Beckey
Seattle: Mountaineers, 1973

Alaska
Alaska mountain guide
J. Vincent Hoeman
[c. 1971]